American Arrivals

Publication of the Advanced Seminar Series
is made possible by generous support from
The Brown Foundation, Inc., of Houston, Texas.

**School of American Research
Advanced Seminar Series**

Richard M. Leventhal
General Editor

American Arrivals

Contributors

Caroline B. Brettell
Department of Anthropology, Southern Methodist University

Leo R. Chavez
Department of Anthropology, University of California, Irvine

Nancy Foner
*School of Public Affairs, Baruch College, City University of New York and
Department of Anthropology, Purchase College, State University of New York,*

Nina Glick Schiller
*Department of Anthropology, University of New Hampshire
and the Max Planck Institute of Social Anthropology*

Jennifer S. Hirsch
Departments of International Health and Anthropology, Emory University

Patricia R. Pessar
American Studies Department, Yale University

Richard A. Shweder
Committee on Human Development, University of Chicago

Alex Stepick
*Department of Anthropology and Sociology and the Immigration and Ethnicity
Institute, Florida International University*

Carol Dutton Stepick
Immigration and Ethnicity Institute, Florida International University

Marcelo M. Suárez-Orozco
Harvard Immigration Projects, Graduate School of Education, Harvard University

American Arrivals

Anthropology Engages the New Immigration

Edited by Nancy Foner

School of American Research Press
Santa Fe

James Currey
Oxford

School of American Research Press

Post Office Box 2188
Santa Fe, New Mexico 87504-2188

James Currey Ltd

73 Botley Road
Oxford OX2 0BS

Director: James F. Brooks
Executive Editor: Catherine Cocks
Manuscript Editor: Kate Talbot
Design and Production: Cynthia Welch
Proofreader: Sarah Baldwin
Indexer: Sylvia Coates
Printer: Maple-Vail Book Group

Library of Congress Cataloging-in-Publication Data:

American arrivals : anthropology engages the new immigration / edited by
Nancy Foner.— 1st ed.
    p. cm. — (School of American Research advanced seminar series)
  Includes bibliographical references and index.
  ISBN 1-930618-33-6 (alk. paper) — ISBN 1-930618-34-4 (pbk. : alk.
paper)
  1. Immigrants—United States—Research. 2. United States—Emigration
and immigration—Research. 3. Anthropology—Research—United States.
I. Foner, Nancy, 1945- II. Series.
JV6465 .A53 2003
304.8'73—dc21

                        2003013210

British Library Cataloguing in Publication Data:

American arrivals : anthropology engages the new immigration. — (A School of American
    Research advanced seminar)
    1. Immigration—United States—Research 2. Anthropology—Research—United States
    3. United States—Emigration and immigration—Research
    I. Foner, Nancy, 1945– II. School of American Research
    304.8'73

    ISBN 0-85255-942-9 (James Currey cloth) — ISBN 0-85255-943-7 (James Currey paper)

Library of Congress Catalog Card Number 2003013210
International Standard Book Numbers 0-930618-33-6 (cloth) and 0-930618-34-4
(paper). First edition 2003.

1 2 3 4 5   07 06 05 04 03

Cover illustration: *Shoppers*. Oil on linen by Nina Talbot © Nina Talbot

Contents

Figures and Tables

Acknowledgments

The essays presented here were first written for a School of American Research advanced seminar called "Anthropology and Contemporary Immigration," which was held in October 2001.

I would like to thank the seminar participants for their essays and engaging discussions, as well as for their responsiveness and commitment to the project throughout the rewriting and publishing process. My thanks, as well, to Josh DeWind, who as a discussant brought to the seminar insights from his work in anthropology and his role as director of the International Migration Program at the Social Science Research Council.

At the School of American Research, President Richard Leventhal was a gracious host. Director of Academic Programs Nancy Owen Lewis and coordinator Leslie Shipman ensured that the arrangements went smoothly and that the meeting provided an opportunity for intellectual interchange and discussion in a relaxed and enjoyable setting. Catherine Cocks, editor at SAR Press, shepherded the manuscript through the production process with great efficiency and good spirit. She went above and beyond the call of duty in carefully reading the entire manuscript and offering comments that helped with the

ACKNOWLEDGMENTS

revisions. It was a pleasure to work with her and also with James Brooks, director of the SAR Press. Kate Talbot was an excellent copy editor. Finally, thanks to two anonymous reviewers for their many useful suggestions, which have, I believe, made this a better book.

American Arrivals

Anthropology Engages the New Immigration

1

Introduction

*Anthropology and Contemporary
Immigration to the United States—
Where We Have Been and
Where We Are Going*

Nancy Foner

Immigration is one of the most pressing contemporary social issues in the United States. In the past four decades, the massive influx of immigrants, mainly from Asia, Latin America, and the Caribbean, has led to dramatic transformations in American society, changing the nation's cities and a host of social institutions and, of course, altering the lives of the immigrants themselves.

The foreign born now represent more than 10 percent of the nation's population. Together with their American-born children, this group constituted one-fifth of the population of the United States in 2000—56 million people. This is a remarkable figure. If today's foreign born and their children were to form a country, it would have approximately twice the population of Canada and roughly the same as France or Italy (Foner, Rumbaut, and Gold 2000). The arrival of an unprecedented number of Latin American and Asian immigrants has transformed the ethnoracial makeup of the country. In 2001, according to census estimates, Hispanics surpassed blacks as the nation's largest minority group. Asians made up 4 percent of the US population, up from one-half of 1 percent in 1960.

The effects of immigration are nothing short of momentous. Not surprisingly, the huge recent immigration has given rise to a scholarly literature in all the social sciences as the various disciplines try to grasp and grapple with the complexity of the subject. This volume focuses on the role of anthropology—in particular, social/cultural anthropology—in understanding this crucial new phenomenon. It explores the contributions anthropologists have made to the study of US immigration and, perhaps more important, the contributions they can continue to make in this field. As the number of immigrants to the United States increases—and as more and more anthropologists study the global migrants in our midst—the time is ripe to reflect on where migration anthropology has been and where it is going: to evaluate the discipline's perspectives, theories, and methods as they pertain to US immigration and to begin developing a research program for the future.

This book is the product of a weeklong advanced seminar at the School of American Research in Santa Fe, New Mexico, in October 2001. The authors discussed their essays there and later rethought and revised them in light of the group meeting and readers' responses. Like the seminar, the volume is organized so that each chapter considers migration from the vantage point of a particular anthropological theme, approach, or subfield: migration and globalization (Marcelo Suárez-Orozco, Chapter 2), gender (Patricia Pessar, Chapter 3), transnational migration (Nina Glick Schiller, Chapter 4), immigrant education (Alex Stepick and Carol Dutton Stepick, Chapter 5), urban contexts (Caroline Brettell, Chapter 6), medical anthropology (Leo Chavez, Chapter 7, and Jennifer Hirsch, Chapter 8), and the moral challenges of cultural migration (Richard Shweder, Chapter 9).

These topics are of fundamental concern to anthropologists of contemporary US immigration, yet they are not, of course, the only ones that have been addressed in the literature. This book is not meant to be an exhaustive review of all migration anthropology or an in-depth analysis of the full range of topics of concern to anthropologists study-ing migration to the United States. However, the authors inevitably touch on several related areas, for example, the family and household (Pessar) and ethnic/racial identities and relations (Brettell, Stepick and Stepick). Presenting a unified theoretical perspective was not the goal of the seminar, nor is it the purpose of this book. The contributors do not speak with one voice but bring different theoretical approaches and concerns to their analyses. As they tackle particular issues, the authors analyze and assess concepts, questions, methodological approaches, and theoretical views that guide the work of anthropologists of contemporary US immigration. Thus, all the chapters, whether or not they are explicitly framed in terms of immigration to the United States, have relevance for understanding the new American arrivals. The chapters show the broad range of anthropological concerns and interests and underscore the particular strengths that anthropologists bring to the immigration field.

In this introduction, I start out by situating anthropological studies of contemporary US immigration in the context of a developing interdisciplinary field of migration studies and in the context of significant changes within anthropology itself. I go on to review where anthropology has been with regard to earlier rural-urban migration research and the ever-expanding body of work on contemporary US immigration. I end by suggesting directions for future research as more anthropologists turn to the study of "mobile subjects" in the United States and seek to carve out a distinctive role for anthropology while also contributing to an emerging interdisciplinary project on immigration. Throughout, I draw on and highlight the themes discussed by the authors in this volume and also consider other areas and issues of concern in migration anthropology.

INTERDISCIPLINARY EXCHANGES AND DISCIPLINARY CHANGES

Asking about anthropology's contribution to US immigration studies is, in some ways, an old-fashioned—indeed, atavistic—approach in these days of interdisciplinary programs and projects, from cultural and feminist studies to various ethnic-studies specialties. A field of immigration studies is, in fact, in the making. The Social Science Research Council Committee on International Migration has sought to promote the "theoretical coherence of immigration studies as an interdisciplinary subfield within the social sciences" (DeWind 2000:70). It has organized conferences and working groups to "enhance the field's interdisciplinary coherence by reinforcing intellectual and professional connections between researchers" (DeWind 2000:72).

Inevitably, immigration specialists are crossing disciplinary boundaries and drawing on theoretical insights—and empirical data—from fields other than their own as they tackle particular problems (Foner, Rumbaut, and Gold 2000).

Certainly, there is great value in the mix of disciplines in immigration studies. "Creative" and "empowering" are the words one sociologist uses to describe involvement in multidisciplinary working groups, conferences, and intellectual exchanges (Waters 2000:45). Moving beyond the bounds of their particular discipline can lead scholars to ask new questions, see old problems in new ways, and go beyond what are sometimes the limited concerns of their own fields. If, as Alejandro Portes (1997:802, 803) notes, theoretical advances arise out of the ability to reconstitute a perceptual field and to identify connections not previously seen, the interdisciplinary thrust of so much immigration research may be particularly productive as it brings new perspectives to bear on familiar issues, incorporates insights from different fields, and promotes the kind of "distance from reality" that he argues is important "in order to identify patterns lost at close range."

Interdisciplinary exchanges do not occur in a vacuum. Each discipline brings a particular history to the table, including the role US immigration has played, and continues to play, in the field (Brettell and Hollifield 2000). Because immigration to the United States is a core theme in American sociology, it occupies a centrality in that discipline that it does not have in anthropology. (For example, at the 2002 annual meetings of the American Sociological Association, twenty-one sessions and eleven roundtables focused on US immigration, compared with eight sessions at the 2002 annual meetings of the American Anthropological Association.) Also, it is not surprising that immigration has been a major topic in American history for many years, given its critical role in the making of the United States.

Although studying the United States and migration is nothing new in anthropology, the traditional emphasis, especially in dissertation research, has been on cultures outside the United States (other than the study of Native Americans).[1] Until recently, immigration to the United States has not been a major topic of concern. When I was a graduate student at the University of Chicago in the late 1960s, it was virtually unheard of to get the blessings of the department (not to mention a grant) to do fieldwork on a non–Native American group in the United States. As Sherry Ortner (1991:163) notes, the only such project to get department backing when she was a student at the University of Chicago was a study of American drag queens, and "one could argue that this was only because drag queens were seen as so exotic and other that they might as well have been Australian aborigines." Anthropologists who work in the United States, as Micaela di Leonardo (1998:127) puts it, have been perceived within the profession as "inauthentic" anthropologists. "There is a pervasive sense that those who engage in [Americanist research] cannot or will not go abroad.... The United States, from the vantage of anthropology departments, is too often considered a playground, an R&R site...." (di Leonardo 1998:67).

Anthropologists face a further challenge when they retreat to their disciplinary base, for anthropology itself has been in turmoil after many years of soul searching. (The focus here is on social/cultural anthropology. Still another debate is just how or whether to integrate the four fields of archaeology, physical anthropology, linguistics, and cultural anthropology.) For one thing, anthropology's so-called traditional constituency—non-industrial societies—is being transformed as globalizing forces dramatically affect even the most far-flung corners of the world, from New Guinea and African villages to Inuit outposts in northern Canada. Villagers in the South Pacific island kingdom of Tonga, for example, regularly watch American television programs and videos, and more than one quarter of the entire population of Tonga now lives in the United States (Small 1997:52).[2] As Marcelo Suárez-Orozco notes in Chapter 2, one aspect of globalization is the astoundingly high level of worldwide migration as people from developing countries—seeking to realize what he calls "structures of desire" and "consumption fantasies" that cannot be met by local economies—move to the metropolises of the developed world. Today, Turkish cultural formations are as ubiquitous in parts of Frankfurt as in Istanbul, and Mexican culture is thriving in New York and Los Angeles.

Urban anthropology is now an accepted subdiscipline within the field. The Society for Urban Anthropology, recently transformed into the Society for Urban, National and Transnational/Global Anthropology, has nearly doubled its membership in the past few years. It has become more acceptable, and respectable, for anthropologists to conduct their research, including their "first" research, in the United States. It is noteworthy that a few years ago the Society for the Anthropology of North America (SANA) was founded as a section of the American Anthropological Association. No less a figure than Clifford Geertz (1997:3) predicts that in the future, anthropology will no longer be defined by a concern with the distant or exotic: There will be an "increased extension of ethnographic approaches to the study of modern industrialized societies, including our own."

Partly owing to these changes, anthropology's founding figures are often prophets without honor in their own home, no longer seen as relevant, given their concerns with Trobriand Islanders, Tallensi clansmen, and Nuer cattle-keepers of a bygone age. Worse, the founding anthropologists have been subject to attack. Among the many critiques launched against figures of the stature of Bronislaw Malinowski, A. R. Radcliffe-Brown, and E .E. Evans-Pritchard are that they were mired in the policies of empire and imperialist expansion, that they ignored or minimized the role of women, and that their static, structural-functionalist approaches portrayed closed, timeless societies—in Eric Wolf's (1982) phrase, "people without history"—and ignored or downplayed the effect of colonial rule and other historical changes. One example cited is Margaret Mead's portrayal of the societies she studied in New Guinea in the 1930s as timeless cultures largely unaffected by the outside world, even though when she did her fieldwork, more than half the Chambri (Tchambuli) men between the ages of fifteen and forty-five were away, working as migrant laborers (Brettell 2000a:97).

Critics of a political-economy persuasion complain of the founding fathers' (and mothers') inattention to flux, change, and wider political and economic processes and structures in which so-called traditional societies were embedded. The postmodern critique lambastes the classic figures as positivists who told false or at least highly biased "truths" and imposed rigid, static categories and formulations on what, in reality, are constructed, fluid, and contested meanings and events. I would not go so far as Adam Kuper (1999:223) in saying that the postmodern movement has made young ethnographers so nervous that they can hardly be persuaded to go into the field at all. However, it has certainly called into question the anthropological enterprise and "ethnographic authority."

This leads to the important questions of methods. Some fifty years ago, in his introductory lectures on social anthropology, Evans-Pritchard (1962:11) wrote that "the social anthropologist studies primitive societies directly, living among them for months or years." This emphasis on long-term fieldwork—and participant observation—has been the hallmark of social/cultural anthropology. Quite apart from the postmodern concern about whether it is even possible to truly understand a culture different from one's own, the fact is that anthropologists do not have a monopoly on ethnographic research or participant observation. The early twentieth-century studies of the Chicago school of sociology, which can be said to have established the field of immigration studies in the United States, were based on ethnographic methods (Stepick and Stepick, Chapter 5). Qualitative sociology is a growing enterprise; even some political scientists engage in participant observation fieldwork. Many historians collect oral histories; a few have been doing studies that involve participant observation research in the present (for example, see Camarillo n.d.). If scholars in other disciplines have been adopting what anthropologists generally think of as "our" methods, anthropologists have also been adopting "theirs." More than twenty-five years ago, Talal Asad (1973:12) noted that the "anthropologist is someone who studies societies both simple and complex; resorts to participant observation, statistical techniques, historical archives and other literary sources; finds himself intellectually closer to economists or political scientists or psychoanalysts or structural linguists...than he does to other anthropologists." This kind of "agnosticism"—or, perhaps more accurately, eclecticism—with regard to methods has become even more pronounced in recent years and is evident in many anthropological studies of immigration.

ANTHROPOLOGY AND MIGRATION— THE EARLY POST-WAR YEARS

Anthropologists' interest in immigration to the United States has a long history. The field's iconic figure, Margaret Mead, may have written her dissertation on Polynesia, but before that, in 1924, her master's thesis compared intelligence test scores of English and non-English–speaking Italian-American children in her New Jersey hometown. She concluded that the much higher scores of English speakers indicated the power of cultural factors (di Leonardo 1998:83). Another

9

of anthropology's founding figures, Franz Boas, who was a critic of the race concepts of his day, secured money from the Dillingham Immigration Commission for a study showing that the physical characteristics of southern and eastern European immigrants changed in the United States, contrary to notions of ideal racial types unmodified by environments (di Leonardo 1998:163). Mead and Boas were writing at the time of the last great wave of immigration to the United States, when anthropology was in its infancy. When anthropology began to establish itself and flourish in the American academy, in the 1940s, 1950s, and 1960s, immigration had slowed to a trickle. Only in recent years, since the massive post-1965 influx, have anthropologists, in any significant number, turned their attention to immigration to this country.

Yet to leave it at that would be a mistake. Although hardly any anthropologists in the three decades following World War II were studying immigrants in the United States, many were involved in research on rural-urban migration elsewhere. Unfortunately, as Glick Schiller (Chapter 4) observes, anthropologists often disregard the discipline's own rich history of migration studies, and some even write as if the ethnographic study of migration, complex societies, and transborder processes is new to anthropology. Nothing could be farther from the truth. As Caroline Brettell (2000a:97) notes in her review of anthropological theorizing on migration, anthropologists had to pay attention to migration "because in those regions of the world that had traditionally been their arenas for ethnographic fieldwork—Africa, Oceania, and increasingly Latin America and the Caribbean—people were beginning to move in significant numbers from the countryside to the growing urban centers of the underdeveloped and developing world." Of importance here is that the ethnographic and theoretical insights of this early work can shed light on the analysis of contemporary US immigration.

Ties to home communities were a prominent feature of the early, first-wave urban anthropology literature. William Shack's comments in the 1973 collection *Urban Anthropology* are an example of a common orientation in anthropological analyses of the time: "Even after living in an urban environment for periods of up to a generation or more, Africans in town retain their tribal identity and membership in the rural society. They think in terms of the hinterland: and a great deal of the social and economic activities of African townsmen are directed towards forming and keeping alive urban-based tribal institutions which function to maintain ties of kinship with the rural village where they ultimately propose to retire" (Shack 1973:251).

One concern was whether urban migrants were sojourners or settlers. Anthropologists documented cyclical or seasonal patterns of movement between home communities and urban areas for many groups, trying to understand the factors propelling people to migrate at certain life stages and to return at others. For example, in his study of the African population of the Copperbelt of Zambia in the 1950s, J. Clyde Mitchell (1973) examined how physical distance between rural areas and town and the efficacy of transportation services affected migrants' continued participation in events and affairs of their rural home. The whole question of return was a dominant one. Did people return for good? If they did, when? Why? For those who remained in the city, why did a return ideology often loom large? (For example, see Plotnicov 1967.) Linked to the question of return was an interest in the nature and effect of economic, political, and familial ties that urban migrants retained to their home areas. Ethnographic accounts in urban Africa and elsewhere revealed that migrants not only sent money home but also often maintained wives and children there and sometimes even exerted political influence in their rural community. Urban research also focused on hometown associations and their role in keeping ethnic/tribal allegiances alive and in undertaking projects to improve the living standards of rural kinsmen (for example, Little 1965).

Sociologists in the United States asked how immigrants and their children became American; first-wave urban anthropologists asked how, in Philip Mayer's (1961) phrase, "tribesmen became townsmen" (see also Gluckman 1961). Put another way, American sociologists focused on how immigrants became incorporated into American social institutions and the dominant national culture. Key questions for anthropologists were whether modernization theory held up in light of evidence from rural-urban migration in third world countries, whether detribalization was the inevitable outcome of the movement of rural dwellers to cities, and whether and to what extent universal urban social and cultural patterns could be discerned in Africa, Asia, and

Latin America. Contrary to predictions of modernization theory, anthropologists showed that the extended family did not disappear in the urban context, nor did village or tribal-based kinship patterns and ideologies, even though they often changed in form, function, and meaning in the city. For example, Edward Bruner (1970) showed that patrilineages continued to be important among the Toba Batak who migrated to Indonesian cities. In Africa, the institution of polygyny did not necessarily atrophy in town, with men sometimes "deploying" wives between town and country (see Parkin 1974 on the Luo of Kenya).

Of course, much changed when people moved to cities. Urban anthropologists studied these processes, too, in virtually every sphere of social and cultural life, from family and kinship patterns to politics and religion. Foreshadowing the contemporary interest in gender and migration, early urban anthropologists wrote about the changing position of women in the urban context, particularly the greater freedom and opportunities for economic independence available to women in town (for example, Little 1973). A literature on urban ethnicity probed the dynamics of ethnic identity and loyalty. Among the topics studied were the symbols of ethnicity that developed in towns, the different meanings of ethnicity for various subgroups (such as classes) within migrant populations, and the use of ethnicity by urban political elites and entrepreneurs for their own political and economic ends (see Cohen 1969).

Even the topic of the second generation, now so prominent in US sociological studies, figured in the earlier work. In her study of the Mossi in the Ghanaian city Kumasi, Enid Schildkrout (1974) argued that ethnicity was expressed mainly in a kinship idiom among first-generation migrants but that the second-generation, born in town, did not make a close association between kinship and ethnicity. Studies of urban ethnicity also explored the intricacies of social relations within and between ethnic groups—at work and in neighborhoods, formal associations, and families. To what extent did urban migrants live out their lives in "ethnic," "tribal," or "village" worlds? Did they become "detribalized," to use the term prevalent in urban African studies in the 1960s and 1970s?[3]

Partly out of a concern to understand inter- and intra-ethnic interaction in towns, many anthropologists used and refined network analysis as a way to chart the dynamic nature of urban migrants' social ties. Some advocated situational analysis—detailed and close study of concrete and specific situations—to reveal social processes and conflicts in action and to illuminate the significance of tribal/ethnic affiliation in particular contexts (for example, Mitchell 1956; Van Velsen 1967). As Mitchell (1956:1) wrote in his classic account of the *kalela* dance in the Copperbelt of Northern Rhodesia, "by working outwards from a specific social situation on the Copperbelt, the whole social fabric of the Territory is...taken in." In general, as more anthropologists turned to research in cities, they began to discuss how to do fieldwork there and to ponder what new approaches might be needed (Foster and Kemper 1974). Mitchell (1966), among others, argued for the use of surveys in urban areas. Like other anthropologists, he saw them as useful in refining and deepening generalizations derived from extensive and intensive fieldwork. Ethnography, with its "total immersion," close personal relationships with informants, and observation of behavior, remained key.

Although urban anthropologists focused on the urban side of the migration chain, they did not neglect the rural end. Of concern, as I already mentioned, were the reasons people left rural areas and the influence that migrants continued to exert there even though they were not physically present. Often, anthropologists had research experience in both the sending and receiving communities. When James L. Watson (1977) edited *Between Two Cultures,* a collection by anthropologists who had researched problems of migration and ethnicity in Britain in the 1970s, the common thread tying together the ethnographic chapters on different groups was that the contributors had research experience at both ends of the migration chain, in the home society and in Britain. Yet another component of migration studies in anthropology also included both rural and urban areas: the study of ethnic diasporas. A major issue in the study of various diasporas was how cultural and social patterns from the home country or region were transformed as migrants settled in vastly different places around the globe. One example was the edited volume *Caste in Overseas Indian Communities* (Schwartz 1967). This examined how caste ideology and practice changed in importance in overseas communities, including those characterized by indentured migration (in the West Indies, Fiji, Mauritius, and South Africa) and those with a history of "passenger" migration (South and East Africa). The focus was not on the urban context—in the Indian case, many migrants went to rural destinations—but on the social, economic, cultural, and political dynamics of the places where Indians settled.

ANTHROPOLOGISTS AND US IMMIGRATION

With the rapid growth of immigration to the United States in the past four decades, anthropologists have increasingly turned their attention to migration issues on their own home turf. The interest in immigration in the United States is a logical extension of developments in the post–World War II period as urban anthropology blossomed to document rural-urban migration in Asia, Africa, and Latin America. It is also part of the attempt in anthropology in recent years to understand the effect of contemporary globalizing processes, which, in Suárez-Orozco's phrase, are delivering the "exotic" to the anthropologists' own backyard. As part of his broader discussion of the factors underlying the new mass migration to the United States and other "wealthier centers of the northern hemisphere," Suárez-Orozco (Chapter 2) notes the role of globalization in creating transnational capital flows that migrants tend to follow; encouraging new tastes, consumption practices, and lifestyle choices through new information and communication technologies; perpetuating and reinforcing unequal patterns of economic development in various regions of the world; and making mass transportation more affordable.

Just as social networks play a role in the migration process, anthropologists' research-based networks in migrants' home communities have figured in their studies. Many anthropologists' interest in immigration grew out of their original research in the community of origin. Some anthropologists literally followed informants as they moved to the United States; others found their informants turning up only a bus or subway ride away. Whatever the reason, anthropologists were among the first social scientists to chronicle and analyze the experiences of the latest arrivals. In 1979, for example, Constance Sutton and Elsa Chaney edited a special issue of the *International Migration Review* that focused on Caribbean migration to New York. (Revised versions of the articles in this issue, many by anthropologists, were published in the volume *Caribbean Life in New York City,* which appeared in 1987.) As Sutton

(1987:22) noted in her introductory chapter, "Studies by anthropologists of Caribbean life in New York City are part of a larger trend in today's practice of urban anthropology which teaches that the field (of study) is not elsewhere but everywhere." The 1976 special issue of *Anthropological Quarterly* on women and migration, edited by Judith-Maria Buechler, was the first collection of papers on this theme and brought together research on migrant women in the United States and Europe.

As it happens, I was a contributor to both these collections, and my route to immigration research is typical of the path taken by many other anthropologists. I conducted dissertation research in a Jamaican rural community; several years later I did research among Jamaican migrants in London (Foner 1973, 1978). A few years after this, I studied Jamaicans in New York (Foner 1983, 1985, 1986, 1987a).[4] Other Caribbeanists had similar experiences: Constance Sutton (Sutton and Makiesky 1987), who started her career doing research in Barbados, subsequently wrote about Barbadians in New York; Linda Basch (1987, 2001), whose "first" research was in the Caribbean, later turned to study migrants in New York; and Karen Fog Olwig (2001) also extended her research from the Caribbean to New York. It is not just Caribbeanists who have made the sending society–receiving society journey. For example, Maxine Margolis (1994, 1998) went from fieldwork in Brazil to study of Brazilians in New York; Johanna Lessinger (1995), originally a researcher in India, turned her attention to Indian migrants in New York; and Paul Stoller (2001, 2002), having worked in West Africa, has recently been writing about West African traders in New York. A focus on immigration in the United States does not mean that anthropologists cut off ties and interests in the sending society. Many have continued to return, and they maintain an active research program both "here" and "there." Moreover, many anthropologists studying US immigration who did not begin their careers in the country of origin have subsequently done fieldwork there. Many have developed research strategies that include both sending and receiving communities, for example, Patricia Pessar (Grasmuck and Pessar 1991) on Dominicans; Nina Glick Schiller (Glick Schiller and Fouron 2001a) on Haitians; Rachel Adler (n.d.), Jennifer Hirsch (n.d.), and Roger Rouse (1991, 1992) on Mexicans; and Cathy Small (1997) on Tongans.

That so many anthropologists who study migration in the United States have had field experience at both sides of the migration chain has shaped their research and theoretical frameworks. They are particularly sensitive to the links that migrants maintain with their home societies, and they are concerned not only with migration's effect on those who move to the United States but also with the consequences for those left behind. Some anthropologists are even reluctant to use the term *immigrant* because of its association with one-way movement and permanent settlement. Instead, they prefer *migrant* or, in some cases, *transmigrant,* to highlight the ongoing connections to the home society (see Glick Schiller, Chapter 4).[5] In US legal parlance, immigrants are those legally admitted to the United States with an immigrant visa for permanent residence status, as opposed, for example, to refugees who enter under different provisions or non-immigrants who are admitted on temporary visas for purposes such as travel, study, or business (see Kraly and Miyares 2001:35). In using the term *immigrant,* I do not have this strict legal definition in mind, nor do I mean to imply that settlement is necessarily permanent. Rather, immigrants are persons who are born outside the United States and move there to live and often work, even if the move turns out to be temporary and even if they retain strong ties to the home country and frequently return there.

It is not surprising that the first major work on transnationalism among US immigrants was written by anthropologists—all three of whom had field experience in both the host and sending societies—and that anthropologists are often guided in their research by transnational perspectives on migration (see Basch, Glick Schiller, and Szanton Blanc 1994; Glick Schiller, Basch, and Blanc-Szanton 1992a). Anthropological writing on contemporary transnational migration can be seen as a logical development of the early urban anthropology studies I have mentioned. In Chapter 4, Nina Glick Schiller traces the foundations of the anthropology of transnational migration to, among others, the ethnographies of urban migrants by Manchester school anthropologists. Linda Basch (2001:121) has also written of her debt to early studies of the African Copperbelt: "Copperbelt migrants were entering into an urban social system while at the same time maintaining their social ties and identifications with their regions of origin. In trying to capture the experience of these migrants, Copperbelt researchers discussed a wider social field that encompassed both the rural and urban areas of [then] Northern Rhodesia."

A transnational perspective conceptualizes migration as part of a pattern of transnational connection. The focus is on the processes by which many migrants—whom Glick Schiller calls "transmigrants"— become embedded in their new land and simultaneously develop and maintain familial, economic, social, organizational, religious, and political relations that span nation-state borders (Chapter 4). Glick Schiller and her colleagues have suggested the term "transnational social field" to encompass the way multiple actors create and sustain multistranded, interlocking social networks and relationships in two or more states as they "become part of the fabric of daily life in more than one state, simultaneously participating in the social, cultural, economic, religious, or political activities of more than one locality." In Glick Schiller's formulation, a transnational social field includes not only those involved in transnational activities but also "persons who have networks to transmigrants, but may not themselves maintain social relations across borders."

A growing number of anthropologists are documenting transnational practices, ideologies, and social fields as a way to understand the migration experience among particular groups in the United States, as well as to contribute to "theorizing migration" (for example, Basch, Glick Schiller, and Szanton Blanc 1994; Glick Schiller, Basch, and Blanc-Szanton 1992a; Glick Schiller and Fouron 2001a; Kearney 1995; Mahler 1998; Mahler and Pessar 2001; Ong 1999; Rouse 1992). In her chapter, Glick Schiller identifies two waves of recent scholarship on transnational migration. The first wave of research attempted to prove that there was a specific migrant experience that could be called "transnational migration." The second wave is moving beyond this question to examine topics such as the similarities and differences between transnational migration today and in earlier periods, the role of migrants in politics and nation-state building projects in home countries, and the extent to which forms of transnational connection continue across generations.

Studying migrants in both sending and receiving societies has also sensitized anthropologists to continuities and changes in social and cultural patterns in the United States. Because of their familiarity with the cultures in migrants' home communities, they are attuned to subtle, as well as dramatic, changes that take place in this country. This has been true of research on racial and ethnic identities (for example, Abusharaf 2002; Basch 1987; Foner 1985, 1987a, 1998a and b; Shokeid 1988; Stafford 1987; Sutton and Makiesky 1987), family and kinship (for example, Holtzman 2000; Pessar 1999b; for an overview, see Foner 1999), and religion (for example, Guest 2003; Hepner 1998; McAlister 1998; Walbridge 1996; Wellmeier 1998; Zane 1999). Anthropological studies of health care, too, have examined the way premigration cultural notions influence migrants' attitudes toward and use of American health-care institutions, as well as their use of folk-healing practices (for example, Gonzalez 1986; Guo 2000; Laguerre 1984). As Leo Chavez discusses in Chapter 7, immigrants bring with them beliefs and behaviors about health, illness, and appropriate treatment that may be unknown to US medical practitioners and conflict with notions of illness and treatment in the US system of health care. Familiarity with the home community brings another benefit: It reduces the risk that anthropologists will assume a timeless past of tradition there and makes them more sensitive to historical transformations that have occurred in the place of origin (Hirsch 2000 and this volume, Chapter 8).

Then there is gender. Anthropologists have been in the forefront in theorizing about the significance of gender in migration and in insisting that migration is a gendered process (Pessar, Chapter 3).[6] The studies have generally focused on the roles and experiences of migrant women and on how their status, relative to men, changes with migration. As Brettell (2000a:109) has noted, "Much of this research can be squarely situated in relation to analytic models at the heart of feminist anthropology—the domestic-public model that explores women's status in relation to different spheres of activity and the model springing from Marxist feminism that addresses the interrelationship between production and reproduction. Among the questions explored are whether wage earning serves to enhance the power and status of immigrant women within their households, whether greater sharing of household activities emerges as a result of the work obligations of women, and how changes in employment, family structure, and life style affect women's own assessments of their well-being."[7]

In contrast to some of the earlier literature on migrant women, there is now an increasing awareness that simple models of female emancipation, on one hand, or unliberated femininity, on the other, are serious distortions (Pessar, Chapter 3). Anthropologists have been exploring the losses and burdens, as well as gains and benefits, that women experience after migration; the continued influence of premigration gender ideologies and practices; and how changes may affect not only the resources and style with which women and men bargain but also what they bargain for (Foner 2000; Hirsch 2000:370; Pessar 1999b). Lately, anthropologists have sought, in Sarah Mahler and Patricia Pessar's words, to bring a "gendered optic to transnational studies" as a way to benefit both the study of transnational processes and the study of gender. The articles, in a special issue of *Identities*, edited by Mahler and Pessar, describe "how gender operates in... transnational contexts and why" and evaluate whether "gender relations and ideologies [are] reaffirmed, reconfigured, or both across transnational spaces" (Mahler and Pessar 2001:441).

Closely linked to gender issues, as Pessar points out in Chapter 3, is the study of family and kinship networks and household organization (see also Brettell 2000a). Anthropologists have written about the way family networks stimulate and facilitate the migration process, the role of family ties and networks in helping immigrants get jobs when they arrive in the United States, and the role of families in developing strategies for survival and assisting immigrants in the process of adjustment, providing a place where newcomers can find solace and support in a strange land and pool their resources as a way to advance. Along with increasing interest in gender and generation, there is awareness that immigrant households and families are not just havens in a heartless world but places where conflict, contestation, and negotiation also occur.

Less focused on one particular issue are the increasing number of ethnographic studies by anthropologists that, in time-honored fashion, are based on in-depth fieldwork and long-term familiarity with particular populations. These chronicle a variety of cultural and social patterns and processes—for example, on Brazilians (Margolis 1994, 1998), Chinese (Chen 1992; Guo 2000; Wong 1982, 1998), Dominicans (Bailey 2001; Hendricks 1974; Pessar 1995b), Haitians (Glick Schiller and Fouron 2001a; Laguerre 1984; Stepick 1998), Hmong (Donnelly

1994; Koltyk 1998), Indians (Lessinger 1995), Israelis (Shokeid 1988), Khmer (Smith-Hefner 1999), Koreans (Park 1997), Mexicans (Chavez 1992), Nuer (Holtzman 2000), Salvadorans (Mahler 1995a and b), Soviet Jews (Markowitz 1993), Sudanese (Abusharaf 2002), and Vietnamese (Freeman 1995). Also in the tradition of participant observation and community studies, a number of anthropological projects on recent immigrants have explored relations between established residents and newcomers in neighborhoods, schools, and workplaces, pointing to barriers and conflicts, as well as ties and common interests that bridge boundaries (see Goode and Schneider 1994; Lamphere 1992; Lamphere and Stepick 1994; Park 1997; Sanjek 1998, 2000; Stepick et al. 2003). A few have analyzed new cultural festivals and events (see Lessinger 1995; Sanjek 1998; Schneider 1990). Whether engaged in fieldwork in schools, neighborhoods, or homes, anthropologists have also been interested in the experiences, problems, and prospects of the children of immigrants—as Alex and Carol Stepick make clear in Chapter 5 (also see Gibson 1988; Gibson and Ogbu 1991; Maira 2002; Matute-Bianchi 1986; Olsen 1997; Stepick et al. 2001; Suárez-Orozco and Suárez-Orozco 1995, 2001). Some anthropologists have specifically focused on the experiences of refugee populations who have been displaced by war and violence and have been resettled in communities throughout the United States (for example, Haines 1989, 1996; Hopkins and Donnelly 1993; Rollwagen 1990).[8] Others have explored what Chavez calls the "shadowed lives" of undocumented immigrants (for example, Chavez 1992; Mahler 1995a and b; Margolis 1994, 1998; Stoller 2002).

Anthropology's tradition of cross-cultural analysis and comparison is also evident in some recent work on immigration. I, for one, have been involved in a variety of comparative projects, comparing the West Indian migrant experience in New York and London (Foner 1983, 1985, 1986, 1998a and b) and contemporary immigrant New Yorkers with those of a century ago (Foner 2000). Closely related is the "city as context" framework, first elaborated in a 1975 special issue of *Urban Anthropology* but, unfortunately, still relatively unexplored. In general, the "city as context" approach emphasizes the unique features of particular cities in urban research. With regard to immigration, Jack Rollwagen (1975) criticized studies that implicitly assume that the life of an immigrant group will be exactly the same regardless of the city in which the group lives—what he called "the city as constant argument." Rather, he suggested, noticeable contrasts will exist between immigrant groups from the same cultural background who settle in different American cities, if only because the size of the immigrant group and available opportunities in various cities vary. Brettell (2000b and this volume, Chapter 6) points to other features that need to be considered: the city's history of immigration, the proportion of immigrants in the population, and the number from different countries of origin; the spatial distribution of immigrants, including the presence or absence of residential ethnic enclaves, and the degree of segregation in the city's housing market; the structure of the city's labor market and available economic opportunities; the character of racial/ethnic relations in the city; the city's political system and civic institutions; and the particular urban ethos that shapes political, economic, and institutional life. Also important are specific characteristics of immigrants themselves, which vary from city to city—their national and ethnic origins, skill composition, and timing of arrival.

To date, the postmodern turn in much of anthropology has had little effect on US immigration studies in the discipline, although there has been some experimentation with "writing immigration." One example is *Jaguar*, Paul Stoller's (1999) novel, or ethnographic fiction, which moves back and forth between Niger and New York to recount the experiences of West African traders. Another is Cathy Small's (1997) *Voyages*, which tells the story of Tongan migration by going back and forth in time and place, between Tonga and California from the mid-1960s to the 1990s, and examines her own experiences as an anthropologist.[9]

Finally, issues of cultural relativism, a long-term anthropological concern, have come to the fore as well. Richard Shweder, in Chapter 9, draws on perspectives developed during his involvement with an interdisciplinary Russell Sage Foundation/Social Science Research Council working group—"Ethnic Customs, Assimilation, and American Law." Among other questions, the group considered the following: Which aspects of American law affect ethnic minority customs? How much cultural diversity in family practices ought to be permissible within the moral and constitutional framework of the United States? What does it mean for an ethnic custom or practice to be judged "un-American"? How do ethnic minority communities react to official attempts to force compliance with the cultural and legal norms of American middle-class life? (Shweder, Minow, and Markus 2000:viii–ix)

Shweder has written about female genital mutilation, a practice among certain African immigrant groups that has been legally banned in the United States. He asks how much toleration of the practice ought to be reasonable in the context of American scientific, medical, legal, and moral traditions. Tolerance, Shweder (2000:227) argues, "means setting aside our readily aroused and powerfully negative feelings about the practices of immigrant minority groups long enough to get the facts straight and engage the other in a serious moral dialogue" (see also Chapter 9). Jon Holtzman (2000), an anthropologist who has studied the Nuer in Minnesota, grapples with the conflicts between Nuer attitudes to domestic violence and those of US courts of law. In Chapter 5, Stepick and Stepick relate the dilemmas faced, on one side, by Haitian parents who fear charges of child abuse if they beat their children as they would in Haiti and, on the other, by culturally sensitive police officers who do not want to undermine Haitian parents' authority but must enforce the law if Haitian parental discipline exceeds legal bounds. In this regard, Pessar (Chapter 3) raises a fascinating question as to why police intervention in immigrant families over charges of child or spousal abuse looms so large in many migrants' discourse on life in the United States when, in fact, such intervention by the police and other state authorities is relatively infrequent. The threat or actual intervention by state authorities, she argues, not only pits one system of morality against another but also challenges family members' claims to holding a more elevated morality than that of white Americans. It unsettles the household, which many migrants see as a repository and maintainer of ethnic culture, gives the family's weakest members new leverage through appeal to the state, and undermines the authority of parents and/or husbands.[10]

WHERE DO WE GO FROM HERE?

This brings us to the future. What directions will anthropologists take—and, more important, should they take—as a growing number branch into research on migration to the United States? Is there a distinctive role for anthropologists in immigration studies? What contributions can they make?

The Push to Interdisciplinary Work and the Pull of the Discipline

As I have indicated, anthropologists enter a field of immigration studies that is increasingly interdisciplinary in nature. One sign of the increasing cross-fertilization of disciplines is that anthropology's theories, methods, and approaches are influencing work in other social science areas. Social scientists of all stripes are adopting transnational perspectives on migration that were first elaborated by anthropologists and are examining and developing them from their own disciplinary standpoints. Ethnographic research—which cultural anthropologists have long seen as the basic method in their field (cultural anthropologists, practically by definition, do fieldwork)—is shared with many immigration specialists in other disciplines, especially in sociology. Whereas some sociologists use survey research methods to document the scope and actual frequency of transnational practices (Portes 2001; Portes, Haller, and Guarnizo 2002), others rely on ethnographic techniques of participant observation and intensive interviews to explore the forms and consequences of transnationalism. Some have even combined ethnographic studies of immigrants in the United States with home-society research (for example, see sociologists Goldring 1998; Levitt 2001a; Smith 1998). Other ethnographer sociologists have explored a wide range of topics among various immigrant groups. These include family lives and social networks (Bacon 1996; Kibria 1993; Menjivar 2000), ethnoracial identities (Kibria 2002; Vickerman 1999; Waters 1999), and gender roles (Hondagneu-Sotelo 1994, 2001).

When reading the work of a social scientist in the immigration field, it is sometimes difficult to determine—from the methods used to the literature cited—his or her specific discipline. This is a healthy development. Interdisciplinary collaboration in research and theory building is what the social sciences at the dawn of the new millennium are all about. Anthropological studies of immigration, as Suárez-Orozco argues in Chapter 2, need to systematically reckon with the approaches and findings of colleagues in allied disciplines. Anthropologists are particularly receptive to interdisciplinary work because they come from a discipline that has long been open to borrowing from and collaborating with other fields. Latin American and Caribbean anthropologists, for example, are typically immersed in the history, sociology, political science, and economics literature pertaining to the society or culture they study. The same goes for specialists in other parts of the world. Likewise, anthropologists focusing on the United States should, as a matter of course, be expected to be familiar with work in other disciplines; in *Exotics at Home,* Micaela di Leonardo (1998:16) rightly criticizes those who have a "casual disregard of the America known to other scholars."

None of the contributors to this volume engage in this kind of narrow, discipline-bound approach. Virtually all have been involved in interdisciplinary collaborations in their work in immigration. Many have co-authored books on migration with social scientists in other fields, including Patricia Pessar's well-known account of Dominican migrants, *Between Two Islands,* with sociologist Sherri Grasmuck (Grasmuck and Pessar 1991); Alex Stepick's award-winning book on Miami, *City on the Edge,* with sociologist Alejandro Portes (Portes and Stepick 1993); Richard Shweder's volume *Engaging Cultural Differences,* edited with legal scholar Martha Minow and psychologist Hazel Markus (Shweder, Minow, and Markus 2002); Caroline Brettell's volumes on immigrant women, edited with sociologist Rita Simon (Simon and Brettell 1986), and migration theory, with political scientist James Hollifield (Brettell and Hollifield 2000); and my book on multidisciplinary perspectives in immigration research, edited with sociologists Rubén Rumbaut and Steven Gold (Foner, Rumbaut, and Gold 2000).

In Chapter 3, Pessar makes clear that the study of gender and migration is not an exclusively anthropological project and has involved other social-science disciplines. She deliberately uses the term "feminist ethnographers" to refer to scholars who share certain epistemological assumptions and research strategies associated with feminist scholarship and anthropological fieldwork, whatever their discipline. Studies of the second generation inevitably address theories elaborated in sociology concerning incorporation and assimilation, including segmented assimilation, and are informed by sociological surveys of immigrant children's school achievements and aspirations (see Stepick and Stepick, Chapter 5). My own work on race and ethnicity has been influenced by historical studies of "whiteness" in American society—which bring out the contingent nature of race and how groups initially disparaged as racial outsiders eventually become part of the racial/ethnic majority—and by sociological studies, including research on residential segregation (Foner 2000, 2002).

I could go on, but the point, I think, is clear. As di Leonardo (1998:365) observes, "just as genuine citizenship is innately internationalist, responsible scholarship is innately interdisciplinary." Yet, as we all know, citizenship in nation-states is not dead—and neither are disciplinary boundaries. An inherent tension exists between the push to interdisciplinary work and the pull of the discipline. Anthropology, like other social sciences, has a particular tradition, a series of classic works, and issues of theoretical and methodological concern that inform and guide research. There is great value in being steeped in these traditions and founding works and being engaged in debates that are central to, and enhance and enliven, the discipline. A greater awareness of the methodological, comparative, and conceptual contributions of the early anthropology of urban migrants is bound to raise questions and offer insights that will enrich contemporary research. Apart from intellectual considerations, the structure of American academic life dictates that we join professional associations in a particular discipline and that we belong to departments that tend to be defined by those disciplines. Given these realities and the growing number of anthropologists focusing on immigration, the time is ripe to evaluate how anthropology fits into an interdisciplinary project on immigration and to set out a research program for the future.

The Ethnographic Approach and Central Issues in Migration Anthropology

Although anthropologists cannot claim "ownership" of fieldwork or ethnographic methods, they are more likely to rely on ethnographic research than sociologists, historians, political scientists, or economists. By *ethnographic research* most anthropologists mean fieldwork involving participant observation and intensive interviews, although often other techniques, such as life histories, genealogies, and network analysis, are also involved (for a somewhat different definition and conceptualization of ethnographic methods, see Glick Schiller, Chapter 4).[11]

To anthropologists, participant observation is an essential part of ethnography—and ethnography does not consist of only in-depth interviews, certainly not just in-depth interviews conducted by assistants. The anthropologist who is conducting ethnographic research does many (sometimes all) of the interviews, incorporates participant observation into the project, and is engaged in long-term contact with the people being studied. This approach has its downside in that it limits the number of people a particular researcher can study and the ability to make generalizations for broad populations—what Stepick and Stepick (Chapter 5) call the "chasm" between the ethnographic particular and broad generalizations. However, anthropologists believe that in-depth study of a small number of people over time provides insights into their beliefs, values, and social relations, as well as the complex way they construct identities in specific contexts. Through participant observation, it is possible to see, as Bronislaw Malinowski observed long ago, that the way people behave is not always the way they say that they behave.

Of course, anthropologists studying migrants in the United States typically supplement their fieldwork with census and other quantitative data, if only to help interpret their ethnographic encounters and to place their field data in a larger context. A number have incorporated social surveys in their research projects. For example, in their Miami study of immigrant youth, Stepick and Stepick (Chapter 5) combined survey research with long-term participant observation and intensive interviewing. Chavez (Chapter 7) describes his involvement in a California study of cancer and Latinas that, in addition to ethnographic interviews, involved a random-sample telephone survey that, among other things, yielded information on demographic patterns. Large-scale surveys, as one observer notes, are "certainly necessary in migration research since it is only through such studies that the relative (quantitative) importance of different phenomena, the distribution of characteristics and their relationship between variables can be ascertained" (Gunilla Bjern, quoted in Brettell and Hollifield 2000:12). Looking ahead, more anthropologists will likely seek to collaborate with sociologists and other social scientists trained to conduct large-scale surveys and analyze census materials and national data-sets. No doubt, most anthropologists will contribute by providing an ethnographic dimension to the studies. This, after all, is our specialty—and we should highlight it.

The great benefit of ethnographic fieldwork is its up-close, in-depth knowledge of the day-to-day lives of individual people, and we should continue to emphasize this strength in our work on immigration. Ethnographic research is critical in developing reliable survey questions and should, as Raymond Smith (2001:58) notes, precede the design of questionnaires and "not be regarded as a supplementary source of anecdotes to support conclusions drawn from the survey." Building on anthropology's strengths, Jennifer Hirsch (Chapter 8) suggests that anthropologists collaborate with one another to conduct multisited, long-term fieldwork in both sending and receiving communities as a way to appreciate the complex dynamics of social and cultural change in the places from which migrants come, as well as the places where they go. To this I would add the value of coordinated field studies among migrants in multiple destinations, in the home country and in more than one "host" society—Indians in Bombay, London, and New York, to mention just one of many possibilities.

Ethnographic research not only brings people—their perspectives, social relations, and problems—to life. Ethnographic studies can also reveal subtleties in meaning and behavior that large-scale surveys often miss or, in some cases, get wrong. Revealing in this regard is a recent article by Alex Stepick and his colleagues using data from a large-scale survey of the children of immigrants in Miami. Stepick and his co-authors were able to interpret and add to the survey data precisely because they had conducted extensive ethnographic work among Haitians in southern Florida and in Miami-Dade County schools. In a few instances, the self-reported survey data were misleading. Although many Haitian students claimed on the survey not to know Creole well, Stepick and his colleagues (Stepick et al. 2001:244) state that "we have never witnessed a Haitian child who did not understand his or her parents' Creole." Similarly, the survey data on ethnic self-labeling showed only a small number of Haitian students claiming an African-American identity, but a disjuncture existed between self-labels and behavior. Most Haitian adolescents' behavior reflected Americanization as they dressed and acted "more African American" (Stepick et al.:260; see also Suárez-Orozco and Suárez-Orozco 2001:10–11 on the limitations of self-reported survey data in studying the children of immigrants). When it comes to women's position in the family, Pessar (Chapter 3) argues that structured surveys have similar problems in that they may lead to a deceptive picture of family unity and consensus. Ethnographic studies, she suggests, are better able to capture the complex, contradictory nature of family dynamics, including the contestation of gender inequalities. As for religion, surveys that ask respondents to check off one category of affiliation may also be suspect. Surveys of Chinese New Yorkers requiring one response—for example, Protestant, Buddhist, or Catholic—miss the way Buddhism, Daoism, and Chinese popular religious beliefs are intertwined and are closely integrated in family and household activities (Guest 2003). In Chapter 4, Glick Schiller argues that self-reported responses on surveys may minimize the importance of transnational ties. Those involved in transnational political or religious activities that are politically suspect, for example, may be reluctant to reveal these involvements to survey researchers.

Whatever the topic of study, it often takes people a long time to open up to researchers asking questions—and several hours of patient interviewing before intimate details come pouring forth (Smith 2001:59). Long-term participant observation brings out the messy realities of day-to-day living—the inconsistencies and contradictions in beliefs and behavior, as well as the many ways they shift and change over time and in different contexts. In Chapter 5, Stepick and Stepick note that direct observation over four years allowed them to appreciate how immigrant youth could be ashamed of their home culture among peers yet embody it within the home and how they could be alienated from and have bitter conflicts with their parents yet still care deeply for them and be strongly attached to the family. In the study of transnational migration, Glick Schiller argues in Chapter 4 that ethnography, because of its long-term engagement within the social networks of immigrants, is well-suited to revealing whether and how individuals maintain transnational connections over time (see Adler n.d.).

As the immigrant influx continues to change notions of race and ethnicity in the United States, the subject of racial and ethnic identities is an important one for ethnographic studies. They can show the shifting and situational nature of these identities, the meanings people attach to them, and how these identities evolve in the context of changing social, economic, and political conditions. A growing literature focuses on panethnic identities—Hispanic and Asian, in particular—among immigrants and their children. However, one-shot surveys are of limited value in capturing the complex dynamics involved. Ethnographic research is required in order to reveal how and why panethnic identities become salient in particular contexts—how they can be invoked or put aside in different moments for different purposes and take on different meanings, depending on the circumstances or sites of interaction (for example, see the ethnographic studies by sociologists Itzigsohn [n.d.] and Kibria [2002]).

Ethnographic research can uncover trends or patterns that inform other studies, including large-scale surveys. Insights gained from fieldwork can revise or modify theoretical perspectives and lead to new theoretical understandings and conceptualizations of migration processes and their effects. The very serendipity and flexibility involved in fieldwork can have theoretical benefits. Anthropologists often report that they go into the field to study one thing but end up focusing on another in response to new situations that were not expected within the initial set of assumptions guiding their project. In Chapter 4, Glick Schiller points out how the research she first used to describe Haitian transnational migration was initially developed with other concerns in mind. In the course of this research, she became aware of how migrants were "building and maintaining transnational social fields." Ethnographers, as Glick Schiller notes, inevitably impose categories as they observe and record data, but these categories and hypotheses are constantly tested in the field as they "continually question, explore, and reformulate their understanding of the relationship between variables and even the choice of variables as the research proceeds."

Ethnographic research can illuminate virtually every area of concern in immigration studies, from the construction of racial and ethnic identities to gender, family relations, politics, work, and religion. A qualitative approach has enabled anthropologists to make important contributions to the study of the second generation, and in the future we should be seeing more ethnographic studies of the experiences of immigrants' children in their communities and schools. Through fieldwork, anthropologists can provide in-depth research on how the children of immigrants grow up in what Sunaina Maira calls "multiple realities," navigating different cultural worlds and calling on different models of behavior in different settings (cited in Prashad 2000:131; see Maira 2002). Anthropologists are also well positioned to examine the multifaceted nature of racial and ethnic identity formation and reformation among immigrant and second-generation youth, as well as the combination of factors that affect school achievement, which is so critical to their future. Some of the most sensitive portrayals of relations between immigrant parents and their American-born children come from novels by second-generation authors (for example, Garcia 1992; Jen 1991; Lee 1995; Ng 1993; Ng 1998). Rich, detailed ethnographies can shed additional light on the sources of conflict, as well as identification, reciprocity, and caring between the generations (see Stepick and Stepick, Chapter 5).

Roger Sanjek's (1998, 2000) New York City research brings out the benefits of fieldwork in communities where multiple cultural, racial, ethnic, and linguistic streams interact. Drawing on a long-term ethnographic team study of native whites, African Americans, and immigrants in Elmhurst-Corona, Queens, Sanjek's work points to several productive research sites and topics, including local politics, housing markets, houses of worship, public rituals, and retail shopping and commerce. The focus on multiethnic and multicultural neighborhoods shows that immigrants do not live out their lives in isolation from the native born but that there are many important points of contact, some marked by conflict and tension, others by accommodation, cooperation, and peaceful coexistence. Fieldwork projects in workplaces and other institutional settings can also elucidate the kinds of relations that develop between immigrants and established resident Americans and among immigrants in different ethnic/racial groups (for example, see Haines and Mortland 2001; Lamphere 1992; Lamphere and Stepick 1994; Stepick et al. 2003).

Ethnographies of intergroup dynamics can reveal not only sites of contention and consensus but also processes of identity construction and incorporation. It is not just a question of how immigrants identify themselves. Also important are how established residents perceive and label immigrants and how such perceptions both reflect and influence the relations that evolve between them. A study of Muslims in New York's Harlem offers tantalizing clues as to how African Americans are readjusting their visions of the African continent, which figure in their own identities, in response to the increasing presence of West African immigrants (Zain 2002). Research on African American–African relations is just one topic that requires further study. Becoming American, as Stepick and his colleagues (2003:25, 143) put it, is not a one-way street. Their study of Miami points to the role of intensive, long-term, direct observation in revealing how interaction between newcomer immigrants and Americans affects the nature of Americans' self-identity. Miami is an especially fascinating case, given how thoroughly Latinization has transformed the region.

The Question of Culture

Obviously, anthropology's contribution is not just a matter of an ethnographic approach and perspective. Any discussion of possibilities for a migration anthropology must consider the concept of culture. After all, part of the anthropologist's toolkit is a sensitivity to cultural patterns and cultural differences—even though the culture concept has never been defined in terms on which all anthropologists agree (see Borofsky et al. 2001; Kuper 1999). In Chapter 4, Glick Schiller defines *culture* as encompassing social relations, social structure, and transgenerationally transmitted patterns of action, belief, and language. Shweder (2001:437) uses *culture* to refer to community-specific ideas about what is true, good, beautiful, and efficient that are socially inherited, customary, and constitutive of different ways of life. In grappling with cultural questions concerning migrants in Europe, Unni Wikan (2002:86) defines *culture* as norms and values that are contested and contestable, preferring the adjectival form, *cultural*, in recognition of cultural differences in outlook and life-ways among people who also have much in common. And these are only three definitions!

The very notion that cultures are "manners of doing things, distinct and characteristic" has, like so much else in anthropology, come under attack (Geertz 1995:42). As Clifford Geertz (1995:42–43) eloquently puts it,

> Questions...rain down...on the very idea of a cultural scheme. Questions about the coherence of life-ways, the degree to which they form connected wholes. Questions about their homogeneity, the degree to which everyone in a

tribe, a community, or even a family (to say nothing of a nation or a civilization) shares similar beliefs, practices, habits, and feelings. Questions about discreteness, the possibility of specifying where one culture, say the Hispanic, leaves off and the next, say the Amerindian, begins. Questions about continuity and change, objectivity and proof, determinism and relativism, uniqueness and generalization, description and explanation, consensus and conflict, otherness and commensurability—and about the sheer possibility of anyone, insider or outsider, grasping so vast a thing as an entire way of life and finding the words to describe it.

However, as Geertz (1995:43) also notes, "whatever the infirmities of culture ('cultures,' 'cultural forms'...) there is nothing for it but to persist in spite of them. Tone deafness, willed or congenital, and however belligerent, will not do."[12] For analytic purposes, I think that it is useful to distinguish, as Geertz (1973a) has done, between culture as values, ideas, and symbols and a fabric of meaning in contrast to social structure, or the existing network of social relations. The fact is that the cultural understandings and orientations migrants bring with them help to shape their reactions to and actions in their new home. Rarely, however, do these orientations persist unchanged; they are restructured, redefined, and renegotiated in the new setting. Indeed, migrants may construct their own versions of tradition as they reconceptualize the past to make sense of current experience and to speak to current dilemmas and issues (Yanagisako 1985:247). An important task for anthropologists is to tease out both the cultural legacies and the cultural changes among migrant populations in the United States and to document how distinctive patterns develop that are a mixture of old and new—what some theorists have called "cultural hybrids," products of a process that has been seen as analogous to "creolization" (see Foner 1999).

This does not mean that culture should be viewed in isolation—in either explaining cultural changes that emerge in the migrant setting or understanding the influence of culture on migrants' behavior. It is imperative to bear this in mind. Kuper (1999:xi) puts it well when he writes that "some form of cultural explanation may be useful enough, but appeals to culture can only offer a partial explanation of why people think and behave as they do, and of what causes them to alter their ways. Political and economic forces [and] social institutions…cannot be wished away, or assimilated to systems of knowledge and belief."

In Chapter 8, Hirsch makes a strong case for the need to situate analyses of culture in the context of structural or institutional constraints and class, gender, and generational divisions. In general, a dynamic interplay exists among structure, culture, and agency— creative culture-building takes place in the context of external social, economic, and cultural forces in the new environment and the cultural understandings, meanings, and symbols (and social practices) immigrants bring with them from their communities of origin. If the US context is critical, so, too, there may be a transnational dynamic as new cultural hybrids are formed among migrants who manage their lives both "here" and "there"—and as the cultural patterns that develop in the United States also reshape the culture of the home community (see Levitt [2001a] for an analysis of the effect of the social practices and cultural models immigrants acquire in the new setting—what she calls "social remittances"—on villages in the Dominican Republic). Global events and links between the global and the local should also be considered. In the wake of September 11, interest in Muslim communities in the United States has increased. One question concerns the way the World Trade Center tragedy and political events in the Middle East have affected Muslim migrants' religious identity, ritual practices, and the meanings attached to these practices.

Although none of the contributors to this volume focus on religion, this is a "natural" theme for anthropologists studying migrants in the United States, given religion's important role in the discipline. Certainly, anthropology's rich body of literature on religion can bring insights to the analysis of religious symbols, meanings, and rituals in the migrant setting. Anthropologists can contribute to understanding the complex combination of continuities and changes in religious beliefs, identities, and practices in specific cases. (See Ebaugh and Chafetz [2000] and Warner and Wittner [1998], edited volumes by sociologists, based on ethnographic research in immigrant congregations in the United States and including contributions by several anthropologists.)

Do some migrants become more "religious" in the United States? If so, is this because religion is a more important identity marker or a key symbol of identity and representation of homeland culture? What forms does religious involvement take in the migrant context? What role does religion play in the constitution of immigrant/ethnic group identities, including new panethnic identities, and in other aspects of migrants' lives? These are only a few of the questions that await further study.

In line with postmodern concerns in anthropology, we should be seeing studies of negotiated and contested meanings and social prac-tices—processes that stand out as immigrants construct new cultural forms and social arrangements in the context of change. A focus on cultural contestation, negotiation, and reinvention will enrich the field as long as agency is not overemphasized at the expense of structural cir-cumstances and constraints—and as long as shared cultural symbols, meanings, and values are not slighted in the quest to document multi-ple perspectives, resistance, and struggle. Also on the table are inter-pretive analyses and "readings" of immigrant rituals, performances, texts, and cultural symbols as a way to elucidate the dynamics of change, conflict, and adaptation in immigrant communities and the forms and nature of transnationalism. Good examples, from across the Atlantic, are articles by social anthropologists in a special issue of *Global Networks,* edited by Katy Gardner and Ralph Grillo (2002). These explore the transnational practices of migrant families through analyz-ing the performances of and meanings attributed to life-course rituals, including weddings and death rituals, among migrant households and families in Britain and also in their countries of origin.

A "reading" of ethnic festivals and cultural performances, as Brettell notes in Chapter 6, can tell us not only about ethnic identity and ethnic expression but also about the ways different immigrant populations mark their space in American urban landscapes. As a vari-ant of this approach, the study of social situations, or specific incidents or series of incidents, as dynamic processes (of the sort elaborated decades ago by Manchester school anthropologists) can also illuminate the development of and changes in cultural orientations and social relations among migrants.

To date, anthropologists have shied away from, and generally been highly critical of, assimilation theory. Yet their focus on culture can contribute to new conceptualizations that emphasize the remaking of American society and culture. Sociologists Richard Alba and Victor Nee (2003) argue for a notion of assimilation that sees immigrants as "reshaping the American mainstream." In their view, American culture must be viewed as a composite: "Although cultural elements from the earliest groups have been preserved—in this sense, there is great cultural continuity—elements contributed from subsequent immigrant groups have been incorporated continually into the mainstream."[13] Alba and Nee barely scratch the surface in showing how this is happening today and only briefly mention cuisine and popular forms of entertainment and artistic expression. A more exhaustive cultural analysis would find such influences in other domains of American life. Who better than anthropologists to tease out the ways that immigrants are remaking and transforming the dominant American culture today and its variations in particular cities and regions? Who better to chart the creation of "hybrid cultures" among young people in different places as members of the second generation grow up, go to school, and socialize with children of immigrants from a variety of countries and cultures and with children of long-established Americans (see Kasinitz, Mollenkopf, and Waters 2002)? Moreover, anthropological studies can deepen our understanding of what sociologist Ruben Rumbaut (1997b) calls the "paradoxes of assimilation," for example, how "becoming more American" can be bad for immigrants' health as they change their diets, exercise routines, and other patterns in the United States or can harm their academic chances as they spend more time watching television and hanging out with friends and less time studying (see also Chavez, Chapter 7).

Closely related are issues of cultural relativism, another anthropological bailiwick that is bound to stimulate studies of how immigrants, with their particular values and standards, confront US laws, rules, and norms in courts, hospitals, government agencies, and other institutional settings. What sorts of conflicts develop between "immigrant" and "mainstream" values, and in what contexts? How have these conflicts been handled by US agencies and institutions? How do immigrants respond? These are not just academic questions. They have policy implications. As experts on particular migrant groups, anthropologists sometimes find themselves called on to provide advice to and speak for the populations among whom they work, as Jennifer Hirsch discusses in Chapter 8. What are the dilemmas confronting anthropologists who are sought after by governmental and other organizations as cultural experts on migrants? How can anthropologists negotiate the tensions between theoretically rigorous ethnographic work and politically engaged, or applied, anthropology?

Richard Shweder, in Chapter 9, takes a decidedly forthright position in the face of the increasing number of moral challenges posed by cultural migration to the United States. Many Americans in dominant groups may be morally outraged and intolerant of the "different" customs of immigrant minority groups. In fact, legal actions may criminalize some of these customs. Shweder discusses a few examples, such as attempts to outlaw animal sacrifice in the Santeria church in Florida and to punish Afghans in Maine for kissing their children's genitals. In this context, Shweder argues that anthropologists have a responsibility to share what they know about other cultures with the American public—and more than that. In his view, they should be involved in—and take a stand on—normative public policy debates by representing "the native point of view" and engaging a normative agenda for a multicultural society in an informed, rigorous way.

Shweder raises several controversial issues in his chapter. Not all anthropologists would agree with his relatively benign depiction of the consequences of female genital surgeries—or on what stand to take and policies to support regarding them. Many would not concur with his critique of anthropologists such as Wikan (2002). On the basis of her involvement in cases with Middle Eastern and South Asian girls in Norway, Wikan contends that state agencies should uphold universal rights for children and women to protect them from oppressive cultural practices such as forced marriages. Appeals to culture and traditional mores, Wikan (2002:24) argues, can end up victimizing weaker members of the group, such as women and children, who are not given a say but "are compelled to do as 'culture' bids." Whatever one's position on these issues, a great virtue of Shweder's chapter is that it highlights, in a dramatic way, the kinds of moral questions anthropologists will increasingly confront in their research on migrants in this country.

These questions are especially likely to arise in medical anthropology studies. Hirsch notes how her expertise was sought by the Centers for Disease Control and Prevention, which was dealing with a syphilis outbreak among Mexican migrants in rural Alabama. Chapter 8 describes her concerns about how to respond in this case and in other situations in which anthropologists are expected to emphasize the role of culture. Certainly, we still have much to learn about how the health-related beliefs and practices immigrants bring from their home cultures affect interactions with the American health-care system—for example, when immigrants and medical personnel differ in their understandings of the causes and implications of biomedically recognized diseases. In this regard, a fascinating question concerns the weaving together of traditional healing and modern medical practices in the American setting and why some migrants (in certain contexts) prefer traditional healers and others, such as one of the Mexican women Hirsch describes, seek out and even overuse modern medical technology.

Again, culture is not all-important or all-determining. Both Chavez and Hirsch worry that an overemphasis on culture in medical anthropology will obscure the role of the political economy of the US health care system and pervasive structural inequalities in American society that affect the health of the poor, migrant and non-migrant alike. In Chapter 8, Hirsch argues that by exaggerating the importance of culture in determining health outcomes, anthropologists "can do a real disservice to those for whom we presume to speak." A medical anthropology of immigration must consider not only immigrants' (and biomedical practitioners') cultural beliefs but also how factors such as immigrant legal status, education, and income affect access to health insurance and medical services and how migrants' living and work conditions affect their health outcomes. Leo Chavez (Chapter 7) tells of his frustrations in developing a culturally sensitive intervention program to increase Latina women's use of breast self-examination and mammography. Even though the program made the women more aware of the value of preventive care and the use of cancer-screening exams, Chavez and his collaborators could do nothing about the cost of screening or lack of medical insurance, to name two of the structural barriers the immigrant women faced in trying to access health care. In addressing work conditions that affect migrant health, Hirsch (Chapter 8) has been developing a project with the Hispanic Health Coalition in

Atlanta to improve occupational safety and health among construction day laborers. Plans for the project include a training program to educate contractors and subcontractors about workplace safety and their legal obligations to provide a safe working environment.

Transnational Migration, Gender Dynamics, and Comparative Approaches

Anthropologists have already made significant contributions to our understanding of transnational migration, yet two of the challenges ahead are to clarify how transnational practices affect migrants' lives and their involvements in US communities and organizations and to investigate whether, and how, migrants transform both home and host countries as they maintain engagements in both places. In this regard, Pessar notes that we need to know more about how grandmothers and other kin deal with caring for children left behind, including rebellious youth sent "home" by distraught migrant parents. Glick Schiller calls for more research on the effects of remittances on those who send them and those who receive them and on transnational migration's influence on nation-state building projects in migrants' homelands. Among the many issues she raises for further study are how migrants navigate issues of legal rights and identity when they maintain homes and businesses and participate in political affairs in more than one nation-state; how transnational religious networks and organizations, as well as religious practices and belief systems, develop and operate within what she calls "transnational social fields"; and whether and how transnational connections continue across generations (see Levitt and Waters 2002). How are the lives of children of immigrants shaped by their parents' transnational attachments? Are there changes as the children reach adulthood, marry, enter the workforce, and raise children of their own? These and other questions will benefit from the comparative study of transnational practices among different migrant groups in the United States. (For beginning attempts at such comparisons in the sociological literature, see Guarnizo, Sanchez, and Roach 1999; Itzigsohn 2000; Levitt 2000; Portes, Haller, and Guarnizo 2002).

Another area for further study is what Pessar (Chapter 3) calls the "analysis of gender across transnational space." Already, anthropologists are beginning to develop analytical frameworks and research strategies that position gender more centrally within the study of transnational migration. Does transnational migration—and the maintenance of strong links to the home community—reinforce premigration gender ideologies and norms? Or does it lead men and women to question these ideologies and norms and develop new meanings and understandings of gender roles? When we speak of "premigration" patterns and practices, how have they undergone changes in recent years? What roles do migration and transnational linkages play in these changes? As part of the effort to avoid simplistic—and triumphalist—accounts of women's gains after migration, Pessar recommends research that historicizes and documents the nature of, and potential inconsistencies within, premigration gender regimes and also probes migrants' social memories, which are so important in understanding how they measure continuity and change in gender ideologies and practices.

Note that I refer to men and women. A challenge for the future, as Pessar (Chapter 3) observes, is to build on and branch out from a concentration on female immigrants to apply gender-inflected research questions and analytic constructs to both men and women. In addition, gender should not be studied separately from other aspects of migrants' lives. (As Pessar also warns in her chapter, gender analyses should not be confined to "the woman's panel" at conferences or the "woman's chapter" in books.) There is a need to develop theoretical and analytical frameworks that can capture "the simultaneity of the impact of gender, race, ethnicity, nationality, class, and legal status on the lives of different immigrants" (Pessar 1999b:69). Among the many topics that can benefit from attention to gender are the role of social networks in shaping migration patterns, the effect of racial and ethnic inequalities in the United States, the experiences and educational outcomes of the children of immigrants, and relations between immigrants and established residents.

Although studies of gender and migration are branching out beyond the traditional domains of the household and workplace, these areas have certainly not been exhausted. In line with anthropologists' longstanding interest in family, kinship, and household organization, a host of topics awaits further study, including marriage choices and patterns, the dynamics of intergenerational relations, and family and household rituals. These can illuminate how migrants construct and reconstruct family lives in the United States in the context of external social and economic forces and premigration cultural frameworks. These studies can also bring out, as Pessar writes in her chapter, how household members' orientations and actions are not only guided by norms of solidarity but also informed by hierarchies of power along gender and generational lines. Also on the agenda is research that analyzes how government legislation and policies affect the formation, unification, and material well-being of immigrant families.

Finally, anthropologists' cross-cultural and comparative perspective suggests other fruitful research directions. In the immigration field, there is a tendency to assume that the findings and analyses of studies on a particular group in one location hold true throughout the United States. Such assumptions are often unwarranted (see Foner 2001a). Building on the "city as context" approach, anthropologists are well equipped to conduct investigations that explore how and why the experiences of specific groups differ from one city to another. As Brettell observes in her chapter, anthropology is a discipline rooted in an understanding of place, and cities are places that differ in myriad ways that may be significant to the processes by which immigrants are incorporated. Each immigrant destination is distinct from any other in important ways, reflecting, among other things, the ways in which geographic and historical particularities shape immigrant flows—their skill composition, the diversity of the groups, and the timing of arrival—and the effects of particular social, political, and economic institutions and structures on the options available to arrivals from abroad (see Waldinger 2001:4, 22).

By uncovering the differences and similarities between groups in various locations, a comparative approach can illuminate the special features of both the individual group and the place being examined. At the same time, it enlarges our theoretical understanding of the kinds of institutions and processes being compared, from the dynamics of identity construction to economic and political incorporation (see Fredrickson 1997:24). Such comparisons should, as Hirsch observes, include newer migrant-receiving cities, such as Atlanta, and not just places like New York, Los Angeles, and Miami, which have already been the subject of considerable study.[14] In fact, anthropologists would do well to turn their attention to the immigrant experience in some of the "new Ellis Islands," which were largely unaffected by immigration until recently. They should also consider suburban areas, which are the first stop for a growing number of newcomers today. (For example, see the essays in Haines and Mortland [2001]; Koltyk [1998] on the Hmong in Wausau, Wisconsin; and Mahler [1995b] on Salvadorans in Long Island suburbs).

Other comparisons can also help us better understand and conceptualize the migrant experience. Within one city, comparisons of different migrant populations can provide insights into the way a distinctive blend of meanings, perceptions, and patterns of behavior emerges among each group (see Foner 2001b).[15] Comparisons of immigrants and non-immigrants can be designed to bring out the role of factors such as social class and race among both populations (see Hirsch, Chapter 8). There is also the possibility of historical comparisons, such as my study of New York City, which compares contemporary immigrants with those who came a century ago (Foner 2000). Going beyond the United States, cross-national comparisons can point to the particular ways that the US context and the US position in the global economic and political system shape the migrant experience. My comparisons of West Indians in New York and London have demonstrated the importance of context, especially the racial context, in West Indian migrant identities, achievements, and social relations. Other cross-national comparisons are sure to provide additional insights into a broad range of questions, from various aspects of immigrant incorporation to the dynamics of transnational and diasporic ties.

The chapters in this volume, in sum, make clear that anthropologists bring their special skills, perspectives, and approaches—and a long-term involvement in migration—to the study of contemporary US immigrants. This is an exciting time in the immigration field. We live in a world on the move; hundreds of thousands of people from all over the globe enter the United States every year. A major task for social scientists is to chart and explain the experiences of the newcomers as they create new lives for themselves in this country while also, in many cases, continuing to participate in institutions, projects, and relations across national borders. Just as the move to the United States irrevocably alters immigrants' lives, so, too, the millions who have arrived in recent decades are reshaping America in profound ways and also transforming their homelands. Anthropologists have already made significant contributions to understanding these changes. There is every reason to expect this trend to continue, even to accelerate, as anthropologists, in conversation and sometimes collaboration with scholars in other disciplines, try to make sense of the many transformations that immigration has created.

Notes

1. A count of all US dissertations between 1930 and the mid-1990s, according to di Leonardo (1998:374), shows single-digit representation for non–Native American work until 1978, with proportions hovering around 15 percent thereafter.

2. This does not mean, of course, that globalization has led to a homogenization of the world. Foreign cultural forms are interpreted, translated, and appropriated according to local conditions of reception (see Inda and Rosaldo 2002a).

3. Early work wrestled with the conceptual differences between "tribe" and "ethnic group," as Brettell (2000a:114) notes in her review article.

4. In my New York research, I interviewed several people from the Jamaican village I had studied in the late 1960s. The teacher with whom I had boarded came to New York in the 1970s (where she worked as a home attendant), and I benefited enormously from my many talks with her.

5. In her chapter, Glick Schiller argues that the term *transmigrant* should be reserved for those persons who, having emigrated from one nation-state to another, live their lives across borders, participating simultaneously in social relations that embed them in more than one nation-state. Transmigrants develop and maintain multiple types of relationships—familial, economic, social, organizational, religious, and political—that span borders. In her formulation, those who are "truly immigrants" cut their ties and refuse to look behind them.

6. An anthropologist—Patricia Pessar (1999b)—was invited to write the paper assessing the stock of knowledge, core theoretical issues, and unresolved empirical questions on gender and immigration for the Social Science Research Council conference on the state of theory and research in the field of international migration. Not surprisingly, another anthropologist—Nina Glick Schiller (1999a)—was asked to write a paper on transnationalism.

7. There is hardly an anthropological account of recent immigrants to the

United States that doesn't touch on questions pertaining to gender. See Brettell and de Berjeois (1992) for a review of the literature on anthropology and the study of immigrant women, as well as the articles in Simon and Brettell (1986). Also see Pessar (1999b) for a review and an appraisal of work on the role of gender, households, and social networks in the migration process.

8. A special unit of the American Anthropological Association, the Committee on Refugee Issues (CORI), was founded in 1988. It extended its focus to immigrants in 1996 and changed its name (but not the acronym) to the Committee on Refugees and Immigrants. In late 2002, it became part of the Society for Urban, National, Transnational/Global Anthropology.

9. Also see Aihwa Ong's chapter in *Women Writing Culture* (which presents her own life, along with the stories of two other emigrant Chinese women). She aims to "capture the specific diasporic articulation James Clifford calls 'traveling-in-dwelling, dwelling-in-traveling'" (Ong 1999:351).

10. For a detailed discussion of West Indian immigrants' attitudes to US laws and practices concerning corporal punishment, based on an ethnographic study in New York, see Waters (1999:220–241). West Indian parents believe that the government tries to deprive them of their chosen technique for disciplining their children without offering any alternative for teaching respect and good behavior to teenagers.

11. For a sampling of definitions of ethnographic methods in anthropology, see Arvizu (2001), Kottak (1999), Peacock (1986), and Salzman (1999).

12. In his introduction to a "conversation about culture" in the *American Anthropologist*, Robert Borofsky (2001:433) argues that rather than seek the concept's underlying essence or reality, we should view it as a conceptual tool that can be applied in various ways for different ends with different effectiveness.

13. As Suárez-Orozco notes in Chapter 2, German Americans, Italian Americans, and Irish Americans all left deep imprints on the molding of American culture. Today in the United States, we eat, speak, and dance differently than we did thirty years ago, in part because of large-scale immigration.

14. This is not surprising. These three cities are among the most popular destinations for recent immigrants. A notable feature of the recent immigration to the United States is its high degree of concentration in a small number of states and metropolitan areas. More than half the immigrants who came during the 1990s settled in and around New York City, Los Angeles, San Francisco, Chicago, Miami, Houston, and Dallas. The recent immigration is overwhelmingly urban and suburban, as opposed to rural, in destination. In 2000, twenty-five of

the nation's large metropolitan regions accounted for nearly three-quarters of all immigrants (Alba and Denton 2002).

15. This includes comparisons of immigrants from different groups within the same country of origin, for example, Trinidadians/Guyanese of East Indian versus African ancestry.

2

Right Moves? Immigration, Globalization, Utopia, and Dystopia

Marcelo M. Suárez-Orozco

Over the past decade, globalization has intensified worldwide economic, social, and cultural transformations. Globalization is structured by three powerful, interrelated formations: (1) the postnationalization of production and distribution of goods and services, fueled by growing levels of international trade, foreign direct investment, and capital market flows, (2) the emergence of new information and communication technologies that place a premium on knowledge-intensive work, and (3) unprecedented levels of worldwide migration that generate significant demographic and cultural changes in most regions of the world.

Globalization's puzzle is that although many applaud it as the royal road for development (for example, Friedman 2000; Micklethwait and Wooldrige 2000; Rubin 2002), it is generating strong currents of discontent. In large regions of the world, globalization has become a deeply disorienting and threatening process of change (Bauman 1998; Soros 2002; Stiglitz 2002). Globalization has generated the most hostilities where it has placed local cultural identities—including local meaning systems, religious identities, and systems of livelihood—under siege. Argentina is a case in point. After a decade of cutting-edge free market policies, the economy of the country that was once the darling of such embodiments of globalization as the International Monetary Fund and World Bank imploded. At the beginning of the twentieth century, Argentina was one of the ten wealthiest countries in the world, yet it ended the century in default, with more than 40 percent of the population at poverty level. By early 2003, an estimated 50,000 *cartoneros* were living off the cartons they gathered every night from trash cans in Buenos Aires, one of the world's most elegant cities.

First and foremost, globalization is about movement. Its emerging regime—mobile capital, mobile production and distribution, mobile populations, and mobile cultures—is generating deep paradoxes. Regions of the world such as East Asia seem to have prospered immensely under globalization's regime (see Table 2.1, World Bank 2001). Yet, in the Argentinas of the world, the forces of globalization have conspired to intensify patterns of inequality and human suffering (Dussel 2000; Mittelman 2000; Nader 1993). The last decade of the twentieth century witnessed vast economic growth in the rich nations, especially the United States, but roughly 25 percent of the population of the developing world continued to live in desperate poverty, on less than a dollar a day (refer to Table 1.1). China's meteoric integration into the global economy has significantly reduced poverty, but, as in much of Latin America, globalization has also increased inequality (World Bank 2001:1).

There is a strong and somewhat amorphous, eclectic anti-globalization ethos, ubiquitously named, articulated, and performed in varied contexts, from Seattle to Genoa and Buenos Aires. Its message seems structured by a common grammar: The global project is destabilizing, disorienting, and threatening to large numbers of people the world over.

Yet, even though many hate what they see in globalization, others are seduced by its promise. Here is another paradox of globalization: As it continues to penetrate the local cultural imaginaries of poor developing countries, even if it destabilizes local economies and livelihoods, globalization generates structures of desire and consumption fantasies that local economies cannot fulfill. These twin factors, globalization's uneven effects on the world economy and the emergence of a global imaginary of consumption, are behind the largest wave of immigration in human history. Globalization's paradoxical power lies in its

TABLE 2.1

*Population Living below US $1 per Day in Developing Countries
1990 and 1998*

	Number of People below US $1 a Day (Millions)		Poverty Rate (%)	
	1990	1998 (Estimate)	1990	1998 (Estimate)
East Asia	452.4	278.3	27.6	15.3
Excluding China	92.0	65.1	18.5	11.3
South Asia	495.1	522.0	44.0	40.0
Sub-Saharan Africa	242.3	290.9	47.7	46.3
Latin America	73.8	78.2	16.8	15.6
Middle East/North Africa	5.7	5.5	2.4	1.9
Europe and Central Asia	7.1	24.0	1.6	5.1
Total	1276.4	1198.9	29.0	24.0

Source: World Bank. Global Economic Prospects and the Developing Countries 2000.

manufacture of both despair and hope. Millions of people, though, must realize their hope elsewhere, as migrants.

Globalization's discontent also visits the "other half," the wealthy, advanced, postindustrial democracies, which have, arguably, benefited the most under its reign. In the advanced, postindustrial democracies, the unprecedented, growing, and seemingly uncontainable migratory flows generated by globalization over the past decade are, alas, experienced as threatening and disorienting to local cultural identities and sensibilities. This is the case in most of western Europe, the United States, and Australia, where anti-immigrant sentiment and xenophobia have emerged as potentially explosive political and social concerns. The general move to the political right in Europe over the past few years can be linked to the fears and anxieties generated by globalization, immigration, and crime. Somewhat monomaniacal anti-immigrant parties in western Europe have gained momentum over the past decade: the Vlams Bloc in Belgium, the Freedom Party in Austria, the People's Party in Denmark, and, of course, in May 2002, the Front National in France. Voters in California overwhelmingly approved Proposition 187, a new law that denies illegal immigrants a host of publicly funded services, including schooling children. In mid-2001, Australia denied a ship in distress, carrying hundreds of asylum seekers, entry to its ports. To paraphrase Tolstoy, globalization is making all the families of the world unhappy in the same way.

In this chapter, I examine certain anthropological concerns related to large-scale immigration and the flow of labor within the paradigm of globalization—a paradigm that will continue to attract the attention of anthropologists and allied social scientists in the decades to come (Inda and Rosaldo 2002b; Suárez-Orozco, Suárez-Orozco, and Qin-Hilliard 2003). First, I explore the parameters of the phenomena called "globalization." Next, I turn to the topic of large-scale immigration and examine recent scholarly debates in a variety of social science disciplines, including (but not limited to) cultural anthropology. Last, I examine several cultural processes of change facing those who pursue their fortunes beyond their national boundaries—the area ripest for important anthropological theoretical and empirical work in the future.

GLOBAL ANXIETIES

The study of globalization is generating considerable academic interest in a variety of disciplines, including anthropology, economics, sociology, political science, law, and education—for example, Appadurai 1996; Bauman 1998; Baylis and Smith 1997; Castles and Davidson 2000; Giddens 2000; Hardt and Negri 2000; Inda and Rosaldo 2002b; Jameson and Miyoshi 1999; King 1997; Lechner and Boli 1999; O'Meara, Mehlinger, and Krain 2000; Sassen 1998.

The term *globalization* in its current usage is quite broad and lacks well-defined epistemological, theoretical, and empirical boundaries. Even though the idea of globalization has gained increased circulation in the social sciences and is pregnant with potential—especially for theorizing broad processes of social change, from Detroit to Delhi—we cannot fully mine its analytic use until we attend to basic definitional and theoretical matters. Anthropologists, for example, tend to approach the problem of globalization in relation to their long-term interest in social organization and culture. Globalization detaches social practices and cultural formations from their traditional moorings in bounded (often national) territories. Globalization decisively undermines the once imagined neat fit of language, culture, and nation. One hundred years ago, European and Euro-American anthropologists took long journeys to remote locations to study exotic social institutions and cultural beliefs. Globalization now delivers the "exotic" to the anthropologist's own backyard. In plain sight, Turkish cultural formations—language, marriage, kinship, ritual practices—are as ubiquitous in parts of Frankfurt as they are in Istanbul. Likewise, Mexican culture is now thriving in New York City. New York culture is alive in Puebla, Mexico, via the cash and social remittances—that is, the social practices and cultural models immigrants acquire in the new setting and remit back home (Levitt 2001a). Hence, we have witnessed over the past decade the emergence of an anthropological taste for topics such as immigration (Chavez 1992; Foner 2000, 2001e and f; Pessar 1995b; Roosens 1989), transnationalism (Basch, Glick Schiller, and Szanton Blanc 1994; Gupta and Ferguson 1992; Mahler 1995a), cultural hybrids (Canclini 1995), delicious dualities (Zentella 2002), and unsettling cultural conflicts (Shweder 2000; Wikan 2000), all brought about by globalization.

Anthropological involvement with the study of cultural forms and dispersal across time and space has a long history. Much of the early literature privileged the study of "culture contact" and "cultural borrowing" via trading, migrations, invasions, or conquest. Franz Boas's (1911b and 1940) early efforts, which resulted in the firm establishment of American anthropology as a major scholarly discipline in the early decades of the twentieth century, centered around theoretical debates over the "diffusion" (versus "multiple invention") of cultural forms (such as a fishing hook, folktale motif, or kinship term) across distinct culture areas. This work was critical to the dismantling of earlier extravagant and racist theories of stages in the cultural evolution of societies. Today, few anthropologists focus their theoretical or empirical work on culture areas or patterns of cultural diffusion per se. However, there is a strong genealogical line of continuity of anthropological concerns with the movement of people, cultural facts, and artifacts over time.

Political theorists, including political anthropologists, are focusing on the emergence of international systems, such as human and civil rights, reaching beyond the confines of individual nation-states. An Argentine torturer accused of committing crimes against humanity in his own country can now be arrested in Mexico and tried in Spain, as happened in February 2001 (Robben n.d.). Political theorists have also begun to examine how new deterritorializing processes shape the course of political fortunes in many parts of the world. Peoples in diaspora—Mexicans in Los Angeles and Dominicans in New York, for example—are emerging as powerful agents across national boundaries. Dual-citizenship agreements—the ability to maintain citizenship rights in more than one nation-state—are complicating the politics of belonging and making them more interesting (Castles and Davidson 2000).

Dominican politicos, for instance, have long been cognizant that election campaigns in their country need to be waged as much in New York, where Dominicans are now the largest immigrant group, as in Santo Domingo. Mexican politicians are now joining the new global game. In late December 2000, newly elected President Vicente Fox spent a day at Mexico's busy northern border personally welcoming some of the 1.5 million immigrants returning home for Christmas—as well as performing and telecasting a new strategic approach to paisanos living in the United States. Under the Fox administration, the more than eight million Mexican citizens living in the United States are no longer an afterthought (or an embarrassment) to Mexican national pride. Likewise, the Salvadorian political leadership carefully takes into consideration the needs and voices of the Salvadorian diaspora in the United States. As a rough formula, a million people in the diaspora translates to nearly a billion dollars in remittances sent home every year. This might help explain the newfound interest among Salvadorian and Mexican politicians in cultivating ties with their brothers and sisters living in the United States. The old adage "all politics is local" is now anachronistic.

For the purposes of this chapter, I define *globalization* as processes of change simultaneously generating centrifugal (as the territory of the nation-state) and centripetal (as supra-national nodes) forces that result in the deterritorialization of basic economic, social, and cultural practices from their traditional moorings in the nation-state. Because globalization involves a kind of "post-geography" (Bauman 1998), mapping it is futile. Different regions of the world are, at once, implicated in multiple, overlapping globalization processes. Although *globalization,* by definition, refers to economic, social, and cultural processes that are postnational, I do not mean to suggest that it augurs the demise of the state apparatus. It is, I think, subtler than that.

Nation-states seem to respond to processes of globalization by displaying new forms of hyper-presence and hyper-absence. Globalization challenges the workings of the nation-state in various ways, from undermining national economies to making anachronistic traditional ideas of citizenship and of cultural production (Castles and Davidson 2000; Sassen 1998). In important ways, states appear hyper-absent qua the forces of globalization, for example, when billions of dollars enter and exit national boundaries with the apparatus of the state having little say over the course of these flows. On the other hand, states are responding to globalization by hyper-displays and performances of power. Arguably one of the most globalized spots in the world today and, alas, one of the most heavily trafficked international borders in the world is the vast region that both unites and separates the United States and Mexico. It is also one of the most heavily guarded borders in history (Andreas 2000). The militarization of the border at a time of record border crossings suggests a process more complex than the simple erosion or demise of the nation-state. In the places that matter, where states bump into each other, hyper-presence seems to be in full force. This is the case in post–September 11 United States, in post-Schengen Europe, and in Japan. (Per the Schengen agreement, there are no longer internal border controls among European Union member states. Hence, a French citizen needs no passport or visa to travel to Spain, and vice-versa.) Even though, internally, Europe has become borderless, external controls—that is, keeping would-be migrants from outside Europe—have intensified (Andreas and Snyder 2000). To claim that the state is waning is to miss one of the more delicious paradoxes of state performance.

What, if anything, is new about globalization? Is globalization simply modernization on steroids? Is it Westernization in fast-forward? Is it imperialism now driven by the extraordinarily high octane of American hyper-power? Alternatively, is it a phenomenon or a set of phenomena of a completely different order? Prominent scholars have claimed that globalization is best conceptualized as part of a long process of change, perhaps centuries in the making (Coatsworth 2002; Mignolo 1998; Sen 2000; Taylor 2002; Williamson 2002).

Two of globalization's three main currents represent continuity with previous processes of economic, social, and cultural change, but the third suggests a new and heretofore unseen force. Globalization is the product of new information and communication technologies that connect people, organizations, and systems across vast distances. In addition to creating and instantaneously circulating vast amounts of information and data, these technologies hold the promise of freeing people from the tyranny of space and time. These new technologies are rapidly and irrevocably changing the nature of work, thought, and the interpersonal patterning of social relations (Turkle 1997).[1]

In other ways, though, globalization now seems to mimic previous cycles of integration. For example, the globalization of capital is nothing new. If anything, it was more impressive one hundred years ago than it is today (Coatsworth 2002; Taylor 2002; Williamson 2002). At the beginning of the new millennium, financial markets, direct foreign investment, capital flow, and the production and distribution of goods and services continue to be highly globalized.

According to the World Bank (2001:1), a "growing share of what countries produce is sold to other foreigners as exports. Among rich or developed countries, the share of international trade in total output (exports plus imports of goods relative to GDP) rose from 27 to 39 percent between 1987 and 1997. For the developing countries it rose from 10 to 17 percent." Likewise, foreign direct investment (that is, firms making investments in other countries) overall "more than tripled between 1988 and 1998 from US$ 192 billion to US$ 610 billion"(ibid). From the time you woke up this morning to the time you go to bed tonight, more than a trillion dollars will cross national boundaries (Friedman 2000). The archetypical American car, the Chevrolet Camaro, is now a thoroughly globalized product. It is built nowhere and everywhere; the capital, labor, and parts originate in multiple continents. It is a car "on the move," so to speak, from its very conception. The global market is also generating global tastes. McDonald's now is Brazil's largest employer (Schlosser 2001). Market forces seduce and manipulate in even the remotest parts of the world with stunning results.

Another feature of globalization that seems to continue an old story is large-scale immigration. Globalization is about deterritorialization not only of markets, information, symbols, and tastes but also of large and growing numbers of people. Large-scale immigration is a world phenomenon that is transforming Africa, Asia, Europe, and the Americas. Sweden, a country of nearly nine million people, now has roughly one million immigrants. Approximately 30 percent of Frankfurt's population is immigrant. Amsterdam, by the year 2015, will be 50-percent immigrant. Leicester, England, is about to become the first city in Europe where "whites" are no longer the majority. Long held as the exception to the North American and European rule that immigrant workers are needed to maintain economic vitality, Japan is now facing a future in which immigrants will play a significant role (Tsuda 1996, 2003). Asia and Africa have large numbers of asylum seekers, refugees, and displaced persons (UNHCR 2001).

Globalization is the general backdrop for any understanding of the anthropology of immigration. At the turn of the millennium, an estimated 175 million transnational immigrants and refugees are living beyond their homelands. Globalization has increased immigration in a variety of ways. First, transnational capital flows tend to stimulate migration; where capital flows, immigrants follow (see, inter alia, Sassen 1988). Second, the new information, communication, and media technologies at the heart of globalization tend to stimulate migration because they encourage new cultural expectations, tastes, consumption practices, and lifestyle choices. Would-be immigrants imagine better opportunities elsewhere and mobilize to achieve them. Third, deeply globalized economies are increasingly structured around a voracious appetite for foreign workers. Fourth, the affordability of mass transportation has put the migration option within the reach of millions who, heretofore, could not do so. In the year 2000, approximately 1.5 billion airline tickets were sold. Fifth, globalization has stimulated new migration because it has produced uneven results. In Zhou and Gatewood's (2000:10) excellent summary,

> Globalization perpetuates emigration from developing countries in two significant ways. First,…capital investments into developing countries transform the economic and occupational structures in these countries by disproportionately targeting production for export and taking advantage of raw material and cheap labor. Such twisted development,

characterized by the robust growth of low skilled jobs in export manufacturing, draws a large number of rural, and particularly female workers, into the urban labor markets.... Second, economic development following the American model in many developing countries stimulates consumerism and consumption and raises expectations regarding the standard of living. The widening gap between consumption expectations and the available standards of living within the structural constraints of the developing countries, combined with easy access to information and migration networks, in turn create tremendous pressure for emigration....Consequently,...capital investments in developing countries have resulted in the paradox of rapid economic growth and high emigration from these countries to the United States.

Any anthropological consideration of globalization must reflect upon the pains it has generated in certain regions of the developing world, perpetuating unemployment and further depressing wages (Bauman 1998; Dussel 2000). On the winning side of the new globalization game, jobs have increased in certain regions of the world. These jobs include the knowledge-intensive sector of the new economy and more traditional jobs in service and agriculture. The growth in jobs in globalization's winning zones has acted as an unstoppable vacuum, pulling millions of immigrants—skilled and unskilled, legal and illegal—from the developing world into the wealthier centers of the Northern Hemisphere.

LIVES BEYOND NATIONAL BOUNDARIES

In recent years, there has been renewed interest in the study of human migration (Suárez-Orozco, Suárez-Orozco and Qin-Hilliard 2001a). Anthropologists have made significant theoretical contributions to the study of immigration. For example, see George DeVos's work on immigration and minority status in comparative perspective (DeVos 1992; Kleinberg and DeVos 1973; Lee and DeVos 1981), Nina Glick Schiller's collaborative work on immigration and transnationalism (Basch, Glick Schiller, and Szanton Blanc 1994; Glick Schiller,

Basch, and Blanc-Szanton 1992a; Glick Schiller and Fouron 2001a), and John Ogbu's work on immigration and anthropology of education (Ogbu 1974, 1978; Ogbu and Matute-Bianchi 1986). Sociologists, demographers, and labor economists are also conducting important new research on immigration in the social sciences. The next generation of anthropological studies of immigration will be increasingly required to reckon systematically with the approaches and findings of our colleagues in allied disciplines and to continue making a case for the unique perspectives emerging from the ethnographic process. Interdisciplinary collaborations between allied social scientists are likely to provide the increasingly sophisticated scholarly frames now needed to deal with the complexities of immigration in the global era.

During the last decades of the twentieth century, most major nation-states saw the topic of immigration emerge as a significant issue with important public-opinion, policy, and research implications. Migration, from the Latin *migrare,* meaning "to change residence," has been a defining feature in the making of humanity from our very emergence as a species in the African savanna. Social scientists have traditionally defined *migration* as the more or less permanent movement of people across space (Petersen 1968). In the language of the social sciences, people "emigrate" out of one location and become "immigrants" in a new setting.

The idea of migration as the permanent movement of people across space suggests several important concerns. First is the relative permanence of immigrants in a new setting. For many (perhaps most), immigration represents a final move; for others, it is a temporary state before eventually returning "home." A central feature of the great transatlantic immigration that took place between Europe and North and South America from the 1890s until the 1910s was the high proportion of people who returned to Europe. By some accounts, more than a third of the Europeans who came to the Americas went back "home" (Moya 1998).

Sojourners represent another pattern of labor flow in which temporality defines immigration. They are the many immigrants who move for well-defined periods of time, often following a seasonal cycle, and eventually return home. Large numbers of migrant workers have followed this pattern—from African workers in the Sub-Saharan region to Mexican agricultural workers in California (Cornelius 1992).

A third type comprises the many new immigrants wordwide who constantly shuttle back and forth. In recent years, certain scholars of immigration have argued that new transnational and global forces structure the journeys of immigrants in more complex ways than previously seen. Anthropologists have been at the forefront of this conceptual and empirical work (for example, Basch, Glick Schiller, and Szanton Blanc 1994). This research suggests that many immigrants remain substantially engaged (economically, politically, and culturally) in their newly adopted lands and in their communities of origin, moving back and forth in ways seldom seen in previous eras of large-scale immigration (Suárez-Orozco 1998).

The idea of immigration as movement across space also requires elaboration. Viewed anthropologically, immigration involves a change in residency and a change in community. Over the years, scholars have concentrated on two major types of large-scale migration: *internal migration* (within the confines of a nation-state) and *international migration* (across international borders). Although many scholars would argue that the large-scale movement of people within a nation-state is a phenomenon of a separate order from the large-scale movement of people across international borders, the differences between these two broad types of migration are often quite blurred.

Frequently, internal migrants share many characteristics with international migrants: Many move from rural villages to urban centers, many experience linguistic and cultural discontinuities, and many face the same bureaucratic and legal restrictions and discriminations international migrants do. Much attention has been focused on international migration. Today, though, most immigrants are internal migrants staying within the confines of their nation-states (China, Egypt, and Brazil have experienced high levels of internal migration). In fact, in spite of the impression that the majority of international migrants are heading to the developed world (that is, Europe and North America), most immigration today is an intra-continental (that is, within Asia, within Africa) phenomenon. China alone has an estimated 100 million internal migrants who, in many ways, experience circumstances similar to those that transnational migrants face when moving across countries (Eckholm 2001:10). Some of the most important anthropological contributions to the study of immigration have focused on internal migration (for example, Brandes 1975; Colson 1971; Kemper 1977; Morgan and Colson 1987; and Scudder and Colson 1982).

MOVING ON—THE CAUSES AND CONSEQUENCES OF LARGE-SCALE IMMIGRATION

Scholars of immigration have generally theorized patterns of migration flows in terms of economic forces, social processes, and cultural practices (Suárez-Orozco, Suárez-Orozco, and Qin-Hilliard 2001a). Social scientists who privilege the economic aspects of immigration have examined how variables such as unemployment, underemployment, lack of access to credit, and, especially, wage differentials are implicated in labor migration (Dussel 2000; Suárez-Orozco, Suárez-Orozco, and Qin-Hilliard 2001b). Anthropologist Jorgé Durand, working with an interdisciplinary team of colleagues, has argued that international migration emerges as a risk management and diversifying strategy deployed by families and communities hoping to place their eggs in various territorial baskets (Massey, Durand, and Malone 2002). Changing cultural models about social standards and economic expectations have also been implicated in why people migrate (Moya 1998). In many cases, people migrate to actualize new consumption and lifestyle standards.

In nearly all advanced, postindustrial economies, bifurcated labor markets have worked as a powerful gravitational field, attracting many immigrants to work in the low-wage, low-status, and low-skilled secondary sector. Anthropologist T. Tsuda (1996, 2003) has noted that in Japan immigrant workers are sometimes called "3 k workers"; *3 k* is for the Japanese words meaning "dirty, demanding, and dangerous." When certain sectors of the opportunity structure are culturally coded as "immigrant jobs," they become stigmatized, and native workers tend to shun them almost regardless of wage dynamics. What would it take, in terms of wages, to make backbreaking work such as strawberry picking in California *not* an immigrant occupation?

Anthropological scholars of immigration have long maintained that cultural and social practices can generate—and sustain—substantial migratory flows. In many regions of the world, such as Ireland and Mexico, migration has been an adulthood-defining rite of passage

(Durand 1998; Massey, Durand, and Malone 2002). In some cases, people migrate because others—relatives, friends, and friends of friends—migrated before them. The best predictor of who will migrate is who has already migrated. Transnational family reunification continues to be a critical vector in immigration today. In the year 1996, 915,900 immigrants were formally admitted in the United States. Among them, 594,604 were family-sponsored immigrants (Suárez-Orozco 1999). Since the early 1970s, family reunification has been one of the few formal ways to migrate into Europe (Suárez-Orozco 1994).

A number of studies have examined how transnational migratory social chains, once established, can generate a powerful momentum of their own. As Patricia Pessar explains in Chapter 3, gender is deeply implicated in the making of these chains. Established immigrants lower the costs of subsequent immigration because they ease the transition of new arrivals by sharing crucial economic, linguistic, and cultural knowledge—about job openings, good wages, fair bosses, and dignified working conditions (Waldinger 1997).

Other recent research highly relevant to anthropological concerns engages the theoretical debate over the role of immigrant workers in the global, postindustrial economy. In the context of the increasingly advanced, knowledge-intensive economies of today, are low-skilled immigrant workers anachronistic? Are immigrant workers a leftover from an earlier era of production?[2]

The comparative research of anthropologist "Gaku" (T.) Tsuda and political scientist Wayne Cornelius on the use of immigrant labor in two paradigmatic postindustrial economic settings—San Diego County, California, US, and Hamamatzu, Japan—suggests a remarkable convergence in patterns of growing reliance on immigrant labor, in spite of marked differences in national context (for example, see Cornelius 1998). These data reveal a pattern of an enduring, indeed voracious, postindustrial demand for immigrant labor. Cornelius (1998:128) concludes, "As immigrants become a preferred labor force, employers do more to retain them, even in a recessionary economy."

These data suggest that immigrant workers become desirable to a wide variety of employers for three basic reasons. First, immigrants are willing to do low-pay work with little or no prospects for upward mobility, work that is boring, dirty, or dangerous but critical, even in firms involving highly advanced technologies. Second, employers perceive immigrant workers quite favorably, as reliable, flexible, punctual, and willing to work overtime. Often, employers prefer them to native-born workers. Third, immigrant transnational labor-recruiting networks are a powerful method for "delivering eager new recruits to the employer's doorstep with little or no effort on his part" (Cornelius 1998:128).

We have a reasonable understanding of how love (family reunification) and work drive immigration. On the other hand, the role of war and its relations to large-scale migratory flows has been generally neglected. Yet throughout history war and international migration have been closely linked. The threat of labor shortages during World War II led to temporary labor-recruiting efforts to attract much-needed immigrant workers to the United States (Calavita 1992). The resultant "*bracero*" program became a powerful force in building—via family reunification—a Mexican migration momentum that eventually turned into the largest and most powerful immigration flow into the United States in the twentieth century (Suárez-Orozco 1998).

In the aftermath of World War II, many of the major northwestern European democracies, such as Germany and Belgium, developed "guest worker programs" to recruit foreign workers, initially in southern Europe and subsequently in the Maghreb region of North Africa and in Turkey (Suárez-Orozco 1994, 1996). These programs came to an end in the early 1970s, but family-reunification and chain migration continued to bring immigrants from North Africa into Europe for years.

The Cold War deterred immigration, because of strict Iron Curtain controls, yet generated large population displacements. The robust Cuban diaspora in the United States can be traced more or less directly to the Cold War (Molyneux 1999). The low-intensity warfare in Central America during the 1980s generated the largest wave of emigration in the region's history. As a result, there are now more than a million Central American immigrants in the United States (Suárez-Orozco 1989b). In the 1990s, the ongoing conflicts in Zimbabwe and Angola generated large-scale migratory flows, especially into South Africa. The recent war in Afghanistan resulted in major population displacements (nearly two million Afghans). As of mid 2003, the Iraq war seems not to have generated the huge population displacements that previous warfare has tended to create.

Natural disasters have also displaced populations and started new migratory flows. The 1999 hurricanes, which devastated much of Central America, initiated significant flows of emigrants into North America.

GLOBAL FLOWS AND THE STATE

Whether social scientists examine the case of internal or international migrants, there is a consensus that the apparatus of the nation-state is decidedly implicated in migratory processes: by what the state does and by what it cannot do. States are in the business of regulating the movement of people, internally and internationally. The right to leave a country, to emigrate, is a recent phenomenon (Moya 1998).

Nation-states regulate, monitor, and police the inflow of international immigrants across borders. Large-scale international immigration is, in significant ways, the product of nation building. Argentina, Australia, and Israel come to mind as archetypal examples. Likewise, the reconfigurations of national boundaries have historically and contemporaneously generated large-scale migratory flows. The partition of British India into Pakistan and India stimulated one of the "largest migrations in human history" (Petersen 1968:290). More recently, the disintegration of the former Yugoslavia led to massive, mostly involuntary migratory movements.

In the area of international migration, nation-states generate policies designed to establish who is a legal or an illegal immigrant, who is an asylum seeker, a refugee, and a temporary guest worker. States regulate how many immigrants are legally admitted every year. The United States, for example, has admitted an average of nearly a million legal immigrants annually since 1990. On the other hand, legal immigration into northwestern Europe was greatly curbed following the oil crisis of the early 1970s (Cornelius, Martin, and Hollifield 1994; Suárez-Orozco 1996).

States also regulate the flows of asylum seekers, those escaping a country because of a well-founded fear of persecution. Agents of the state decide who is formally admitted as a refugee. In the post–Cold War era, there has been an explosive growth in the numbers of asylum seekers worldwide. For example, some 369,000 foreigners requested asylum in Europe during the year 1998. Only a small portion of those seeking asylum are eventually granted formal refugee status.

In recent years, many postindustrial democracies—including the United States and throughout northwestern Europe—have developed new strategies to deal with increasing numbers of asylum seekers (Suárez-Orozco 1994). For example, the 13,000 Kosovars who arrived in Germany in mid-1999 were given a three-month, renewable Temporary Protective Status on the condition that they not apply for refugee status, in effect, forfeiting all the rights and entitlements that come with formal refugee status. Similar arrangements were made for asylum seekers from Bosnia.

In the face of growing numbers of asylum seekers and a widespread public concern that many of them are economic refugees in search of a better life in wealthier countries, various countries have put into place new formal and informal strategies. Many of these new strategies seem to be designed to prevent asylum seekers from accessing safe countries, where, under Geneva Convention agreements, they would have the right to a fair hearing.

The high-seas interdiction program put into effect in the United States in the early 1990s is an example. The strategy was conceived to prevent large numbers of Caribbean (especially Haitian) asylum seekers from arriving in US territory, or even within its territorial waters, where they could establish certain legal protections. Apprehension in international waters and return to Haiti leave asylum seekers with little practical recourse under international law. In Europe, a similar strategy has been to deem certain areas in international airports not part of the national territory. For example, parts of the Zaventem airport are not technically Belgian territory but are considered to be international territory. Asylum seekers entering such airports have been turned back because they were said to remain in international territory and, therefore, did not come under the jurisprudence of the Geneva Convention (Suárez-Orozco 1994).

Although advanced, postindustrial democracies are likely to continue facing significant numbers of asylum seekers, the majority is in the developing world. For example, at the beginning of the millennium, there were more than three million asylum seekers in the African continent.

The state does wield substantial power regarding internal and international migration, but in certain areas it faces strict limitations in the management of human migratory flows. Nowhere are these limitations more obvious than in the state's inability to control illegal immigration. In many parts of the world, undocumented or illegal immigration has become a permanent problem that periodically emerges as an unsettling political issue.

In the United States, for example, it is estimated that by the turn of the millennium there were seven million illegal immigrants. In Europe, the number of illegal immigrants is a more carefully guarded secret because of its dangerous political connotations. Most hard-core, right-wing political parties in Europe, including France's Front National, Belgium's Vlams Bloc, and Austria's Freedom Party, revolve around anti-immigration (illegal) platforms. In the 1990s, these once marginal parties made substantial gains with electorates quite concerned about the problem of undocumented immigration.

The enduring problem of illegal immigration in many parts of the world suggests that immigration is now structured by powerful global economic factors, social forces, and cultural practices that seem impervious to state actions such as controls of international borders (Andreas 2000; Cornelius, Martin, and Hollifield 1994). Transnational labor-recruiting networks, enduring wage differentials between nation-states, changing standards of consumption, family reunification, and war generate a powerful migratory momentum not easily contained by unilateral, or even multilateral, state interventions to curb it.

THE VARIETIES OF THE IMMIGRANT EXPERIENCE

When settled in a new country, how do immigrants fare? The United States, as the ur-country of immigration, provides an interesting case study. It is the only advanced, postindustrial democracy where immigration is at once history and destiny. The intensification of globalization in the past decade—arguably responsible for the greatest peacetime expansion of the US economy—coincided with the largest number of immigrants in history (US Bureau of the Census 1999). By the year 2000, the foreign-stock (the foreign born plus the US-born second generation) population of the United States was nearly 55 million people (Portes and Rumbaut 2001), more than 32.5 million of them foreign-born. Two dominant features characterize this most recent wave of immigration: its intensity (the immigrant population grew by

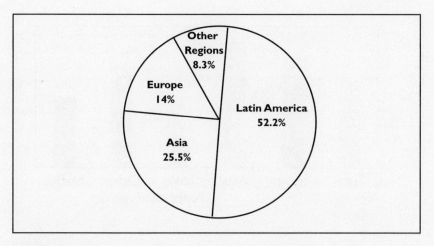

FIGURE 2.1

Distribution of the foreign born by region of birth (2002). Source: Current Populatoin
Survey, 2002. PGP-3. US Census Bureau.

more than 30 percent in the 1990s) and the radical shift in the sources
of new immigration. Until 1950, nearly 90 percent of all immigrants
were Europeans or Canadians. Today, more than 50 percent of all
immigrants are Latin American, and more than 25 percent are Asian—
from regions of the world where globalization has generated especially
uneven results (see figure 2.1).

Immigrants to the United States today compose a heterogeneous
population defying easy generalizations (Suárez-Orozco and Suárez-
Orozco 2001). They include highly educated, highly skilled individuals
drawn by the explosive growth in the knowledge-intensive sectors of the
economy. They are more likely to have advanced degrees than the
native-born population (see figure 2.2).

These immigrants come to the United States to thrive. These immigrants, especially those originating in Asia, are among the best educated and skilled folk in the United States. They are over-represented
in the category of people with doctorates. Fully half of all entering
physics graduate students in 1998 were foreign-born.[3] In California's
Silicon Valley, 32 percent of all the scientists and engineers are immigrants (Saxenian 1999). Roughly a third of all Nobel Prize winners in
the United States have been immigrants. In 1999, all (100 percent!) US

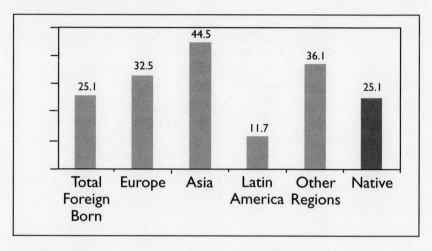

FIGURE 2.2

Percent of the immigrant population with a bachelor's degree or higher by origin (2000).
Source: Current Population Survey, March 2000. PGP-3. US Census Bureau.

winners of the Nobel Prize were immigrants. With the exception, perhaps, of the highly educated immigrants and refugees escaping Nazi
Europe, immigrants in the past tended to be poorly educated and more
unskilled than today's immigrants (Borjas 1999). Never in the history
of US immigration have so many immigrants done so well so fast.
Within a generation, these immigrants are bypassing the traditional
transgenerational modes of status mobility and establishing themselves
in the well-remunerated sectors of the US economy.

At the same time, the new immigration group contains large numbers of poorly schooled, semi-skilled or unskilled workers, many of them
in the United States without proper documentation (illegal immigrants). In the year 2000, more than 22 percent of all immigrants in the
United States had less than a ninth-grade education (see figure 2.3).

These are workers, many of them from Latin America and the
Caribbean, drawn by the service sector of the US economy, where there
seems to be an insatiable appetite for foreign folk. They typically end
up in poorly paid, low-prestige jobs often lacking insurance and basic
safeties. Unlike the low-skilled factory jobs of yesterday, the kinds of
jobs usually available to low-skilled immigrants today do not hold much
realistic promise for upward mobility (Portes 1996:1–15). These immi-

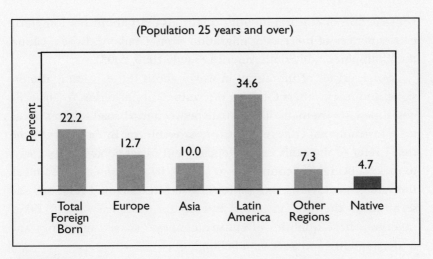

FIGURE 2.3

Percent of the immigrant population with less than the ninth grade completed by origin (2002).

grants tend to settle in areas of deep poverty and racial segregation (Orfield 1998, 2002). Concentrated poverty is associated with the "disappearance of meaningful work opportunities" (Wilson 1997). When poverty is combined with racial segregation, the outcomes can be dim (Massey and Denton 1993:3).

CULTURE MATTERS

In all countries facing immigration, there have been major debates surrounding the cultural and socioeconomic consequences of large-scale population movements. In the United States, a palpable concern, not always fully articulated, relates to how the new immigrants—the majority of whom are non-English speaking, non-European people of color migrating in large numbers from the developing world—will culturally adapt to and transform their new country. In western Europe, there are similar concerns about the cultural adaptations of large numbers of immigrants coming into the Judeo-Christian continent from the Islamic world (Suárez-Orozco 1991b). The anxieties about the long-term vicissitudes of Islam in Europe have been greatly accentuated since September 11, 2001. Likewise, in Japan, a country where mythologies of racial and cultural homogeneity are deeply implicated in the construction of cultural identity, questions exist about the long-term consequences of increasing migration from Thailand, Korea, China, the Philippines, and South America (Tsuda 1996, 2003).

Some critics of immigration worry about the economic dimensions, and many others focus on the cultural implications. Analytically, it is sometimes useful to differentiate between two broad spheres of culture: instrumental culture and expressive culture. By *instrumental culture,* I refer to the skills, competencies, and social behaviors necessary to make a living and contribute to society. By *expressive culture,* I mean the values, worldviews, and patterning of interpersonal relations and sensibilities that give meaning and sustain the sense of self. Taken together, these qualities of culture generate shared meanings and understandings and a sense of belonging.

In the instrumental realm, globalization seems to be stimulating a worldwide convergence in the skills necessary to function in today's economy. In Los Angeles, Lima, or Lagos, the skills required to thrive in the global economy are fundamentally the same. These include communication skills, higher-order symbolic and cognitive skills, as well as habits of work and interpersonal talents common in any cosmopolitan setting. The ability to work with the culturally "other" is also a skill that will be increasingly remunerated, thanks to globalization.

Immigrant parents worldwide are very much aware that if their children are to thrive, they must acquire these skills. In math, children the world over will need the higher-order skills to master, at a minimum, fractions, decimals, line graphs, probabilities, and other basic statistics. In literacy, they will need the ability to read and understand complex instructions and manuals and to convey ideas in writing (in some cases, in more than one language). In logic, they will need problem-solving skills to address various possible outcomes by formulating and testing hypotheses, given certain antecedent conditions. Nearly everywhere, the ability to work with computers and with people from different linguistic, ethnic, and racial backgrounds will be essential for thriving in the workplace (see Murnane and Levy 1996, especially Chapter 2). Immigration for many parents represents nothing more, and nothing less, than the opportunity to offer children access to these skills.

THE ACCULTURATION DEBATE

Although immigrant parents encourage their children to cultivate the instrumental aspects of culture in the new setting, many are ambivalent about their children's exposure to some of the expressive cultural elements. During the course of our research with immigrant families in the United States, it has not been difficult to detect that many immigrant parents strongly resist a whole array of cultural models and social practices that they consider undesirable in American youth culture. These include cultural attitudes and behaviors they deem to be anti-education, anti-authority, and anti-family, for example, sexually precocious behaviors and the glorification of violence. Many immigrant parents reject this form of acculturation (Suárez-Orozco and Suárez-Orozco 2001).

If *acculturation* is superficially defined as acquiring linguistic skills, job skills, and participation in the political process, the consensus on these shared goals is universal. If, on the other hand, we choose a broader, more ambitious definition of *acculturation* as also including the realm of values, worldviews, and interpersonal relations, a worthy debate ensues.

The first issue that needs airing is the basic question of "acculturating to what?" Taking the United States as a point of reference, we can observe that American society is no longer, if it ever was, a uniform or coherent system.[4] Because of immigrants' diverse origins, financial resources, and social networks, they end up gravitating to very different sectors of American society. Some are able to join integrated, well-to-do neighborhoods, but the majority experience American culture from the vantage point of poor urban settings. Limited economic opportunities, toxic schools, ethnic tensions, violence, drugs, and gangs characterize many of these environments. The structural inequalities in what some social theorists have called "American Apartheid" are implicated in the creation of a cultural ethos of ambivalence, pessimism, and despair (Massey and Denton 1993). Asking immigrant youth to give up their values, worldviews, and interpersonal relations to join this ethos is a formula for disaster.

For those immigrants who come into intimate contact with middle-class, mainstream culture, other trade-offs occur. New data suggest that many immigrant children perceive that mainstream Americans do not welcome them and, in fact, disparage them as undeserving to partake in the American dream (Suárez-Orozco 2000). Identifying wholeheartedly with a culture that rejects you has its psychological costs, usually paid with the currency of shame, doubt, and even self-hatred.

Even if middle-class, mainstream Americans wholeheartedly embraced new immigrants, it is far from clear that mimicking their behaviors would prove to be, in the long term, an adaptive strategy for immigrants of color. Mainstream, middle-class children are protected by webs of social safety nets that give them leeway to experiment with an array of dystopic behaviors, including drugs, sex, and alcohol. On the other hand, for many immigrant youth, without robust socio-economic and cultural safety nets, engaging in such behaviors is a high-stakes proposition in which one mistake can have lifelong consequences. A white, middle-class youth caught in possession of drugs is likely to be referred to counseling and rehabilitation, but an immigrant youth convicted of the same offense is likely to be deported.

The current wave of immigration involves people from fantastically diverse and heterogeneous cultural backgrounds. Beneath surface differences, a common grammar can be identified among groups as culturally distinct from one another as Chinese, Haitian, and Mexican immigrants. The importance of the family in driving and sustaining immigration and the emphasis on hard work and optimism about the future are examples of shared immigrant values. (For an overview of recent research on immigration and family ties, see Falicov 1998; Rumbaut 1996; Suárez-Orozco and Paez 2002 [especially Chapters 12, 13 and 14]; Suárez-Orozco and Suárez-Orozco 1995; and Suárez-Orozco, Suárez-Orozco, and Qin-Hilliard 2001c. For an overview of immigrant optimism and achievement orientation, see Kao and Tienda 1995.)

These three aspects of culture come to the fore in the process of immigration. Consider, for example, the case of immigration and the family. Many immigrants come from cultures in which the family system is an integral part of the person's sense of self. Family ties also play a critical role in family reunification, a significant force driving the new immigration. Furthermore, after immigrants settle, many emotional and practical challenges force immigrants to turn to one another for support, accentuating family ties (Suárez-Orozco and Suárez-Orozco 2001).

Hard work and optimism about the future are also central to immigrants' raison d'être (Kao and Tienda 1995; National Research Council 1998; Rumbaut 1995; Steinberg, Bradford Brown, and Dornbusch 1996; Suárez-Orozco 1995). Their most fundamental motivation is to find a better life, and they tend to view hard work as essential to this. That many immigrants do the impossible jobs native workers refuse to consider is an indication of just how hard they are willing to work. Immigrant family ties, work ethic, and optimism about the future are unique assets that should be celebrated as contributions to the total cultural stock of the nation.

Countries unable or unwilling to tolerate or, indeed, thrive in the context of immigration-related changes need to carefully reconsider their dependence on immigrant labor. The one fundamental law of immigration is that it will change everyone involved: the immigrants and those among whom they settle. In the United States and Europe today, we eat, speak, and dance differently than we did thirty years ago, in part because of large-scale immigration. However, change is never easy. The changes brought about by the new immigration require mutual calibrations and negotiations.

Rather than advocate that immigrants, especially their children, abandon all elements of their culture as they embark on their uncertain assimilation journey, a more promising path is to cultivate and nurture the emergence of new hybrid identities and transcultural competencies.[5] These hybrid cultural styles creatively blend elements of the old culture with that of the new, unleashing fresh energies and potentials.[6]

The skills and work habits necessary to thrive in the new century are essential elements of acculturation. Immigrant children, like all children, must develop this repertoire of instrumental skills. At the same time, maintaining a sense of belonging and of social cohesion with their immigrant roots is equally important. When immigrant children—be they Algerians in France, Mexicans in California, or Thais in Japan—lose their expressive culture, social cohesion is weakened, parental authority is undermined, and interpersonal relations suffer. The unthinking call for immigrant children to abandon their culture can result only in loss, anomie, and social disruption.

In the archetypical country of immigration, the United States, emerged the model of unilineal, or "straight line," assimilation. The bargain was straightforward: Please check all your cultural baggage before you pass through the Golden Gate. In that era, the young nation was eager to turn large numbers of European immigrants into loyal citizen workers and consumers. It was an era of nation building and bounded national projects.

Even then, however, accounts of immigrants rushing in unison to trade their culture for American culture were greatly exaggerated. German Americans, Italian Americans, and Irish Americans have all left deep cultural imprints in the molding of American culture. Even among fifth-generation descendants of the previous great wave of immigration, symbolic culture and ethnicity remain an emotional gravitational field (Glazer and Moynahan 1970).

Beyond the argument that maintaining the expressive elements of culture is symbolically important and strategic from the point of view of social cohesion, another argument is worth considering. In the global era, the tenets of unilineal assimilation are no longer relevant. Today there are clear and unequivocal advantages to being able to operate in multiple cultural codes, as anyone working in a major corporation knows. The ability to transverse cultural spaces has social, economic, cognitive, and aesthetic advantages. Dual consciousness has instrumental and expressive benefits. Immigrant children are poised to maximize their unique advantage. Although many view their cultural—including linguistic—skills as a threat, I see them as precious assets to be cultivated.

Large-scale immigration is both the cause and consequence of important cultural transformations. Immigration, I emphasize, inevitably leads to cultural changes and accommodations among both new arrivals and native citizens (Ainslie 1998). Immigration can be said to be the consequence of cultural change in that new cultural tastes and changing cultural conceptions of what is an acceptable standard of living have been implicated in large-scale migratory flows (Massey, Durand, and Malone 2002; Sassen 1988). Culturally, immigrants not only significantly reshape the ethos of their new communities (Ainslie 1998; Gutierrez 1998) but also are responsible for significant cultural transformations "back home" (Durand 1998). As certain immigration researchers (for example, Levitt 2001a) have argued, in many settings, immigrant "social remittances" profoundly affect the values, cultural models, and social practices of those left behind. Because of mass transportation and new communication technologies, immigration is no longer structured around the "sharp break" with the country of origin that once characterized the transoceanic experience (see Ainslie 1998; Suárez-Orozco and Páez 2002). Immigrants today are more likely to be at once "here" and "there," bridging increasingly unbounded national spaces (Basch, Glick Schiller, and Szanton Blanc 1994). In the process, they are transforming both home and host countries.

Increasingly transnational immigration will need to be framed in the context of powerful—and, as of yet, little understood—global formations. New patterns of capital flows, new information technologies, new patterns of communication, changing cultural expectations, and the ease and affordability of mass transportation are generating dynamics that transverse the traditional boundaries of the nation-state. Global capitalism is increasingly characterized by "borderless" economies predicated on transnational capital flows, newly opened markets, and immigrant-dependent economic niches. All these factors would suggest that immigration is certain to remain a vital social phenomenon in the new millennium.

Notes

1. Yet another paradox of globalization is that as it unites, it deeply divides the world between those who can access and manipulate the new technologies and those who are left behind, "stuck," so to speak, in local contexts (Bauman 1998).

2. Few topics have generated as much controversy as the economic consequences of large-scale labor migration. Do immigrants help or hurt the economies of their new countries? Do immigrants carry their own weight, or do they represent a burden to citizens and other established residents? Do complex, postindustrial economies need low-skilled immigrant workers, or have they become redundant? Much of the recent scholarship on immigration and the economy has tended to focus on concerns such as the fiscal implications of immigration, immigrant competition with native workers, and immigration and wages. Another important theme has been the economic integration and progress of immigrants over time (Borgas 1999; Espenshade 1997; National Research Council 1997; Suárez-Orozco, Suárez-Orozco, and Qin-Hilliard 2001b).

The research findings on the economic consequences of immigration are somewhat contradictory. Some economists claim that immigrants are a burden to tax payers and an overall negative influence, especially on advanced, postindustrial economies (Huddle 1993). Others suggest that they continue to be an important asset (Simon 1989).

A recent study on the economic, demographic, and fiscal effects of immigration by the US National Research Council (NRC) concludes that in the American setting, "immigration produces net economic gains for domestic residents" (National Research Council 1997:3). Not only do immigrants "increase the supply of labor and help produce new goods and services," but their presence also "allows domestic workers to be used more productively, specializing in producing goods at which they are relatively more efficient. Specialization in consumption also yields a gain" (National Research Council 1997:3–4). The NRC estimates that the immigration-related "domestic gain may run on the order of $1 billion to $10 billion a year" (National Research Council 1997:5). Given the size of the US economy (about seven trillion dollars), it is clear that immigrants will neither "make it" nor "break it."

In fiscal terms, the NRC data suggest, "immigrants receive more in services than they pay in taxes" (National Research Council 1997:7). The panel estimates that "if the net fiscal impact of all U.S. immigrant-headed households were averaged across all native households the burden would be...on the order of $166 to $226 per native household."

The NRC study and other studies conclude that even though immigration is a plus in overall economic terms, low-skilled new immigrants have contributed to a modest drop in the minimum wage of low-skilled workers. They found that a 5-percent drop in wages since 1980 among high-school dropouts could be attributed to the new immigrants. However, no evidence exists to suggest that new immigration has "hurt" the economic condition of native minority workers, such as African-Americans (National Research Council 1997:5).

Other studies examine the issue of the socioeconomic progress made by immigrant workers. The research of Dowell Myers tracks, over time and across generations, various dimensions of the economic adaptations of immigrant-origin men in a region of the world heavily impacted by immigration, the state of California. His work explores three sequential outcomes: educational attainment, occupational mobility, and earnings. In fundamental ways, the recent Mexican immigrant experience in Southern California seems to replicate earlier patterns of immigrant adaptation. Yet, in other ways, Myers's findings suggest new—and disturbing—patterns.

Myers's research reveals that, upon arrival, Mexican immigrant men tend to be poorly educated, work in low-skilled occupations, and earn low incomes. Myers finds that over time immigrant men make modest improvements in their economic condition. However, he also suggests that important changes occur across younger cohorts within the first generation. These changes, according to Myers, are strongly related to the much higher educational attainment of immigrant children. In other words, Myers finds an old story with a new set of characters: Poorly educated immigrant men make modest gains over time, but their children are able to attain more education in the new country.

Still, Myers's data reveal a disturbing new pattern: Among the children of immigrants, higher education "does not appear to fully convert into higher occupational status or earnings; and higher occupational status translates even less well into higher earnings. These under-returns are most pronounced for the more recent arrivals from Mexico and for young cohorts, including native-born, both of whom newly entered the labor market in the 1970s and 1980s." Myers concludes, "The social implications of these falling returns to education and occupation are regrettable, because the declining reward system may discourage other" immigrant children from investing in schooling as the route for status mobility (Myers 1998:188).

3. See "Wanted: American Physicists," *New York Times,* July 23, 1999, p. A27. Of course, not all these foreign-born physics graduate students are immigrants. Some will return to their countries of birth, but others will surely go on to have productive scientific careers in the United States.

4. I concur with Alejandro Portes (1996:1) when he argues that we can no longer assume that new immigrants will assimilate into a coherent mainstream. He articulates a critical question that is now in the minds of many observers of immigration: "The question today is to what sector of American society will a particular immigrant group assimilate? Instead of a relatively uniform 'mainstream' whose mores and prejudices dictate a common path of integration, we observe today several distinct forms of adaptation. One of them replicates the time-honored portrayal of growing acculturation and parallel integration into the white middle class. A second leads straight in the opposite direction to permanent poverty and assimilation to the underclass. Still a third associates rapid economic advancement with deliberate preservation of the immigrant community's values and tight solidarity."

5. I concur with Teresa LaFromboise and her colleagues (1998) on the need to reconceptualize what they call the "linear model of cultural acquisition."

6. Margaret Gibson (1988) articulates a theoretical argument on immigrant transculturation and a calculated strategy of "accommodation without assimilation" in her study of highly successful Sikh immigrants in California. For a theoretical statement on the psychology of ethnic identity and cultural pluralism, see Jean S. Phinney (1998).

3

Anthropology and the Engendering of Migration Studies

Patricia R. Pessar

Migration studies encourage collaboration across disciplines (for example, Grasmuck and Pessar 1991; Massey, Durand, and González 1987). Such collaboration has challenged migration scholars to develop theories and methods reflective of the conceptual frameworks and explanatory strategies informing research in disciplines such as anthropology, sociology, history, political science, law, and economics. In most cases, scholars of international migration have shared a common concern: to elucidate the nature of those structures and processes that generate and sustain cross-border migration and condition its effects. They also explore continuities and changes in the lives of immigrant and refugee populations, as well as the structures of socioeconomic opportunities and constraints that pattern the incorporation of newcomers and their children into the host society and place of origin.

Within this shared project, a dynamic and evolving division of labor among migration scholars has developed. Within this division of labor, anthropologists have been at the forefront in insisting, first, that women be accorded their rightful place among the subjects of our research and, second, that theories of migration recognize the fact that migration is a gendered process (Brettell and DeBerjeois 1992; Grasmuck and Pessar 1991).[1] It is not surprising that anthropologists should have spearheaded such revisionism. First, anthropologists were pioneering in the development of feminist theory and research methods (Martin and Voorhies 1975; Reiter 1975; Rosaldo and Lamphere 1974; Visweswaran 1997). Second, because of the discipline's concern with theorizing the relationship between structure and agency, ethnographers found binary models of migration on maximizing either actors or macro political-economic structures wholly inadequate. Their research pointed to the importance of mediating units such as households, families, and social networks. These, they argued, facilitated and sustained international migration, as well as channeled its effects. Feminist ethnographers, in turn, challenged the ways in which much of the scholarship on migration, in general, and on households and social networks, in particular, neglected important matters of gender hierarchies, inequality, and conflict.

I should note that I use the term *feminist ethnographers,* instead of the more generic term *anthropologists,* advisedly. I refer to that group of scholars who, irrespective of discipline, share certain epistemological assumptions and research strategies associated with the traditions of feminist scholarship and anthropological fieldwork.[2] These include the conviction that quantitative, positivist approaches to social science research commonly fail to contextualize the data collected or redress gender-linked biases in research design.

Feminist scholarship often aims to uncover those gendered beliefs, structures, and practices that constrain the individual and collective pursuits of women and men. Ethnographic enquiry that positions people's meanings and understandings at the center facilitates the defining of solutions that reflect and respect local knowledge (Benmayor, Torruellas, and Juarbe 1997).

Feminist ethnographers have operated on three fronts. They have explored why and how migration is a gendered process. They have demonstrated how a concern for gender increases our understanding of the causes, consequences, and processes of international migration. In certain instances, their scholarship has even overturned widely held beliefs about migration that were the product of earlier research in which gender was not treated (Pessar 1999b; Wright 1995). Last, they have contributed to scholarship on women and on gender by exploring how women's status vis-à-vis men is affected by migration structures and processes and by deconstructing the notion of an essentialized female subject.

THE MIGRANT AS MALE

To underscore the existence of gender bias in the literature on migration, in the mid-1980s I wrote, "Until recently the term 'migrant' suffered from the same gender stereotyping found in the riddles about the big indian and the little indian, the surgeon and the son. In each case the term carried a masculine connotation, unless otherwise specified. While this perception makes for amusing riddles, the assumption that the 'true' migrant is male has limited the possibility for generalization from empirical research and produced misleading theoretical premises" (Pessar 1986:273).[3]

To appreciate why women were largely absent from empirical research and writings produced in the 1950s, 1960s, and early 1970s, it is useful to review the theoretical assumptions guiding much of the migration scholarship produced by anthropologists and other researchers of that period.[4] Most scholars were influenced by neoclassical theory. According to one popular variant, those individuals with the ability to project themselves into the role of "Western *men*" headed off to the cities where they could attain the benefits of modern life (Lewis 1959; Redfield 1955). Males, these scholars alleged, were more apt to be risk takers and achievers, and women were portrayed as guardians of community tradition and stability.[5] Hence, in Everett Lee's (1966:51) seminal "push-pull" theory of migration, we learn that "children are carried along by their parents, willy-nilly, and wives accompany their husbands though it tears them away from the environment they love."

Migration research of this period also suffered from the more general tendency to disregard women's contributions to economic, political, and social life. As June Nash (1986:3) writes, "Whether investigators were influenced by neoclassical, Marxist, dependency or developmentalist paradigms, they tended to stop short of an analysis of women's condition in any but the most stereotyped roles in the family and biological reproduction."

Not surprisingly, researchers of the day designed studies of immigrant populations that included only male subjects. Therefore, in the introduction to their book on migrant workers in Europe, John Berger and Jean Mohr (1975:8) wrote, "Among the migrant workers in Europe there are probably two million women. Some work in factories, many work in domestic service. To write of their experience adequately would require a book itself. We hope this will be done. Ours is limited to the experience of the male migrant worker." In 1985 we find Alejandro Portes (Portes and Bach 1985:95) explaining that the surveys he conducted throughout the 1970s with Mexicans and Cubans in the United States had to be restricted to male family heads: "We felt at the time that an exploratory study, directed at comparison of two immigrant groups over time, would become excessively complex were it to encompass all categories of immigrants. In subsequent interviews, however, respondents were also used as informants about major characteristics of other family members, in particular, their wives." A male bias also existed in the works of many immigration historians of the period who assumed that only male immigrants' lives were worthy of official documentation and scrutiny (Handlin 1951; Howe 1976) or that the history of male migrants was gender-neutral, making it unnecessary to treat women at all, except, perhaps, in a few pages on the family (Bodnar, Weber, and Simon 1982).

SCHOLARSHIP ON IMMIGRANT WOMEN

After feminist scholarship gained a foothold in migration studies, it flourished. Today we have a rich and varied corpus exploring women and migration. However, there is a downside. Scholarship on immigrant women has been ghettoized—considered a subfield in migration studies as a whole and in the specific bodies of literature on migration within the individual social science disciplines. We see such ghettoizing at play when the organizers of major migration conferences convene separate "women's" panels on gender and migration or families and migration. This reflects and reinforces the assumption that gender, along with other mutually constituting structures of difference, such as race and nationality, will not be adequately treated in all panels on diverse topics such as labor force participation, citizenship, and modes of socioeconomic incorporation (see Hirschman, Kasinitz, and DeWind 1999). The challenge remains to build on and branch out from a concentration on female immigrants in order to apply appropriately gender-inflected research questions, analytical constructs, and methods to both men and women (see Gabaccia 1992). In this way, we will manage to produce not only comprehensive and truly gendered accounts of migration structures, processes, and outcomes but also works in which the gender specificity of labor migration becomes something to be explained rather than simply assumed.

Feminist migration scholars have contributed to this larger goal in a variety of ways. Studies ranging in scale from the examination of gender-segmented labor markets (Morokvasic 1993; Sassen 1996; Tienda, Smith, and Ortiz 1987) to accounts of the gendered body as a site for contests over the meaning of, and appropriate redress for, violations of human rights (Bhabha 1996) have occasioned critiques of gender-neutral aspects of larger theories of immigration and refugee displacement. Of special note is feminist research that has effectively challenged previous understandings of particular migration systems and structures, for example, studies of southern African migration. This work points to the inadequacy of earlier scholarship, which, mostly because of its blindness to gender, found the roots of women's poor socioeconomic status solely in its function for capitalism (Wolpe 1975). Drawing upon a socialist feminist theory of gender relations, a new group of researchers developed a more complex and nuanced explanatory model. This work demonstrates that women's subordination and immobility were related to the mutually reinforcing benefits that men,[6] capital, and the state derived from imposing these constraints.

A GENDERED APPROACH TO HOUSEHOLDS AND SOCIAL NETWORKS

Although ethnographers have focused on diverse and interlinking units of analysis, the household and social networks have received the greatest attention. This owes, in part, to anthropologists' long engagement with matters of kinship and social organization and to feminist migration scholars' embrace of socialist feminism—with its emphasis on matters of production and reproduction. Of the various conceptualizations of the household available in social science literature, two perspectives have had a disproportionate impact on migration studies. The first portrays the household as a moral economy of sorts, exhibiting social solidarity and income pooling among members. The second perspective, although not contradictory to the first, emphasizes the role households play in developing strategies for survival—which usually means strategies aimed at maximizing economic gains and adapting to larger structural inequities.

Inspired by feminist scholarship, critics have objected to the notion that migrant households are organized solely on principles of reciprocity, consensus, and altruism. They have countered that even though household members' orientations and actions may sometimes be guided by norms of solidarity, they may equally be informed by hierarchies of power along gender and generational lines. Therefore, the tension, dissention, and coalition-building these hierarchies produce within the migration process also must be examined (Grasmuck and Pessar 1991). A particularly graphic example of a lack of consensus among household members is provided by Pierrette Hondagneu-Sotelo (1994). She describes a young Mexican wife whose fear of abandonment by her migrant husband leads her to pray that he will be apprehended by the Border Patrol and sent back home to her.

Hondagneu-Sotelo is right when she asserts that many have assumed, rather than empirically demonstrated, that individual acts of migration emanate from collective, household decision making. I suspect that this problem is rooted not only in researchers' assumptions about collective household action but also in their willingness to take informants' statements at face value rather than interpret them dialogically. To advance broader claims to being a family that is both respectable and economically secure, rural inhabitants frequently draw upon the rhetorical trope of a unitary household, under the undisputed authority of the patriarch, when speaking to "outsiders" about the actions of their own household members (Grasmuck and Pessar 1991; Rouse 1986). Frequently, research findings on the postmigration status of women and men are a product of the research methods used. That is, structured surveys may yield portraits of family unity and consensus regarding women's subordination. Ethnography, on the other hand, should prove more adept at capturing dynamic and often contradictory processes in the reproduction and contestation of gender inequalities (see Pessar 1995a).

Certain economists, demographers, and sociologists have also turned to the study of migrant households. These proponents of the "new economics" of migration dispute the neoclassicists' assumptions that individuals emigrate only to redress imbalances in international wage rates. Rather, these researchers argue that the true decision-making unit is the *household*, not the autonomous individual. This "collective unit" seeks not only to maximize anticipated income but also to minimize risks and loosen constraints associated with a variety of market failures extending well beyond the labor market—for example, future markets, capital markets (Taylor 1986).

Unfortunately, because the "new economists" take a relatively narrow view of the parameters of migrant households' cost/benefit analyses, they miss the important role assumed by domestic political economies in these calculations. For example, when unmarried Dominican women urge their parents to allow them to emigrate alone, parents weigh the threat to the family's reputation posed by the daughter's sexual freedom and possible promiscuity against the very real economic benefits her emigration will bring. Similarly, in assessing the benefits of return migration, many Dominican immigrant women assess the personal gains from settlement and blue-collar employment in the United States against the expectation of "forced retirement" back on the island (Pessar 1995b).

Scholars who adopt the moral economy perspective tend to view households as essentially passive units whose members are collectively victimized by the larger market economy. We see this vision in the pioneering work of Claude Meillassoux (1981) on African migrant households and domestic communities. Significantly, he recognized that the domestic and productive activities of the migrant wives who remained in rural communities were essential for the social reproduction of male migrant labor on a seasonal and generational basis. Although Meillassoux acknowledged that women who engage in non-capitalist activities within the household and migrant community are in a contradictory and exploited relationship vis-à-vis the capitalist economy, this observation did not lead him to analyze the equally exploitative social and economic relations *within* migrant households. With such a model of passive and unitary households, we are totally unprepared to account for "transgressive" practices, such as the decision of many Kikuyu women to migrate alone to a nearby city rather than accept the onerous burden of maintaining homes and lands over the duration of their migrant husbands' and fathers' prolonged absences. Nici Nelson (1978:89) describes these exploited women as "voting with their feet."

More than twenty-five years after the publication of Meillassoux's work, we still continue to compile case studies documenting the social reproduction of migrant labor by labor-exporting households (Dandler and Medeiros 1988; Griffith 1985; Soto 1987). In much shorter supply, however, are treatments of the strains and limitations on the perpetuation of a labor reserve. We need, for example, comparative research on whether and how the "enforced" immobility of migrant wives and sisters is contested by women responding to the increased demand for female labor in domestic service and export-oriented industries at "home" and in immigrant-dominated sectors abroad (Grasmuck and Pessar 1991; Mills 1997; Nelson 1992). On the other hand, we must also deconstruct femininity and infuse it with hierarchies of power. This enables us to better capture the ways in which certain categories of women have become actively involved in the processes of subordination and immobility of other women, as when mothers seek to safeguard the reputations of their place-bound daughters and to control their labor (Wright 1995). Finally, there is a paucity of literature on the limits to grandmothers and other kin's willingness and capacities to care for the children left behind and to "resocialize" rebellious youth sent "home" by their distraught migrant parents (Basch, Glick Schiller, and Szanton Blanc 1994; Guarnizo 1997a).

By contrast to depictions of the passive household acted on by external forces, the second perspective (the strategizing household) presents us with a unit that continuously seeks to adjust itself to the larger socioeconomic and ecological system. Although this rendering of migrant households holds the promise of addressing the role of structure and agency in the migration process, critics lament the "veneer of free choice" built into the concept of strategies. Moreover, the model of the economic-maximizing household fails to specify how strategies actually develop within the confines of the household (Bach and Schraml 1982). Failing a specification of the mechanisms of strategy evolution, the implication is that the unit has no dissention over objectives (Dwyer 1983; Rouse 1986; Schmink 1984).

Addressing the matter of free choice, authors such as Charles Wood (1981, 1982) and Kenneth Roberts (1985) have countered that household sustenance strategies emerge out of an interplay between factors that are internal to domestic units and over which their members have some degree of control (such as consumption needs and available labor power) and forces that lie beyond the household unit and are far more resistant to the intervention of migrant household members (such as job opportunities, inflation, and land concentration). Others have suggested that our formulations of contingent agency within migrant households need not, and should not, be restricted to solely economic or material constraints. In addition, they point to cultural constructs such as kinship, gender, and class ideologies. These, too, shape and discipline household members and, as a consequence, influence how they individually and jointly perceive abstractions such as "consumption needs" and "labor power" and how they interpret and experience the range of opportunities and constraints external to the household. Moreover, these symbolic constructs strongly condition the type of strategies that can be imagined and orchestrated both individually and collectively (Fernández-Kelly and García 1990; Grasmuck and Pessar 1991; Kibria 1993; Pessar 1995a). Along these lines, we need more research on how images, meanings, and values associated with gender, consumption, modernity, and "the family" circulate within the global cultural economy (Appadurai 1990) and how these "ideoscapes" and "mediascapes" are interpreted and appropriated in varied sites by different household members in ways that either promote or constrain mobility (Brennan 2001; Mills 1997).

Finally, the claim that the "immigrant family" in the United States is an adaptive social form assumes an immigrant household already firmly in place (Pérez 1986). It diverts our attention from the important task of analyzing legislation and government policies that effectively block or limit the formation, unification, and material well-being of immigrant families (Espiritu 1997; Garrison and Weiss 1979; Hondagneu-Sotelo 1995; Hondagneu-Sotelo and Avila 1997; Mohanty 1991). We also need to turn a critical gaze on the accompanying rhetoric that makes these initiatives "thinkable" and credible (Chavez 2001; Chock 1996). For example, researchers have interpreted recent immigration and welfare legislation as measures intended to denigrate and discipline immigrant women in the United States and to orchestrate a return to the subsidies that "stay-at-home" wives afforded during the *bracero* program (Chavez 1998; Hondgagneu-Sotelo 1995; Naples 1997).

Researchers sensitive to gender difference have begun to challenge the popular notion that social networks operate in a neutered fashion. We see this misguided assumption clearly represented in those studies of family migration networks that assume that the effects of family networks on individual migration are equivalent for all household members (Taylor 1986). This approach fails to recognize that individuals' access to networks and individual network exchanges are rights and responsibilities informed by gender and kinship norms. As sociologist David Lindstrom (1991:26) correctly observes, "migration networks involve not only the provision of migration assistance, but the reproduction of social roles as well." In the case of the Mexican rural communities he studied, norms of family honor and beliefs that women are inferior and require surveillance mitigated the mobilization of family networks for women's migration. Yet, with declining household incomes, such patriarchal norms frequently had to be weighed against the much-needed earnings that migration of a wife or daughter might bring. According to Lindstrom, to resolve this contradiction, rural households came to depend on a far more limited number of effective network connections mobilized for aiding a female migrant than was the case for her male counterparts. Unlike fathers and sons, responsibility for women's migration and settlement could rarely be delegated to distant kin, friends, or a *coyote*—an individual who could not be confidently charged with the responsibilities of protection and control. In this way, women's mobility was far more restricted than men's because women had to depend almost entirely on the prior existence and willing mobilization of close family migration networks (for example, a migrant father or brother).

Critics also dispute the common assumption that networks are socially inclusive and maintained by kin, friends, and compatriots motivated by obligations and norms of social solidarity. A counternarrative suggests that migrant social networks can be highly contested social resources, not always shared even in the same family (Hondagneu-Sotelo 1994; Menjívar 2000). On this score, Hondagneu-Sotelo (1994) found that migrant networks were traditionally available to Mexican males. Now that women have developed independent female networks, it is not uncommon for family and household members to use entirely different social networks. This access to alternative networks may be very significant for those women who seek to escape the patriarchal vigilance and control characterizing traditional family networks.

IMMIGRANT WOMEN AND EMANCIPATION

No doubt affected by the timing of anthropologists' initial engagement with the topic of women and migration, ethnographers were greatly influenced by standpoint theory. This theory holds that there are "common threads of female experience" (Hartsock 1987) and these produce gender identification between female ethnographers and their subjects, thereby minimizing or erasing differences of race, ethnicity, class, or sexual orientation. Among the shortcomings of this brand of feminism were the tendencies of scholars to generalize from a white, heterosexual, middle-class subject position (see Rosaldo 1980) and to frame research questions regarding migrants in light of this former subject position. A case in point is the disproportionately large body of literature that addresses how immigrant women's wage work blurs the purported gender divide between the private and public spheres, thereby facilitating greater parity between immigrant men and women. As critics have noted, the initial assumption regarding separate private/domestic and public spheres misrepresented the experiences of many households. In these units, women's participation in income-generating activities within and outside the household was both common and crucial to the maintenance of its members.

Such a move by what have been called "second wave" or "Western, emancipatory" feminists to give voice and agency to women was, and is, laudable. Yet it was hobbled from the start by a universalist conception of a global sisterhood whose traits and particular struggles represented only a small segment of this sisterhood. Second wave feminism also erred in its conviction that gender was an autonomous system that universally and equally oppressed all women.

A third wave of feminist scholarship was needed to correct these faulty premises. In many cases, minority and postcolonial scholars insisted that gender is embedded in, and interacts with, other systems of power and stratification, such as ethnicity, race, and class (Collins 1990; Mohanty 1991; Zinn et al. 1986). These revisionists noted that, in as much as power flows in more than one direction, the oppressed can also be the oppressor, the victim, or the victimizer, depending on the particular axis of power under consideration (Kibria 1993). It was also understood that women and men's identities and experiences needed to be contextualized and studied with regard to interlocking forces such as patriarchy, state and global capitalism, state formation, and nationalism.

This is a tall order and one that anthropology has much to offer. Examining the dynamic relationships among systems, institutions, groups, and individuals has long been central to anthropology's holistic epistemology. Moreover, there is a growing appreciation that for many gender is envisioned and lived not only in local and national spaces but also in transnational ones. As the final section of this chapter discusses, anthropologists' multisited ethnographies offer a strategy to investigate this latter phenomenon.

Developments in third wave feminism have proved far more conducive to explaining those seeming inconsistencies or contradictions in the experiences of many immigrant women than earlier theories of gender inequality and women's emancipation. For example, rather than view the struggles of many immigrant women to maintain intact nuclear families and to reproduce the patriarchal bargain as evidence of a traditional and, as yet, unliberated femininity, researchers have come to interpret these subjectivities and practices in a wholly different light. They conclude that in many cases these struggles represent acts of resistance against those forces within the dominant society that threaten the existence of poor, racialized immigrant families (Zavella 1987; Zinn et al. 1986).

Only by recognizing the multiple positionings and consciousness of new immigrants do we come to appreciate the importance of conjugal households and their partners' commitment to the "patriarchal bargain." Multiple external forces buffet immigrant families. Legislation informed by racist and sexist discourse has, in the past and present, severely challenged the survival and well-being of immigrant families (Chavez 1998; Hondagneu-Sotelo 1995; Mohanty 1991). Immigrant men are increasingly frustrated and scapegoated. They expect, and are expected, to be the breadwinner. Yet they frequently face structural impediments that block the fulfillment of this role. As the following quotation attests, this has sobering implications for the successful performance of masculinity. In the words of an unemployed Salvadoran male immigrant, "Believe me, I feel as if my hands are tied, and my head ready to explode from the tension and disappointment. I don't want to be a *mantenido* [supported by the wife]. I don't feel like a man, I feel like a lady, and excuse me, but that's really terrible, insulting for a man who's used to providing for his family" (Menjívar 1999:612).

We are reminded here of Patricia Fernández-Kelly and Ana García's (1990:148) assertion that "[f]or poor men and women the issue is not so much the presence of the sexual division of labor or the persistence of patriarchal ideologies but the difficulties of upholding either." Whether through choice or necessity, large numbers of immigrant women have also assumed wage-earning responsibilities. Yet, contrary to the assumptions of mainstream white feminists, these women's pursuit of employment often results from severe economic need and, as such, expresses vulnerability far more than strength within the home and marketplace (Fernández-Kelly and García 1990). This does not mean, as Evelyn Nakano Glenn (1986) reminds us, that immigrant women may not simultaneously experience the family as an instrument of gender subordination. Indeed, their frequent attempts to use wages as leverage for greater gender parity in certain arenas of domestic life attest to this fact. The dilemma confronting many immigrant women, it would seem, is to defend and hold together the family while attempting to reform the norms and practices that subordinate them (Glenn:193).

Although poor immigrant families may experience difficulties in upholding a patriarchal division of labor and may often suffer socially and materially as a consequence of men's unemployment, upwardly mobile couples confront the opposite challenge: the "contradiction" that dual wage earning poses for households that have achieved, by their standards, a middle-class standing. In certain Dominican and Cuban immigrant families, for example, women's "retirement" to the domestic sphere is a favored practice for marking the household's *collective* social advancement (Fernández-Kelly and García 1990; Pessar 1995a). Many Dominican women I knew who agreed to leave wage employment viewed their alternatives as either an improved social status for the entire family through their retirement or improved gender relations (as wives) through their continued wage work. In leaving the workforce, many of the most conflicted women chose to place immigrant ideology (with its stress on social mobility) and traditional family domestic ideology (with its emphasis on both patriarchy and collective interests) before personal struggle and gains.

Of course, such actions contradict the feminist tenet that women's interests are best served by positioning themselves in both the household and workplace (Feree 1990). Yet some of my informants saw themselves struggling on another front to challenge the distorted and denigrating cultural stereotypes about Latino immigrants held by many members of the majority culture. Several female informants actively resisted these negative stereotypes by symbolizing the household's respectability and elevated social and economic status in a fashion common to the traditional Dominican middle class: They removed themselves from the visible productive sphere. Their stance echoes a broader claim advanced by Yen Le Espiritu (1997:6) and others: In a hostile environment, "some women of color, in contrast to their white counterparts, view unpaid domestic work—having children and maintaining families—more as a form of resistance to racist oppression than as a form of exploitation by men."

Relatively few studies address the question of whether migration promotes or hampers a feminist consciousness (Shukla 1997). Most report, not surprisingly, that the majority of the immigrant women studied do not tend to identify as feminists or participate in feminist organizations (Foner 1986; Hondagneu-Sotelo 1995; Pessar 1984). Immigrant women, we are told, base their dissatisfactions and complaints about life in the United States on injustices linked to class, race, ethnicity, and legal status discrimination more than gender. For example, according to Nancy Foner (1986), her Jamaican female informants experienced racial and class inequalities more acutely than those based on gender, and this sense of injustice gave them a basis for unity with Jamaican men. Moreover, the many domestic workers in their ranks felt no sense of sisterhood with their upper-middle-class white employers, whose "liberation" these immigrant women facilitated by providing inexpensive child care so that their female employers could compete in the male occupational world (Foner 1986). Nonetheless, Hondagneu-Sotelo's (1995:197) point is well taken when she concludes that although none of the Mexican immigrant women she interviewed "identified 'gender subordination' as a primary problem, rearrangements induced by migration do result in the diminution of familial patriarchy, and these transformations may enable immigrant women to better confront problems derived from class, racial/ethnic, and legal-status subordination. Their endeavors may prompt more receptiveness to feminist ideology and organizations in the future."

I agree with Hondagneu-Sotelo's more processional approach. In fact, I am unsettled to see my own early 1980s research on Dominican immigrants, which reported little, if any, collective action around problems of gender inequality, cited many years later as an example of *an overall* lack of gender consciousness among Dominican immigrant women. To mitigate such generalizations, I have attempted in later work to better contextualize and historicize my earlier claims. Accordingly, I describe the growth of self-help and feminist associations that took hold as the ethnic community in New York City consolidated over the course of the 1980s and 1990s (Pessar 1995b; Pessar and Graham 2001).[7] This points to a larger matter: the need to better historicize and contextualize our claims regarding continuities and change in pre- and post-migration gender ideologies, relations, and practices.

When anthropologists and other scholars of immigration take the next, much-needed step to investigate feminist organizing in multiethnic and transnational contexts, they will find themselves in the position to advance theory. As Daiva Stasiulis (1999:183) observes, we require a conceptual framework that can analytically "deal with not merely the plurality but also and more importantly the positionality of different nationalisms, racisms, ethnocultural movements, and feminisms in relation to one another." Such an approach will aid our understanding of the possibilities and limitations of transnational and interethnic solidarities within the women's movement, through highlighting the existence of alternative feminisms and exploring the extent to which feminist projects are complementary or contradictory (Stasiulis 1999).

The study of culture and its social reproduction and contestation is central to the discipline of anthropology. Yet the bulk of research on gender and migration has focused on matters of gendered agency, paying far less attention to issues of identity and to those symbolic constructs out of which identity and experience are forged (see Gross,

McMurray, and Swedenburg 1996; Matthei and Smith 1998). I refer to constructs such as religious discourses, educational texts, media productions, and popular culture. These are imposed on our subjects with the aim of rendering wholly natural and timeless a given gender regime, with its accompanying hierarchies of power, inclusions and exclusions, forms of bodily activity, and structures of feeling and desire. Following Sherry Ortner (1996), in attending to these important matters, we must take stock of not only hegemonic gender ideologies but also counterhegemonies. Too frequently, narratives of immigrant women's relative gains, viewed against immigrant men's losses, read unwittingly like triumphalist modernization tracts. One way to avoid avoid such misrepresentation is for researchers to do a far better job of historicizing and documenting the pre-migration nature of gender hegemonies and counterhegemonies. There is also a need to explore those internal inconsistencies and contradictions at the levels of meaning and performance of masculinities and femininities. These pre-emigration slippages and tensions are crucial to an analysis of gender and migration because they come into play when immigrant men and women confront and negotiate the opportunities, constraints, and contradictions of the gender regimes operating in the host society (Pessar 2001).

When conducting such studies, as I found in my research with Guatemalan refugees and returnees, it is wise to include not only past ethnographic accounts of pre-migration gender regimes but also infor-mants' social memories about gender ideologies, identities, and prac-tices. I reached this conclusion after noting the contrast between many ethnographic reports of gender complementarities and interdepen-dence among indigenous Guatemalans and those reports of refugee and returnee men and women who described far more oppressive and patriarchal pre-exile beliefs and practices. Consequently, I advise that "while pre-exile, ethnographic accounts of gender relations in indige-nous communities are useful in pointing out (likely) variations in gen-der ideologies and practices, and in documenting patterns that may be reconstituted in returnee households and communities, they are only part of the picture. The returnee[s']...social memories [crafted in large part with the tools for critical gender analysis provided by the internationals they met in refugee camps] are equally important, if not more so. It is against these potent images of patriarchal men and victimized women that many returnee women (and) men now gauge how far they have come in constructing more equitable gender relations" (Pessar 2001:466).

Often, ethnographic research on gender and migration restricts its engagement largely to immigrant and ethnic subjects and institutions. Far less in evidence are treatments of "borderland encounters" (Ortner 1996) between immigrant women and men and members of the host society. This alternative approach has the virtue of placing "'us' and 'them' within the same frame and subjects all parties to the same analytical scrutiny" (Ortner 1996:211). It underscores how reciprocal representations of the "other" with respect to gender (and other interlinking axes of difference) reveal tensions and contradictions in the ideologies, practices, and distribution of power within the lives of immigrants and native-born populations. On this score, important works in cultural studies and ethnic studies (for example, Anzaldúa 1990; Espiritu 1997; Lowe 1996) alert us to the fact that representations of majority white American men and women and those of immigrants and ethnics of color may be mutually constituting. Therefore, ideological representations of gender and sexuality are central in the exercise and perpetuation of patriarchal, racial, and class domination, as when representations of Asian men as both hypersexual and asexual and Asian women as both super-feminine and masculine are used to define, maintain, and legitimate white male virility and supremacy.

For their part, immigrants of color and new ethnics also draw discursively upon white bodies and the bodies of their own women to engage in the politics of national/ethnic pride and belonging and to resist racism. Although earlier colonial and racist ideologies featured sexually promiscuous women of color, contemporary immigrants in the United States reverse the tables. Filipinos and Vietnamese, for example, assert the morality of their communities by denouncing the sexual improprieties of American society and white women and praising the sexual restraints of their own ethnic cultures and women. Ethnographers have noted that this rhetoric and accompanying discipline lead to restrictions on the autonomy, mobility, and personal decision making of immigrant daughters. Moreover, because immigrant and ethnic women are often charged with the responsibilities to transmit and maintain ethnic traditions (di Leonardo 1984; Gabaccia 1994), young women who veer from acceptable behaviors may be labeled "non-ethnic," "untraditional," and, even worse, as betrayers of their cultures and homelands. Yen Le Espiritu (2000) is right when she concludes that this move by immigrant communities to resist racism through an emphasis on their own morality and through restrictions on women's sexuality produces its own contradictions. One of the most severe is its casting the family as a site of potentially the most intense conflict and oppressive demands in immigrant lives.

In my opinion, the link between resistance to subordination and racism and immigrant groups' reclaiming the moral high ground provides a lens through which to interpret the tremendous emotion and dread reported among immigrant men and some women when they discuss state intervention over charges of child and spousal abuse. I do not intend to minimize the very real danger and humiliation such police intervention poses, but I am interested here in exploring why such infrequent encounters with the law are mentioned so frequently in immigrant discourses on life in the United States. If, as suggested above, the policing of morality in immigrant families creates a force field along gendered and generational lines, the enforcers of this regime are no doubt frustrated by the knowledge that their families' weakest members can gain leverage by appealing to a powerful state (Menjívar 2000; Waters 1999). At a more symbolic and ethical level, the threat or actual intervention by state authorities pits one system of morality (with respect to domesticity, gender, and generation) against another. It threatens to unsettle the household experienced as a repository of and maintainer of ethnic culture. It also challenges the claims that family members possess a more elevated morality than their white American counterparts. Last, it undermines the supremacy of the male patriarch over his household.

For young women, the consequences of the strong disciplining of their sexuality and geographical mobility can be paradoxical. Those very gender inequalities that root girls to home and reward female compliance may actually contribute to their academic success (Foner 2000; Suárez-Orozco and Suárez-Orozco 2001). The socialization girls receive in being cooperative, compliant, and passive may be rewarded by their teachers in overcrowded and understaffed inner schools.

Although girl's domestic responsibilities may reduce time spent at home on schoolwork, it does remove them, unlike their brothers, from the unsavory features of street life (Foner 2000). Reflecting the differences in experiences these gendered social geographies create, Mary Waters (2001) found that second-generation West Indian boys discussed being black American in terms of racial solidarity and rigid racial boundaries. The boys' more adversarial form of African-American identity was born out of repeated incidents of social exclusion, harassment, and denigration at the hands of white Americans. Within the school context, this adversarial stance had a chilling effect on academic achievement. For example, West Indian second-generation males were more likely than their female counterparts to suffer social stigma if they spoke standard English among friends; they were more likely to report that they accused others of "acting white" (Waters 2001). Although girls also faced exclusion on grounds of race, they discussed being American in terms of the freedom they sought from strict parental control. For girls, education and, subsequently, relatively well-paying jobs were means to acquire this much coveted freedom. In short, the ways in which second-generation females respond to the constraints placed on their sexuality and physical mobility may position them to acquire the education needed for the social mobility eluding their parents and brothers.

GENDER AND TRANSNATIONAL MIGRATION

As of late, anthropological theories and research methods have become far less fixed to unitary locales and individual nation-states. As anthropologists have turned their sights on subjects who cognitively, socially, and/or physically cross multiple geographical and cultural borders, some have enquired how structures of difference and power rooted in nationality, race, class, and gender are both reproduced and reconfigured within and across transnational spaces. To date, there has been far less movement toward developing an analytical framework capable of stimulating and guiding such research with respect to gender and transnational migration than has been the case for matters of national belonging, racialization, and class formation (Basch, Glick Schiller, and Szanton Blanc 1994; Rouse 1995). This is a challenge several colleagues and I have taken up over the past few years. I close this chapter with a presentation of the framework Sarah Mahler and I developed to help us better study gender across transnational space. We call this model "gendered geographies of power" (Mahler and Pessar 2001).

The first building block of our model is called "geographical scales." This spatial term captures our understanding that gender operates simultaneously on multiple *spatial, social, and cultural* scales (for example, the body, the family, the state, gender hegemonies, and counterhegemonies) across national and transnational terrains. The disciplining force and seeming immutability of any given gender regime are reinforced through repetition in the ways in which gender is embedded and reenacted between and among these scales. Important questions emerge when the phenomenon of transnational migration is added to the mix. When geographical scales are distributed across transnational space, do this multiplication and dispersal produce even greater opportunities for the reinforcement of prevailing gender ideologies and norms, or does transnational migration provide openings for men and women to question hegemonic notions of gender, to entertain competing understandings of gendered lives, and to communicate these new understandings across transnational spaces? Although we require much more research to begin to answer these questions, preliminary work indicates that gains for women or men may be uneven and contradictory (Goldring 2001; Pessar 2001). For example, Georges Fouron and Nina Glick Schiller (2001) find that poor Haitian immigrant women's remittances and gifts elevate their social status back home to an extent previously unimaginable. Yet, paradoxically, their material contributions help to maintain a Haitian state that systematically discriminates against women.

The analytical construct of "social location" is the second component of the model. It refers to persons' positions within power hierarchies created through historical, political, economic, geographic, kinship-based, and other socially stratifying factors. *Gender* is underscored in the framework's title because gender organizes human actions such as migration yet is frequently ignored. For the most part, people are born in a social location that confers on them certain advantages and disadvantages. For example, Sarah Mahler (2001) shows how migrants from a very remote region of El Salvador must struggle harder than migrants from urban areas to build and sustain transnational ties. However, hierarchies are not built just at the national or supra-national level. Hierarchies of class, race, sexuality, ethnicity, nationality, and, of course, gender operate at various levels that affect an individual or group's social location. In other words, multiple dimensions of identity also shape, discipline, and position people and the ways they think and act. In sum, our model takes as its foundation the obvious, but not always stated, fact that people—irrespective of their own efforts—are situated within power hierarchies that they have not constructed.

The third step in building this conceptual framework is to examine the types and degrees of agency people exert, given their social locations—hence, our focus on gendered geographies of *power*. Here Doreen Massey's (1994:149) concept of "power geometry" proves quite helpful. She observes that the particular conditions of modernity that have produced time-space compression have also placed people in very distinct locations regarding access to and power over flows and interconnections between places—similar to our observations above. Then she goes further to foreground agency, as when people exert power over these forces and processes that affect them. Some individuals "initiate flows and movement, others don't; some are more on the receiving-end of it than others; some are effectively imprisoned by it.... [There are] groups who are really in a sense in charge of time-space compression, who can really use it and turn it to advantage, whose power and influence it very definitely increases [such as media moguls and the business elite]...but there are also groups who are also doing a lot of physical moving, but who are not 'in charge' of the process in the same way at all. The refugees from El Salvador or Guatemala [for instance]" (D. Massey 1994:149).

There are also those who do not move at all yet feel the effects of time-space compression and those who both contribute to this condition and are imprisoned by it. The latter instance is vividly documented in Denise Brennan's (2001) study of Dominican sex workers who contribute to a German and even international sexual aesthetic yet almost never get to see Germany for themselves.

Massey helps us to see not only how people's social locations affect their access to resources and mobility across transnational spaces but also how they initiate, refine, and transform these conditions. To her "power geometry" and our "social location" and "geographic scales" we add two final dimensions to complete our particular notion of gendered geographies of power. First, we view agency as affected by both extra-personal factors and quintessentially individual characteristics, such as initiative. Two people may hail from equally disadvantageous social locations, but one—owing to her own resourcefulness— will exert more influence than the other. Second, we argue that the social agency in which we are interested must include the role of cognitive processes such as the imagination, as well as substantive agency. In the foreground of what people actually do transnationally are imaging, planning, and strategizing; these must be valued and factored into people's agency. Moreover, some people may not take any transnational actions that can be objectively measured (such as remitting funds, writing letters, or joining transnational organizations), yet they live their lives in a transnational cognitive space. A concrete example would be youth who envision themselves as becoming migrants to such a degree that they stop attending school, seeing very little utility in education if they are to work overseas. Perhaps they do migrate at a later date, translating their imagination into reality. Even if they never realize their dreams, their leaving school cannot be fully understood without reference to their imagined lives as migrants. Therefore, for studies examining global agency, we advocate a consideration of both transnational cultural economies (Appadurai 1990) and *cognitive,* as well as corporal, actions. In doing so, we readily acknowledge the difficulty in detecting and measuring such intangible efforts.

To summarize, "gendered geographies of power" is a framework for analyzing people's social agency—corporal and cognitive—given their own initiative and their positioning within multiple hierarchies of power operative within and across many terrains. Although this framework is not applicable to transnational contexts only, we feel that it is especially useful for analyzing these contexts in light of their complexities. Thus, we can speak of a gendered geography of power that maps the historically particularistic circumstances a specific group of people experiences, and we can analyze these on multiple levels. However, we can also contemplate a less particularistic gendered geography of power wherein different groups are located vis-à-vis macro-level processes, such as global economic restructuring, and can trace their efforts and ability to influence these processes. In short, the framework is intended to aid scholarly analysis of gender across transnational spaces for case studies and comparative investigations.

CONCLUSION

Theory development and research on migration can only benefit from doing away with "the woman's panel" or "woman's chapter." Instead, we must ensure that all aspects of migration are subjected to a thorough gendered analysis based on the understanding that "gender as a social system contextualizes migration processes for all immigrants" (Hondagneu-Sotelo 1999:566). For example, this means that panels on migration and politics would systematically interrogate how constructions and practices of masculinities and femininities organize the political lives of immigrants. The same would hold for treatments of labor force participation, education, and so on.

In this chapter, I have reviewed several contributions to migration studies and feminist studies by ethnographers who have positioned women and gender centrally within their research. These scholars have greatly advanced our understanding of migration as a gendered process. Nonetheless, it is time to add complementary perspectives to our socialist feminist framework that are more attuned to issues of cultural production and contestation, to encounters between immigrants and established residents, and to the construction of transnational subjects and agencies. Such an expanded framework promises to enhance theorizing on gender and migration, expose migration researchers to new debates and advances in feminist and gender studies, and augment the audience for scholarship on gender and migration.

Notes

1. For a more comprehensive review of largely ethnographic works that seek to engender our understanding of international migration, see Pessar (1999a and b). Also see Buijs (1993), Morokvasic (1984), Phizacklea (1983), and Simon and Brettell (1986).

2. The work of certain sociologists has been particularly important to these developments. Charles Wood (1981), for example, was a pioneer in critiquing gender-neutral portraits of migrant households. Ethnographic research by sociologists such as Pierrette Hondagneu-Sotelo (1994, 2001), Nazli Kibria (1993), and

Luin Goldring (2001) has greatly advanced our understanding of the ways in which constructions of masculinities and femininities organize migration and migration outcomes.

3. This chapter includes certain materials previously published in Pessar (1999a and b) and Mahler and Pessar (2001).

4. It should be noted that for several decades the United States has attracted proportionately more female migrants than other labor-importing countries and that women constitute the majority among US immigrants from Asia, Central and South America, the Caribbean, and Europe (Donato 1992; Houston, Kramer, and Barrett 1984).

5. Researchers neglected Ernst Ravenstein's (1985, 1989) early observations on the differences between women and men in his "migration laws." In the 1880s, for example, he declared that women were more likely than men to migrate short distances.

6. B. Bozzoli (1983) argues that gender relations proved central to households' resistance to full proletarianization. However, this move depended on male appropriation of female labor.

7. See Jones-Correa (1998) for an analysis of the contrastive social benefits Latin American immigrant men and women seek from organizational life. The author argues that in an attempt to recapture pre-emigration social status (in the context of current male downward mobility in the United States), men tend to join transnational immigrant organizations. Women fill the breach by assuming the role of intermediaries between the immigrant community and the surrounding society.

4

The Centrality of Ethnography in the Study of Transnational Migration

Seeing the Wetland Instead of the Swamp

Nina Glick Schiller

Anthropologists were among the first scholars to propose "a transnational perspective for the study of migration" (Glick Schiller, Basch, and Blanc-Szanton 1992b). Today the study of transnational migration is a shared project that stretches across disciplines, with scholars in anthropology, sociology, geography, and history employing the same terms and, to some extent, citing one another's work. However, terms such as *globalization, transnationalism, transnational community, transnational network, transnational social field, deterritorialization,* and *transmigrant* often are deployed differently and are undefined. The definitional jungle is difficult to traverse because within it lies a methodological quagmire. Although one scholar's wetland is another's swamp, the current moment seems an appropriate time to survey the development of the field, clarify concepts, and explore issues of methodology. In this chapter I explicate theoretical, methodological, and substantive contributions ethnographers have made to the study of transnational migration and suggest future directions for research. Exploring the epistemological assumptions residing within ethnographic approaches to transnational migration, I briefly note the venerable but often forgotten history of migration studies within anthropology. Before beginning these various explorations, I define some of the key terms of transnational migration studies.

To underscore the ethnographic perspective on transnational migration, I contrast it to the way the same topic appears when approached by means of social surveys. Even though the ethnographers who study migration are not a homogenous lot and there has been valuable cross-fertilization among the practitioners of different methodologies, ethnography is, I argue, the most appropriate methodology for the study of transnational migration. Ethnography is a methodology that includes more than participant observation. Ethnographers obtain and use a variety of quantitative data and utilize various kinds of questionnaires. However, they do this in a very different relationship to theory, and their understanding of the ways in which categories of data are defined differs from the positivist approach of other social scientists (Schensul, Schensul, and LeCompte 1999).

DEVELOPING A TRANSNATIONAL PERSPECTIVE FOR THE STUDY OF MIGRATION

At the end of the 1980s, scholars in a number of disciplines, including anthropology, cultural studies, and geography, became fascinated by the various flows of people, ideas, objects, and capital across the territorial borders of states. Anthropologists working in the United States proposed a new paradigm for the study of migration, called "transnationalism" (Glick Schiller, Basch, and Blanc-Szanton 1992b and c; see also Kearney 1991; Rouse 1991). As early as 1916, Randolph Bourne had used the term to describe the transborder relations of immigrants to the United States. Political scientists addressed the topic in the *Annals of the American Academy of Political and Social Science* in 1986. By 1990, anthropological use had begun (Georges 1990; Glick Schiller and Fouron 1990).[1] However, not until the 1990s did the term refer to an approach to the study of migration and become a topic of sustained interest in migration studies. The new paradigm in migration made visible the multiple, cross-border relationships of many migrants, enabling researchers to see that migration can be a transnational process.

Building on research on Caribbean migration that Basch had conducted with Caribbean sociologists (Basch et al. 1990), Linda Basch, Cristina Blanc-Szanton, and I (Glick Schiller, Basch, and Blanc-Szanton 1992c:1) called persons who live their lives across borders "transmigrants." Not coincidentally, some of the first scholars to conceptualize transnational migration worked in the Caribbean and Mexico, two areas of the world that had long, continuous histories of migration and cultures of migration. It was easier for scholars working in those two settings to break out of the dominant paradigm that assumed that persons could belong to only a single country and that US migrants had to choose between their home country and the new land.

Anthropologists emerged as key theorists of transnational migration by drawing on a heritage of ethnographies of migration. This heritage may surprise persons in various disciplines who believe that anthropologists' concern has been with social actors living in local, "traditional" settings (Morawska 2001b:3–4). Even in anthropology, the long, rich history of migration studies often goes unacknowledged, and one can find anthropologists who write as if the ethnographic study of migration, complex societies, and transborder processes is something new to their discipline (Marcus 1986; Rosaldo 1989). In fact, ethnographers of migration have long maintained a creative tension with certain mainstream currents in anthropology and sociology and offer a critique of both.

The ethnographic study of transnational migration is rooted in a different, older definition of culture than that adopted by prominent anthropologists such as Clifford Geertz and Arjun Appadurai and an increasing number of anthropology textbooks. Many contemporary anthropologists define culture as a system of meaning, discarding or downplaying the study of social relations and social action. Because social relations are at the foundation of transnational migration, it is not surprising that most ethnographers who study people living their lives across borders deploy a broader, older, Tylorian concept of culture that encompasses social relations, social structure, and transgenerationally transmitted patterns of action, belief, and language. Utilizing this more encompassing approach to culture, anthropologists who studied migration in past generations developed several topics central to the current study of transnational migration, including the diffusion of ideas and material culture through migration, social networks, and social fields.

Transnational migration studies focus on the nature and impact of relationships—economic, religious, political, and social—that embed people in two or more societies. In 1990, a network of scholars, most of whom were anthropologists, met in a conference at the New York Academy of Sciences and established four vital points: (1) Nation-states continue to shape transmigrant actions and identities, (2) the nature, pattern, intensity, and types of transnational connections of migrants vary with class, gender, and generation, (3) states often try to encompass and redirect the transnational activities of migrants, and (4) continuities, as well as differences, exist between contemporary and past patterns of transnational migration (Feldman-Bianco 1992; Georges 1992; Glick Schiller, Basch, and Blanc-Szanton 1992c; Lessinger 1992; Ong 1992; Richman 1992; Rouse 1992; Sider 1992; Sutton 1992; Wiltshire 1992).

Subsequently, many scholars embraced the concept of transnational migration articulated at this conference and cited the resulting publication. However, the focus on the multiple social relationships of migrants sometimes became lost in the general excitement over the new paradigm. The tasks of distinguishing patterns of variation within transnational migration and comparing past and present periods of transnational migration were not prioritized. Also ignored were the previous several decades of research, much of it ethnographic, that documented (but did not highlight) transnational connections.

Instead, scholars turned to a celebration of the contemporary moment of globalization. In the euphoria sparked by the new, rapid, global flows of ideas and information via computers, satellites, and the Internet, a small but significant core of scholars spoke of a postmodern moment (Appadurai 1990; Kearney 1991). This sparked what I have called the "dissing" of previous paradigms. We heard about disjuncture, dislocation, displacement, disengagement, disconnection, deterritorialization, and the dismantling of the old stabilities, knowledge, conventions, and identities. The past was static; the present was fluid. The past contained homogenous cultures; we lived in a world of hybridity and complexity. Before, anthropology studied small isolated societies; now the world was our terrain.

Both those who emphasized the postmodern moment and those who were less sanguine about the libratory potential of transnational processes linked these processes to a new stage of capitalism. Marked by the restructuring of production, distribution, and consumption, the new stage of capitalism was understood to be globally stimulating increased levels of migration and inducing and facilitating both the home ties and diasporic connections of persons who had migrated across international borders.

With the celebratory postmodern rhetoric now behind us, we can sort out the relationship between contemporary globalization and the emergence of the transnational framework for studying migration. It is now clear that in the 1990s we were experiencing two discrete but inter-related types of novelty. First, we were shifting our paradigm; we had changed the analytical framework we used to conceptualize migration. Second, although globalization is not new, the end of the twentieth century marked a period of intensive global restructuring of capitaliza-tion that facilitated, and again made necessary, a large number of migrants' maintaining some type of home tie or other transborder con-nection and organizing their lives around these connections. Extensive migrant interconnection across state borders had been part of an ear-lier period of globalization in the late nineteenth and early twentieth centuries but had been obscured by the assimilationist paradigm that came to dominate migration studies (Foner 2000, 2001c and e; Glick Schiller 1999a, b, and c; Goldberg 1992). With a new period of global-ization, the transnational ties of migrants were again visible and even more significant.

The enthusiastic reception of David Harvey's *The Condition of Postmodernity: An Enquiry into the Conditions of Cultural Change,* published in 1989, marks the moment when the paradigm changed for many in anthropology and related fields such as cultural studies. Harvey, a geo-grapher, explicitly linked changing structures of capital accumulation, which he called "flexible accumulation," with transformations in the nature of cultural processes. The paradigm change spawned the devel-opment of several other related fields of study: transcultural studies, diaspora studies, and globalization studies. Soon studies developed of transborder family, business, and historical connections that stretch across multiple nation-states and connect sets of individuals to one another by means of identity narratives (Nyiri 1999; Ong 1999; Smart and Smart 1998).

As various interdisciplinary studies of cross-border interconnections developed, some scholars did not distinguish transnational migration from other forms of transnational connection (Cohen 1997). However, there are good reasons to view transnational migration studies as a distinct field of research within the more general study of transnational processes. Transnational migrants, or transmigrants, establish sets of social relations across borders and maintain them over time, even across generations. Diaspora studies began by identifying narratives of identity legitimated by myths of common origin and global dispersal (Clifford 1994; Tölölyan 1991; the journal *Diaspora*). Globalization studies focus on the worldwide flow of capital, goods, and ideas.

DEFINING THE TERMS

Before going further, I will define my terms. The definitions I propose emerged from comparative ethnography that documented the existence of the phenomenon. *Transnational processes* can be defined as political, economic, social, and cultural processes that extend beyond the borders of a particular state and include actors that are not states but are shaped by the policies and institutional practices of particular states (Glick Schiller and Fouron 1998, 1999; Mato 1997).[2] These processes are much broader than migration and include flows of goods, information, and political influence. In contrast to transnational processes, *global processes* affect the earth's inhabitants, wherever they may reside. These processes cannot be reduced to specific networks of connection across the borders of specific states. They vary greatly, affecting cultural and biological processes and their interface and shaping our environments, as well as our relationships to our physical and cultural environments and to one another. Global processes include cultural transmission such as media messages via satellite television or the Internet, environmental changes caused by increased emission of gasses into the atmosphere, and the dissemination of ideologies, from neo-liberalism to religious fundamentalism. At different times in the past 500 years, the intensity of global processes has varied. The term *globalization* is most useful as a way to speak about the periods of intensified integration of the world through systems of production, distribution, consumption, and communication (Mittleman 1996).

In our initial work, my colleagues and I spoke about transnationalism to emphasize the qualitative changes brought about when migrants develop a multiplicity of transnational relations. We argued that migration can be conceptualized as transnationalism when migrants develop and maintain multiple relations—familial, economic, social, organizational, religious, and political—that span borders (Basch, Glick Schiller, and Szanton Blanc 1994a; Glick Schiller, Basch, and Blanc-Szanton 1992b and c, 1995). Transnationalism is fully developed only when people establish transnational relationships and interact with persons other than kin, but kin ties are often the foundation for myriad types of non-kin social relationships.

The term *transnationalism* proved problematic, however. There are many forms of transnational processes beyond migration, and migrants themselves participate in a range of transnational processes and connections. Moreover, migrants may engage in multiple, ongoing connections across borders without engaging in political activities that link them to the nation-state.

Distinguishing transmigrants from migrants who have very different experiences of connection and incorporation has proven useful. *Transmigrants* are those persons who, having migrated from one nation-state to another, live their lives across borders, participating simultaneously in social relations that embed them in more than one nation-state. Activities and identity claims in the political domain are a particular form of transmigrant activity that is best understood as *long-distance nationalism* (Glick Schiller and Fouron 2001a). In some cases, individuals maintain hometown ties but avoid a connection with any form of a nation-state–building process, although states are increasingly striving to encompass such relationships (Kearney 2000).

Some writers have taken up the term *transnationalism* for both transnational migration, which they term *transnationalism from below,* and the cross-border activities of states and multinational corporations, which they label *transnationalism from above* (Smith and Guarnizo 1998). Again, the attempt at clarity has opened another set of problems and debates. *Transnationalism from below* is often used to signal transmigrant practices that constitute a transgressive or grassroots type of transnational connection. In actuality, migrants represent a wide range of classes and political and economic interests. Many transmigrants work to maintain existing systems of power. Even poor migrants may support or participate in struggles against oppressive circumstances in one location while being committed to status hierarchies and systems of exploitation in another (Goldring 1998).

Whatever terms are adopted, the decade of discussion has made the following four points clear. First, not all persons who migrate become embedded in more than one location. Some are truly immigrants, cutting their ties and refusing to look behind them. Others are sojourners, who circulate, earning money or temporary political protection outside a homeland. They maintain transnational networks but do not become simultaneously incorporated in two or more nation-states (Diminescu 2002; Morokvasic 1996). Second, people may be incorporated in both the old land and the new and may publicly identify with only one of these locations. That is, a gap can exist between incorporative behavior and a conscious political project. The degree to which a person who has emigrated maintains transnational connections or becomes embedded in more than one location varies over time. Third, migrants can participate in transnational political networks that evoke a homeland without maintaining political relationships to that homeland. Often, it is only when people become well embedded in their new land that they participate in transnational political connections to the old one and become long-distance nationalists.

Fourth, certain identity processes of migrants are global instead of transnational. For example, people who live in disparate parts of the world and imagine themselves as a single, diasporic people who share a common history but do not maintain any form of social networks that connect them to one another or to a specific homeland state are engaged in a global, not transnational, process of identity construction. A diasporic consciousness that develops after movement and oppressive conditions, such as the aftermath of seventeenth-to-nineteenth century African slavery, can create potent imaginaries that motivate political action and personal self-presentation. Some members of a population who share a diasporic identity not focused on a homeland, in particular conditions, may become involved in a specific project of transnational nation-state building. This describes the transformation of much of US Jewish life during the development of the Zionist movement and the growth of the state of Israel. Some members of the African diaspora may become committed to building a particular African state. On the other hand, other members of the same population, who maintain a diasporic identity and see themselves as part of a global population, may never engage in specific transnational processes linked to that identity. They neither build transnational networks nor participate in any form of transnational connection to a particular homeland. For example, I maintain a Jewish identity, built on a sense of common history, but do not personally participate in transnational networks that connect me to Israel or to people organized around a Jewish identity in other states.[3]

To facilitate the conceptualization and analysis of the multiple transborder relationships within which transmigrants live their daily lives, my colleagues and I suggested the term *transnational social field* (Basch, Glick Schiller, and Szanton Blanc 1994a; Glick Schiller, Basch, and Blanc-Szanton 1992b and c). (Rouse [1991, 1992] preferred the term *circuit*.) *Social field* is a more encompassing term than *social network*. Networks are generally understood to be chains of social relationships that extend from a single individual. Network analysis is egocentric; it directs our attention to the density and types of relationships of a specific individual. In contrast, the analysis of *social field* is sociocentric. We focus on alterations in social actions, ideas, and values as people are linked together by means of multiple interlocking networks (Glick Schiller 1999a). The concept of a social field enables us to visualize the simultaneity of transmigrant connections across the borders of two or more states. We investigate the ways in which transmigrants become part of the fabric of daily life in more than one state, simultaneously participating in the social, cultural, economic, religious, or political activities of more than one locality (Fouron and Glick Schiller 1997; Glick Schiller and Fouron 1998, 1999).

Transnational social fields are not metaphoric references to altered experiences of space; they comprise observable social relationships and transactions. Multiple actors with very different kinds of power and locations of power interact across borders to create and sustain this field of relationships. Persons who live within transnational social fields are exposed to a set of social expectations, cultural values, and patterns of human interaction shaped by more than one social, economic, and political system. Noting that the multistranded social networks make up a transnational social field enables us to distinguish between transmigrants, who have direct personal networks that stretch across borders, and those who live within social relationships shaped by transnational connections but do not, themselves, maintain such connections.

In the effort to popularize the concept of transborder social connection, many researchers turned to the term *transnational community*. The term is user-friendly but also poses difficulties. First, various researchers use *transnational community* to describe very different kinds of social formations. Portes (1997:812) refers to transnational communities as "dense networks across political borders created by immigrants in their quest for economic advancement and social recognition." Vertovec (n.d.) argues that a transnational community is a collectivity that lies between networks of individual actors, or transnationalism from below, and the cross-border activities of states, or transnationalism from above. Faist (2000a:196) has categorized the transnational community as one form of "transnational space," using the term to encompass various instances of connection through "collective representations." In his approach, the same term applies to the transnational village described by Levitt (2001a and b), linked by ongoing forms of observable connections, and the Jewish diaspora, an ideological construction of collectivity.

After several decades of community studies in which the community was approached as both object and sample, many anthropologists concluded that the term *community* obscures more than illuminates, confounding ideology with sociality and impeding the analysis of political and economic power (Silverman 2002). (The concept of community as object and sample comes from Conrad Arensberg [1965].) Rather than describe a location or local political unit, the word *community* evokes an ideology of shared interests. The term *community* leaves unmarked the exploitative class relations and divisions of wealth and status that stratify a population. It also obscures the various links between the state and community elites that enable these elites to constitute and maintain their exploitative relations within the "community." By deploying the term *transnational community* to encompass all studies of transnational social fields, researchers begin with an assumption of commonality before it has been demonstrated through research. A transnational social field does not necessarily constitute a community. Certainly, some people who maintain transborder relations invoke an ideology of community, and in those instances it makes sense to use the term and investigate the reasons for this invocation of solidarity.

EPISTEMOLOGICAL ISSUES—THEORY, METHOD, CONCEPTS, QUESTIONS

As the study of transnational migration matured, debate on questions of theory and method commenced. Survey researchers and social researchers trained to dismiss ethnography as "vignettes" ignored, misunderstood, or even derided the developing study and theory building of the initial research on transnational migration (Kivisto 2001). Portes, Guarnizo, and Landholt (1999:218–219) state that "it is not enough to invoke anecdotes of some immigrants investing in businesses back home or some governments giving their expatriates the right to vote in national elections to justify a new field of study." They insist that the study of transnational migration is legitimate only if evidence exists that "significant proportions of persons are involved in the process and that the process persists over time." The implication of these statements is that ethnographic research has not provided and cannot provide these forms of empirical evidence. Underneath the dismissal of ethnographic data as anecdote are significant differences in epistemology and notions of the way theory is developed and tested.

Addressing methodology, Guarnizo, Portes, and Haller (2002:2) state that "the main difficulty with the field of transnationalism, as developed so far, is that its empirical base relies almost exclusively on case studies. While useful, these studies invariably sample on the dependent variables, focusing on those who take part in the activities of interest to the exclusion of those who do not take part in them. The result is to exaggerate the scope of the phenomenon by giving the false impression that everyone in the studied communities is becoming a transnational."

In point of fact, most ethnographic studies of migration have not been studies only of transmigrants. They have been case studies, but case studies of migrating populations that included, but were not limited to, transmigrants and their social fields. The difference between ethnographic and survey approaches to transnational migration is not an exclusive focus on "the dependent variable" but a distinctively different idea about how to build and test theory and about what migration theory is trying to explain. The choice of the dependent variable reflects the question under investigation. Ethnographers and survey researchers studying transnational migration have approached the topic of migrations with a different set of questions from that of many other survey researchers.

There are three domains of difference between ethnographic and survey approaches to the study of transnational migration: (1) theory and hypothesis testing, (2) the influence of methodological nationalism in defining the questions studied, and (3) the nature of data.

Theory and Hypothesis Testing

The distinctions between ethnographic and social survey methodologies are often falsely reduced to the difference between qualitative and quantitative research. As Schensel, Schensel, and LeCompte (1999) point out, this contrast distorts and conceals that which distinguishes ethnography from other research methods, a characteristic highlighted by the way in which ethnographers approach the study of transnational migration. In fact, many ethnographers conduct surveys and obtain and use a variety of quantitative data. Some survey researchers conduct ethnography before they conduct a survey. However, ethnographers and survey researchers differ in their understanding of the relationships between theory and data collection. The differences are so fundamental in the area of theory building that survey researchers often believe that ethnographers can merely suggest interesting lines of inquiry; they cannot produce verifiable data.

Most ethnographers and survey researchers would accept the definition of theory offered by Stephen Reyna, an anthropologist and the founder of the journal *Anthropological Theory*. Reyna sees theory as generalizations that are high in scope and abstraction and that state relationships between concepts so as to explain observed occurrences (Reyna 1994, 2002; see also Wallace 1971). Ethnographers rarely utilize grand theory, but they do deploy what Merton (1968) termed "middle level theory," beginning their research with a formulation of relationships between variables, based on past research and reading. (However, high-level abstractions such as those about the nature of power and the power of culture are certainly within the domain of anthropology [Reyna 2002].) This use of theory, sometimes called "formative theory" or "grounded theory," was explicated by the Manchester school ethnographers, such as Jahn Van Velsen (1967), who developed the extended case-study method. More recently, Michael Burawoy (1991a and b, 1998), a sociologist, has championed this approach.

Formative theory connects "concepts that can explain what causes, predicts, or is associated with a central problem or topic under investigation" (Schensul, Schensul, and LeCompte 1999:2). It "helps to organize observations and interviews into units, patterns and structures, attributing meaning to otherwise disconnected social facts" (Schensul, Schensul, and LeCompte 1992:2).

In their use of formative theory, ethnographers do not differ from other empirically oriented social scientists.[4] The differences arise in the ways and means of building and testing theory. In ethnography, systematic explanations of the relations between variables are constantly explored and reformulated in the course of research. The formative theory of ethnographers not only builds on previous observations and generates hypotheses from them but also produces new hypotheses from within ongoing observations. Those who deploy social surveys and test theory from a statistical sampling of a database generally operate with a model of science that proposes that deductively inferred hypotheses must be generated before a study begins. Data collection then verifies or fails to confirm the initial hypothesis. Ethnographers, too, generate hypotheses, but during the research, they continually question, explore, and reformulate their understanding of the relationship between variables and even the choice of variables. This process enables ethnographers to change research questions as new situations, not expected within the initial set of assumptions, present themselves. To social scientists who limit hypothesis testing to the statistical manipulation of variables, ethnography is not science, at least not good science.

For example, the initial research I used to describe Haitian transnational migration had been formulated to study the forces that shape ethnogenesis among Haitian immigrants in New York and various migration histories and patterns of incorporation in the Caribbean. It was not a case study of the transnational migration, and the dependent variable was Haitian/United States–based ethnicity (Glick Schiller et al. 1987). However, in the course of this research, it became clear to me that a variety of migrants were building and maintaining transnational social fields and beginning to articulate identities that reflected this form of social location (Glick Schiller and Fouron 1990). When I was able to conceptualize transnational migration, I altered the direction of my subsequent research and analysis, which contributed to a new theoretical perspective. The new theoretical perspective on migration was then taken up by a range of scholars who further theorized the conditions that lead migrants to develop social, political, economic, and religious networks extending between nation-states (Goldring 1998; Mahler 1998; Smith and Guarnizo 1998). In short, a theory of transnational migration was developed and tested by ethnographers within the course of ethnographic research. Its utility stands apart from and does not require statistical verification. Portes, Haller, and Guarnizo (2002:278) have claimed that ethnography can provide only "a few descriptive examples and their possible determinants" but social surveys can validate the theoretical claim of the significance of transnational migration. Such a stance reduces all ethnographic research to the status of exploratory and denies its capability to develop and substantiate theory.

The Influence of Methodological Nationalism

Ethnographers of transnational processes have questioned the fundamental assumption of mainstream social sciences and the humanities that the nation-state is the natural unit of analysis (Basch, Glick Schiller, and Szanton Blanc 1994a; Kearney 1991; Rouse 1991). By calling for an "unbounding" of social science, we have challenged established theories of immigrant incorporation. Discarding prevailing theories of modernization and assimilation, we have linked changes in the world economy to changes in patterns of migrant incorporation and have called on researchers to envision social relations that stretch across national borders and boundaries. Andreas Wimmer and I (2002a and b) have proposed the term *methodological nationalism* to critique the nation-state bias of mainstream academics and their tendency to identify with the interests of their own nation-state. We define *methodological nationalism* as "the assumption that the nation/state/society is the natural social and political form of the modern world" (Wimmer and Glick Schiller 2001a:301). We have argued that nation-state–building processes have fundamentally shaped the ways immigrations have been perceived and received. In turn, these perceptions have influenced (but not completely determined) social science theory and methodology and, more specifically, its discourse on immigration and integration.

Influenced by methodological nationalism, sociological theories of migration have generally sought to explain why various populations migrate and the subsequent degree and rate of assimilation into a new nation-state (Alba and Nee 1999; Morawska 2001a). Sociological theorists began with a classic push-pull theory, positing that certain factors within a sending society push individuals to migrate and another, discrete set of factors within a receiving society impel individuals to move and settle in a new home. Subsequent theorists critiqued this approach from a variety of perspectives. Reconciling competing explanations, D. S. Massey has recently spoken of the multiple determinants of migration, including various kinds of economic micro-level decision models, world systems theory, social capital theory, and the theory of cumulative causation (D. S. Massey 1999). Despite their apparent differences, both the initial theory and Massey's approach share the basic, generally unstated assumption that people normally and naturally stay in one place. They assume that stasis is both the ordinary and the desired human condition. In this perspective, the migrant exists outside the norm, in a liminal state, and assimilation into the new society is natural and desirable.

Rejecting the foundational notion of stasis that pervades much of sociological theory and leads down the path of methodological nationalism, many ethnographers of migration have generated a different set of questions, building on the work of several generations of anthropologists who have studied migration. Anthropologists have played a key role in these developments because, since the very beginning of the discipline, anthropologists have studied the physical and cultural implications of the movement of populations and the flow of ideas and material objects (Boas 1940; Kroeber 1944; Lowie 1937; Schapera 1947). This anthropological acceptance of contact and diffusion as a norm through human history is perhaps linked to the disciplinary interest in the migration histories that mark the emergence of the human species and the development of systems of signification.

The twentieth-century diffusionist school of anthropology read the entire history of cultures as one of migration (Perry 1923; Smith 1933). The diffusionists are often used as a model of theory gone awry. If their writings are remembered at all, it is to provide a striking example of how European scholars tried every possible means of dismissing indigenous creativity all around the world. However, Boas, Lesser, Kroeber, and many other US anthropologists also worked with diffusionist theories. Within this early anthropology are useful insights on which the scholars who developed the transnational perspective in anthropology built. Deploying a global vantage point, the diffusionists did not naturalize the borders of the nation-state. They neither used a particular state as their unit of analysis nor equated the borders of the nation-state with the boundaries of society, economy, or culture. Their work reminds us that the sanctity of borders and boundaries is recent in human history and anthropological theory (Moch 1992).

With the demise of all forms of diffusionist theory by the 1950s, most social scientists retreated into a social science bounded not only by the territorial borders of a single nation-state but also by an identification with the nation-building project of that state. Modernization theory, developed during the Cold War, contrasted a premodern, unchanging, traditional world to modern industrial society, positing that the modern era was one in which all societies would shed their local cultural differences and archaic, authoritarian political systems as they became economically more developed and stepped into the modern world (Apter 1965; Rostow 1960). The modern world was made up of stable, discrete nation-states. In this framework, nation-states were increasingly normalized as the natural outcome of economic development within several variants of anthropology.

In the United States, some anthropologists championed community studies that approached communities as if each stood as a fixed social order within a folk-urban continuum (Redfield 1955, 1967). The community study method failed to examine the ways in which the community studied was shaped by colonialism and by a larger political structure that enforced intensive exploitation and imposed and maintained unequal political and social relationships. British social anthropologists developed structural-functional approaches to what they called "tribes," thereby positing stasis within discrete and unrelated societies.

To a certain extent, the ethnographies of transnational migration were written in opposition to the stasis theorists in sociology and anthropology. Even before the beginning of transnational migration studies, many ethnographers began their study of migration with a different set of questions. We were influenced not only by the strengths of diffusionist theory but also by Max Gluckman, the Rhodes-Livingston studies, and the Manchester school. These earlier researchers documented persisting ties of kinship within African urban life and the networks of connection that migrants maintained with their tribal identities and rural areas of origin. They asked not what causes migration but rather why people maintain or construct home ties when they migrate. What motivates people to live their lives so that they can be simultaneously rural and urban, townsmen and tribesmen, or "traditional" and "modern" (Mayer 1961)? Using ethnographic studies and social anthropology, these scholars developed network studies, situational analysis, the extended case-study method, and other process approaches to complex societies and colonial relationships (Barnes 1954, 1969; Epstein 1958, 1967, 1969; Gluckman 1958, 1967; Mitchell 1956, 1969; Turner 1957). Studies of Puerto Rican migration and rural-urban migration in Latin America were also important in initiating an ethnography of migration. They, too, had a history and trajectory situated outside the assimilationist and modernization framework (Lewis 1966; Padilla 1958; Roberts 1978).

Beginning in the 1970s, scholars of migration—primarily, but not exclusively, anthropologists who built on concepts of networks and kinship—began to document continuing transnational connections (Eades 1987; Gonzalez 1988; Grasmuck and Pessar 1991; Kearney 1986). However, until the 1990s, no widely accepted terminology was available to foreground and theorize transnational ties. When an anthropological theory of transnational migration did emerge, it developed directly from the ethnographic evidence.[5]

Ethnography versus Social Survey—The Nature of Data

Many researchers who rely on survey methods define ethnographic observations as anecdote. It is true that anthropologists sometimes begin an academic article with a vignette from their personal observations. Such portraits of social relations are not equivalent to journalistic observation. They represent examples of patterned, frequently observed behaviors and are selected because of their typicality. Anthropologists ascertain typicality of behavior not on the basis of a delimited set of self-reported frequencies of particular behavior but from their ongoing observations, over time and within a range of contexts, of what people do, differentiated from what they say that they do. Anyone who has responded to a survey questionnaire immediately realizes how the predefined choices shape and distort one's responses and how, after the fact, one remembers other aspects of one's behavior. There is also behavior one prefers not to report or that one does not consider relevant.

Like all social scientists, ethnographers impose categories as they observe and record data. However, these categories are constantly tested in the field, and, increasingly, field data are also contextualized by the writer, who identifies her or his own social positioning so that the reader can take these particular biases into account. Evidence provided on the basis of a survey done without corroborating participant observation is emic data. It is a respondent's self-presentation and cannot be equated with observed behavior. As Marvin Harris pointed out, it is methodologically important to distinguish between emic and etic observations and, for good ethnography, to include both forms of data. "Emic operations have as their hallmark the elevation of the native informant to the status of the ultimate judge of the adequacy of the observer's descriptions and analyses. Etic operations have as their hallmark the elevation of the observer to the status of ultimate judge" (Harris 1979:33). The ethnographer must have a sense of daily activities based on observation, as well as self-reported descriptions.

Consistent and sometimes very important differences exist between observed behavior and verbal reports. This is why participant observation is an essential part of ethnography, although ethnography cannot rely only on participant observation and must include ethnographic interviews and surveys. Observation is also part of an ethnographic interview, and the ethnographer records in field notes not only what the respondent says but also all the interactions observed in the course of the interview.

These points are particularly important in the study of transnational migration. There are many reasons for the discrepancies between self-reported responses and the actual behavior of migrants who maintain various forms of transnational connections. Some are political. For example, persons who seek or are granted political asylum on the grounds that they can no longer safely reside in their homeland may report that they have little or no contact with those left behind. Acknowledgment of an ongoing homeland connection could undercut their political claim or persona. In these situations, even family ties may not be discussed, and questions about transnational kinship become political questions. Such connections become apparent to an ethnographer who observes and sometimes helps facilitate telephone calls, the purchase of calling cards for the home country, and the sending of various kinds of remittances.

People engaged in political activities organized to change the political situation in a homeland may not report their activities if these are defined as subversive either at home or abroad. Transnational economic activities may not be acknowledged because people involved in the informal economy or even with formal businesses may use kinship networks to restock their business, avoiding taxes and bureaucracies. Transnational religious activities may not be acknowledged when the religion in question has become politically suspect, as in the case of Islam since the United States and the European Union declared a global war on terrorism. Haitian practitioners of Haitian and other Afro-Caribbean or Afro-Brazilian religions, which differ from mainstream belief systems, may not readily disclose their transnational religious networks and practices to a survey interviewer who is a stranger. All these types of connections become apparent to the ethnographer.

In understanding and assessing the significance of transnational migration, it is important to remember that at particular times, migrants may speak of their expectation of returning home or emphasize their desire to settle in the new land. Their emphasis at any one time reflects an array of factors, including the current immigrant or refugee policies of the country of settlement, the current political situation in the homeland, and a host of personal and economic motivations. The self-ascription of migrants as immigrants or temporary sojourners is important data, influencing what respondents choose to disclose about themselves in response to a questionnaire. However, these emic statements must be accompanied by data about the actual development and range of the respondents' transnational connections: familial, economic, religious, social, and political. Ethnography, because of its daily, long-term engagement within the social networks of immigrants, is well suited to discover whether and how specific individuals within a study population maintain multiple transnational connections over time.

The loss or misrepresentation of information is only one of the difficulties in studying transnational migration through survey research. Another is the inability of synchronic surveys to document social process. Providing a single snapshot of a response cannot tell us how an individual will respond over time and in a variety of situations. Multiple surveys over time allow for the possibility of ascertaining a pattern of response; at best, they turn a snapshot into a slide show. The representations never become a moving picture.

What is at stake in these methodological discussions becomes clearer when looking at how the various methods lead to different assessments of the significance of transnational migration. Using probability surveys of Colombian, Dominican, and Salvadoran immigrants in the United States that reduce the study of transnational migration to frequent economic transactions or direct participation in homeland political parties or hometown associations, Portes (2001:183) argues that "participation in transnational economic and political activities is exceptional." On the basis of this type of data, he concludes that there is "limited numerical involvement of immigrant groups in transnational activities" (Portes 2001:182). Transnational family connections are excluded from any measure of transnational connection as nothing new and therefore useless in accessing the importance of the contemporary phenomena of transnationalism. Itzigsohn et al. (1999) provide a broader definition by including occasional interactions reported in surveys and differentiating between broad and narrow transnationalism. Using this approach, Itzigsohn (2002) finds that 63 percent of Dominicans in New York and in Providence, Rhode Island, have transnational connections. In general, however, those who seek to study transnational migration on the basis of survey data have found themselves arguing that transnational migration is significant despite its rarity.

Ethnographers see different things. We are able to watch as transnational family connections become the foundation for many other kinds of interconnection. By studying not only the actors who maintain transnational organized or economic activity but also the social field that includes persons who have networks to transmigrants but may not, themselves, maintain social relations across borders, ethnographers judge that the transnational connections of migrants and their descendants are widespread and significant.

When researchers accept the concept of a transnational field of social relations, they enter into a research domain that is best explored by ethnography. There are two interrelated reasons for this. First, economic, political, religious, familial, and personal transnational relationships may involve an array of interconnected actors. Second, when we acknowledge that the study of transnational migration includes examination of a specific kind of social field that we must trace within the same research frame, five sets of actors emerge: (1) circulating migrants within a transnational network who travel between their new land and homeland, (2) transmigrants who maintain multiple connections across borders and who may or may not travel, (3) immigrants and their descendants who may maintain only one or two types of transnational connections, such as family and friendship, (4) immigrants and their descendants who do not maintain their transnational connections but participate in networks with people who do maintain such ties, and (5) circulating migrants, transmigrants, and immigrants and their descendants who utilize various forms of media, including the Internet, to obtain information about the homeland and utilize this information in their day-to-day interactions and decision making.

Research into a transnational field extends into all the domains we understand to be social: reproduction, gender, socialization, economics, politics, religion, and identity. If we judge the significance of the phenomena of transnational migration on the basis of numerical assessments taken from surveys of the number of people who report one or even several specific, frequent kinds of transnational activity—

whether business transactions or formal membership in transnational political organizations—we miss the significance for public policy and for the development of a new way to theorize society, one not restricted by the boundaries of a nation-state.

THE SECOND WAVE

Within the past few years, a second wave of research on transnational migration has moved beyond the efforts to prove that a specific migrant experience we can call "transnational migration" exists, to ask a new series of questions. The second wave has also revisited the question of this form of migration's novelty. Because of ethnography's strengths in studies of transnational migration, anthropologists have much to offer. The second wave has begun to ask the following questions, which constitute a significant and exciting agenda for further research.

In what specific ways is the current period of transnational migration similar to and different from previous periods in which migrants constructed transnational social fields? As increasing numbers of scholars have turned their attention to the transnational connections of previous waves of migrants, it has become clear that a wealth of data are available about transnational migration between various regions of the world at the end of the nineteenth century and that many areas of similarity exist between past and present (Chan 1990; Cinel 1982; Lamphere 1987; Lesser 1999; Morawska 1987, 1989).[6] These data indicate that transnational migration becomes important in periods of intensive globalization. However, most analysts stress the novel aspects of the current transmigrant experience, despite the evidence of previous periods of transnational connection. They attribute this novelty to the new period of global capitalism, the effect of new technologies, or the interrelationship between a restructured global capitalism and the new technology (Foner 2002; Portes, Guarnizo, and Landholt 1999; Smith 1998). More detailed investigation is needed here, including investigation of the changing role of various states in the midst of globalization. Ethnography provides insights into the processes of everyday forms of state formation, which involve both simultaneous incorporation into the daily activities of a new society and continuing multiple connections with the incorporative practices of other states.

What are the relationships between transnational migration and poverty? We know that persons who migrate are rarely among the poorest or least educated of a society; a long-distance move requires certain economic, social, and cultural capital. However, we know much less about the effects of the burden of remittances on class formation in the old land and the new and on the life possibilities of migrants (Sider 1992). Remittances are widely acknowledged as a source of foreign exchange for many poor states, but systematic study of the role of migrants in sustaining the political and economic viability of the sending nation-states has just begun. We need to explore the role of remittances in sustaining families, localities, and whole nation-states as various forms of state services are withdrawn. Poverty studies, development studies, and transnational studies must be brought together to explore the effect of remittances on transmigrants and those they left behind (Conway, Bailey, and Ellis 2001; Fouron and Glick Schiller 2001a and b). Moreover, we must explore the relationship between deepening poverty in certain countries and localities and the inability of specific sets of actors to access transnational social fields. It is important to document that as communication technologies have grown, so have disparities of access to these technologies. Different regions of an emigrant-sending country, various classes, and men and women may have differential possibilities of establishing and maintaining transnational connections (Mahler 2001). By investigating the tensions and unities within networks over time and across space, we can explore the class tensions that develop within family networks and between actors within a single transnational social field.

What is the role of transmigrants in sustaining nationalist ideologies and nation-state–building projects within contemporary global capitalism? To what degree are transmigrants implicated in the contemporary resurrection of ideologies of blood, race, and nation as they participate in forms of long-distance nationalism? How is it possible for migrants to live as "flexible citizens" or to navigate a world still divided into nation-states of very different degrees of power (Ong 1999)? In *Nations Unbound: Transnational Projects, Post Colonial Predicaments, and Deterritorialized Nation-States,* my colleagues and I argued that "by living their lives across borders, transmigrants find themselves confronted with and engaged in the nation-building processes of two or more nation-states"

(Basch, Glick Schiller, and Szanton Blanc 1994a:22). Second wave scholars of transnational migration have increasingly returned to this theme. They have provided further evidence that nation-states remain significant units of analysis in the study of transnational migration; migrants from certain states avoid contact with sending states, and migrants from other states participate in various kinds of home country politics (Tölölyan 2001). With this understanding, a scholarship of long-distance nationalism has begun.

The concept of long-distance nationalism, popularized by Anderson (1993, 1994) and increasingly employed by scholars of transnational migration, provides an analytical lens that brings into focus the ways in which transmigrants relate to their homeland and to different sectors of the homeland population. Skrbis (1999), describing the ideology and practices of Croatians in Australia, Fuglerud (1999), studying the connections of Tamils to the struggle in Sri Lanka, and Georges Fouron and I (2001), in our study of the Haitian ideology of blood and nation, have found this term useful and have documented the global significance of long-distance nationalism as a political ideology and set of practices. Long-distance nationalism links together people living in various geographic locations and motivates or justifies their taking action in relationship to an ancestral territory and its government. Through such linkages, a territory, its people, and its government can constitute a transnational nation-state.

We are seeing the flourishing of a politics in which ancestral identities are made central by diverse sets of actors, including emigrants of different classes, political refugees, leaders of homeland governments, and intellectuals (Ali-Ali, Black, and Koser 2001; England 1999; Klimt 2000). In past periods of extensive transnational migration, disparate actors also contributed to ideologies and practices of long-distance nationalism (Bodnar 1985; Glick Schiller 1999c; Wyman 1993). However, important new questions are raised by the current revitalization of long-distance nationalism during a period in which financial institutions, multinational corporations, and various forms of regional and global trade agreements transcend borders and state-specific regulations to a greater degree than ever before.

Citizenship and civil society became two hot topics among scholars at the turn of the twenty-first century, and some observers began to talk about "postnational citizenship" (Soysal 1994) as if the allocation of citizenship was no longer linked to state power. In contrast, researchers of transnational migration began to explore the ways various sectors of transmigrants navigate issues of legal rights and identity as they live in more than one nation-state (Grahm 2001; Nyiri 1999). Approaching the topic from a very different angle, Karen Olwig (1997) has stressed that although people may leave home and live across borders, notions of home continue to be linked to the land left behind. Space and place can be locations of connection instead of representations of identity. Bill Maurer (1995) has looked at the ways, through concepts of blood and descent, even small, weak states may restrict access to citizenship among migrants from other countries while extending it to nationals living abroad.

How is gender constituted within transnational social fields, and how is it linked to the reconstitution of notions of family, race, and nation? In a special issue of *Identities: Global Studies in Culture and Power,* Patricia Pessar and Sarah Mahler address questions of the reconstitution of gender categories and the challenges to and reinforcement of gender hierarchies within transnational contexts, including transnational migration (Mahler and Pessar 2001; see also Kelherer 2000; Matsuoka and Sorenson 2000). Over the years, feminist scholarship has linked the personal to the political and explored the connections between the domestic domain and the public arena. The different and gendered strategies of men and women in migration are increasingly being explored (Grillo, Riccio, and Salih 2000; Hondagenu-Sotelo 1998, 1999). Recently, scholars have begun to examine the emotional toll paid by transmigrants when states, such as the Philippines, rely on the export of labor to the extent that, to support their children, women must leave home, construct transnational households, and raise their children from afar (Salazar-Parreñas 2001). Feminist analysis is also now examining the mutual constitution of nation and gender in transnational spaces as gender is lived by transmigrants embedded in two or more nation-states (Fouron and Glick Schiller 2001b). In Chapter 3 of this volume, Pessar takes the discussion further by linking gender to recent scholarship on the embodiment of race and nation.

Do forms of transnational connection continue across generations, extending our concepts of transnational migration and family? A concept of transnational social fields leads to a re-evaluation of the concepts of the second generation and of family in migration. When transnational social fields are established, kin relations and children who live within such fields are reshaped by that experience. Children in such social fields become a transnational second generation. Much research is yet to be done about the children socialized within transnational social fields. A growing body of research on the second generation in the United States reveals that youths may choose between several identity options: rejection of the identity embraced by their parents, a hyphenated identity, and identification only with their homeland (Waters 1999; see also Levitt and Waters 2002). In Europe, social surveys of the children of migrants in England, France, and Germany indicate that the majority of youths in the sample identify with their parent's home country but most have multiple identities (Heckman 2001).

Ethnography is essential to explore the degrees to which these choices of members of the second generation reflect their experiences within the transnational social fields of their family and to explore the links between identity and transnational social relationships. We need to know whether the identities of members of this generation change as they age, marry, raise families, and move into a range of social and occupational settings, including transnational social fields established by their own generation. Georges Fouron and I (2001a) have hypothesized that young people who grow up within a transnational terrain develop a sense of self that has been shaped by personal, family, and organizational connections to people "back home." Participation in transnational social fields can link children of immigrants to broader processes that define them as a political constituency that can act on behalf of its "home country."

The question of transnational connections extending across generations and the topic of transnational family are just beginning to come together in an important new area of scholarship (Chamberlain 2002). Researchers working on data about transnational migration to Europe have begun to theorize aspects of transnational migration through the lens of family dynamics. They speak of "frontiering" to emphasize "the crisscross and clash of cultural values that is ongoing within transnational families" (Bryceson and Vuorela 2002:13). Theirs is not a unilineal model of assimilation through generations but a dynamic view of a complex cultural process of differentiation and belonging that takes place within the terrain of more than one nation-state.

What is the relationship between the transnational social field built by migrants and various forms of transnational religious networks, organizations, ideologies, and activities? Evidence of the transnational networks of migrants can be found in studies of Islam in Europe, the building of churches or temples in the homeland with funds from transmigrants abroad, and the support of Hindu nationalism by non-resident Indians in the United States (Carter 1997; Chan 1990; Lessinger 2003; Levitt 2001b; Yalçin-Heckmann 1997). Most studies of migration and religion have focused on the role of organizations. Recent work by Peggy Levitt explores the way migrants use religious organizations to maintain transnational connections in complex relationships with various states and their nation-state–building projects. Much work is to be done to link the descriptions of religious networks to the growing body of research on other aspects of transnational social fields and to explore the belief systems and religious practices that develop within transnational social fields (van Dijk 2002).

RE-ENVISIONING OUR CONCEPT OF SOCIETY

Morawska (2001a) proposes a conceptualization of migration as "structuration" to posit the continuing dynamic between structure and agency that extends into a transnational domain. Faist (2000a and b), reasoning along similar lines, strives to conceptualize a domain of cross-border social relations that he glosses as "transnational social spaces" instead of societies. Both Guarnizo (1997b) and Landolt (2001) refer to a "transnational social formation." Much work remains to put aside the blinders of methodological nationalism and develop a concept of systematic and structured transnational social processes and relationships. The concept of social field enables us to envision how people can simultaneously be incorporated into two or more nation-states yet live within ongoing social relations that are not coterminous with any polity. Ethnographies of simultaneous migrant incorporation can provide the building blocks for a reformulation of our concept of society. In this reformulation, states remain significant as repositories of varying degrees of power but are not coterminous with the domain of social relations, which extends transnationally. The study of transnational migration opens a pathway to differentiate between polity and society in ways that can advance social theory.

THE FUTURE—REINTEGRATING TRANSNATIONAL MIGRATION INTO TRANSNATIONAL STUDIES

Analytically, it is necessary to study transmigrants as a specific set of transnational actors and explore the nature and significance of the transnational fields they establish. However, too much research on transnational migration has stood apart from the work being done on other forms of transnational processes. Contemporary transnational migration exists in a context in which many people around the world watch the same televisions shows, are besieged by the same advertise- ments, long for the same commodities, and find their states penetrated and their dreams of a brighter future constrained, altered, and defaced by the same set of global corporations, financial institutions, and regu- latory transnational agreements.

Transmigrants also participate in or confront a series of other transnational actors, including the personnel of corporations, non- government organizations, religious organizations, and social move- ments for global change. Since the 1970s, anthropologists and other social scientists have been writing about the global assembly line, the international division of labor turning an ethnographic eye to deindus- trialized US cities, the entrance of women into the *maquedora* export processing industries of Mexico, the emerging free-trade zones in the Caribbean and Asia, and the effects of structural adjustment policies (Harrison 1997; Nash and Fernández Kelly 1983; Ong 1987; Rothstein and Blim 1992).

The world systems framework, which became so influential among anthropologists in the 1970s, served as a critique of modernization dis- courses but did not encourage analysts to examine global cultural processes, transnational connections, and migration. The time has come for scholars of transnational migration to document the intersec- tion of a multiplicity of transnational processes.

In developing the study of transnational migration, ethnographers must continue to build on the methodological and theoretical strengths of past generations of anthropological studies of migration and homeland connections and learn from and contribute to transnational studies. We must not only develop the study of transnational migration but also place our research more centrally in the field of transnational studies and globalization, understanding that transnational migration is but one aspect of past and current moments of globalization. Studies of the continuing role of states and nationalism must be an important part of this scholarship, but we must move beyond methodological nationalism and neither naturalize the nation-state nor conflate its interests and projects with our own. Only then can the ethnographies of transnational migration enable us to reconceptualize society and think beyond the conceptual and political constraints of the current world order.

Notes

1. Note that in Europe, at about the same time, anthropologists such as Mirjana Morokvasic (1996) also began to speak of transnational migration, although without calling attention to a new paradigm.

2. The word *international* is generally used to refer to state-to-state relations. Another term that has recently received attention is *cosmopolitan*, which usually refers to persons who are global in their perspective, rejecting loyalty to any particular nation-state or region. They differ from internationalists. Although cosmopolitans may identify with global capitalists, internationalists historically have rejected their own nation-states to identify with a worldwide struggle of workers for economic and social justice.

3. I should note that I do live in a transnational social field that includes such networks. My father's mother's brother's children and their descendents settled in Israel and exchange email and visits with my father's sister and her children in the United States, who strongly identify with Israel. This definitely influences my identity and actions, although it has led me to repudiate Zionism (Glick Schiller and Fouron 2001).

4. This same point is imbedded in the challenge to mainstream historiography made by Thistlewaite (1964), who began a revisionist history of Atlantic migration (Gerstles 1999).

5. I should note that writing about transnational migration does not necessarily free analysts from identifying with the interests of a nation-state in their politics and social science. It is certainly possible to study transnational migration and continue to accept as normal and identify with the nation-state as the unit of

analysis, legitimating and reinforcing methodological nationalism (for example, see Kovisto 2001).

6. Immigrants in the previous stage of globalization, at the turn of the twentieth century, entered into politics in the United States motivated, at least in part, by the desire to support and strengthen the struggles or national welfare of their home country (Bodnar 1985; Kwong 1987:101). In Latin America, also an important area of migration settlement in the nineteenth- to early twentieth-century movement from Europe, there is a history of transnational connection that is only now beginning to be re-evaluated (for example, see Lesser 1999; Gonzalez 1992).

5

Becoming American

Immigration, Identity, Intergenerational Relations, and Academic Orientation

Alex Stepick and Carol Dutton Stepick

Henri was born in Haiti and migrated to the United States with his family before he started school. He is a 1.5 generation immigrant; that is, he immigrated at a young enough age to be enculturated primarily in his adopted country. A star student throughout high school, he graduated from Harvard University in 2000 and spent the following year working for Americorps, "to help his community." In 2002, Henri entered medical school. He has a brother now at Harvard and a brother who graduated from Northwestern University. His father is a janitor and his mother a domestic. The brothers attribute their success to their parents, who unfailingly pushed them to pursue academic excellence. Henri and his brothers personify the archetypal immigrant student, high achieving with a positive orientation toward education.

Marie, also a 1.5 generation Haitian immigrant, was a high school English Honors student and an excellent gospel singer. Marie appeared to embody the ideal immigrant adolescent profile, an outstanding student, close to her parents, and deeply involved in church activities. Then she showed signs of assimilation—she acquired an African American boyfriend. In her parents' eyes, a boyfriend, especially an

African American boyfriend, meant that she was no longer serious about her education. In their eyes, Haitian girls are not supposed to express interest in boys until they have finished school. Her parents, supported by their church, suspended all her privileges, accused her of no longer being Haitian, and ultimately forced her to move out of the house. Not surprisingly, Marie's grades dropped dramatically.

In high school, Henri and Marie replicated the positive stereotype of immigrant students.[1] Yet Henri continued to succeed and Marie was derailed. Marie's parents, along with many other immigrant parents, blame the process of assimilation, particularly what they perceive as Americanization. Immigrant parents often feel that their children are rejecting them and their home-country culture. Increasingly, academic studies agree with immigrant parents' evaluation of the negative effects of American culture on their children (Landale and Oropesa 1995; Landale, Oropesa, and Gorman 1997; Portes and Rumbaut 2001; Rumbaut 1997a).

If you listen to the children, however, you hear a more complex, nuanced interpretation. The children of immigrants frequently articulate ambivalence toward American culture. As Louis, recently arrived from Haiti in the ninth grade, stated, "I don't like the fact that the American culture gives children so much power over their parents. The parents' authority is undermined. They can't tell their children what to do."

Many immigrant youth present a paradox. The standard line, both in the academic literature and in immigrant communities, is that immigrant students outperform native minorities. Our work and that of others demonstrate that immigrant students typically have high educational aspirations and put forth considerable effort in school. Their educational outcomes, however, do not always match their aspirations. Many do excel, but the academic achievement of many immigrant students regresses toward the low mean for native minorities.

In 2000, the first and second generations of immigrants and their children totaled 56 million persons—one out of every five Americans (Portes and Rumbaut 2001:xvii; Suárez-Orozco and Suárez-Orozco 2001:1). As the United States continues to accept large numbers of immigrants, most of whom are of school age or have school-age children, the integration of children of immigrants into the US educational system continues to be important. The children of immigrants will continue to influence the constant efforts to reform the US educational system; their successes or failures in school will also affect their own lives and the general character of the United States. Moreover, many immigrant youth do not fit the positive stereotype of being high achieving and positively oriented toward education. An anthropological approach enables us to address this issue by moving beyond correlates of educational attainment that are readily measurable, such as GPA and parental education, to the concrete processes and interaction of factors that produce those correlations.

This chapter concentrates on variation within minority groups and specifically explores the factors distinguishing individual students whose ethnic/national background is the same but who express different orientations toward school. Many forces may be involved, but in this chapter we focus on the youths' relationship to American peers and culture, including the powerful forces of prejudice and discrimination, and to their parents and homeland culture. We focus on these relationships because they are important in understanding immigrants and education and because they highlight the particular contributions of an anthropological approach to understanding immigrants and education. We rely primarily on a longitudinal project in Miami, Florida, among the area's primary immigrant groups; African Americans were a control group to substantively illustrate selected relationships.[2]

We argue that prejudice against newcomer immigrants compels them to assume the behavior and appearance of American adolescents. To the parents of immigrant children and many others, immigrant youth appear to have thoroughly absorbed and accepted American culture as they adopt American eating habits and dress—as they walk the walk and talk the talk. These changes cause a backlash in most immigrant parents, who fear that their children have abandoned home-country values and fail to appreciate opportunities in the United States. As a result, adolescent children of immigrants have shifting identities. The labels they use to describe themselves change over time. As they mature, these labels shift from an identification with US peers to a greater reflection of their (or their parents') homeland. Ironically, at the same time, their behavior and cultural preferences increasingly echo their American peers. Their maturation reveals a disjuncture between the apparent, Americanized presentation of self and an increasing awareness of the importance of their cultural roots and differences from their American peers. Deciding whether to conform to a peer culture that rejects education is a common choice confronted by many immigrant youth. Their relationships to adults while working out these conflicts critically affect whether they can maintain the positive academic orientation and achievement commonly associated with immigrant students. This chapter concludes with a discussion of how the primarily anthropological methods associated with ethnography specifically aid this analysis.

This chapter is based on a project on immigrant youth begun in 1989 with research among Haitian high school students. Subsequently, this expanded to incorporate the other major immigrant and native minority youth groups in Miami, Florida (Stepick and Stepick 1999). The project grew out of twenty years of fieldwork in Miami among various immigrant and non-immigrant communities. In the fall of 1995, we began a longitudinal, qualitative project, "The Academic Orientation of Immigrant and Native Minorities," in four high schools in the Miami-Dade County public school system.[3] Research began with a sample of 300 students then entering high school. The population consisted of Haitians, English-speaking West Indians, Nicaraguans, Cubans, Mexicans, and African Americans. We included documented and undocumented immigrants. Using participant observation and intensive interviewing, we sat in high school classes and "hung out" with students between classes and after school. We interviewed not only students but also their teachers, counselors, administrators, and parents.[4] We combined the quantitative methods of survey research with long-term participant observation and intensive interviewing because we see these methodological tools as complementary, rather than in opposition. We have gained the benefits of large-scale survey data, particularly their ability to generalize reliably to a broad population. Ethnographic methods, associated primarily with anthropology, can reveal how questionnaires mislead because of improper selection and/or wording of questions and how complex processes are better seen through intensive, long-term fieldwork. Finally, we believe that ethnographic methods are best suited for probing individuals' meaning and interpretation of events.

ANTHROPOLOGY AND IMMIGRANT EDUCATION

Anthropologists have made critical contributions to the understanding of immigrants and education. In a series of critical works, Ogbu (1978, 1982, 1983, 1987a and b) maintains that native-born and immigrant minorities can be categorized into three types—autonomous, immigrant, and caste-like—each having a different cultural and academic orientation.[5] Ogbu (1987b) argues that caste-like minorities, such as African Americans, have created a style of cultural inversion that repudiates derogatory images projected on them by the dominant white populations. In addition to African Americans (Ogbu 1987a), other caste-like minority groups that have been studied and academically perform below the norms of the majority population include Koyukon Athabascans of the Alaskan interior (Scollon and Scollon 1981), Native American Utes (Kramer 1991), West Indians in Great Britain (Tomlinson 1983), Crucians in St. Croix (Gibson 1991), Turkish "guest workers" in West Germany (Castles 1984), Finnish students in Sweden (Paulston in Gibson 1993; Skutnabb-Kangas 1981), Maoris in New Zealand (Titus 2001), Koreans in Japan (Lee 1991), and Burakumin in Japan (Shimahara 1991).

The academic orientation of many new immigrants to the United States appears to be the opposite of caste-like minorities. Those most likely to succeed are first-generation immigrants. Usually, they have been in their newly adopted country long enough to learn the language well, and they maintain a cultural orientation that conceives of education as a primary pathway to success. Matute-Bianchi (1986) found that Mexican immigrants perform much better than US-born Mexican Americans (also see Suárez-Orozco and Suárez-Orozco 1995). Similarly, students from Central America were found to succeed in spite of tremendous personal and family traumas in their home countries (Suárez-Orozco 1987a and b, 1989a and b). Gibson (1989) determined that immigrant Sikh school children face tremendous discrimination but those who identify with their homeland culture do better academically. Indochinese school children succeed in school precisely because their parents pass on cultural values that encourage achievement (Caplan, Choy, and Whitmore 1989, 1991, 1992; Gold 1992). Also, Portes and Rumbaut (1993, 2001) determined that in San Diego and Miami recently immigrated students tend to have higher GPAs than those born in the United States. East Asians and Asian Indians in Britain (Gibson 1993; Ogbu 1978; Tomlinson 1989), Polynesians in New Zealand (Penfold in Ogbu 1993), "down islanders" in St. Croix (Gibson 1991), and Turks and Finns in Australia (Inglis and Manderson 1991) academically surpass native minorities.

In the 1990s, anthropologists and some sociologists using qualitative methods demonstrated that not all immigrants are alike. In general, immigrant students may do well academically, but not all are outstanding students. National origin differences can be significant, even among those classified as being in the same US ethnic group, such as Hispanics. Both Cubans and Mexicans in the United States may be Hispanic, but pre-1980 Cuban immigrants came from higher-class backgrounds than most Mexican immigrants and appear to succeed more, academically (Portes and Bach 1984; Suárez-Orozco 1987c; Suárez-Orozco and Suárez-Orozco 1994). There can also be variation within a national origin group. Korean immigrants to the United States come from a higher socioeconomic class than Koreans in Japan and perform better academically (Kim 1984). Portes and Rumbaut (2001) found that Cuban students in private schools had much higher GPAs and lower dropout rates than Cuban students in public schools.

How immigrants are perceived and received by the host society also affects their educational achievements. Cubans and Haitians have migrated to and settled in the same place, Miami. The federal and local governments, however, have received them in dramatically different ways, conferring many benefits on Cubans that are withheld from Haitians. Although socioeconomic background differs between the two groups, their dissimilar receptions have contributed more significantly to Cubans' being among the nation's most economically and politically successful groups and Haitians' being one of the least successful (Portes and Stepick 1993).

For immigrant adolescents who look like native-born, caste-like minorities (that is, "black" and "brown" immigrants), the tension between maintaining an immigrant cultural orientation with an associated positive academic orientation, on the one hand, and assimilating to a native-born minority, adversarial academic orientation, on the other, can be difficult and perplexing. Bryce-LaPorte (1993), Foner (1985, 1987a, 1998b), Kasinitz (1992), Kasinitz, Battle, and Myares

(2001), Portes and Stepick (1993), Waters (1999), and Woldemikael (1985, 1989) all find that black immigrants experience conflict over identifying with their native culture versus that of African Americans.

Others also have found variation in academic orientation within particular groups. For example, in earlier research we found that some Haitian students expressed the stereotypical immigrant enthusiasm for education and others, in the same city and even the same neighborhood, developed an adversarial orientation toward school (Stepick 1998; for the case of Vietnamese, see Zhou and Bankston 1994). In general, the concept of segmented assimilation has asserted that immigrant youth who are classified as similar to native minorities (for example, black immigrants and African Americans) and who live in inner-city, minority neighborhoods might assimilate to the oppositional subculture of inner-city, minority youth (Portes and Zhou 1993). According to the concept, such youth would assume the behavior of African Americans (Portes and Stepick 1993; Stepick 1998).

Central to understanding divisions among immigrant youth is the distinction between academic orientation or engagement and academic achievement. Academic achievement reflects accomplishments, such as grades and test scores. Academic orientation reflects aspirations, effort, and values.[6] It is possible that students who perceive education as important when they enter school do not achieve for a variety of reasons. Students may try to excel but fail because of language difficulties or lack of experience with formal education. They may also respond to peer pressure that devalues education or may encounter cultural incongruities, such as a school's failure as an institution to address their peculiar needs and problems adequately (Trueba 1987a and b, 1989; Trueba, Jacobs, and Kirton 1990; Trueba, Spindler, and Spindler 1989). We expect that a positive academic orientation is critical but not always sufficient for academic achievement.

Different ethnic/racial groups tend to have distinctive cultural orientations.[7] Although immigrants may live in the same neighborhoods as caste-like minorities, they view education as worthwhile because they typically maintain a dual frame of reference (Ogbu 1991:10; Suárez-Orozco 1989a and b, 1991a). Rather than emphasize the prejudice and discrimination they encounter in the United States, they compare the opportunities in the United States with those in the less developed or more troubled economies in their homelands. The immigrants interpret economic, political, and social barriers in the United States as temporary problems they will overcome with hard work and education (Ogbu 1991:10). Although maintaining an immigrant cultural orientation can be interpreted as resistance to assimilation, it appears to promote the attainment of human capital, specifically through education (Portes and Zhou 1992; Zhou 1994; Zhou and Bankston 1994, 1998) or entrepreneurial endeavor (Hurh and Kim 1984; Light 1972; Waldinger 1989b).

For our purposes, we conceive of adolescents' academic and associated cultural orientation as a meaning system that stipulates goals (D'Andrade 1984:88–119) and as a loose consensus about values and norms, reflected in outwardly obvious and sometimes symbolic areas such as language use and dress. Frequently, cultural orientation includes more internalized or less self-conscious values and attitudes toward, for example, education, authority, the broader society, family, and one's co-ethnic group. Academic orientations express cultural conceptions of academic achievement and the formal educational system. Yet all members of an ethnic/racial group do not share them uniformly; these vary within minority groups. For example, not all African Americans assert an adversarial academic orientation, nor do all immigrants possess a positive one. Moreover, most students are likely to identify fully with neither a positive nor an adversarial relationship (Eckert 1989; Eisenhart and Graue 1993).

As we consider selected factors influencing the acquisition and maintenance of cultural capital, cultural orientation, and associated academic orientation, we follow other anthropologists in conceiving of these cultural factors as embedded in a cultural ecological process (Dehyle 1987; Delgado-Gaitan 1989; Delgado-Gaitan and Trueba 1991; Gibson 1987; Suárez-Orozco 1987c and d, 1989a, 1990; Suárez-Orozco and Suárez-Orozco 1994, 2001; Trueba 1987a; Trueba, Spindler, and Spindler 1989). By this, we simply mean that culture is not free-floating, a *sui generis* phenomenon independent of social, political, economic, and other factors. Cultural orientation may be partially autonomous, but also it is likely to alter as circumstances change. Immigrant youth may arrive in the United States with a positive orientation toward school, but the social, economic, and political circumstances confronting them may collide with and alter that positive orientation.

The first of these immigrant cultural ecological factors we address is the host society's perception and treatment of new immigrants. Broadly, this includes how immigrants are welcomed or rejected—in our case, how the school system and peers interact with immigrant youth. We specifically argue that prejudice and associated discrimination are among the most powerful factors influencing cultural and academic orientation.

PREJUDICE AND IDENTITY

"They dress all funny." "No matter what, you make fun of them." "Look at old pictures of all of us, all of our weird shoes and weird ways, customs, before we found out what's in style." These are the words of three Nicaraguan youth who had been in the United States five to ten years (Konczal 2001).[8] Newcomer Haitians are referred to as "just-comes" and "boat people." Nicaraguans are *"indios"* and *"tira flechas."* Recently arrived Cubans are "reffies" or "rafters." Mexicans are "wetbacks." Regardless of where they come from, the most recently arrived children of immigrants face discrimination.

As reflected in the comments of the Nicaraguan youth, the response of new immigrants is to shed their newcomer identity as quickly as possible, to adopt "what's in style" and become similar to and accepted by their new peers. They learn to speak unaccented English. If they live in a predominantly African-American area, it is Black English. If they live in a Latino neighborhood, it is "Spanglish," occasionally referred to as "Cubonics" in Miami. They learn to dress appropriately, abandoning their usually more conservative, "nicer," "reffie" clothes for what is in style.

These behaviors reflect complex changes in self-identity. When we began our ethnographic fieldwork with a cohort of ninth graders, most conceived of themselves first as individuals. If they did assume a label, it was within the subculture of American adolescence. They were jocks, nerds, snobs, cool, or out-of-it before they were Nicaraguan, Nicaraguan-American, or Hispanic, for example. The younger the child, the less aware he or she tended to be of external labels generated by non-peers. These students had little or no idea of the concept of racial or ethnic identity. They knew that their parents were from a foreign country and that many of the students themselves were also born there. They also had learned that in the United States others would perceive and frequently label them with the panethnic labels of *Black* or *Hispanic*.[9] Identity within their school- and age-based peer groups critically affected their lives, but young immigrant teens often were uncertain about what label best fit them. In a fundamental, profound, and, probably to most social scientists, surprising sense, young immigrant adolescents in south Florida did not know who they were ethnically or, at least, how they should label themselves. As they grew older, they became more aware, sophisticated, and complex in their adoption and potential instrumental use of ethnic labels and identities.

Emmanuel, a graduate research assistant, passed out a survey on school violence to a class at the predominantly Haitian high school King High.[10] One open-ended question asked students to indicate their racial or ethnic identity. A number of students asked Emmanuel, who is Haitian, to explain what the question meant, a query that he and other researchers on the project frequently received when they asked adolescents in Miami for their ethnic identity. Emmanuel decided to explain to the entire class that racial or ethnic identity meant how you view yourself, whether you are Haitian, African American, Black, or "whatever." Seemingly satisfied, the students set about filling in the questionnaire. One black student was soon walking along the rows of desks, looking over other students' shoulders at their answers. When he turned in his questionnaire, Emmanuel noticed that he had not indicated his racial or ethnic identity. One-on-one, Emmanuel asked him why he had avoided that question. He replied in perfect, unaccented, adolescent American English, "Okay, okay, I'm going to answer the question," retrieved his questionnaire, and filled in *White*.

A perplexed Emmanuel queried, "Surely you don't see yourself as white, do you?" The student responded, "I know I'm not white, but I don't want to reveal my identity." Emmanuel continued, "Well, where were you born?" The student simply replied, "The United States." Emmanuel tried another approach: "Where were your parents born?" This time the student replied, "In Haiti, but I am ashamed to say that."

A few months later, at a high school a couple miles away that has proportionally fewer Haitians and serves a more working- and middle-class population, one of the Haitian teachers of English as a Second

Language (ESL) organized a Haitian Flag Day celebration. About 1,000 kids poured into the auditorium. Most attending the celebration were recent arrivals, still enrolled in ESL classes. Many who filled the school auditorium were dressed in Haiti's national colors of red and blue, in T-shirts emblazoned with *Quis Queya* (the aboriginal name for the island Haiti shares with the Dominican Republic), or in stereotypical peasant garb (blue denim and straw hats). To open the program, one young man with a distinct Haitian accent welcomed everybody with the standard Haitian greeting, *"Sak pase?"* ("What's happening?") In unison, the crowd roared the standard response, *"N'ap boule!"* ("We're burning/rolling!") The loudspeakers then blared the Haitian national anthem as flag bearers and dancers paraded down the center and side aisles. The program consisted mainly of native Haitian music and folk dances, most danced solely by young women in red and blue costumes. The dance steps were derived primarily from Haiti's religious heritage of Vodou. By American standards, the movements are suggestive, pelvically oriented with many thrusts. The crowd loved the whole display and jumped up out of its seats, stabbing the Haitian flags in the air.

Visibly dismayed, the teachers frowned their disapproval from the edges of the auditorium, like prison guards waiting for a riot. A week earlier another high school had erupted in violence while protesting the school's administration. Although Haitian Flag Day was a celebration, not a protest, the barely controlled, boisterous energy alarmed the administrators. The vice principal cut short the assembly by announcing that rules had to be followed and that the students had to respect and act according to rules of conduct. She never said which rules were in danger of being broken, leaving some with the impression that having fun and showing pride in being Haitian might be against the rules.

Discrimination against newcomers from peers and adults creates shifting self-identification for the children of immigrants. Recent arrivals are the most likely to feel and proclaim a national identity. In school (with the exception of English-speaking West Indians) they are placed in ESL classes that temporarily provide some protection from anti-newcomer prejudices. However, as revealed in the example of Haitian Flag Day, prejudice against Haitians can still surface in the adult staff. Nicaraguans in ESL classes appear to be oblivious to the epithets and prejudices against them. Even though the term *reffie* was ubiquitous outside ESL classes, in four years of fieldwork it was never once heard within an ESL classroom (Konczal 2001).

We found that Nicaraguans eschew their heritage when they graduate from ESL into mainstream classes, where they are likely to be confronted with discrimination. Marlon was born in Managua, Nicaragua, and had been in the United States nine years when our research began. He maintained that he did not remember much about Nicaragua, that he did not know what its capital was, and that his parents are reffies, to whom he doesn't speak that much. He declared that he never speaks Spanish to his friends (Konczal 2001). Those adolescents who have been in the United States five to ten years are the ones most likely to reject their cultural roots and thoroughly assimilate into the local peer culture. During the early 1990s, Haitian leaders in Miami feared that they were losing Haitian youth to the inner-city, oppositional youth culture (Stepick and Stepick 1994). An early report on Nicaraguans made similar claims for them (Fernández-Kelly and Schauffler 1994). Similarly, our ethnographic work revealed that a subset of youth is selectively acculturating by learning to be "cool" and as much like the local majority population as possible. For Nicaraguans, the local majority is Cuban. For Haitians, it is African American. These youth appear to be engaged in segmented assimilation.

When we examined those who had been in the United States more than ten years, we observed an opposite trend, especially among those who were doing well in school. In the high school we studied that has the highest concentration of Haitians, through the 1990s an increasingly large group of Haitian students insisted on speaking Creole, even in the presence of African Americans. They wore conservative, non–hip hop dress styles to school and pressed for more school activities that would reflect Haitian culture. Similarly, Nicaraguans attending a predominantly Cuban-American high school came to interpret derogatory epithets as jokes. Cesar, who was born in the United States, explains, "Well, to me it doesn't really happen. They don't really tell me, 'Oh, spear thrower,' this and that. The only persons that do that is, like, basically my friends when we play around" (Konczal 2001). The Nicaraguans who are second generation or have been in the United States for more than ten years feel that being Nicaraguan is not an obstacle in school or to their ultimate success. In a focus group held just before they graduated from high school, all the participants whom we identified as Nicaraguan claimed that they were a mix of Hispanic, Latin, Spanish, and Nicaraguan and that, most importantly, "they [the labels] are all the same."

The identity of immigrant youth seems to evolve: from homeland nationalism upon arrival, to shame of the homeland, and after about ten years in the United States, to renewed pride in the homeland. In general, as the children of immigrants mature, they become increasingly likely to adopt a hyphenated label. As an older Haitian teenager who has been in this country all his life explained, "Just because a person wants to become an American, you know, doesn't mean they have to forget their heritage and everything," or as an older Nicaraguan teenager stated, "No matter what, I'm both Nica and American. If you're from another country, that's your home. It's in my blood. I'm not totally American. I'm not into all that white stuff" (Konczal 2001).

Shifts in self-identity labels during the high school years also contradict the presumptions of unilineal assimilation predicting that immigrants will become more Americanized with time. Although more than 10 percent of the 300 students in our research identified themselves as American at the beginning of the research, hardly any claimed to be American near the end of their high school careers. Most who had labeled themselves as American at the beginning shifted to a hyphenated identity.

Contrary to predictions of the segmented assimilation perspective, only a small proportion of black children of immigrants in the survey identified themselves as Black or African American. It is a cliché in Miami to hear a Caribbean immigrant proclaim, "I didn't know I was black until I came to the United States." Race is recognized in the Caribbean, but in the United States it assumes an unparalleled prominence (Waters 1999). Nonetheless, at the beginning of the research, less than 15 percent of West Indians and Haitians embraced a Black or African-American identity. The categories Hispanic and Latino are unfamiliar to most Latin American immigrants when they arrive in the United States (Portes and Truelove 1987). No Cubans in our high school sample claimed to be Hispanic or Latino. Only one-fourth of the Nicaraguans and Mexicans adopted the Latino or Hispanic label.

Paradoxically, the dominant local group, Cubans, and the most discriminated against, Haitians, tended to adopt the same type of identity, as hyphenated Americans. Cubans and Haitians, however, met at the hyphen coming from different directions.

Over time, Haitians became more willing to acknowledge their national origins. Many Haitians began high school trying to hide their Haitian heritage, being what their peers referred to as "cover-ups" or "undercovers." However, many undercovers ended high school revealing and even reveling in their Haitian heritage. Two factors, one structural and another individual, enabled this positive transformation of relationships and attitudes. First, changing demographics meant that Haitians had become the overwhelming majority within one of the high schools studied and a substantially growing number in two of the other schools we studied.

By the mid-1990s, King High School's African Americans, formerly the majority, were estimated to be less than 20 percent and maybe as little as 10 percent of the student body. Those African Americans who slandered, denigrated, and intimidated Haitians lost the protection of being in the majority. They no longer had the power of numbers to enforce their discrimination against Haitians. In the early 1980s, when Haitians constituted a small minority of the student body, Haitians had little recourse when insulted. Within the school's circumscribed environment of student relationships, African-American students dominated. They could demean Haitians as unworthy newcomers, lower than the lowest of American society. Haitians could not readily retort. Although Haitian newcomers may have had pride in their Haitian origins, they had no mechanism for convincing their African-American peers that they deserved respect. The majority student culture simply devalued what Haitians valued and accomplished. Speaking more than one language (Haitian Creole and French) was inconsequential if one could not speak English, especially hip, colloquial Black English. Being well dressed in French styles meant being a sissy or too fancy for an American high school. Being respectful and submissive toward teachers was inappropriate for the majority student culture. As members of a minority, Haitians could not combat negative interpretations of their culture.

For most immigrant groups, some of these immigrant cultural

traits, such as respect for teachers and learning, are rewarded by larger institutions, particularly teachers and family. However, the broad anti-Haitian prejudice in south Florida diluted teachers' appreciation of Haitian students. Some teachers recognized the positive traits of Haitians and rewarded them, but others occasionally uttered anti-Haitian remarks or "balanced" their positive evaluation of Haitian students with critical comments.

Haitian parents could not adequately support their children's expression of Haitian cultural values, either. Not only did they confront pervasive prejudice, but also the vagaries of immigration often split families, with one and sometimes even both parents remaining in Haiti while the children were in Miami. Single parents or relatives had difficulty reinforcing values and discipline. In Haiti, not only were both parents usually available but also extended family members who could punish misbehaving children. The generally anti-Haitian immigration policy of the United States deters extended family members from immigrating, making the presence of these relatives less likely.

These forces combined in the 1980s to convince many Haitian students to abandon their heritage. To survive as adolescents and get along with their African-American peers, they had to cover up, to assimilate, the sooner the better. The immediate power of African-American students within the school, reinforced by the broader American society and complemented by the diminished power of Haitian families, compelled the submission of Haitian students.

Although African-American students had power within the context of school to oblige Haitians to assimilate, outside school they remained a disempowered minority. Haitian adults in the workplace, for example, made no efforts to assimilate to African American culture. Because of the power of Cubans in Miami, Haitian adults were more likely to learn Spanish than Black English. Even within the school, teachers and administrators urged Haitians to Americanize into mainstream American culture and to speak standard English instead of Black English. In the broader Miami context, beyond the school peer culture, African Americans did not dominate Haitians or anyone else. Only when they constituted a majority within the narrow confines of student culture did African-American, inner-city youth culture exercise dominant power. Although Haitian student numbers have increased and

African-American power to discriminate immediately against Haitians has diminished, a legacy of ghetto style and adversarial attitudes toward education continues for some Haitians.

Besides the changes occasioned by demographics, individual Haitian students' achievements also underlay their reassertion of Haitian culture. The students who forcefully and self-consciously promote Haitian culture tend to be those who have been most successful in high school, the ones who are in the advanced classes or have achieved success in sports. They have mastered being both African-American and Haitian. They cannot be "dissed" (disrespected) or ridiculed for not being like African Americans.

In contrast, in the basic-level classes, where students have not demonstrated academic or extracurricular accomplishments, students are more likely to present problems for teachers. They tend to exhibit the negative attitude toward education attributed to inner-city, poor African Americans. One teacher maintained that there were few problems in her upper-level classes. "However," she added, "problems occur when the class consists predominantly of Haitian females who have been here long enough to speak the language without an accent—especially if they are limited in academic potential and/or interest. Nothing seems to help in that situation."

Cubans moved toward the hyphen from another direction; they became hyphenated Americans from a position of power. Of the groups studied, Cubans were the most likely to perceive themselves as simply "American" early in their high school years. In Miami, Cubans are "the Americans," the dominant local group that sets the standards. Miami's Cuban enclave has achieved unprecedented gains for first-generation immigrants. Cubans have the highest per capita income of any Hispanic group in the United States. They have the highest rate of business ownership. They also control local government and represent south Florida in the US House of Representatives and the state legislature. In Miami there are as many Latino radio stations as English-language ones, and as many people watch the nightly news in Spanish as watch the top-rated English-language station.

Miami Cubans so thoroughly dominate the local scene that young Cuban children of immigrants often do not realize that they may be different from the rest of America. They can presume that everyone outside Miami is just like them, until they are forced to confront the biases of "mainstream America." The case of Elián Gonzales, the Cuban rafter boy who became the focus of national attention in 2000, jolted Cubans into the realization of how different they may be. As Cubans rallied to keep the boy in the United States, non-Cubans in and outside Miami retorted that the boy should be reunited with his father in Cuba. Miami was filled with passionate arguments and demonstrations as local Spanish-language television covered the issue literally non-stop.[11] Polls revealed that the overwhelming majority of non-Cubans were angered by and opposed to Miami Cubans' strident opposition to the US government's efforts to return the boy to his father. In response, many Miami Cuban youth who had previously thought of themselves as American suddenly embraced their Cuban roots. After Elián was returned to Cuba, Vivian, a Cuban teen, concluded, "The Americans [meaning non-Hispanic whites], it's like this is their country and we're not part of this. We are visitors. Just that, we're not Americans. We're from other places. We don't belong here." Onan, a Nicaraguan, added, "I think what she's trying to say is no matter how hard you try, you're always going to be from another country. We're not going to be American American. We're going to be Latin."

As for Nicaraguans and Mexicans, they have arrived in the most successful Latino community in the United States. From the outside, Miami may appear to be Latino or Hispanic, but from the inside, national origin makes a difference. As the leader of a Nicaraguan organization proclaimed, "Nicaraguans are discriminated against in south Florida. No politicians want to hear what we have to say. I don't know why. They ignore us.... Every year we go to Washington to lobby, but they won't listen! There are several [bold] Cuban organizations, and they each receive millions of dollars per year" (Konczal 1999). The father of one of the Nicaraguan adolescents in our study claimed that he was fired from his job because he was Nicaraguan. He added, "Cubans get more opportunities. They are able to move up in the work place easier" (Konczal 2001).

Nicaraguan adults tended to see discrimination from the federal government as well as on a day-to-day basis, for example, at work. The youth were more likely to think that anti-Nicaraguan discrimination was limited to the federal government. On a local level, they get along with Cubans. At the school we studied that was predominantly Hispanic, Nicaraguans often hang out with Cubans, form close relationships with them, and date and even marry Cubans. No Nicaraguan in our sample had exclusively or even primarily Nicaraguan friends. More than half the Nicaraguans in our sample claimed that at least one of their closest friends was Cuban. As one stated, "We're all Hispanics." Similarly, none of the Nicaraguan students thought that teachers discriminate against them. According to school district statistics, more than 50 percent of the staff at the high school attended by our Nicaraguan sample was Hispanic. Accordingly, Nicaraguan students felt that teachers did not discriminate against them, "because they [the teachers] are Hispanic, too, or they're of Hispanic descent" (Konczal 2001).

For Nicaraguan youth, being Hispanic in Miami presents opportunities unavailable to Haitians or African Americans. Nicaraguan youth see Miami as a place where they are more likely to succeed than in other parts of the United States. Those adolescents who worked claimed that discrimination was based on age. Management and co-workers treated them unfairly, they believed, because they were teenagers. None declared that they were discriminated against for being Nicaraguan. Grace stated, "I think here in Miami we're not going to have a problem. But I think if we move probably to Colorado, Michigan, and stuff, they'll discriminate against any Hispanics." Adopting a Hispanic, as opposed to Nicaraguan, identity moves them closer to the Cuban majority and the community's center of power.

Mexicans are in a different social position. With more than 31 percent living below the poverty line, people of Mexican descent have the highest poverty rate in Miami-Dade County (Boswell 1994). In contrast, the income of Cubans is nearly on a par with that of non-Hispanic whites. Except for a small minority of professionals and middle-class individuals, most Mexicans live away from the urban area of Miami. They concentrate in the southern end of the county, which was hardest hit by Hurricane Andrew in 1992 and has been least affected by Cubans. Mexicans in Miami-Dade County experience conditions similar to those confronted by Mexicans in the southwestern United States twenty years ago. They work mostly in agricultural fields, nurseries, construction, daycare, and informal sector jobs. The lower-income, predominantly agricultural Mexican children of immigrants attend semi-rural schools where the administration and teachers are primarily Anglos.[12] They do not enjoy the relative luxury, as do Nicaraguans and Cubans, of having primarily Latinos teaching them. Unlike in urban Miami, personnel in the schools attended by Mexicans view Spanish as detrimental to a young person's education. Rather than encourage students to retain and increase their understanding of their culture, many school officials and teachers view Spanish speakers as having a "language deficiency," as one math teacher put it (Morgan 2001).

We have argued that the prejudice against newcomer immigrants compels them to assume the behavior and appearance of American adolescents. Children of immigrants first move from a national self-label toward primarily a hyphenated and occasionally even simply an "American" identity label. However, as they mature in high school, feel more self-confident and capable in their new environment, and, especially, become more aware of and subject to prejudice, many shift back toward a national label. Those who claimed to be simply American more likely refer to themselves as hyphenated Americans. Many who assumed a hyphenated label revert to a national label.

Yet there is a disjuncture between self-labels and behavior. The self-labels are becoming less American, but the behavior of these youth is undoubtedly becoming more Americanized in most respects. They speak better English and prefer English to their native language. They may still go to church, but they prefer English-language services and are likely to try out new churches, different from the ones their parents attend. They are also more apt to have friends of the opposite sex and from other ethnic groups and to listen to American music, with its suggestive lyrics. Females are likely to dress in a more sexually provocative manner. To the immigrant youths' parents and many others, the children of immigrants appear to have thoroughly absorbed and accepted American youth culture, specifically in their preference for English, new styles of dress, and gender relations and occasionally in their expressions of independence and challenges to parental authority. Parents often do not see the disjuncture between children's American-oriented cultural preferences and continued appreciation of their parents. Parents fail to recognize their children's declaration of identity through self-labeling that increasingly reverts to a home-country emphasis. Instead, parental concern for their children's future creates a backlash when the parents fear that the transformations they do recognize mean their children's abandonment of home-country values and failure to appreciate the opportunities in the United States.

INTERGENERATIONAL RELATIONS

In the first ethnographic examples presented here, Marie's parents booted her out of the house because she had become "too Americanized." Her parents perceived Marie as rejecting their values and them. Marie's case is extreme but hardly unique. Beatriz, a Mexican who was unable to accept parental rules, proclaimed, "I ain't living with my mother no more. I got into a fistfight with my father, and my mother was on my back, so I went to hit my mother. But I couldn't cuz she's my mother, you know, so I just walked out."

Nearly all adolescents have conflicts with their parents, and these usually revolve around differing values, such as the importance of education or expression of sexuality. Immigrant parents, however, usually maintain a fundamentally different value system. For example, parents assume that they have unquestioned authority over their children. Moreover, immigrant parents are apt to be ignorant of normative and legal limits, such as restrictions on physical punishment. Immigrant parents are also less likely to know about and to be able to access mediating institutions, such as school counselors or psychologists. As a result, parent-child conflict in immigrant households can be severe and can easily result in extreme consequences.

Among our Latino samples (Cuban, Nicaraguan, and Mexican), children of immigrants in conflict with their parents were less likely than Haitians to be kicked out of their family households. Instead, children from split families (for example, through divorce) might go to live with the other parent. In some cases, the parents and child would simply agree to disagree. Marlon, a Nicaraguan, referring to his parents' claims, said, "Well—I don't speak to them much. I'm never home." Diana, another Nicaraguan, had a very positive relationship with her parents the first few years after she arrived, but she had become alienated by the end of high school: "I'm not tight with every family member individually.... You see I'm *verrry* independent."

Some children of immigrants, along with native minorities, are able to work out a good relationship with their parents. Even though their parents do not like the way they dress or the music they listen to, they are able to communicate with one another and overcome differences. These children express strong, positive emotions for their family. When Diana, the Nicaraguan teen, was new to the United States, she maintained that her sister was her best friend, with whom she enjoyed going to church youth group parties. She described her mother as "my precious mom" (Konczal 2001). Alicia, a Mexican, worked with her mother on the weekends selling orchids at a local farmers market. When her mother was unable to go to the farmers market, Alicia took charge of selling for the day. Isabel, another Mexican, respected her mother and would not purposely disappoint her. She recounted her mother telling her, "'I know everybody gets mad at me at times for being strict,' but she's, like, 'you hafta understand. You know, I worry.' She goes, 'Isabel, you don't know how many things pass through my head,' and I [Isabel] started realizing, well, that's true, you know. I wouldn't wanna be home thinking a lot of things 'bout my child at two o'clock in the morning and everything" (Morgan 2001).

Even those who have difficult relationships with their parents still love and appreciate them. Marie, whose Haitian parents threw her out of the house, was not rejecting her parents by having a boyfriend. She loved her parents. She loved going to church with them. She saw herself as Haitian, or at least Haitian-American, not American or African-American. In our research, even those youth who dressed hip-hop style, joined gangs, took drugs, and adopted what their parents regarded as the worst of American culture were not necessarily rejecting their parents or their parents' culture. Yves, a Haitian who sported a thoroughly hip-hop style, with extra baggy pants, cornrows, gold teeth, and a bandana on his head, explained, "That [dressing hip hop] doesn't mean you any less of a Haitian than the next person that wear a tie and shoes like my father does. It's your pride and knowing where you came from, where you going, and how you have to help others, and by speaking Creole, by doing certain things. That's how you know a Haitian."

For immigrant parents to realize that their children are not rejecting their home culture through these new American behaviors, however, parents and children need to communicate. Louis, a recently arrived Haitian who deplored the permissiveness of American culture, added, "Haitian parents don't talk to their children. Children don't feel comfortable with their parents. When they have a problem, they can't talk about it with their parents. There is no respect for children. In the parents' view, children never say something good."

Alan, who had been in the United States for two years, concurred: "Haitian parents are not friends with their children. That can lead the children to do bad things."

A group of Cuban and Nicaraguan students complained, "Hispanic parents don't let you do anything!" One added, "My parents don't realize, this is America! When I have kids, I'm gonna give them some space. Let them be independent!"

Suzanne felt that her mother treated her "like a little child too much." When asked whether her mother was behaving like a Haitian or an American regarding parental control, she replied, "Like a Haitian. She thinks like a Haitian in the old days. To her, a girl should start dating at twenty-one. This creates a lot of conflict between me and her. I am eighteen. She doesn't think I should be dating. We argue. When boys call me at home, she doesn't like that."

However, Suzanne herself is caught between two cultural models that define the adolescent years quite differently, as childhood in Haiti and as emergent adulthood in America. Suzanne sees it this way: "Children have too much freedom in the American culture. Way too much. They take advantage of it. In the Haitian culture, I think children have too little freedom. You can't do nothing. Like in the Haitian culture, they have been living in school and church. They don't let you go out with your friends."

Suzanne looks forward to college, perhaps in Chicago, as "going away from my parents, having an experience on my own, and living by myself."

Some Haitian adolescent children actually perceive their parents' child-rearing practices as potentially leading to downward segmented assimilation. Marcelene, born in the United States of Haitian parents, asserted, "Their authoritarian way drives you away from them. You can't talk to them. This can lead you to do bad stuff."

The children of immigrants may be in intense conflict with their parents but still care very much for them and feel that family is important.[13] They are caught in a contradiction. They want to advance the traditional value that, as they mature, they will cease to be dependent children and will assume some responsibility for contributing to the family. At the same time, they are absorbing the common American notion that adolescence is a period in which individuals move from dependence to independence and responsibility primarily for themselves. The conflict they embody does not reflect a diminution of feelings for family but an intensification of negative ways of relating.

Immigrant parents also express ambivalence. One day, for example, Robert's mother was crying over the phone to our research assistant, not knowing how to cope with the cultural conflicts she faced. She claimed that her son did not have sufficient interest in school, and she feared that he was getting into trouble. She was willing to pay for a private school, but her son wanted to continue at the public high school. She wanted to force him to go to the private school but feared his response. She confided, "I feel caught up between two forces. On the one hand, I have to prevent the police from coming to my doorstep, which means that I need to help my son so that he does not engage in criminal activities. On the other hand, I have to prevent HRS [Human and Rehabilitative Services, now the Department of Children and Families] from coming to my doorstep. This is a really difficult situation for me."

If this mother punishes her son harshly by enrolling him in the private school and beating him, as she would in Haiti, she could face charges of child abuse. If she protects him from the police for his petty misdemeanors, she herself risks facing the police and still not avoiding Florida's Department of Children and Families. Police and social workers report numerous examples of disrespectful children shouting, "I'll call the authorities and charge you with child abuse if you hit me!" as parents get ready to strike them. When police arrive, they face a dilemma. They have received multicultural training and know that the parent is attempting to exercise authority according to Haitian standards. The police do not want to undermine that authority. They sympathize with the Haitian parents' concern that if they cannot control their offspring, the children may fall prey to the vices of gangs, violence, drugs, and crime. However, the police must enforce the law, and Haitian parental disciplinary standards frequently exceed the bounds of US law (Stepick 1998; Stepick et al. 2001).

These ethnographic examples are confirmed by survey results demonstrating that the children of immigrants who report high levels of conflict with their families still highly value their families (compare with Portes and Rumbaut 2001:199; Stepick et. al. 2001). The battlegrounds center first on relatively superficial, symbolic cultural patterns such as dress but often expand to include challenges to parental authority and, especially for females, expressions of sexuality. Parents, who frequently have less knowledge of American culture than their children, feel caught in a double bind. If they discipline their children in the relatively authoritarian fashion of their home country, their children or school personnel may report them to US authorities for child abuse. If they fail to use discipline, they worry that their children will lose interest in education and become involved in the negative aspects of life in the United States, such as drugs, gangs, and sex and pregnancy.

In summary, desire for acceptance by their peers is the first motivation for Americanizing, but the children of immigrants also appreciate and seek the individual freedom enjoyed by American adolescents. They feel that their parents are too controlling, that they are being denied the delights available to American adolescents. For nearly all the immigrant children in our sample, these expressions of becoming American engender conflict with parents.[14] Some youth manage to maintain good relations, but for others, such as Marie, relations become too strained and destroy a positive academic orientation. For youth to balance the opposing pulls of American culture and family/homeland culture, the parent-child relationship must be close and trusting. Youth must be able to confide in and receive support from the adults for the difficult, seemingly disjunctive choices they face. If the relationships are positive, the youth are likely to maintain the stereotypically positive academic orientation of immigrants. If relationships with their parents and other adults become characterized by conflict, their academic orientation is likely to turn negative.

ACADEMIC ORIENTATION AND ACHIEVEMENT

Marie's case demonstrates that intergenerational conflict can have a profoundly negative effect on academic orientation and achievement. Conversely, the success of Henri and his brothers at Harvard and

Northwestern indicates how parents can play a significant role in supporting a positive academic orientation and subsequent achievement. Henri's parents repeated daily that education was the way to get ahead.

If asked directly, students claim to have a positive academic orientation. Virtually all declare that school is important, and equal numbers state that they want to become professionals. Positively oriented students attend school consistently, complete their class work and homework, and participate in school functions and extracurricular activities. Alicia, a Mexican, commented, "I do pretty well because I love school. I have a passion for learning. All my teachers in eighth grade said, 'You love learning. That's why I love having you as a kid [student]'" (Morgan 2001). Similarly, Carlos, a Nicaraguan, was talking with his friends about students who were trying to get out of class for one reason or another. When asked whether he wanted to get out of class, too, he quickly replied, "I can't miss school, especially Algebra II" (Konczal 2001).

In contrast, negatively oriented students may be enrolled in school but have poor attendance records. Sometimes these adolescents withdraw from school when they reach working age. Beatriz, a Mexican, confided, "And last year I wouldn't come to school at all. I would go, like, on Monday, and I wouldn't come back 'til two weeks later" (Morgan 2001). When Gustavo, a Nicaraguan, was asked about the future, he asserted, "I don't know what I'll be doing a year from now. I can't see into the future" (Konczal 2001). Teresa, also a Mexican, stated that she wants to complete high school but has failed a number of required classes, regularly misses class, and "smokes out." When asked directly about whether she thought that she would graduate from high school, she paused and slowly responded, "I want to, but the way things are going for me, no. Every time my brothers get in problems, I always end up getting into them, too" (Morgan 2001).

Intergenerational relations are certainly not the only factor influencing academic orientation and achievement, but we did find it to be important for many, regardless of other characteristics. Students who persisted in maintaining a positive academic orientation had an adult in their life with whom they felt they could communicate.

Despite working very long hours, Alicia's mother, who completed fewer than six years of formal education in Mexico, noted, "I push them [her daughters]…so my goal is for them. I want to see them go to college. I really want to see them in a luxury car, be something in life better, you know?" She expected her children to graduate from college and be successful. She attended all of Alicia's volleyball games. Usually, she was the only parent in attendance (Morgan 2001). Nicaraguans in an ESL class demonstrated the link most self-consciously and directly in essays about their New Year's resolutions. A majority proclaimed that they sought "to get good grades, to get a good job, and to help my family" (Konczal 2001).

We also found some differences by national origin. With the highest dropout rates and lowest GPAs, Mexicans did far worse in school than any other group. In our small sample of thirteen Mexican-origin girls, only four graduated from high school within four years (Morgan 2001). Of the remaining groups, Haitians performed the worst and West Indians the best. These differences reflect, we think, local contextual variation in the host society's view of particular immigrant groups, their insertion into the local economy, and their family's socioeconomic characteristics.

We believe that Haitians performed poorly because of the prejudice and discrimination they face. Also, their parents have very low-level educational backgrounds (even compared with other immigrant groups). West Indians face some of the same racial discrimination as Haitians but have the advantage of being native speakers of English, and their parents are likely to have relatively higher levels of education.

Mexicans contrast with the other Latino groups in our study. The Mexicans we studied are in the same countywide public school system as Nicaraguans and Cubans, but they are in a very different social world. Most Mexicans live at the county's southern edge in an agricultural area away from the urban core that Cubans dominate, and most have roots as migrant laborers. Some still follow the crops, and many live in "migrant labor camps," even though they may no longer migrate seasonally. Mexican youth's parents are more likely to have long-term experience in the United States as return migrants, and many parents cannot even conceive of their children being able to go to college. Veronica, an excellent photographer, noted how her father inadvertently discourages her aspirations: "I want to go to college, but my dad tells me, 'Where you going to live?' and tells me that working and going to college is hard. He tries to tell me the reality" (Morgan 2001).

Not surprisingly, Mexican youth perceive fewer opportunities and have lower aspirations and, subsequently, lower achievement than all other groups we studied. Although nearly everyone interviewed in other groups claimed that they wanted to be some kind of professional, such as a doctor, a lawyer, or an engineer, most Mexicans in our sample aspired to lower-level, white- or blue-collar jobs, such as secretary or mechanic. A few maintained that they wanted only to be a mother. Again, not surprisingly, Mexicans had the highest rate of truancy. As Isabel explained, "Because it's, like, last week—not last week but—no, it wasn't last week. I forgot what week it was. I only came to school, like, for two days. You know, I make up excuses to tell my mom. I don't want to go to school—I'd rather just stay home" (Morgan 2001).

ANTHROPOLOGY AND IMMIGRANT EDUCATION

Our primary goal has been to address the sources of variation among the children of immigrants of similar ethnic/national backgrounds in their academic orientation and achievement. We have focused on the relationships of children of immigrants to their American peers and peer culture and to their own parents. We have used primarily ethnographic examples to demonstrate the evolution of their self-identity and behavior and the consequences for their relationship with their parents.

The variation in academic orientation and achievement is complex, as are relationships among the factors producing that variation. Qualitative, ethnographic methods, which are the primary methods of anthropology, are particularly adept at probing behind simple statements that education is important. Long-term participant observation can reveal the inconsistency between students' assertions and their actual day-to-day behavior. Only through participant observation, for example, could we discover the disjuncture between students' Americanized behavior and their reclaiming of more ethnic and national self-identity labels. Similarly, anthropological methods are particularly skillful at revealing the conflicting sentiments of immigrant students toward their parents, their simultaneous desires to enjoy American adolescent freedoms and to respect their parents' wishes and home culture.

The integration of qualitative methods with the quantitative methods more typical of sociology can not only reveal complex dynamics but also aid in producing valid generalizations. Our work was primarily ethnographic, which we supplemented with surveys and intensive interviews and focus groups. Our argument rests primarily on the presentation of ethnographic particulars across specific, varying contexts, but we also benefited from complementing that with quantitative data. Social scientists who use surveys more commonly strive for generalizations based on large surveys of individuals frequently conducted by survey research firms or assistants who may never meet or may interact only briefly with any of the respondents. Survey data are good at presenting a broad picture, at producing generalizations for broad populations—the type of statements that, incidentally, the media and often the funders of research desperately seek.

Anthropology has always grappled with the chasm between the ethnographic particular and scientific generalization. Early anthropology pontificated on primitive societies. Franz Boas and other early anthropologists began a counter-movement that emphasized ethnographic particularism and the difficulties, if not impossibility, of generalizing beyond one case embedded in a particular context. When later anthropological generations reverted to broad generalizations concerning peasant societies or even a particular society, albeit with a firmer empirical base, similar reactions resulted, including the postmodernist insistence on context and specificity. The most immediate difference in most anthropological research and that of more quantitatively oriented social science research is, therefore, the kind of data emphasized. Anthropologists and others who use qualitative data tend to present what its detractors label as only "anecdotes" and what we feel is fundamental reality, at least as far as observers are capable of apprehending, comprehending, and reporting it. Those who use surveys and other data from large samples tend to report more abstract summaries, what many qualitatively oriented researchers deride as decontextualized bits and pieces. Good quantitative methods, however, rely fundamentally on anthropological methods.

Social science hypotheses, interpretations, conclusions, and theories ultimately rest on empirical observations or, at least, the presumption of empirical observations. Surveys, interviews, and focus groups do not observe behavior directly. Rather, they rely on individuals honestly reporting their beliefs and behavior. Participant observation, the method primary to anthropological ethnography, relies on direct observations. Moreover, anthropologists and others who employ qualitative methods typically observe directly over long periods of time. Four years spent directly observing immigrant youth enabled us to understand how new immigrants can feel ashamed of their home culture among peers yet embody it among family, how self-identity can change across contexts and through time and seemingly be at odds with immigrant youths' cultural expressions in their dress and language, how immigrant youth can be alienated from their parents and endorse American "freedoms" yet still love their parents and seek to retain something of their home culture's values, and how immigrant and minority youth can proclaim the value of education yet make no effort in their classes and even fail them.

Anthropological participant observation and interviewing over a long time revealed the evolution of what turned out to be a complex process of academic orientation, parent-child relations, and assimilation. Only by observing and directly talking to immigrant youth and their parents over time could we both observe actual behavior and determine how they interpreted the process. Their interpretations proved crucial to our resolving the inconsistencies between immigrant youths' Americanized behaviors and their continued pride in their home culture.

Potentially, quantitative research could have accomplished the same thing, but it would have been much more difficult and required a lot of luck. Not only would the research have had to be longitudinal, but also the researchers would have had to know all the right questions before administering their questionnaires. For an issue as complex as immigrant youth and education, an extraordinarily long survey instrument would be necessary. After administering the survey, the researchers would still be confronted with the daunting task of which questions from the long list are the truly relevant ones for analysis. Quantitative researchers have developed sophisticated techniques, such as factor analysis, to reduce data complexity, but these remove the researchers yet one more step from direct empirical observation and are still subject to interpretation in their implementation.

Frequently, when quantitative researchers notice a longitudinal, unanticipated trend, such as the movement away from American-oriented toward more homeland national labels, they must resort to hypotheses not based on their own empirical data, because they may not have asked all the relevant questions or the data reduction techniques yield ambiguous results. Qualitative researchers who conduct longitudinal research, on the other hand, observe the changes as they are occurring and have an opportunity to collect data to explain them.

In a key article on immigration studies' methods, the sociologist D. S. Massey (1987) argued that good survey questionnaires always rely on ethnography, although the reliance is frequently unrecognized. When we did our first survey of Haitians in Miami, we included a standard survey question: Are you currently working? Although we knew that many Haitians were unemployed, the results still surprised us. More than 70 percent replied that they were not working. Further interviewing revealed that unemployment was high, but not that high. The problem was the wording of the question and Haitians' conceptions of "currently working." Haitians replied yes to that question only if they were working full-time at a permanent job. Working less than forty hours a week, even if one had been doing so for years, was not considered "currently working." Similarly, working sixty hours a week but at a job that was likely to end, such as agricultural labor, was also not considered "currently working." Moreover, being self-employed in what academics call the informal sector was considered not "currently working." To get at the meaning of "currently working," we needed to ask a series of questions: Are you currently working? Are you currently working part-time? Are you currently working temporarily? Are you engaged in a *ti-djob* (Creole for "informal sector work")? Are you doing anything else that generates income? When we asked these questions, the unemployment rate declined by more than 50 percent. We learned to make these distinctions after a period of participant observation. We could then incorporate our understanding into a survey questionnaire.

Immigration researchers frequently borrow and mix methods. Ethnographic methods, not survey research, were the basis of the Chicago School centered in the Sociology Department of the University of Chicago, before surveys became the predominant tool of sociology. Even though anthropology and sociology have tended to diverge methodologically since then, overlap is still considerable. Moreover, there have been calls recently to mix methods, particularly to embed ethnography within sample survey research (Hernandez and Charney 1998; National Science Foundation 1995). In short, anthropological methods embedded in the Chicago School established the field of immigration studies in the United States. More recently, they have been an integral, if not always recognized, component of most immigration research. In current work focusing on education and the children of immigrants, anthropological research in league with other qualitatively oriented research is at the forefront of understanding the keys to the academic success or failure of millions of new Americans. Qualitative methods have revealed processes critical to the adaptation process of immigrant students. Combining the insights of qualitative findings with quantitative survey research permits generalizations to larger populations.

Notes

1. Although an important distinction exists between people who are immigrants (born abroad) and children of immigrants (born in the United States to at least one immigrant parent), for convenience we refer to both as *immigrants.*

2. The broader project focuses on (1) school policies and practices (analyzed in Acherman-Chor 2001), (2) social capital, which includes the relationships we address in this chapter, and (3) individual and contextual variables, which include age, gender, years in the United States, immigration status, and neighborhood (analyzed in Konczal 2001; Morgan 2001; Stepick et al. 2001).

3. Funding was provided by NSF SBR-9511515, the Andrew Mellon Foundation, the Carnegie Corporation, and the Spencer Foundation. Alex Stepick was the principal investigator and Carol Dutton Stepick the director of field research. Stan L. Bowie was also a co-investigator. This chapter relies heavily on the doctoral dissertations of two research assistants associated with the project, Lisa Konczal (2001) and Jane Morgan (2001). We are also grateful to the other research assistants who have contributed to the project: Rose Bebon, Gillian Dixon-Dawkins, Deborah Dyer Teed, Emmanuel Eugene, Paula Fernández, Dora Acherman-Chor, Sonia Rivas, and Karla Mendieta. Yves Labissiere was associated with the project as a postdoctoral fellow. For earlier reports of this research, see www.fiu.edu/~iei/. Also see Stepick et al. 2001.

4. Our research was parallel to that of Portes and Rumbaut's *Children of*

Immigrants (Portes 1996; Portes and MacLeod 1996a and b; Portes and Rumbaut 1996, 2001; Portes and Schauffler 1996; Rumbaut and Portes 2001). They surveyed children of immigrants in Miami-Dade and Broward Counties in Florida and in San Diego, California, in 1992 and again in 1995. In 2001–2002 they were in the process of doing a third round with their sample. Their primary technique was a survey of the students, although they supplemented this with open-ended interviews with some parents. Our intensive research with groups in addition to Haitians began four years later. We replicated their surveys, but our primary technique was participant observation. We also conducted intensive interviews with parents, teachers, and administrators. We included African Americans in our sample. Our research is similar to Suárez-Orozco's project in New England and northern California, which began approximately one year after ours, and to another project, directed by Margaret Gibson in Santa Cruz County, California, that focuses on peer relationships. A few ethnographic examples and many analytic themes we present here come from our earlier research, reported in Stepick (1998) and Portes and Stepick (1993).

5. Ogbu conceptualizes autonomous minorities as those who are not being subordinated and are not characterized by disproportionate and persistent school failure. Such groups include the Amish, Jews, and Mormons. Although important in many respects, autonomous minorities are not part of our research design.

6. Suárez-Orozco uses the term *academic engagement,* which he divides into behavioral and cognitive dimensions. We make substantially the same distinction, except that, for us, engagement is behavioral and orientation is cognitive.

7. A consensus exists among anthropologists that race is not a biological category and has an ontological status no different from ethnicity. Most societies, including the United States, still distinguish race and ethnicity, maintaining, for example, that the black/white distinction is fundamentally distinct from the Jewish/Arab one. Although we believe that the black/white distinction is fundamental in US society, it is socially constructed and not biological (Sanjek and Gregory 1994). To acknowledge the social difference the label *race* makes while recognizing that the category is not biological, we employ the adjective *ethnic/race.*

8. We use *immigrant youth,* or more specifically *Nicaraguan youth,* for convenience to refer to a much more complex category. More accurately, in this particular case we are referring to youth of Nicaraguan descent. This includes not only people born in Nicaragua but also those born in other countries, such as the United States, who have at least one parent born in Nicaragua. More generally, it

could even include those who have (and who recognize) one ancestor born in Nicaragua. In our sample, though, everyone we refer to as Nicaraguan was either born there or had at least one parent born there. The same applies to the other national labels we use, such as *Cuban* or *Haitian*. We do not use the phrase *youth of Nicaraguan descent* because it is wordier and not used in everyday speech by anyone we know. *Immigrant youth* refers to both those born abroad and those born in the United States to at least one immigrant parent.

9. Incidentally, Miami has very few Asians, less than 2 percent. As a result, they were not part of our research design.

10. The names of all schools and immigrant students are pseudonyms. The name of the research assistant is not a pseudonym.

11. Miami's local English-language television covered the story extensively, certainly more than did media in other US cities, but not quite non-stop.

12. *Anglo* is the term generally used in Miami for what may otherwise be labeled as *non-Hispanic whites*. Because so many Cubans identify with their Spanish roots, *Euro-American* or simply *white* does not distinguish Cubans from *non-Hispanic whites*. Although the category *Anglo* includes many who do not have English roots, most notably Jews, it remains preferred over the more cumbersome *non-Hispanic white* (see Grenier and Stepick 1992).

13. Foner (1978) makes a similar argument concerning Jamaican immigrants and youth in London.

14. These relations are primarily with parents, as in the preceding examples, but not necessarily. Occasionally, the relationship can be with an older sibling, an aunt, an uncle, or even a non-relative, such as someone from church, a teacher, or a coach.

6

Bringing the City Back In

Cities as Contexts for Immigrant Incorporation

Caroline B. Brettell

Many years ago I published an article titled "Is the Ethnic Community Inevitable?" (Brettell 1981). This article, which compared first-generation Portuguese immigrants in Paris, France, with those in Toronto, Canada (places where I had carried out ethnographic field research), was sparked by my unease in applying theory that had been developed to explain the settlement and incorporation of immigrants in North American cities to the European context, at least a particular European context as I saw it at the time I was studying it. I wrote of this discomfort as follows:

> When I arrived in Toronto to conduct my research, I brought with me all the baggage of traditional participant-observation anthropology. I looked for an ethnic neighborhood, and my search was rewarded by the Kensington Market area in downtown Toronto. In Kensington, Portuguese stores, a Portuguese church, Portuguese restaurants, and Portuguese families are all clustered together. I had found my "Little Portugal" just as Herbert Gans and William Foote Whyte had found their "Little Italies" and

others their "Chinatowns and Cabbagetowns." But when I arrived in Paris, I found no "Little Portugal" which had carved out its own social niche within the great French metropolis. Not only was I forced to adopt new methods of research,[1] but I also had to revise my entire theoretical perspective on immigration and on the patterns of settlement of foreigners in cities. It was necessary to come to terms with the urban structures themselves as they influence the lives of newcomers. It was also necessary to view the formation of a "community," be it a geographical community or one based on social networks, as a strategy appropriate in some situations and inappropriate in others. Individuals choose to associate or identify themselves with one another. What factors make such a choice advantageous? What institutions make it possible or likely? (Brettell 1981:1)

Having made this observation, I then endeavored to delineate distinct urban forms as these relate to variables such as the history and geographical patterns of growth, the place of any city vis-à-vis the nation of which it is a part, the degree of industrialization, the location of labor markets, the nature of housing, and the social composition of city residents. I contrasted the horizontal stratifications of Toronto, as a grid city, with the vertical stratification patterns of some parts of Paris within the *peripherique* highway that circumambulates the city and creates a boundary between the urban core and the surrounding Region Parisienne.[2] I compared the employment patterns of Portuguese immigrants in these two cities with the structural differences outlined, focusing on the residence patterns these generated. Portuguese newcomers to Toronto settled in the houses immediately surrounding Kensington. Many Portuguese families in Paris lived in concierge lodgings or sixth-floor maid's rooms scattered across the eighteen *arrondissements* of the central city. This dispersal was fundamentally linked to patterns of female employment.

I also contrasted the pluralistic multiculturalism of Canadian immigration policy, which promotes and nurtures ethnic distinctiveness, with the more assimilationist emphasis on "becoming French" that characterized French immigration policy. Broadly speaking, French policy promoted residential dispersal and was linked to an expressed fear of the emergence of *"ghettos à l'americaine."* At the time, the French were making every effort to avoid concentrating families of similar national background in public housing projects being built in the Parisian suburbs.

The article addressed the institutional foundations of ethnic communities as well, arguing that community implies a set of organizations within which social interaction can occur or with which group membership can be identified. I was thinking particularly of voluntary associations, such as clubs, churches, special schools, and commercial establishments. At that time, I noted, "the restaurants, small stores, and travel agencies that are ethnic domains in America remain French in France as a result of a law prohibiting non-French citizens from opening and operating such establishments, and as a result of the traditionally heavy concentration of the French themselves in the tertiary sector of the French economy and society" (Brettell 1981:12). I drew attention to the fully Portuguese parishes in Toronto and contrasted them with the Portuguese-language masses held in side chapels of Parisian churches. National histories of religion were, in other words, equally important to consider. All of this led me to the conclusion that the ethnic community, in either a geographical or social network sense, was not necessarily inevitable and that we, as scholars, had to focus carefully on the conditions for its emergence.

The Paris of today is different from the Paris of a quarter-century ago. The Portuguese, who have produced a second, if not a third, generation by now, have also changed, but to my knowledge there is still no "little Portugal" within the perimeter of the city.[3] Furthermore, Paris does contain distinctly ethnic neighborhoods. Even at the time I carried out "first field work" in France, other ethnic groups (particularly those of North African origin) had the beginnings of such neighborhoods, the Goutte d'Or of the 18th *arrondissement* being the prime example. Finally, this research was carried out in an era of anthropology that preceded concepts of unbounded and transnational cultures and communities, and one might want to rethink my arguments in light of these new conceptualizations. None of these changes, however, invalidate the need to examine critically the theories we develop to analyze the incorporation of immigrants into cities in one cultural context as we draw on them to sharpen our understanding of similar processes in another. Taking account of "the city as context" is absolutely vital to comparative anthropological study of immigrants and the immigration process.[4]

The concept of the city as context was formulated within anthropology when the subfield of urban anthropology was still in its infancy and was part of the challenge to distinguish between anthropology *in* cities and anthropology *of* cities, or as Ulf Hannerz (1980) phrased it, "the city as the locus," not the focus, of urban anthropology (see also Howe 1990; Kemper and Rollwagen 1996). In his introduction to a special issue of the journal *Urban Anthropology* devoted to the city as context, Jack Rollwagen (1975:3) questioned the assumption that all cities are similar and, therefore, have no bearing on the life of the immigrants who settle there. John Gulick (1975:11) noted that "the literature is full of references to 'the city' or 'urban society' as if a homogenous or monolithic entity were being talked about." Gulick (1984), building on observations made a decade earlier by Anthony Leeds (1973), went on to suggest that a "city as context" approach means linking the macro to the micro.

With the exception of Irwin Press's (1979) study of Seville, and perhaps Richard Fox's (1977) attempt to formulate a typology of cities, the issues raised by the concept of city as context were relatively unexplored within anthropology for more than a decade.[5] However, the new wave of immigrants that entered the United States, especially after 1980, has resulted in a revival of this concept, first by Nancy Foner (1987b) in an edited book of essays about new immigrants in New York (see also Foner 2001e). In her introduction to this book, Foner points to specific social and economic features of this "classic" city of immigrants that shape the experience of newcomers who arrive and settle there. Of course, new immigrants have equally changed the city. More recently, Foner (2000) has added a temporal dimension to her analysis of New York as a city of immigrants by comparing the late nineteenth- and early twentieth-century third wave of immigration with the post-1965 fourth wave. Over the course of a century, New York has changed: Suburbanization has proceeded apace, and Manhattan is no longer the most populous borough; employment and educational opportunities have expanded; neighborhoods are polyethnic instead of monoethnic; no two immigrant groups dominate, as did the Italians and the Jews, who composed the majority of third-wave immigrants; and the population of native-born minorities (African-American and Hispanic) has grown. These changes are significant to the way immigrants of today are incorporated as compared with those of a century ago.

A second important book that focuses on the relationship between cities and immigrants is *Structuring Diversity: Ethnographic Perspectives on the New Immigration* (Lamphere 1992). This volume includes essays based on research in six urban places that have experienced different forms of economic transformation since the mid-1960s—Garden City (Kansas), Miami, Chicago, Houston, Philadelphia, and Monterey Park (California). In her introduction, Louise Lamphere (1992:15) notes that the earliest anthropological research in urban areas "did not utilize macro-level data on unemployment, family income, arrest rates, or school dropout rates to frame a study of a local population. Furthermore, the class structure and political economy of a particular city were not analyzed in order to explore the possible roles that macro-level forces could play in shaping a particular set of behaviors." Lamphere suggests that a new urban anthropology should focus on the connections between the macro and the micro. This is precisely what the authors in this volume do as they explore the changing relationships between newcomers and established residents in different urban contexts.

Sociologists have also been attentive to the importance of urban context. For some time, Roger Waldinger has noted, the study of cities was the study of immigrants, but these became separated. "In a sense, much of the sociological research on the new immigration to the United States is about people who just happen to live in cities, but how the particular characteristics of the immigrant receiving areas impinge on the newcomers is a question immigration researchers rarely raise" (Waldinger 1989a:211). Elsewhere he writes more explicitly that "each immigrant receiving area has its own particular group of newcomers, and the economic and political structures of the immigrant receiving areas are also distinctive" (Waldinger 1996:1078). Waldinger is careful to emphasize that urban structures are not determinative. The interaction of urban structures and the characteristics of ethnic groups shape immigration outcomes.

What all these scholars are suggesting is that the city, a primary destination for most newcomers, should become a key unit of analysis in immigration research.[6] This is particularly appropriate for anthropologists who study immigrants. Anthropology is a discipline rooted in an understanding of place (Appadurai 1988; Gupta and Ferguson 1992, 1997a and b), and cities are important places. They are specific social, economic, political, and cultural fields that have been shaped as much by history as by present-day local, regional, national, and often global economic and political forces. As receiving areas for immigrants, cities differ in myriad ways, and these differences may be important to the process by which immigrants are incorporated. I outline some of these differences here, drawing on several cities as examples of distinctive places. I operationalize the term *context* historically, structurally, culturally, and interactionally.[7]

HISTORY AND GEOGRAPHY—THE TEMPORAL AND SPATIAL DIMENSIONS OF CITIES

Cities differ in the depth of their history as receiving areas for immigrants. This history can, in turn, be related not only to the spatial distribution of newcomers within urban environments but also to a distinct urban identity, a self-conscious definition of being a "city of immigrants." In North America, cities such as New York, Toronto, and Chicago, which have traditional inner-city receiving areas for new immigrants dating back to the nineteenth century, can be contrasted with sunbelt cities such as Dallas and Atlanta, which only recently have begun to experience an influx of more diverse populations and, hence, greater ethnic heterogeneity.

Foner (2000) notes that when Jewish and Italian immigrants started to pour into New York in the latter nineteenth century, there were few alternatives to downtown neighborhoods. "Manhattan's Lower East Side carried the sobriquet of a private city, 'Jewtown,' while there were three Little Italys south of Fourteenth Street. In 1890, over half of New York City's Italians lived in just three wards bordering on Canal Street" (Foner 2000:39). A study of New York's Chinatown in the 1890s reported that "the entire triangular space bounded by Mott, Pell, and Doyers Streets and Chatham Square is given to the exclusive occupancy of these orientals" (cited in Yuan 1966:323). Today, the immigrants have spread out into the boroughs and beyond, but the Lower East Side is still a major receiving area for Chinese immigrants (Kwong

1996). This pattern of ethnic enclaves, as places of residence and business, now characterizes other areas of New York City. These include Washington Heights, where Dominican immigrants live and work and where there are between 1,500 and 2,000 visible Dominican-owned enterprises; the vibrant Korean enclave in Flushing (Min 1998); and "Little Odessa" in Brooklyn's Brighton Beach, where Russian immigrants have gathered.

Such enclaves also heighten a city's identity as a city of immigrants, an image reinforced by demographics. According to the 2000 census, the foreign born constituted 36 percent (approximately 2.9 million) of New York City's population. By the latter 1990s, fully 42 percent of Toronto's population was foreign born (the largest proportion in any Canadian city). For more than thirty years, Toronto has celebrated its diversity with a Day of Multiculturalism, a broad urban festival that gives every immigrant group a place within the larger urban structure. Anthropologists, and also some sociologists, have spent the most time "reading" such festivals and other cultural performances for what they tell us not only about ethnic identity and ethnic expression but also about the way each immigrant population marks its space in the complex landscapes of cities (Brown 1999; Cohen 1993; Kasinitz and Freidenberg-Herbstein 1987; Sanjek 1998; Schneider 1990; Werbner 1996). Kasinitz (1992), for example, discusses the annual West Indian–American Day Carnival parade in Brooklyn as an event that has created a pan-Caribbean ethnic identity by appropriating a public space that used to be the sole purview of Lubavitcher Hasidic Jews.

Spatially concentrated immigrant enclaves are, of course, not limited to older cities of immigration. Miami has a well-developed "Little Havana," and the Kreuzberg area of Berlin, known as "Little Istanbul," is a commercial and residential center for the approximately 200,000 Turkish immigrants in that city, and a place to which Turks develop a stronger attachment than to Germany. In both cases, it is significant that a single immigrant group predominates. Increasingly, cities are characterized by areas that are strictly ethnic commercial centers. For example, Johanna Lessinger (1995) argues that "Little India," located at 74th and 37th in the Jackson Heights area of Queens, is the core of commercial life and social exchange for a residentially dispersed Indian population arriving by subway or car from all over the metropolitan area. Despite "Koreatown" in Los Angeles and the Flushing area of New York, Min (1996:45) argues, the majority of Koreans in these two cities "live in a non-geographical community tied together by ethnic networks that rely principally on Korean churches, alumni associations, and ethnic media." In Dallas, several Korean businesses are concentrated in one area along Harry Hines Boulevard near downtown, but Koreans live primarily in the northern suburbs. In Richardson, an area adjacent to and almost surrounded by the city of Dallas, there are other areas of largely Indian or Chinese shops. These populations used to live nearby but increasingly have moved out to the suburbs, returning to the original area of settlement to do their "ethnic" shopping. In Oak Lawn/ Love Field, a more inner-city neighborhood, African Americans, Latinos, Asians, Anglos, and a substantial gay community are clustered in what was already referred to twenty years ago as a "multiethnic jumble" (Chaze 1983:51). In the Oak Cliff neighborhood in the southern part of the city, Hispanics predominate—mostly Mexicans but also Guatemalans and El Salvadorans.

The presence or absence of ethnic enclaves, whether or not they are residential and commercial centers, and the extent to which they are dominated by a single immigrant population are significant factors in explaining quite distinctive processes of immigrant incorporation (including how social relations are constructed) into urban areas. The unique character of enclaves affects the visibility of immigrant populations and, as a result, how they are represented and received locally.

Greater Washington D.C. offers a final interesting case. According to Robert Manning (1998), 28.6 percent of the Washington D.C. population in 1800 comprised African slaves and a few black freedmen. By 1860, blacks were 20 percent of the population, and more than 75 percent were free. Unlike other East Coast cities, including nearby Philadelphia, the growth in the Washington D.C. population in the final two decades of the nineteenth century was linked to blacks, not immigrants.[8] In other words, this was a metropolitan area that was largely bypassed by the third wave of immigration but rose to the fifth most common destination for legal immigrants in the late 1990s. Whereas one in twenty-two area residents was foreign born in 1970 and one in twelve in 1980, the proportion of foreign born had risen to one in six by 1998 (Pan 1999; Singer et al. 2001).

Despite Washington D.C.'s position today as an important receiving area for legal immigrants, one wonders about the degree to which area residents think of their city as a city of immigrants. In Washington D.C., immigrants are dispersed throughout the metropolitan area rather than concentrated in ethnically homogenous residential enclaves. One D.C. neighborhood, Adams-Morgan (the second highest zip code destination in Washington D.C. given by new immigrants to the INS, after South Arlington [Singer et al. 2001]), is home to recent immigrants, but Asians and Hispanics share this area with African Americans and some whites. The neighborhood is full of ethnic businesses, but in some cases the business owners live elsewhere. The diversity of this neighborhood has a long history, but the pressures of new gentrification are a constant threat (Laura Kamoie, personal communication). Multiethnic neighborhoods and suburban dispersal are factors that may mitigate the visibility on which a self-conscious identity as an immigrant city is constructed. *International city* may be a more appropriate descriptor for Washington D.C.

Historical depth has an additional spatial dimension worth considering. Chicago has been characterized by a unique historical geography of immigration. The early spatial depictions of the process by which immigrants were integrated into this city (formulated by the Chicago School theorists, whose work is at the root of both urban anthropology and urban sociology) referred to run-down "slums" and "immigrant enclaves" located somewhere between the central business district and the working-class and second-generation immigrant settlements that spread out in concentric circles to the suburbs. Distance from downtown was a marker of social and economic mobility, changes in family structure, and other factors associated with immigrant incorporation (assimilation and acculturation, of course, being the concepts used at the time). As members of an immigrant group ascended the socioeconomic ladder, they were able to move out of the central core into higher-status and more ethnically mixed neighborhoods. Some cities are still characterized by this pattern. Others, such as Paris, where the middle and upper classes continue to reside in the central area, are not.[9] More importantly, this pattern is not characteristic of southern

metropolises such as Dallas and Atlanta and is only partially characteristic of New York, although Manhattan, as the "central core," still
receives a significant proportion of newcomers.

Immigrants to the Dallas metroplex often migrate directly to the
suburbs rather than to inner-city neighborhoods, and they have contributed significantly to phenomenal regional growth that now
stretches north of the city toward Oklahoma. The anthropologist Sarah
Mahler, based on her research on Salvadorans on Long Island, has
been most eloquent in drawing our attention to this new phenomenon:
"It seemed ironic that Long Island, with its image of classic white suburbia, would attract such a large, diverse group of immigrants. But suburban areas across the country are attracting immigrants, in small part
because of the safety and aesthetics of the suburbs as compared with
the inner cities, and in large part because jobs have been created in
these areas. Long Island is no exception. Many Asians are also moving
in, deserting areas of New York City, especially Queens; Turks have
come close to monopolizing gas stations throughout the island as well"
(Mahler 1995a:14–15). The research that Mahler and others have conducted among immigrants in suburban areas reflects a major transformation in US postindustrial cities. Suburbs are no longer simply
bedroom communities but "dynamic growth poles of employment,
consumption, leisure, culture and public administration" (Manning
1998:342). A recent study by demographer William Frey for the
Brookings Institution, drawing on data from the 2000 census, notes
that in 65 of the 102 largest metropolitan areas, minorities account for
most of the suburban growth. More than half of Asian Americans in
large metropolitan areas reside in the suburbs, as do half of Hispanics,
but only 39 percent of blacks (Frey 2001:5). Even in 1990, more than
seven times as many immigrants lived in the Maryland and Virginia suburbs as lived in Washington D.C. proper, a trend that continued
throughout the 1990s (Singer and Brown 2001:976; see also Alba et al.
1999; Waldinger 2001:6–7).

Quite recently, the Chicago School model of cities has also been
challenged by urban geographers and urban planners working on
newer but well-known cities of immigration such as Los Angeles and
Miami. These are not cities with commercial cores surrounded by concentric rings of industry and settlement but sprawling and decentral-

ized metropolitan areas fragmented into numerous political and economic jurisdictions. Edward Soja (1992:27) describes Los Angeles as a "polymorphic and centrifugal metropolis, a nebulous galaxy of suburbs in search of a city, a place where history is repeatedly spun off and ephemeralized in aggressively contemporary forms." Wei Li (1998) has coined the term *ethnoburb* to describe the suburban ethnic clusters of Los Angeles. Although ethnoburbs are multiethnic, a single ethnic minority group tends to have significant concentration. As places of business and residence, they are forged, Li (1998:481) argues, "under the influence of international geopolitical and global economic restructuring, changing national immigration and trade policies, and local demographic, economic and political contexts" (see also Davis 1992). Suburban areas can differ as much as urban areas, and these differences should equally become a focus for our attention as we study fourth-wave immigration.

Soja (1996) contrasts Los Angeles with Amsterdam, "the most self consciously centered and historically centripetal city in Europe." He further describes one city as self-consciously multicultural (with its Little Tokyo, a vast Koreatown, a huge and long-established Mexican barrio, a new barrio with a mix of Central American migrants, and a new Armenian community [Soja 1996:443–444]) and the other as a city where diversity is understated. Even multicultural Los Angeles had, as Abelmann and Lie (1995:89) point out, an ethos of whiteness and racial homogeneity for much of the twentieth century. The result of this ethos has been a politics of exclusion—the "systematic segregation and sequestering" of new immigrant workers into ethnic enclaves. I return to the question of ethos later in this chapter, but it is worth stressing here that this is something anthropologists can pursue further with their particular theoretical lenses and methodological frameworks.

The historical depth and spatial distribution of immigration can also shape attitudes toward immigrants, the ways in which people in different cities receive and respond to foreigners in their midst. Of course, this response may not always be predictable. One of the best ways to explore this response is by analyzing local discourse in the media. Portes and Stepick's (1993) understanding of Miami is enriched by their detailed study of how newspapers such as the *Miami Herald* wrote about immigration. A careful examination of this kind of evidence, and how it changes over time, can illuminate whether and how immigrants are viewed as part of any urban context and, ultimately, how an "image" of a city is constructed and controlled. To this we might add analyses of the ethnic media as sites where immigrants construct and represent their own place within an urban context. Finally, Chavez has taken this approach to a national level, focusing his attention on the images on national magazine covers that are, in his view, sites of "cultural production" where political ideas and positions are debated and negotiated (Chavez 2001:46). Local discourse is often framed by national discourse, and any analysis must consider both.

More traditional methods of anthropological research can equally access questions of reception. As part of his argument for integrating the local context into analyses of European reactions to immigrants, Cole (1997) compares the ambivalence of Sicilians in the working-class Albergheria neighborhood of the city of Palermo with the more politicized anti-immigrant stance of residents in northern Italian cities, where nativist and racist graffiti and gang violence target foreigners and *terroni* alike. His explanation for the difference is situated in a complex analysis of class, culture, and political economy. For example, he notes that representatives of churches, unions, and associations in Palermo urge Sicilians to treat immigrants with a tolerance born of the memory of the Sicilian emigration experience. Northern Italian cities, by contrast, have a longer history, both with immigration (including the arrival of hundreds of thousands of southerners in the postwar period) and with labor market segmentation. We need more cross-urban and cross-cultural work on this topic, especially on how urban discourses are shaped by broader national discourses on immigration.

THE SOCIAL CONTEXT—HOMOGENEITY, HETEROGENEITY, INTERACTION, AND IDENTITY POLITICS

In one of the classic monographs of urban anthropology, Abner Cohen (1969) analyzes the ethnic politics of Hausa migrants and traders in the city of Ibadan, Nigeria. Cohen argued that heterogeneous African towns manifested different degrees of political ethnicity, ranging from situations in which "cultural differences between people in the town are...rapidly eroded by various cleavages which cut across ethnic differences and give rise to close cooperation and alignments between men from different ethnic groups...[to] situations where men emphasize their ethnic identity and separateness and adjust within the contemporary setting, in terms of their endoculture" (Cohen 1969:194).

Although Cohen does not fully explain the conditions under which different ethnic or cross-ethnic strategies emerge, his study points to the importance of a close analysis of the social context of different urban environments. How heterogeneous are they? How divided are they? Does one ethnic group hold the reins of local power? How do different ethnic groups relate to one another? When, where, and how do identity politics emerge? In other words, the character of race relations and the balanced or unbalanced distribution of immigrants from one or several sending societies can powerfully influence the experience of immigrants in cities. Waldinger (1989a:214) observed more than a decade ago that of the five main urban receiving areas in the United States, three were dominated by immigrant populations from a single point of origin—the Mexicans in Los Angeles and Chicago and the Cubans in Miami (see also Waldinger 2001). New research is beginning to identify experiences among Mexicans who have recently settled in Los Angeles with those who have settled in the New York City area—the latter not a traditional receiving area for Mexicans but an area with a powerful presence of other Hispanics (Cubans, Puerto Ricans, Dominicans, South and Central Americans). This difference alone will shape processes of incorporation for Mexicans in these two cities.

An additional twist is provided by Washington D.C., a metropolitan area that became, as already mentioned, the fifth most common area of settlement for legal immigrants in the United States in the 1990s but where no single immigrant group dominates. Mexican immigrants represented only 1.2 percent of recent immigrants between 1990 and 1998. On the other hand, Washington has attracted the largest proportional flow of Africans of any metropolitan area in the United States (Singer et al. 2001:12). Washington D.C. is also an urban area with a significant inner-city African-American population. Two important empirical questions need further investigation: (1) How does the small Mexican population interact with other Hispanic groups, especially immigrants from El Salvador, who compose the largest single immigrant group but who comprise only 10.5 percent of newcomers to the area (Singer et al. 2001:4)? (2) How do African immigrants relate to and interact with African Americans?[10]

With regard to the second question, Goode and Schneider's (1994) study of Philadelphia is particularly instructive. At the time of their research, Philadelphia was the fifth largest city in the United States but only sixteenth in the number of immigrants. It drew an average of 7,117 newcomers each year between 1984 and 1986, compared with 92,345 for New York and 57,912 for Los Angeles. In other words, immigrants were less important to its urban dynamic than to cities such as Miami and Chicago. More important, in Goode and Schneider's (1994:4) view, is that newcomers to this "divided city" had to contend with the "large, geographically isolated but socially and politically important African American population…[whose presence] had a profound effect on how immigrants viewed themselves and positioned themselves vis-à-vis the political and socioeconomic structures of the city." In Philadelphia, vital ethnic neighborhoods, complete with specialty shops, festivals, ethnic churches, and local associations, exist within an urban center overlaid with tensions between whites and blacks.

Goode and Schneider also focus on the way that the local political and economic structures have shaped the incorporation of immigrants and the relationship between immigrants and the dominant African-American minority. In particular, they note the declining labor market, the trend to suburbanization (including the location of high-tech industries in the suburbs), the inability of Philadelphia to compete with the more dynamic urban centers to the north (New York) and south (Washington D.C.), the greater reliance on a local tax base compared with other cities of similar size, the weakness of the tourist industry, and the absence of a region for which this city serves as a center. Certain new immigrant groups, the Koreans, for example, have gained economic power through their entrepreneurial activities, but, according to Goode and Schneider, they envy the political power that remains in the hands of the African-American population.[11]

Atlanta is another city divided by race, but with a much more recent history of immigration than Philadelphia. In 1860, the foreign born constituted no more than 6 percent of the population, and most were Irish, German, and English. After the Civil War, according to Rutheiser (1996:88), urban boosters tried to attract only Anglo-Saxon immigrants to the south, and Atlanta was no exception. Despite these efforts, small but significant numbers of Germans, Russian Jews, and Greeks settled between 1865 and 1915. By 1940, only 1.4 percent were foreign born, and in 1960 the figure was 3.2 percent. Only after 1980, Rutheiser claims, did the ethno-racial landscape begin to change as Atlanta became a location for the resettlement of Southeast Asian refugees from Vietnam, Cambodia, and Laos and, in the 1990s, refugees from Afghanistan, Ethiopia, Eritrea, Somalia, and Eastern Europe. In the 1990s, legal and illegal economic immigrants also came to Atlanta, but, Rutheiser (1996:90) concludes, they went relatively unnoticed and are "marginalized from…social and political life" in a city that has had black mayors for some time.[12]

The contrast between the context of Philadelphia and Atlanta and that of Miami is stark because in Miami one immigrant group, the Cubans, is numerically dominant and holds the reins of political and economic power. They have what Eames and Goode (1977:176) referred to as "critical mass"—a strategic population level that provides a foundation on which to build vital institutions and around which to organize for ethnic group action. Portes and Stepick (1993) note the implications of this critical mass for the incorporation of other Latino groups, in particular, the Nicaraguans, who were welcomed because of not only shared "Latinness" but also a shared political ideology (militant opposition to an extreme left regime). The Haitian experience has been quite different. Writing about blacks in Miami, Portes and Stepick (1993:178) observe that "a tangle of conflicting and often contradictory perceptions, attitudes, and interactions yielded a confusing scene where racial solidarity alternated with class and ethnic factionalism as well as economic competition. During [the 1980s], Black Americans became increasingly divided by class, as did Haitians; and both immigrant and native Blacks became increasingly ambivalent toward each other. These contradictory tendencies weakened their common voice, making it all the easier for these groups to be lost in the fray."

Here, it is worth mentioning the work of political scientist John Mollenkopf (1999), who has compared urban political conflicts and alliances in New York and Los Angeles. Mollenkopf argues that New York and Los Angeles differ in the degree to which they have been able to contain social explosion and native backlash in the face of immigration. He offers two fundamental explanations for this difference: (1) The cities are characterized by different political balance among groups. (2) They differ in the "ways in which their political systems create (or lack) incentives for dominant white elites to recognize, incorporate, or co-opt claims from subordinate groups (including new immigrant groups) and for leaders of subordinate groups to accommodate one another" (Mollenkopf 1999:413). In New York, Mollenkopf (1999:413) suggests, "all groups, including whites, have a significant immigrant component, whereas nativity pits groups against each other in Los Angeles." In New York, all groups have access to the political system, whereas access is more limited in Los Angeles. "All groups must fight it out in one, highly partisan system in New York, while Los Angeles County has eighty-eight separate, nonpartisan jurisdictions" (Mollenkopf 1999:413). Anthropologists working on immigrants in cities need to be as attentive as political scientists to the structure of urban politics and the ways urban politics shape the processes of civic participation and group interaction.

The ethnic heterogeneity of a city influences the structure and patterns of intergroup relations. Where no one group dominates in demographic terms, various immigrant groups must forge alliances to achieve economic and political ends. Such alliances often lead to the emergence of panethnic organizations. Anthropologists are especially well-trained and well-positioned to study intergroup dynamics by "reading" what Ulf Hannerz (1980) has referred to as the "drama of cities"— particular events of interaction that reveal points of contention and consensus and, hence, processes of identity construction and incorporation. The riots targeting Korean business owners after the Rodney King trial in Los Angeles provide a good example (Abelmann and Lie 1995; Park 1996). In the multiethnic reality of Los Angeles, the struggles in Monterrey Park over language use also illustrate this. Latinos and Anglos joined together to halt the exclusive use of Chinese in a suburb that was slickly advertised as a "Chinese Beverly Hills" (Davis 1992:207; Soja 1996:447). All the activities circulating around the Elian Gonzalez case in Miami not only offer another example of the "drama of cities" but also reveal differences between Cubans in Miami and those who settled on the East Coast. The conflicts between Cubans, Haitians, and African Americans in Miami following a visit by Nelson Mandela, whom the Cubans viewed unfavorably as being pro Castro (Portes and Stepick 1993:176), offer one more example. In his contribution to the original volume on the city as context, Kenneth Moore (1975:25) argued that the core of urban culture can be understood by studying "the way diversity interrelates in proximity.... It is from this perspective," he suggested, "that we must try to explain urban wholes or urban context."

THE URBAN LABOR MARKET AND THE IMMIGRANT LABOR MARKET

In his comparative study of immigrants in different nations and cities, Jeffrey Reitz (1998) demonstrates that entry-level earnings vary from one country to another and from one city to another within a country, suggesting that labor markets are diverse and attract discrete segments of immigrant populations (see also Ellis 2001). Similarly, Robert Kloosterman (1998:75), in an article on the postindustrial city in Europe, notes that "between cities—even within a single national institutional framework—differences in the economic structure could result in diverging patterns of opportunity for both indigenous and migrant workers. In a former manufacturing city, overall demand for labor may be much lower as a result of de-industrialization than in a city which is traditionally strongly oriented towards service activities." Consideration of the city as context draws attention to such variations in urban labor markets and, as a result, to the economic niches into which immigrants can enter.

One place to start is by drawing a comparison between cities with a vibrant economy and those with a more sluggish economy. Economy influences the number and type of immigrants in an urban context. Providence, Rhode Island, is an interesting case in this regard. One of the oldest cities in the United States, Providence has a deep history of immigration linked to the textile-mill economy of the late nineteenth century and a jewelry industry that survived into the 1940s. Between 1865 and 1900, the population of Providence grew by more than 100,000, largely as a result of the arrival of Irish, German, Italian,

French-Canadian, and Portuguese immigrants. Through much of the late twentieth century, however, Providence was a city in decline, and only recently has it experienced a process of urban renewal and revitalization. Although Colombians and Portuguese were brought to the Providence area after 1965 to work in the textile industry (Lamphere 1987), many of the more recent immigrants to Providence are either secondary migrants (for example, Dominicans, Haitians, and Puerto Ricans moving out of the New York City area) or refugees (Hmong, Cambodians, Liberians, Kosovans). Secondary migrants are employed in the hospitality and health-care industries and, to some extent, in manufacturing. Others have started small businesses. In general, it is not the labor market opportunities (including many low-skill, low-paying, and dead-end jobs) that have attracted recent immigrant groups to this city. Competition from overseas has all but killed the local textile economy, and other manufacturing industries have been in decline. Providence experienced a serious recession in the first half of the 1990s while the economies of neighboring states were booming. Secondary immigrants came to Providence in search of a better quality of life—a lower cost of living, a less crime-ridden environment, proximity to family members—or a government or non-profit program such as Catholic Charities. The arrival of several refugee populations drew hostile comments in the Letters to the Editor section of the *Providence Journal* during the latter 1990s. Entrenched "ethnics," faced with growing Hispanic populations, were calling for the end to bilingual education programs and for the establishment of English as the official language. Power in the city remains in the hands of older immigrants. By comparison with Dallas, Atlanta, or even Boston, Providence is not a city that has attracted high-end (that is, with extensive human capital) immigrants, and this is fundamental to any comparison of immigrants, the immigrant experience, and immigrant reception in different cities.

Providence can be contrasted to a city such as Las Vegas, the fastest-growing metropolitan area in the United States in the 1990s and a city that essentially reinvented itself to keep ahead of the gaming competition that has been increasing in other states and cities across the United States.[13] Much of the population growth has also been the result of internal migration, estimated at 6,000 people per month in the 1990s. These were people drawn by booming construction, convention, and tourism industries. A study conducted by the Department of Comprehensive Planning in Clark County, Nevada (Holmes 1998), showed that 29 percent of the people who moved there in 1993 were from five counties in southern California that received heavy flows of immigrants in the 1990s—Los Angeles, Orange, San Diego, San Bernardino, and Riverside. Some of those moving to Las Vegas are second-generation Mexicans looking for something better than the society and economy of southern California, which was experiencing an economic recession in the early 1990s. As in Providence, these are secondary migrants, although equal numbers of Mexicans come directly to Las Vegas from Mexico.[14]

The Latino population in Clark County, Nevada, grew by 139 percent in the 1990s, from 85,000 to more than 300,000 (Cleeland and Romney 1999). Most Latino adults have found work in the same sectors of the economy as non-Hispanics, and many of these jobs are at union wages in the country's most unionized city. In 1997, 36 percent of culinary workers (whose union is the state's largest and most powerful) were Anglo, 36 percent were Latino, 15 percent African-American, and 12 percent Asian (Rothman 2002:68). As anthropologist M. L. Miranda (1997:126) writes, "The possibility of securing employment in the flourishing tourist and gaming industry of Nevada is a tremendous draw. For immigrants who are not proficient in English, the gaming industry provides employment in unskilled jobs; for those who are bilingual, higher-paying jobs can be had; and for those who have experience in the hotel and gaming industry and are bilingual, there is an opportunity for a great deal of upward mobility. Even people with minimal English-speaking skills have been known to work themselves into higher-paying positions. Jobs that require little skill and English-speaking ability, such as parking lot attendants and waiters/waitresses, because of tips, pay very well in Las Vegas and Reno."

Historian Hal Rothman's (1998:314) observations are equally germane: "Las Vegas became the Last Detroit, the last place in the nation where relatively unskilled workers could find a job after high school, earn a middle class wage, and expect to remain with the company for their entire working life." According to Otto Merida, executive director of the Las Vegas Latino Chamber of Commerce, immigrant couples with little education, few skills, but a willingness to work can earn

$16–18 an hour between the two of them and succeed in Las Vegas, a city where the rate of unemployment is extremely low and the hotel occupancy rate year-round is well above the national average. Las Vegas workers are, in short, "extremely well off by postindustrial blue-collar standards" (Rothman 2002:64).

Latino-owned businesses in Las Vegas doubled in the late 1980s and early 1990s, and Mexican restaurants launched in the Los Angeles area opened branches in Las Vegas. In addition to the labor market opportunities, Los Angeles Mexicans are attracted to the inexpensive housing, short driving distance to work, and low crime. The Latino presence is apparent. "Almost overnight, taquerias, money transfer outlets and immigration consultants have filled strip malls in new immigrant neighborhoods to the north and east of the Strip" (Cleeland and Romney 1999). There are three Spanish-language weekly newspapers, three radio stations, two television networks, and two telephone directories. Strong organizations have developed, the Hispanic middle class is growing, and there is an expectation that the community can soon begin to field more political candidates (Miranda 1997). Schools in Las Vegas have developed bilingual programs. The Las Vegas International Mariachi Festival, celebrated on Mexican Independence Day (September 15), has sold out each year (Miranda 1997). Even the tourist industry began to cater to Latino patrons with excess capital. Indeed, Miranda (1997:182) notes that the Independence Day festivals began as an event "for Latin American high-rollers" and the hotels have been booking more Latin performers. Despite all these changes and the wealth of opportunities, Miranda (1997) cautions that many Hispanic households in the Las Vegas area are still struggling or must have all adult members employed to make ends meet and that the high school drop-out rate is higher than it should be.[15] Overall, though, both Otto Merida (personal communication) and he stress the openness and opportunity in Las Vegas as a city for immigrants.

In many US cities, immigrants participate in the service economy, but they have also spearheaded the revival of small business. Three areas of the urban economy that shape immigrant entrepreneurship have been identified: under-served or abandoned markets, such as those in the inner city; low economies of scale, such as the taxi business; and ethnic goods and services. Immigrant entrepreneurs have moved into urban economic niches that the native born overlook, under-exploit, or shun. The extent to which any immigrant population takes advantage of one or all of these opportunities, and the extent to which enclave economies emerge, varies from group to group and from city to city. Comparisons between populations of the same immigrant group in different urban contexts make this apparent. In New York City, Koreans dominate the greengrocer business, specializing in ready-to-eat fruits and vegetables in bite-size pieces. In Los Angeles, by contrast, Koreans have focused on gasoline service stations, dry cleaning, and liquor stores.

The movement of new immigrants into small business has also been documented in European cities (Boisssevain and Grotenberg 1986; Rath and Kloosterman 2000; Westwood and Bhachu 1988). Ethnic entrepreneurs in cities such as Amsterdam and Berlin are "revitalizing formerly derelict shopping streets by introducing new products and new marketing strategies...fostering the emergence of new spatial forms of social cohesion...opening trade links between far away areas that were hitherto unconnected...and posting challenges to the existing regulatory framework through being engaged in informal economic activities" (Kloosterman, Van der Leun, and Rath 1999:252). Anthropologist Jan Rath and his colleague Robert Kloosterman (2000) call for research on immigrant entrepreneurship that moves beyond an "ethnocultural perspective" to consider the structural aspects of the urban economy, the degree of segregation in the urban housing market, the kinds of social networks that immigrants construct and can capitalize on in their urban context, and the overall institutional framework, including, in many European cities, the nature of the welfare state. As Rath and Kloosterman suggest, the emergence of immigrant entrepreneurs in European cities offers ample opportunity for comparative research. Such research will enable us to test and refine models that have been developed based mostly on research in North American cities.

One such model has to do with the supposed opportunities for social and economic mobility that ethnic enclave economies offer. New research in the United States has subjected this model to more careful scrutiny. Peter Kwong (1998), for example, suggests that, although this might be the case for Korean entrepreneurs in several cities in the

United States (Min 1998) or for the Chinese in San Francisco (Wong 1998), it is a source of enslavement, exploitation, dependence, and limited opportunity for many who live and work in the Chinese enclave in New York. Other research challenges the idea that enclaves and the ethnic solidarity they engender are not necessarily inevitable. Arguing that historical, social, and cultural factors in a localized (that is, city) context must be considered, Patricia Pessar (1995c) demonstrates that marked divisions of social class and nationality preclude the development of an enclave economy among Latinos in Washington. Unlike in Miami or Los Angeles, as mentioned earlier, no single Latino group predominates in Washington D.C.

Pessar's reference to class is important because it suggests that the social and economic characteristics of immigrants who go to one city or another may vary and thus affect incorporation outcomes. There are fewer professionals among the West Indians of New York than among those in Washington D.C. (Foner 2001a:19). There are more middle-class Chinese in the population that has settled in Los Angeles than in the populations in New York and San Francisco (Waldinger and Der-Martirosian 2001:239). These differences should stimulate more careful comparative analysis, across a range of cities, of the interaction between local labor markets and the human capital of specific immigrant groups.

THE CULTURAL ETHOS OF CITIES

Cities can have a unique urban ethos or "collective conscience" (in the Durkheimian sense), that is, a dominant set of values that shapes political, economic, and institutional life and, as a result, both the incorporation of and attitudes toward immigrants. (For a different approach, see Molotch, Freudenberg, and Paulsen 2000.) This ethos can emerge from a specific history of economic and political growth. It can also derive from the larger state or national context or a larger cultural context. To some extent, ethos is also about the way a city looks at itself, represents itself, or constructs its identity. This ethos may have an impact on how immigrants experience a city and how they are incorporated in it.

In some sense, Judith Goode (1990) is dealing with this question of ethos when she describes "two important city-wide models of differ-

ence" in Philadelphia that are important to the process of incorporation—one of the city as a pluralistic mosaic composed of many cultures
and the other as a place polarized by race, racism, and xenophobia.
Similarly, ethos undergirds, at least to some extent, Setha Low's (1996,
1997, 1999) typology of cities and Rutheiser's (1996, 1999) discussion
of Atlanta as a "postmodern city." Rutheiser suggests that any city can
convey certain messages and project certain images, encapsulated in
what he labels its "publi-city" (1996:10). These are often transferred to
the built environment by urban "imagineers," who write the urban text.
The terms *world-class* and *future-oriented,* used by Atlanta boosters, are
similar to those used by Dallas boosters. However, Dallas also projects
another image, as the "can-do" city of business. To what extent, we can
ask, do immigrants absorb this set of values, and how does it shape the
activities they pursue? One self-employed Pakistani informant told me
that he was influenced in his decision to come to Dallas because word
had traveled all the way to his village in Pakistan that Dallas offered lots
of opportunity and was a good place to start a business. Of course, one
must also wonder about the media's effect—specifically in the form of
the television show *Dallas,* which is still being shown in remote parts of
the world. The point is that this ethos, in whatever format it is projected
(locally and internationally), might offer an additional explanation for
entrepreneurship beyond the argument that immigrants become self-
employed as a coping strategy in the face of racism and unemployment
(Waldinger, Aldrich, and Ward 1990).

I explore this question of ethos by briefly addressing three examples. The first is the city of Montreal, a city shaped by a political culture
of "two solitudes." (*Two Solitudes* is the title of a famous novel written by
Hugh MacLennan about the province of Quebec.) Seguin and
Germain (2000:47) argue that the history of Montreal is framed by a
"narrative of contention and opposition between French and Anglo
Saxon cultures" and that this narrative has profoundly shaped the
experience of immigrants. Until the final decades of the nineteenth
century, people of British, Scottish, Irish, and French descent composed the bulk of the city's population, and each group occupied its
own, segregated area of the city. The East End was French-speaking;
the West End was English-speaking, with the dividing line along the
Rue St. Laurent (otherwise known as St. Lawrence Main). In other

words, like Philadelphia, Montreal is a divided city, but divided by language not race.

Into this divided city came Greek, Italian, Jewish, and Portuguese immigrants who created their own ethnic neighborhoods. Between 1951 and 1971, the proportion of the population of non-French or non-British origins residing in Montreal rose from 14.7 percent to 25.1 percent (Ramirez 1997). In the 1970s and 1980s, the attitude toward these newcomers was highly negative in the province because they were largely oriented toward the English-speaking community in Montreal. This resulted in legislation specifically designed to halt the "anglicization" of immigrants. Included was the famous Bill 101, which required attendance at French elementary and secondary schools for all children settled in Quebec, with the exception of children whose parents were educated in English in Quebec or another Canadian province.

Despite these and other measures, the negative attitude toward newcomers survived into the 1990s. It was manifested most publicly in the anti-immigrant comments of Parti Québécois leader Jacques Parizeau after the loss of the second referendum on separation in 1995. A recent illustration occurred in February 2001 when a Bloc Québécois Youth policy paper argued, much to the dismay and disgust of minorities in Quebec, that immigrants and anglophones were a nuisance to the French language and that Quebec must not "dilute" its identity. "French Canadians argued that if the present trend of immigration continued, Francophones would be a minority in Quebec. Thus the negative attitude towards immigrants. Others have argued that French Canadians, because of their cultural homogeneity, close kinship links, and isolation from France, make Quebec a closed society that produces a deeply rooted xenophobia" (Germain and Rose 2000:297).

The majority of immigrants to the province of Quebec have settled in Montreal, a bilingual city within a larger province where French-Canadian culture and the French language are sustained by law and policy, including immigration policy. Canada grants Quebec the power to admit certain categories of immigrants. Quite recently the provincial government announced efforts not only to increase francophone immigration (that is, to favor Haitians, Vietnamese, Lebanese, and Africans from francophone countries, and the like) but also to encourage immigrants to settle in other parts of the province.[16] However, in

Montreal, beneath the surface of bilingualism, beneath the "tension between two cultural and linguistic worlds" (Seguin and Germain 2000:48), lurks a polyethnic city (Meintel 1997; Meintel et al. 1997) and a host of multiethnic urban neighborhoods (Germain et al. 1995). Germain and Rose (2000:239) argue that in Montreal, unlike many other North American cities, the suburbanization of immigrants, "though a growing trend, is still markedly limited" and where it has occurred, there is "a tendency toward clustering in established multi-ethnic suburbs rather than dispersing into new sectors characterized by suburban sprawl and mainly inhabited by francophones."

In Montreal, "the immigrant population is confronted with a series of socio-professional territories which are...structured along ethno-linguistic lines" (Fournier, Rosenberg, and White 1997:114). In a sense, though, immigrants have co-opted the reality of this divide and the ethos of two solitudes to suit their own purposes, creating patterns of interethnic mixing and trilingualism that might be absent in other North American cities among first-generation immigrants. According to the 1996 census, 100,000 Quebec residents lived in households where English was spoken alongside at least one and sometimes two or more other languages. Intermarriage among those of different origins was on the increase. The Quebec Bureau of Statistics reported that in 1996 mixed marriages between English mother-tongue Quebec residents and someone outside their language group outnumbered marriages between two fellow Anglos.

Some researchers have observed that native languages have survived longer in Montreal than in other North American cities because of bilingualism and the "double majority" (Anctil 1984). The same can be said of ethnic identity. Anthropologist Deirdre Meintel (2000:14) argues that Montreal offers "a hospitable environment for perpetuating immigrant ethnic identities. For decades public discourse centered on the ethnic specificity of the Québécois terms of language, culture and identity has dominated the mass media and political life.... The long struggle of the francophone Québécois for recognition of their group identity...has served as something of a paradigm for other ethnic groups."

If second-generation immigrants in Quebec are not *pur laine* (literally, "pure wool," and figuratively, true Québécois), they must identify themselves in another way. "Montreal," Seguin and Germain (2000:47) argue, "makes a particularly interesting subject for the study of cosmopolitanism because of its higher level of multiethnicity coupled with its status as the metropolis of a divided society." In short, immigrant incorporation in a city such as Montreal is fundamentally shaped by the cultural ethos of a self-consciously "distinct" society.

Las Vegas offers another example of a city with a self-constructed and self-conscious image of itself, in this case as the capital of "entertainment tourism." Historian Hal Rothman (1998:290) observes that in the mid-1960s "Las Vegas became the first city in the nation to embrace a service economy, albeit an idiosyncratic one, as its dominant formulation." He suggests that Las Vegas, and more generally the state of Nevada, imported everything, including labor, to nurture its ethos of malleability to suit people's desires. As Las Vegas rebuilt itself in the 1990s, the need for labor to fuel the Vegas ethos increased. First- and second-generation immigrants, among others, responded. "The more labor became extra-local and foreign," writes Rothman, "the easier it became to maintain the illusion of exclusivity at a more profitable bottom line." If the city fulfills the desires of entertainment tourists, it also fulfills the desires of those who have come there to work. For immigrants, the American Dream is attainable in a state that prides itself on individual freedom, maintains a low tax rate, and offers a middle-class way of life to its workers "off the backs" of tourists. The urban ethos of Las Vegas, in other words, is shaped as much by the laws and culture of the state of Nevada as Montreal is shaped by the laws and culture of the province of Quebec.

Just as the Pakistani immigrant was drawn to Dallas by its reputation of being "good for business," immigrants are drawn to the Adams-Morgan area of Washington D.C. by its reputation as a place where diversity is accepted and political activism is nurtured. Refugees from Ethiopia, Southeast Asia, and Central America are among those who have settled in this neighborhood. According to historian Laura Kamoie (personal communication), they are partly drawn to the D.C. area by the possibility for continued political lobbying on behalf of their countrymen and by the certainty that their activities will draw media attention. Hackett (1996:284) mentions the existence in the D.C. area of organizations with such homeland interests.

Equally, in a truly international city, some immigrants (women, in particular) were brought to work as part of the domestic staffs of various foreign diplomats. When these diplomats returned to their countries of origin, some domestic staff members remained and eventually brought family members to join them. Terry Repak (1995) suggests that this is the foundation for Central American immigration to Washington. Refugees from the civil wars in this region joined their co-ethnics in the 1980s. Singer and Brown (2001:981) argue that contemporary African migration to the Washington D.C. area can also be "traced back to the arrival of embassy staff and other international workers to Washington, DC in the 1950s and 1960s." International students also should be added to the mix, students drawn to programs in international service and international polity at Georgetown, George Washington, and American Universities, and, among African immigrants, to Howard University. Many of these students also stayed.

Perhaps most important to this argument about how the culture of government and international politics in Washington D.C. has shaped immigration is that the city grew as a federal bureaucracy rather than through industrial growth and lacked local control over its political affairs (Cary 1996). Without industry, Frances Cary notes (1996:xvi), Washington D.C. drew a larger percentage of skilled and entrepreneurial immigrants than other US cities before 1965. Singer and Brown (2001:978) further suggest that the city's unique political status also shaped immigrant life in early phases of immigration: "Without elected local government, immigrant groups could not turn to local political machines to address their interests as they often did in other cities. Instead, immigrants in Washington had to look to the federal government to deal with local matters."

This is not the full story, however. The majority of newcomers to the D.C. area, particularly those arriving since 1980, have settled in the suburbs. This process is partly explained by what Robert Manning (1998:335) labels "urban apartheid." During the middle decades of the twentieth century, African Americans were pushed into the inner city out of places such as Georgetown and the suburbs as whites took them over. In 1970, 24.7 percent of African Americans in the D.C. area resided in the suburbs, compared with 90.3 percent of whites. "The historic legacy of urban apartheid combined with the lack of an efficient mass transit system for delivering workers from the District to work sites in the suburbs, effectively denied the vast majority of African Americans the opportunity to work and live in the booming satellite cities of Washington, DC until the 1980s" (Manning 1998:339).

Meanwhile, immigration averted a rising labor crisis in the suburbs. According to Manning (1998:346), more than 93 percent of Korean and all other Asian-owned businesses in metropolitan Washington, as well as 89 percent of Hispanic-owned enterprises, are in the suburbs. The settlement of immigrants in the suburbs is, in Manning's view (1998:341), at the foundation of a major social transformation, moving Washington from a "provincial biracial city to an international, multicultural metropolis." Finally, it is worth noting the role of international relief agencies in the region in this process of suburban settlement. "Many Vietnamese, Cambodians, and Laotians were settled in northern Virginia by refugee resettlement organizations due to the availability of housing, social services, and employment" (Singer and Brown 2001:980). This, too, is part of the local/national/international political culture that shapes the immigrant experience in Washington.

CONCLUSION

In this chapter, I have addressed the question of cities as contexts for the reception and incorporation of immigrants. The argument is based on the premise that these contexts differ, in their history of immigration, their spatial dimensions and housing stocks, their political economies, their immigrant populations, and their dominant culture or ethos. Cities may also be differentially affected by state (or provincial) and national policies and institutions. All these factors can shape the experience of immigrant populations and should be a fundamental part of our analyses. For example, these influence the kinds of jobs immigrants take and, therefore, their economic incorporation. These influence where immigrants live, how they construct communities, what languages they use in daily life, how and with whom they forge social relations, and, therefore, how they are socially and culturally incorporated. These influence the kinds of organizations that immigrant groups develop, the opportunities for local political participation, and, therefore, their political incorporation.

The methods of anthropology are best suited to micro-level research in situations of face-to-face interviewing and interaction. In my view, though, no anthropological research on immigration can proceed without attention to more macro-level units of analysis, including "the city." The city must become a focus for research, instead of merely a locus, precisely because it may help to explain differences between, for example, how Mexican immigrants in New York City and Mexican immigrants in Los Angeles live or the integration of Haitians in Montreal and in Miami. Even when similarities are revealed in different urban environments—for example, between Salvadorans in Long Island (Mahler 1995a and b) and in San Francisco (Menjívar 2000), contrasted with those in Los Angeles—we should explore contextual explanations for those shared experiences. When we find that a single immigrant population is being described differently in the same urban context, as in Kwong's (1996) and Zhou's (1992) quite distinct analyses of the Chinese in New York City's Chinatown, we are challenged to address how our theories, and the questions these theories generate, shape what we find. (I am grateful to an anonymous reviewer for helping me with these insights.) Above all else, this chapter stands as a call for the kind of comparative research that has always been at the foundation of the discipline of anthropology. It was with this comparative perspective that I tried, several decades ago, to sort out the similarities and differences between Portuguese immigrants who had migrated to Canada and settled in Toronto with those who migrated to France and settled in Région Parisienne.

This leads me to one final observation. Much of my discussion focuses on the relatively recent phenomenon of direct immigration to the suburbs. We may need to think more profoundly about what we mean by *city* and what the relationship is between a city and its surrounding region. Discussing Washington D.C. without including an analysis of the larger metropolitan region (which crosses several counties and states) is as difficult as discussing Dallas without focusing on the entire metroplex, covering four counties that extend to the north, west, and northwest and encompass several other cities, including Fort Worth. Las Vegas, referred to with increasing frequency as an "All-American metropolis" or the "First City of the Twenty-First Century" (Rothman 2002), is also becoming an urban area with multi-centers, "a harbinger of sorts, albeit sometimes in exaggerated form, of major transformations in contemporary urban economies…[and] constituting a new form of urban settlement" (Gottdiener, Collins, and Dickens 1999:254). These new urban forms present both theoretical and methodological challenges to the anthropological study of immigration.

Notes

Acknowledgments: Preliminary thinking on these issues appears in Brettell (1999, 2000b) and is being explored further as part of the project "Immigrants, Rights, and Incorporation in a Suburban Metropolis," funded by the Anthropology Program of the National Science Foundation project (BCS-0003938). The title of this chapter relates to Hollifield (2000), who argues that political scientists have brought the state back into the study of immigration. I would like to thank the following people for their assistance: Bruno Ramirez and Deidre Meintel, Université de Montréal; Blair Ruble, Woodrow Wilson Center; Marta Martinez, Rhode Island Historical Society; Tony Miranda and Hal Rothman, University of Nevada, Las Vegas; Otto Merida, Hispanic Chamber of Commerce, Las Vegas; Samantha Friedman, George Washington University; Laura Kamoie, American University; and Audrey Singer, Brookings Institution. The author would also like to thank Nancy Foner, the participants in the SAR Advanced Seminar, and the anonymous reviewers for their comments. Finally, I gratefully acknowledge the support of the University Research Council of Southern Methodist University. The grant they awarded facilitated travel and research for this chapter.

1. I came to refer to these methods as "subway anthropology" because I rode the Paris metro and its extensions to most of my interviews.

2. Immigrants were also settling in the larger Région Parisienne, first in impromptu shantytowns (labeled *bidonvilles*) and later in public housing projects *(habitation à loyer moderée)* that were built in the late 1960s and the 1970s.

3. Toronto has also changed. By the mid-1990s, 42 percent of its population was born outside the country. European countries as places of origin have been replaced by Asia, the Caribbean, Africa, and Central and South America. As in many US cities, there has also been a shift in the spatial distribution of new immigrants, with more of them settling in the suburbs in private or public housing, depending on their income (Frisken et al. 2000).

4. This is especially important in the US context because immigration has

contributed most significantly to the growth of major metropolitan areas such as New York, Los Angeles, and Chicago but also Washington, San Francisco, Seattle, Dallas–Fort Worth, and Houston in the 1990s (Holmes 1998). Capturing the first evidence of the impact of the fourth wave of immigration, an article in *US News and World Report* in the early 1980s reported that our big cities were "going ethnic" (Chaze et al. 1983).

5. See also John Gulick's (1967) study of Tripoli. More recently, Rutheiser (1996) has written about Atlanta. His efforts are part of a renewed interest in the city as an object/subject of inquiry. Low (1996, 1997, 1999) adds a new dimension to Fox's typological approach.

6. Two edited volumes worth mentioning are Waldinger and Bozorgmehr's *Ethnic Los Angeles* (1996) and Portes and Stepick's study of Miami, *City on the Edge* (1993). Furthermore, several authors who contributed to a 1998 OECD publication, "Immigrants, Integration and Cities: Exploring the Links," make certain cities (Berlin, Sydney, Stuttgart, Birmingham) the focus of attention. On an international scale, we have, of course, Saskia Sassen's (1991) work on the global cities of London, Tokyo, and New York, centers of technology, financial production, and support services, with urban economies shaped more by translocal economic forces than by local policies.

7. Rapport and Overing (2000:332–333) have defined *context* as "the environment which an individual inhabits before, during and after situations of interaction with others."

8. Manning (1998:333) gives the following figures for 1900:

	Blacks (% of Population)	Immigrants (% of Population)
Washington D.C.	31.1	7.0
Baltimore	15.6	13.3
Philadelphia	4.8	22.7
Pittsburgh	4.5	25.4
Boston	2.1	35.1
Chicago	1.8	34.5
New York	1.8	36.7

9. Body-Gendrot and Martiniello (2000) argue that in many European cities, by contrast with those in the United States, the middle class has not deserted the city centers for the suburbs as extensively. This is important as one considers how immigrants relate to specific urban contexts and, particularly, how they interact with other groups within an urban context.

10. Muller (1998:44) argues that, in general, the conflict between African Americans and immigrants in Washington D.C. has been minimal. He suggests that this may be related to urban employment patterns. One third of all jobs in Washington D.C. and two-fifths of all jobs held by African Americans are for local, state, and federal government. This is the highest percentage in the nation. One half of Hispanics are in service occupations, compared with only a quarter of African Americans. African Americans hold the higher percentage of managerial and professional jobs in D.C., in comparison with other cities. On the other hand, the riot that erupted in May 1991 after a rookie African-American female police officer shot a Salvadoran immigrant should be noted. An African-American member of the D.C. City Council suggested that if Latinos did not like the United States, they should go home (quoted in Chavez 2001:140). Laura Kamoie (personal communication) suggests that in the Adams-Morgan neighborhood of Washington D.C., Ethiopians (the largest population in the United States) and African Americans have sometimes had their differences.

11. In the 2000 census, Philadelphia ranked nineteenth as an intended destination for immigrants. In May 2001, City Councilman James T. Kenney released a plan to attract immigrants to the Philadelphia area, calling it a matter of urban survival. "The plan outlines twelve steps that Philadelphia—which lags behind New York and other large U.S. cities in drawing newcomers—can take to attract immigrants. The plan's most ambitious recommendation would be the creation of an 'Office of New Philadelphians' [that] would assist new arrivals on multiple levels" (Rhor 2001). The new office would be modeled on New York's Office of Immigrant Affairs. Other suggestions were included to move Philadelphia toward being an international city. Jeffrey Passel expressed some reservations about the plan, asking whether "economic vitality causes immigration or immigration causes economic vitality" (Rhor 2001). See Schmitt (2001) for a discussion of a similar plan in Pittsburgh.

12. Los Angeles is another city where the relationships between African Americans and immigrants are important to consider. Soja (1996:448) describes the changes in Los Angeles as follows: "With the growth of Koreatown and Anglo gentrification pushing from the north, and Latinoization obliterating the old Cotton Curtain and spreading through the Watts-Willowbrook-Florence-Compton corridor from the east, black LA has not only been compacted, it has become increasingly polarized, with the richest and poorest African-American communities more visibly locked together in their inequalities than ever before."

13. In 1990, the population of Las Vegas was 852,646; by 1998, it had grown

to 1.2 million. In June 1993, Nevada was first in the rate of growth of construction jobs, most of this around Las Vegas (Miranda 1997). These figures are impelled by a tourist industry that boomed in the 1990s. "In 1996 more than 30 million people passed through the 100,000 hotel and motel rooms in Clark County, leaving a profit of more than 15 billion for the gaming and tourist industry" (Rothman 1998:313).

14. Miranda (1997:126) notes that this trend dates back to the 1960s, when many Mexican Americans came to Nevada not only from California but also from Texas, Arizona, Utah, Colorado, New Mexico, the Midwest, and the East Coast. They came in search of jobs with higher wages and better benefits. Miranda also discusses other Hispanics (Puerto Ricans and Cubans) who have resettled in Nevada. The Cubans brought to Las Vegas their experience in the pre-Castro Havana casino industry.

15. According to Rothman (2002:182):

> The incredible construction boom of the last decade has ballooned the construction labor force to more than 75,000, overwhelmingly Spanish speaking, but wages for the work have stayed at the bottom, as is typical in right-to-work states. "I don't think there's anybody who speaks English who builds houses anymore," said one construction industry veteran. Outside of the realm of well-compensated service labor, many Latinos receive poor pay—if they're fortunate, only the most basic benefits—and remain transient. Wages are in the single-digit dollars per hour. Even entrepreneurial crews find it hard to make decent money. A crew of four "Mexicans," as Latino laborers of every nationality are colloquially called, will frequently split $500 for two and a half days of grueling work sheetrocking a new house in a trendy suburb. These wages offer little hope of eventual prosperity, stability, or ownership of a home like the ones the workers build, but they powerfully contribute to the affordability of housing for everyone else in the Las Vegas Valley. Construction workers are among the few Las Vegas workers left out of "the Last Detroit," this last bastion of remarkable prosperity for the unskilled.

16. According to a May 11, 2001, article in the *Montreal Gazette* ("Too Much English Spoken, Too Few Fleur-de-lis Displayed" by Nicholas Van Praet), there were strong objections in a citizenship swearing-in ceremony in Montreal to the absence of Quebec symbolism and the overemphasis of Canadian symbols. Quebec has discussed granting a simultaneous Quebec citizenship and having a Quebec national anthem.

7

Immigration and Medical Anthropology

Leo R. Chavez

Immigrants trying to negotiate the US medical system give testimony to the truth in Virchow's famous declaration, "All medicine is politics." Viewing immigrants as outsiders who are simultaneously insiders, the larger society often questions their use of medical and other social services. The issue of medical services for immigrants and citizens alike, at least in the United States, is open to such debate because there is no guaranteed "right" to medical care. Even though citizens may feel an entitlement to medical care, many are unwilling to grant this to immigrants. As a consequence, immigrants seeking medical care face restrictive policies, financial tests, and citizenship requirements. Moreover, immigrants often enter the labor force at the bottom, where low incomes, lack of medical insurance, and little available time present obstacles to their use of medical services. In short, immigrants are disadvantageously embedded in a political economy of health care characterized by pervasive structural inequalities (Farmer 1999; Morsey 1996; Whiteford 1996). It is a challenge for anthropologists, particularly those taking a critical approach (Lock and Scheper-Hughes 1996), to explore the influence of culture on immigrants' use of US medical services without minimizing the tremendous role these structural factors play in the lives of immigrants. This chapter highlights several important problems that occur when immigrants interact with the US medical system (also see Hirsch, Chapter 8). I will draw on my own research and that of others for examples of issues that arise from the confrontation of immigrants' cultural beliefs with the receiving society's medical beliefs and practices, the stigma of disease when associated with particular immigrant groups, structural obstacles faced by immigrants seeking medical care, and the limitations of interventions at the individual instead of societal level.

Anthropological interest in immigration is both old and new. Franz Boas, the totemic ancestor of American anthropology, provided a classic example of anthropological research countering public representations of and taken-for-granted assumptions about immigrant characteristics. His research on Southern and Eastern European immigrants in the early twentieth century directly challenged existing scientific and commonsense assertions about the link between immigrants' physical/bodily structures and shapes and their moral and intellectual potential. Using the methods popular at the time, Boas measured the heads of immigrants' children (an example of the "second generation" study so in vogue in immigration research today) and compared them with the immigrants' measurements. He found that the second generation did not resemble the immigrant generation in head shape. As Kraut has noted, "Boas concluded that nutrition and other aspects of living conditions determined these 'racial characteristics' more than heredity" (Boas 1911a; Kraut 1994). A few years later, in the 1920s, the Mexican anthropologist Manuel Gamio carried out investigations into the life and working conditions of Mexicans in the United States (Gamio 1930, 1931). The poignant narratives he collected from Mexican workers provide compelling evidence for the harsh, unhealthy working conditions they endured and the social and political barriers to integration they encountered. (See Chavez [1992] for a discussion of contemporary living and working conditions for farm workers in Southern California. See also Goldsmith [1989]).

Despite these early examples of interest in immigration, anthropological research on immigration waned, perhaps because of the massive reduction in immigration during the Great Depression and World War

II (Pedraza 1996). Just as influential was anthropology's professional identification as the science of the *Other* (read "primitive," "less technologically advanced," "less complex political organization"), of non-Western cultures and societies that had to be "salvaged" before they passed away as a result of the putative, homogenizing march of modernity. An anthropological interest in immigrants returned in the latter decades of the twentieth century, corresponding to worldwide increases in the transnational movements of refugees and people seeking economic opportunities (Brettell and Hollifield, eds. 2000). In the United States, immigration flows have increased steadily since the mid-1960s, reaching about one million legal and undocumented immigrants a year by the end of the twentieth century and into the early twenty-first century (Pedraza 1996). The movement of people has not affected only the United States; it has had global repercussions (Castles and Miller 1998).

Immigration has given anthropologists a window into the ramifications of people's crossing national borders. As the world experiences what has become glossed under the concepts of globalization and transnationalism, anthropologists, and many others, want to understand the implications of the rapid and increasingly efficient movement of people, capital, goods, and information across increasingly porous national borders. In many ways, these movements are constructing a world of linkages, bridges, connections, and hybridizations, all of which are forcing a re-thinking of "the national order of things" (Malkki 1992). At the same time, immigrants often receive an ambivalent welcome when they cross those borders (Chavez 2001). Ground zero in this ambivalence frequently centers in the domain of medical care (and its utilization) and competing, or at least different, cultural beliefs surrounding health, illness, and well-being. In sum, focusing on immigrants can throw into stark relief many theoretical issues central to medical anthropology and anthropology in general.

IMMIGRANTS AND CULTURES CROSSING BORDERS

The movement of people has implications for the physical and mental health of those who move and those among whom they establish themselves. The history of European contact with native peoples in the Americas provides a tragic example of this. The indigenous Americans suffered massive population declines after Europeans arrived in the New World. They were felled not so much by strength of arms as by the silent, unseen germs and viruses brought by the Europeans and their animals. American Indians had no natural immunities for many European diseases, even children's diseases considered relatively harmless, such as measles, swine flu, and chicken pox. The loss in human life is almost beyond our abilities to imagine. By some estimates, as many as 90 percent of certain American Indian populations died after a succession of epidemics and plagues, sometimes before they even met Europeans. Disease went ahead of the Europeans, clearing the land of much of the native population and weakening its capability to withstand the invaders (Kraut 1994). Unfortunately, miners, colonists, and missionaries (and even anthropologists) who come into contact with people in remote areas of the world, such as the Amazon, continue to introduce deadly epidemics to natives (Chagnon 1997). In the Americas, ironically, the Europeans acquired valuable medicinal knowledge from the native *shamans,* or medical specialists, who were very adept at the use of indigenous plants to treat illnesses. Hundreds of indigenous drugs have been listed in the *Pharmacopoeia of the United States of America* and the *National Formulary* (Kraut 1994).

Today's immigrants are less likely to come from Europe and the industrialized nations than from less industrialized countries in Asia and Latin America. Anthropologists have long studied in the places where today's immigrants were born. They have written extensively on practices of folk healers, the use of folk medicine, the nature of folk illnesses, and indigenous beliefs about the body and what it means to be healthy (Rubel and Hass 1996). Not surprisingly, immigrants bring with them beliefs, behaviors, fears, prejudices, values, and established assumptions about both the physical and spiritual worlds that may not correspond to dominant cultural realities in the society at large. This is especially true when their beliefs and cultural assumptions come into contact with the culture of biomedicine.

Anthropologists speak of biomedicine as a cultural system because, like religious systems, ideological systems, and even common sense, biomedicine has the "capacity to express the nature of the world and to shape that world to [its] dimensions" (Geertz 1973b; Rhodes 1996:166; see also Clifford Geertz's [1973b, 1983] discussions of cultural systems). The ethnomedical systems of immigrants can differ from biomedicine in fundamental ways. Modern biomedicine evolved from the Cartesian premise of a mind-body dichotomy. As Lock and Scheper-Hughes (1996:58) noted, in biomedicine, "body and self are understood as distinct and separable entities; illness resides in either the body or the mind.... By contrast, many ethnomedical systems do not logically distinguish body, mind, and self, and therefore illness cannot be situated in mind or body alone."

For some immigrants, the spiritual and the physical are linked together and form the basis for understanding many illnesses, their symptoms, and their cures. Too often, immigrants find themselves facing problems associated with what have become commonplace, postmodern dilemmas. Their health-related beliefs and practices can place them on a collision course with the US biomedical system. Immigrants may have culture-specific beliefs about health, illness, and wellness and culture-specific expectations of patient-healer interaction. When immigrants suddenly arrive at a US hospital emergency room, their beliefs may not be familiar to attending physicians and staff. This is especially true for folk illnesses or culture-bound illnesses.

In their book, *The Culture-Bound Syndromes,* Simons and Hughes (1985:475–497) list 158 illnesses, but even this is only a partial list because every culture, past and present, undoubtedly has one or more culture-bound illnesses. Table 7.1 suggests but a few of the many illnesses typically unrecognized by practitioners of biomedicine but pervasive among the cultures of origin of many immigrants in the United States. Associated with such illnesses are notions about appropriate curing rituals and practitioners (the need, for example, to deal with the spirit world), as well as traditional epistemologies about the relationship between the physical body and the spiritual self.

In *The Spirit Catches and You Fall Down,* Anne Fadiman (1997) has provided a poignant example of how cultures can collide when immigrants seek medical care. This is the story of a Hmong family in Merced, California. One day Lia, a young child born in the United States, suddenly began experiencing seizures. Biomedicine understands this as epilepsy, but the parents attributed this to Lia's soul leaving her body when she was frightened by the loud noise of a closing door. What developed over many years of interaction with doctors, nurses, other medical personnel, and social workers affiliated with a

TABLE 7.1

Selected Folk Illnesses Found among Immigrants in the United States

Folk Illness	Country of Origin	Symptoms
Aire ("vapors")	Peru	Eczema, dermatitis, epilepsy, convulsions, hysteria, paralysis, pneumonia, gastrointestinal problems.
Amok	Malaysia, Indonesia	Violent outbursts, aggressiveness or homicidal behavior, amnesia.
Bilis	Latin America, United States	Anger and rage, nervous tension, chronic fatigue, malaise.
Boufée delirante aigüe	Haiti	Sudden aggressive behavior, confusion, hallucinations.
Cholera	Guatemala	Nausea, vomiting, diarrhea, fever, severe temper tantrum, unconsciousness, dissociative behavior.
Dhat	India, Sri Lanka, China	Severe anxiety and hypochondria associated with the discharge of semen, feelings of exhaustion, weakness.
Empacho	Latin Americans, United States	A gastrointestinal blockage caused by food clinging to the intestinal wall.
Gahsum-ari	Korea	Repressed anger causes insomnia, excessive tiredness, acute panic, fear of death, indigestion.
Koro	South China, Southeast Asia, India (Assam)	Intense anxiety that the sexual organs will recede into the body.
Latah	Malaysia, Indonesia, Japan, Thailand	Hypersensitivity to sudden fright or startle, dissociative or trance-like behavior.
Mal de ojo (evil eye)	Mediterranean, Latin America, United States	A fixed stare from an adult causes fitful sleep, crying without cause, diarrhea, vomiting, fever, in a child or an infant.
Mollera caída (fallen fontanelle)	Mexico United States	An infant's depressed fontanelle causes crying, fever, vomiting, and diarrhea.
Qaug dab peg (the spirit catches you and you fall down)	Hmong	Seizures (generally translated as epilepsy).
Shen-k'uei	Chinese populations	Excessive semen loss causes anxiety, panic, dizziness, backache, fatigue, insomnia.
Sin-byung	Korea	Possession by ancestral spirits causes weakness, dizziness, fear, insomnia, anxiety.
Susto, Haak-tsan, Lanti	Latin America, United States, Caribbean, China, Philippines	A frightening event causes the soul to leave the body, anxiety, irritability, anorexia, insomnia, phobias, trembling.
Taijin kyofusho	Japan	Anxiety, fear that part of the body or body odor gives offense to other people.
Zar	North Africa and Middle East	Spirit possession causes shouting, dancing, hitting the head against a wall, crying.

(Source: Adapted from Simons and Hughes 1985:475–497)

hospital in the Merced area is a story of the deep cultural misunderstandings that can arise even among well-meaning, concerned people. The story also reveals the power struggle that emerged over the parents' compliance with the doctors' advice for medical treatment.

Lia's parents feared the doctors and did not understand the purpose of the powerful drugs that had such visibly negative effects on their daughter. They were reluctant to discuss their fears with medical personnel and quietly administered her medicine in a manner they believed more appropriate, which meant not giving her the medicine sometimes. The doctors turned to Child Protective Services, which removed Lia from her parents' care and placed her in foster care. Although she was eventually returned, this had a devastating effect on her parents, who never understood how anyone could care for their daughter better than they. From the doctors' perspective, it was important that Lia's parents and the Hmong, in general, understand who has final authority over a person's medical well-being. One of the doctors who treated Lia explained why he believed that removing Lia from her parents was necessary: "I felt that there was a lesson that needed to be learned. I don't know if this is a bigoted statement, but I am going to say it anyway. I felt it was important for these Hmongs to understand that there were certain elements of medicine that we understood better than they did and that there were certain rules they had to follow with their kids' lives. I wanted the word to get out in the community that if they deviated from that, it was not acceptable behavior" (Fadiman 1997:97).

Rather than take an adversarial approach to patient-physician interactions, medical anthropologists such as Arthur Kleinman (1980, 1988) advocate that physicians ask a few simple questions of patients in order to understand their explanatory model: What do you call the problem? What do you think caused the problem?[1] Immigrant patients rarely are in a position to ask physicians and other medical personnel these questions. Their interactions with physicians are often limited because of the short time allocated for patient visits, lack of English skills, and fear that such questions might imply a lack of respect for the doctor's knowledge and authority (Chavez 1984).

The story of Lia and her family also indicates the hostile context surrounding the provision of medical services to immigrants. When immigrants are new to an area, as the Hmong were in Merced, even highly educated people such as physicians can be totally ignorant of the historical forces behind their coming to the United States (Fadiman 1997). The Hmong were America's secret army in Laos, where they fought communists during the Vietnam War years. The Hmong believed that, in exchange for fighting, the United States would take care of them and their families. However, public opinion about the impact of immigration can color their reception, including medical care that is grudgingly given. As an obstetrician at the hospital where Lia was treated commented, "I and my friends were outraged when the Hmong started coming here. Outraged. Our government, without any advice or consent, just brought these nonworking people into our society. Why should we get them over anybody else? I've got a young Irish friend who wants to get a US education and wants to work. He can't get in. But these Hmong just kind of fly here in groups and settle like locusts. They know no shame, being on the dole. They're happy here." When appraised of the high rate of depression among the Hmong,[2] he responded, "What do you mean? This is heaven for them! They have a toilet they can poop in. They can drink water from an open faucet. They get regular checks, and they never have to work. It's absolute heaven for these people, poor souls" (Fadiman 1997:235). Attitudes of this kind form the basis of anti-immigrant movements and public policies targeting immigrant use of medical services.

As Lia's story suggests, immigrants' beliefs about health and illness can greatly affect the course of illness and even life expectancy. The work of Arthur Rubel and his colleagues (Rubel, O'Nell, and Ardon 1984) on Mexicans suffering from *susto*, or soul loss, underscores the power of belief. Believing that one is sick, afflicted, or susceptible to disease can have physical implications and determine the course of an illness. *Susto* sufferers became sicker and, in some cases, died earlier than others suffering the same health problems but not experiencing *susto*. The relationship between mind and body is a powerful one we do not fully understand.

Another example of the power of cultural beliefs was provided by David P. Phillips, a sociologist who examined the influence of traditional Chinese beliefs about birth years and their relationship to diseases (Bower 1993:293). For example, Chinese medical and astrological teachings posit that people born in a fire year—which has a 6 or 7 as the final digit—do not do well when they develop heart conditions. People born in an earth year—ending in 8 or 9—are more susceptible to diabetes, peptic ulcers, and cancerous growths. People born in a metal year—ending in 0 or 1—do not do well when suffering from bronchitis, emphysema, or asthma. Phillips and his associates indirectly tested these beliefs by examining the California death records of 28,169 adult Chinese and 412,632 Anglo controls between 1969 and 1990. The Chinese-American death records were further divided into two groups. One group consisted of those who were born in China, resided in San Francisco or Los Angeles, and did not have an autopsy (a procedure shunned by followers of traditional Chinese medicine). The second group consisted of all the others.

The researchers found that Chinese Americans generally died earlier than Anglos if they had the ill-fated pairing of birth year and disease. When examining deaths among Chinese Americans only, those with the astrologically ill-fated pairings of year and disease died from 1.3 years to 4.9 years sooner than Chinese Americans suffering from the same diseases but not born in the "bad" years. When the two groups of Chinese Americans were compared along the dimension of traditional/modern, women born in an earth year who were more likely to hold traditional views died 3.3 years earlier than other Chinese-American cancer victims. Traditional Chinese-American women born in the metal year who suffered from bronchitis, emphysema, or asthma died 8.3 years earlier than Chinese Americans with the same illnesses but born in other years. Although this is indirect evidence, immigrants' beliefs appear to influence the severity of their illnesses. For anthropologists, this research raises more questions than it answers because it is based on aggregated data removed from individual life histories. How and why do beliefs about birth year influence illness trajectories? Did knowing the birth year of a patient affect the way others treated him or her? Did knowing the birth year's association with particular diseases affect the way patients sought and/or followed medical treatment? Does this evidence suggest that these beliefs are founded on truths that we do not perceive or understand?

"Foreign" medical beliefs can become widespread and penetrate mainstream thought. When the Chinese first came to America in the nineteenth century, their use of medicinal plants, animal parts, and acupuncture was strange to non-Chinese and rarely sought outside Chinatown (Kraut 1994). Today, acupuncture is a subject of common discourse and is increasingly sought by non-Asian Americans. Many medical insurance programs pay for acupuncture treatment. What was once the subject of skepticism and humor is now widely accepted as an alternative, effective medical practice. Knowledge of traditional Chinese medicine has traveled in the United States in response to growing interest in alternative medical practices and as part of the cultural baggage of those who immigrate here. *Traditional* does not mean "unchanging," for practices in the home country are also influenced by history and developments in traditional medical practices abroad that find their way back (Zhan 2001).

The complex multidimensional and multidirectional changes experienced by immigrants, the receiving societies, and the societies "back home," with whom immigrants may maintain important contacts, are often reduced to a discussion about assimilation and acculturation, which are typically presented in simple, unidirectional terms. Often it is assumed that over time immigrants will shed as quickly as possible the cultural beliefs and behaviors they brought with them in exchange for "American" beliefs and behavior (Suárez-Orozco 2000). However, it is sometimes more appropriate, and healthier, for immigrants to retain some of their beliefs and behaviors. Ruben Rumbaut (1997a) has summarized the protective aspect of many beliefs and behaviors of immigrants, which has led to a number of paradoxes in the medical literature. High-risk Mexican and Asian immigrant women come to the United States with healthful behaviors, including eating a healthy diet and drinking and smoking less than US-born women. Although these women are poor and often deliver without adequate prenatal care, their children are, relatively speaking, born healthy, with low rates of low birth weight (Markides and Coreil 1986; Rumbaut and Weeks 1989; Rumbaut et al. 1988; Williams, Binkin, and Clingman 1986; Yu 1982). In time, however, their behaviors tend to become "American." They are more likely to take alcohol, smoke cigarettes, eat high-fat foods, and engage in risky sexual behavior. Consequently, less positive birth outcomes are correlated with assimilation. Similarly, Mexican immigrant women are less likely than Anglo women or African-American women to get breast cancer. Perhaps related to diet, exercise, and increased income (Vernon et al. 1985; Vernon et al. 1992), their risk increases with more time in the United States. Japanese men in Japan smoke at twice the rate of American men but are diagnosed with lung cancer at half the rate. For Japanese men in the United States, this rate also increases with time. The reason is not totally understood but might be associated with dietary changes, including drinking less green tea, and the stress of living in a society with markedly greater income inequality than in Japan (Bezruchka 2001). As Rumbaut (1997a) has noted, assimilation can be bad for an immigrant's health.

The cultural beliefs immigrants bring with them are not the only things problematic from the perspective of receiving societies. A recurring problem has been the association of immigrants with disease, which socially stigmatizes them as a threat to the public's health. Recent examples include linking AIDS to Haitian immigrants, mental pathologies to Cuban immigrants, and malaria to Mexican immigrants, but this is not a new problem. In 1870s California, whites blamed Chinese immigrants for the spread of smallpox. In 1900, San Francisco's Chinatown was cordoned off by ropes and guarded by police in an attempt to quarantine the Chinese, who were believed to be the source of bubonic plague (Kraut 1994; Shah 2001). In 1906 New York, Mary Mallon, an Irish immigrant, acquired the nickname "Typhoid Mary," which became synonymous with the health threat associated with immigrants (Kraut 1994). In the first decade of the twentieth century, Italians were associated with outbreaks of typhoid in Philadelphia and polio in New York (Kraut 1994). The larger public often viewed these and other "less desirable" immigrants as threats to public health, a threat isomorphic with characteristics such as foreignness, lack of hygiene, and mental inferiority. The screening of immigrants for contagious diseases was a central component of the Ellis Island experience in the late 1800s. The 1924 immigration law mandated that the consulate in the immigrant's country of origin conduct a medical exam before the immigrant's departure for the United States (Kraut 1994).

The social stigma of carrying unwanted disease has left its mark on contemporary immigrants as well. In the early years of AIDS, little was known of its origin. Haitians, however, became associated with AIDS and were the only nationality to be listed as a risk factor for the disease, raising questions about their suitability for immigration and their ability to donate blood (Farmer 1992). The Cuban refugees who came in the Mariel boat lift of 1980 were stigmatized by characterizations of criminal insanity and homosexuality, both of which were associated with threats to the public and its health (Borneman 1986). Mexican immigrants have been associated with rampant fertility, threatening the public health by overburdening its medical and welfare systems (Chavez 1997; Johnson 1995; Zavella 1997). Once acquired, the stigma of being a health menace can be difficult to shed. Such characterizations can mask actual health needs and the structural factors that cause ill health among immigrants, particularly poverty, crowded living conditions, dangerous occupations, lack of medical insurance, and the burdens associated with pariah status.

CULTURAL MODELS AND DISEASE

Less studied until recently has been the way immigrants' beliefs about biomedically recognized diseases differ from those of physicians and other biomedical practitioners. Between 1991 and 1993, I was co-principal investigator in a large study to examine Latinas' (both immigrant and US-born) beliefs and attitudes about breast and cervical cancer and their use of cancer screening tests (Chavez et al. 1995; Chavez, Hubbell, and Mishra 1999; Chavez et al. 1997). In the first year, we conducted ethnographic interviews with thirty-nine Mexican and twenty-eight Salvadoran immigrant women and compared their responses with those of twenty-seven US-born women of Mexican descent (Chicanas), twenty-seven Anglo women, and thirty physicians in northern Orange County, California (Chavez et al. 1995; Chavez, Hubbell, and Mishra 1999; Martinez, Chavez, and Hubbell 1997; McMullin, Chavez, and Hubbell 1996). These interviews were based on snowball and organization-based sampling. Interviews were conducted in the interviewees' language of preference and typically lasted from two to four hours. In year two of the study, we used these ethnographic interviews to help develop a telephone survey that was administered to a random sample of immigrant and US-born Latinas and Anglo women throughout the county (Chavez et al. 1997; Chavez et al. 2001).[3] The telephone survey totaled 803 Latinas, most of whom were born in Mexico (53 percent) or the United States (32.5 percent), with several

Latin American countries also represented, most notably El Salvador (3 percent) and Guatemala (2.7 percent). In year three, we developed and tested an intervention program targeting breast cancer beliefs and behaviors. Our findings suggested that the perceptions of Latina immigrants and physicians about cancer risk factors can be worlds apart, which has implications for doctor-patient communication, adherence to prescribed regimens, and the effectiveness of interventions to alter existing beliefs.

As part of the interview, we obtained from each informant a list of possible factors that might increase a woman's chances, or risk, of getting breast cancer. (See Chavez, Hubbell, and Mishra [1995] for a full discussion of the methods used.) We then selected the most salient factors listed for each group of women and arrived at twenty-nine risk factors. We asked each informant to rank the factors and to explain her ordering. Table 7.2 shows Mexican immigrant women's top-six ranked risk factors and the top six for physicians.

Mexican immigrant women's most important risk factors for breast cancer were hits or bruises to the breast; excessive fondling of the breast was sixth. The relative significance given to these two risk factors suggests the importance of physical stress and abuse as a cause of cancer in the women's cultural model. As one Mexican immigrant woman said: "Bruises to the breast are bad. The breasts are very delicate, so when a child sucks on the breast and leaves a bruise, it's bad. Hits to the breast can also cause cancer. And when the husband massages or squeezes the breast or sucks on it, that, too, can cause cancer" (quoted in Chavez et al. 1995).

For Mexican immigrants, lack of medical attention ranked second. As one Mexican immigrant woman indicated, this reflects a clear sense of the political economy of medicine: "I don't have insurance. In my opinion, if one doesn't have insurance, it's bad because, well, here cures are expensive, and, well, you know, sometimes for many people what we earn is not enough even to eat and live. So when we have these types of illnesses, we don't go to the doctor because of a lack of money" (quoted in Chavez et al. 1995).

They also emphasized cigarette smoking, birth control pills, and breast implants. These risk factors suggest that the lifestyle choices women make can possibly lead to breast cancer.

TABLE 7.2

The Six Highest-Ranked Breast Cancer Risk Factors for Mexican Immigrants and Physicians in Orange County, California

Risk Factors	Mexican Immigrant Women's Ranking	Physicians' Ranking
Hits/bruises to the breast	1	26
Lack of medical attention	2	11
Smoking cigarettes	3	10
Birth control pills	4	13
Breast implants	5	15
Excessive fondling of breasts	6	29
Heredity, family history	7	1
Getting older	25	2
Having first child after age 30	21	3
Never having a baby	23	4
Obesity	17	5
Hormone supplements	16	6

(Source: Chavez et al. 1995)

Physicians emphasized risk factors found in the epidemiological literature. As Table 7.2 indicates, physicians ranked heredity or a family history of breast cancer first and foremost, followed by getting older (aging), having a first child after age thirty, never having a baby (the preceding two relate to not having the periods of interrupted estrogen production that occur during pregnancy), obesity, and hormone supplements (continued exposure to estrogen).

As Table 7.2 suggests, the correlation between Latina immigrants' views of important risk factors for cancer and those of the physicians is an inverse one. The risk factors ranked as important by the immigrant Latinas were ranked as unimportant by the physicians, who claimed these to be superstition or off the radar of contemporary epidemiological research. The risk factors the physicians ranked as important were generally ranked as unimportant by immigrant Latinas because they were unfamiliar with such notions or did not see any relevance to breast cancer. These and other findings contributed to the development of questions examined as part of the broader survey conducted in year two of our study.

These divergent models of breast-cancer risk factors suggest the difficulty immigrants may encounter when attempting to communicate with physicians. Immigrants and physicians may not understand much about each other's views. Turner (1987) has suggested the existence of a "competence gap" in biomedical knowledge that impedes effective communication between physicians and their patients. This gap can go both ways. Physicians may not be aware of the beliefs informing immigrants' views of disease and risks. Immigrant Mexican and Salvadoran women might have viewed certain risk factors as unimportant because of a lack of basic biomedical knowledge. Also, immigrant women have definite beliefs about behaviors that, in their view, constitute possible risk factors for breast cancer. These beliefs may derive from a multitude of sources: knowledge transmitted among family and friends, popular media, conversations with health practitioners, and cultural beliefs that are much broader than cancer itself. Indeed, Latina immigrants often located their discussion of cancer in the moral, gender, and material contexts of their lives (Martinez, Chavez, and Hubbell 1997).

SOCIAL AND ECONOMIC FACTORS INFLUENCING ACCESS TO MEDICAL CARE

In the United States, immigrants confront a medical system under assault from many directions, which can make obtaining medical care a major challenge. Frequently, this access is relative to the resources immigrants manage to acquire through their participation in the US labor market. We wanted to investigate this in the study of Latina beliefs and attitudes about cancer. Sociodemographic data collected in year two of that study suggest some of the immigrant women's basic medical needs, shown in Table 7.3.

Latino immigrants in Orange County have, on average, demographic characteristics that set them apart from the US-born population, and these characteristics have important implications for their medical needs. As mean ages in Table 7.3 suggest, Latina immigrants are significantly younger than whites. This trend toward an aging population, especially among non-Latino whites, is expected to continue,

Table 7.3

Sociodemographic Characteristics of Latina Immigrants, Latina Citizens, and White Women in Orange County, A Random Sample Telephone Survey, 1992–1993

	Latina Undocumented Immigrants N = 160	Latina Legal Immigrants N = 311	Latina Citizens N = 313	White Women N = 422
Demographic Characteristics				
Median age	27	33	34	41
% Children <18 living with respondent	81	82	62	49
Median years of schooling	9	9	13	14
Median language and acculturation score (5-point scale)	1.0	1.2	4.2	NA
Current Work Status				
% Employed full-time	24	42	53	51
% Employed part-time	14	10	12	12
% Homemaker	44	31	17	18
% Unemployed, seeking work	10	6	5	3
% Unemployed, not seeking work	9	10	9	6
% Retired	0	1	4	11
Spouse's Work Status				
% Employed full-time	67	80	79	80
% Employed part-time	15	6	2	2
% Unemployed, seeking work	16	7	6	3
% Unemployed, not seeking work	3	4	4	2
% Retired	0	2	10	13
Household Income				
% <$15,000	76	46	14	10
% $15,000–$24,999	17	31	23	12
% $25,000–$34,999	4	8	12	10
% $35,000+	1	15	51	68
Medical Insurance				
% Private insurance	21	52	77	85
% Government insurance, Medicare, Medi-Cal, IMS, etc.	18	13	13	14
% Medically uninsured	61	35	10	1
% No regular source of medical care	41	16	4	2

(Percentages may not add up to 100 because of rounding. Source: Chavez et al. 1997.)

with people sixty-five and older expected to increase to 37 percent of the population by 2050 (US Bureau of the Census 1996). The United States will find ever greater proportions of its medical expenditures going toward geriatric care and illnesses related to aging.

However, the majority of immigrants are concentrated in the younger, working-age bracket, especially in the fifteen to thirty-four age group. Few immigrants are sixty-five and older. Latinas are generally younger than Anglo women. In the study, Anglo women were, on average, in their early forties, approaching the end of their reproductive years. Latinas were in their early thirties, but their age varied with immigration status, most undocumented Latinas being in their late twenties. Latinas were in their reproductive years. An indication of this is the proportion of Latinas who had children under age eighteen living with them. As Table 7.3 indicates, more than 80 percent of Latina immigrants and 62 percent of Latina citizens were living with their minor children, compared with only about half the Anglo women. Although this proportion is high for Latina immigrants, it would have undoubtedly been higher if we had included the Latina immigrants who left their young children in their place of origin.

The age structure of immigrants indicates that medical needs center around maternal and child health care for women and work-related problems for both men and women. These demographic trends also suggest an area of possible future conflict in the politics of medical care: To what degree will maternal and child health care—increasingly associated with immigrants—become less of a priority in a society beleaguered by the needs of its aging native population?

Access to medical services in America, especially for non-emergency medical care, depends on the patient's ability to pay. Lacking a government-sponsored, national health-care system, which would guarantee services for all US residents, patients must prove their ability to cover expenses. Patients can cover medical costs out of pocket, with a direct cash payment for services rendered, an exchange more suited to care from a private physician than a clinic or hospital, where medical costs can quickly become exorbitant. Often required for medical services, especially from hospitals, is proof of third-party payment guarantees, which translate as private or government-sponsored insurance programs. Immigrants are usually at a disadvantage when attempting to meet these financial tests, primarily as a result of the nature of their integration into the labor market. However, not all immigrants are equally disadvantaged. Undocumented immigrants are less likely than legal immigrants and Latina citizens (mostly US-born) to acquire the financial wherewithal and insurance coverage necessary to open the door to medical care. Again, let me turn to data I have collected in Orange County, California, to illustrate these points. Orange County is a particularly good place to examine issues of immigrants' access to medical services because it is one of the wealthiest counties in the nation and boasts good access to health services (Warren 1999).

Latina immigrants in Orange County bring with them a range of human capital assets. These influence their participation in the labor market, which, in turn, affects their acquisition of the resources (income and medical insurance) needed for medical services. Two important factors are education and familiarity with the English language. As Table 7.3 indicates, Latina immigrants (both undocumented and legal) had a median of nine years of education. In contrast, Latina citizens and Anglo women had a median of one year and two years of college, respectively. In addition, Latina immigrants scored low on a standard language/acculturation index composed of five questions primarily related to language use. An undocumented immigration status is also a factor limiting labor market participation, especially mobility.

The information on the work status of women interviewees and their husbands provides insight into the disadvantaged position of undocumented immigrants in particular. (Data were collected during a period of recession in southern California.) With about one-quarter of undocumented Latinas working full-time, they were the most likely of all the women we surveyed not to work outside the household. On the other hand, they were more likely to work part-time. Most of their spouses worked full-time but not in the same proportion as the other groups. Their spouses were also much more likely to work part-time than the spouses of the other women. In fact, they were seven times as likely to work part-time as the spouses of Anglo women and Latina citizens and two-and-a-half times as likely as the spouses of legal immigrants. Both undocumented Latinas and their spouses were also more likely to be unemployed and seeking work than all others. These data suggest that a lack of legal immigration status places immigrants in a disadvantaged position in the labor market. Finding steady, full-time employment can be difficult for them, at least in comparison with legal immigrants and US citizens. Also note that, compared with Anglos, few Latina immigrants surveyed were retired, reflecting the disparity in average ages.

Income data for the families of the women we surveyed showed an inverse correlation with changes in citizenship status. Most (76 percent) of undocumented Latinas clustered in the under $15,000 per year category. Legal Latina immigrants managed to move into higher income categories, but most (77 percent) had annual household incomes under $25,000. In contrast, citizen Latinas were found much more often in the higher income categories, and Anglos predominately in the highest income category. All Latina immigrants have generally low incomes, which, when combined with the likelihood of their having children living with them, suggests that they would encounter difficulties covering out-of-pocket the cost of their family's medical care needs.

Undocumented Latina immigrants were also the most likely to lack medical insurance. As Table 7.3 indicates, few undocumented immigrants had private medical insurance, which is typically a benefit of employment. Some did have government-sponsored insurance, usually prenatal care or Medi-Cal for their US-born children. Overall, though, 61 percent of undocumented Latinas were uninsured, lacking one of the main keys that open the door to non-emergency medical care. Legal immigrants fared better, but more than a third lacked medical insurance. Interestingly, one out of ten citizen Latinas did not have medical insurance, whereas almost all Anglos had access to some form of medical insurance. Not surprisingly, many undocumented immigrants did not have a regular source of medical care. Latina legal immigrants were more likely to have a regular source of medical care, and almost all citizen Latinas and Anglos had a regular source of medical care. A regular source of medical care is highly correlated with health status, and lacking such a relationship indicates a problem area in medical service.

ACCESS TO MEDICAL CARE—A TWO-TIERED SYSTEM?

The study of Latinas and cancer sheds light on additional aspects of access to care that are, no doubt, relevant to other groups as well. If we examine the types of services used by those women in the study who did not have a regular source of medical care, a pattern emerges that correlates with the resources (income and medical insurance) available to immigrants and citizens. As Table 7.4 indicates, undocumented Latinas rely first on public health clinics and then on hospital outpatient clinics, followed by private physicians who can be paid in cash "with no questions asked." For a few undocumented Latinas, hospital emergency rooms are the primary source of care, and this is a costly alternative. Latina legal immigrants turn to private physicians most often, but not to the same degree as Latina citizens and Anglos. Latina legal immigrants also rely on public health clinics and hospital outpatient clinics, with some belonging to health maintenance organizations (HMOs). For Latina citizens and Anglos, private physicians and HMOs are the most important sources of regular medical care. To a certain extent, these patterns suggest that a two-tiered system of medical care exists: one for the medically insured and one for the uninsured, for whom access to medical care is a constant problem (National Health Foundation 1995).

For Latina immigrants without a regular source of medical care, the use of medical services also depends largely on their medical insurance coverage. The uninsured with no regular source of medical care often search out a private physician who will take cash up front for minor health problems. For some, the barriers, including cost and even a general lack of knowledge about how to access medical services, can prove to be too formidable. On March 28, 1989, five-year-old Sandra Navarrette died in Orange County of chicken pox, a childhood disease that is rarely fatal in the area. Her parents were undocumented immigrants from Mexico who did not take her to a hospital until it was too late to save her. They had been in the United States only a short time and did not know where to find medical services (Chavez, Flores, and Lopez-Garza 1992). Unfortunately, for many immigrants who lack medical insurance and experience episodic illnesses or injuries, there may be no alternative to the hospital emergency room as the primary source of medical services. However, emergency room costs can quickly outstrip immigrants' meager resources, and hospitals are then left with unpaid bills (Clark et al. 1994).

Not surprisingly, the politics surrounding the provision of medical

TABLE 7.4

Sources of Medical Care for Immigrant Latinas, Latina Citizens, and White Women in Orange County Who Had a Regular Source of Care, A Random Sample Telephone Survey, 1992–1993

	Latina Undocumented Immigrants N = 160	Latina Legal Immigrants N = 311	Latina Citizens N = 313	White Women N = 422
Private physician	21%	44%	66%	77%
HMO	1%	6%	16%	16%
Hospital outpatient clinic	25%	17%	8%	3%
Public/community clinic or health center	45%	30%	9%	3%
Hospital emergency room	4%	0.4%	0%	0.5%
Other	3%	1%	3%	0.2%

(Percentages may not add up ot 100 because of rounding. Source: Chavez et al. 1997.)

services, including the delivery of babies, stimulate some of the most contentious public-policy debates (Berk et al. 2000; Johnson 1996; Johnson 1995; Mills 1994; Rumbaut et al. 1988; Zavella 1997). For example, former governor of California Pete Wilson made cutting off undocumented women from prenatal care one of his central political concerns (Lesher and McDonnell 1996). California's Proposition 187 in 1994 sought to deny undocumented immigrants access to medical and other social services and to compel physicians and other medical personnel to turn in undocumented immigrants seeking medical services to the Immigration and Naturalization Service (Chavez 1997; Martin 1995). Although most of Proposition 187's provisions were never implemented, because of constitutionality issues, it provides a compelling example of the extent to which medical care, and other social services, for immigrants can become embroiled in public controversy and even nativist sentiment (Calavita 1996; McDonnell 1997).

Proposition 187 was ultimately a symbolic statement about the public's unease with increasing immigration, but the 1996 welfare reform law actually denied immigrants, both legal and undocumented, access to many medical and social services (Shogren 1996). Medicaid use illustrates the impact of this reform on immigrants. Between 1994 and 1997, non-citizens' use of Medicaid, an important government program for support of medical needs, dropped precipitously, from 39.8 percent to 32 percent, a 19.6 percent reduction in the proportion of non-citizens using the program. The Medicaid enrollment for citizens stayed steady before and after welfare reform (30.3 percent to 30 percent) (Fix and Passel 1999). This decline occurred among non-citizens who were below 200 percent of the poverty level, which is generally considered the low-income category. Although closing the door on medical and other social services for immigrants may reduce costs for government programs in the short run, having medically under-served people among us is not a wise policy in the long run. Untreated medical problems become more costly with time. Contagious diseases are best cured quickly—illness does not distinguish between citizens and non-citizens. Facing obstacles to conventional treatment, immigrants often resort to home treatment or alternative curers and dispensers of remedies. From the government's perspective, these alternative health-care providers are problematic because they are unregulated by conventional codes of practice and safeguards.

Unregulated health-care providers emerged as a problem area for regulation after several well-publicized cases of unlicensed persons dispensing medicine and possibly dangerous remedies to patients. For example, a common affliction in Mexico and among Mexican immigrants in the United States is *empacho,* described as a blockage of the intestines caused by food becoming stuck. One remedy sold in Mexico and imported to the United States contains high levels of lead powder, which is especially dangerous for children. In addition, "fake" doctors (practicing medicine without licenses) operate out of clinics in immigrant neighborhoods. Their work comes to light when a tragedy occurs, as happened in April 1998 in Santa Ana, California. A thirteen-month-old child died after receiving treatment from a man who had been practicing medicine at a clinic for nearly a year without a license (Reza 1999). Lay people sometimes dispense drugs or injections of medicine at low cost to customers out of the back rooms of neighborhood grocery stores, bodegas, video stores, and other shops (Guccone and Blankstein 2002; Haynes 1997; Terry 1997). Such activities also come to light after tragedy strikes. For example, in Tustin, California, on February 22, 1999, a toddler died after receiving an injection of penicillin administered in the back room of a gift shop (Reza 1999). Although the child was found to have died from dehydration and not the injected medicine, such cases suggest the health risks posed by the use of clandestine medical treatments and highlight the difficulty of finding adequate medical services from conventional providers (Guccone and Blankstein 2002; Weber 1999; Yi and Jack 1999). However, we still do not understand all the factors related to the use of alternative health-care providers (Chavez and Torres 1994).

My own research and that of others suggest that immigrants turn to alternative sources of health care for many reasons. Such providers include spiritual healers who are effective when illness is believed to be related to spirits or when intervention with the spirit world is required (Fadiman 1997; Holliday 2001). Some illnesses may also require traditional herbal medicines and other paraphernalia found in shops (*botanicas* in Spanish) (Holliday 2001). Many folk illnesses require the services of a culturally appropriate healer who can provide the necessary treatment or herbal remedies. In such cases, immigrants' use of healers may reflect a preference based on cultural similarities and appropriateness (Chavez and Torres 1994). This may be particularly true in the case of spiritual healers, with whom patients share religious beliefs (Chavez 1984; Rubel, O'Nell, and Ardon 1984). Other times, immigrants turn to clandestine practitioners or spiritual healers for medically related practices that the larger society looks upon with disdain or stigmatizes, such as female circumcision and animal sacrifice. When this occurs, it can spur societywide debates, even legal cases, over the limits to society's obligation to tolerate questionable cultural practices (see Shweder, Chapter 9).

For Mexican immigrants, medical care in Mexico, which is not that far away, is an appealing alternative. Reasons for crossing the border include cultural factors, such as familiarity, ability to communicate in a common language, and the convenient availability of drugs over the counter without a prescription. In addition, Mexican immigrants find that health practitioners in Mexico "understand" their health problems, sometimes in contrast to a "bad" experience in a US medical encounter (Chavez 1984). Not surprisingly, the Mexican immigrant women (28 percent) participating in ethnographic interviews for our cancer study were more likely than Chicanas (7 percent), Salvadoran immigrant women (4 percent), and Anglo women (4 percent) to have sought care in Mexico for health problems. This proportion is almost identical to that in a study I was involved with in the early 1980s, in which 31 percent of Mexican immigrants (N = 2,013) in San Diego County had gone to Mexico for medical care at least once since coming to the United States (Chavez 1984).

The frequency of immigrants' use of alternative curers is difficult to determine fully. In our cancer study, we asked informants in ethnographic interviews and respondents in the broader survey about their use of alternative curers. Of the 533 immigrant Latinas surveyed, 3.8 percent had been to a folk healer *(curandero)*, herbalist *(yerbero)*, or spiritualist *(espiritualista)*. This was the same proportion as US-born Latinas (also 3.8 percent, N = 260). Interestingly, Anglo women (7.1 percent, N = 422) were more likely than Latinas to have sought care from alternative healers. More interviewees thought that one or more of these alternative healers could cure certain types of cancer: 12.8 percent of Latina immigrants, 15.5 percent of US-born Latinas, and 21.9 percent of Anglo women. As these findings suggest, not only immigrants seek alternative answers to questions about health and spiritual well-being. Anglos and other natives turn to spiritual healers and seek the curing power of crystals, prayers, and other non-biomedical alternatives (Baer 2001; McGuire 1988).

Ethnographic interviews in our study with Latina immigrants suggest that folk healers are good for certain ailments, especially stomach problems and folk illnesses such as *empacho, mollera caída, bilis,* and *susto.* Many Mexicans (26 percent), Salvadorans (29 percent), and Chicanas (15 percent) said that they would go to a *curandero* if a problem required it. Ethnographic interviews also suggest that Mexican and Salvadoran immigrants place much stock in the efficacy of herbal remedies, with almost half the Mexicans (49 percent), Salvadorans (46 percent), and Chicanas (48 percent) indicating that they would seek care from an herbal specialist. Herbal remedies, especially teas or salves, were suggested for a plethora of health problems, including stomach problems, bile problems, nerves, diabetes, colic, diarrhea, skin rashes, congestion, headaches, menstrual cramps, sore throat, kidney problems, and many more. Importantly, seeking care from a doctor did not preclude trying herbal remedies, and vice-versa.

Although some informants said that they went to an herbal special-ist or to Mexico, where good herbal remedies are sold in stores and by street venders, many more indicated that herbal and other remedies are part of everyday knowledge and could be found around the house, bought at a pharmacy, or borrowed from a neighbor. They used teas, especially mint tea *(yerba buena)*, and common remedies such as aspirin, Tylenol, wood alcohol, Vicks VapoRub, and cold medicines. Informants indicated that they would typically try to cure, at home or with the help of a relative or friend, mostly "minor problems" such as colds, sore throats, flu, headaches, stomach aches, fevers, small cuts, abrasions, and sore muscles. As a twenty-seven-year-old Mexican immigrant said, "Sometimes I try to treat [problems] that are not serious [at home]. Let's say someone has a fever. You might try and cure that using Tylenol, or alcohol. That's what we Hispanics use. It's part of our cul-ture. It comes from our parents, who inculcated us, taught us that sometimes a bath and rubdown with alcohol reduces the [body's] tem-perature. That's why we don't go to a doctor, but try and cure a fever with Tylenol and an alcohol rubdown, and that's it."

Importantly, immigrants' social networks serve as a safety net that provides many social and cultural resources, including health remedies, and reinforces ties and solidarity among local neighbors and family (Menjivar 2002). Among our ethnographic interviewees in the cancer study, 18 percent of the Mexican and 21 percent of the Salvadoran immigrants had turned to a friend when they needed medical advice. For example, a sixty-seven-year-old Mexican immigrant woman said, "We have a very close friend who has almost forty years working in the university hospital. And he helps not just us, but everyone who asks him for advice he is ready to help. He advises us because he knows a lot about medicine because he works in an operating room, and he comes and he sees us and gives us advice. For example, my son last Sunday had a bad pain in his stomach, and we called him [the friend], and he told us that it was his appendix and that we should take him immediately to the doctor."

Cecilia Menjivar (2002) has noted that among Guatemalan immi-grants in Los Angeles, health remedies are also part of the resources transmitted by transnational networks. Our ethnographic interviews with Mexican and Salvadoran immigrants support Menjívar's observation. A Mexican immigrant said that, after noting the importance of vitamins for her gastritis, colon, stomach, and bile, she also took something for her liver, which she said "is prepared," noting, "They send it to me from Guadalajara [Mexico]." A twenty-eight-year-old Salvadoran immigrant said, "The majority of remedies I have brought to me from El Salvador. There are many herbs that can be used to cure, for example, for body pains. There are many herbs there that I know how to use, that are sent to me from El Salvador."

In sum, immigrants, such as those from Mexico and other parts of Latin America, often find medical services difficult to access. They face a host of social, economic, and cultural barriers. However, immigrants are resourceful, often turning to the medical knowledge of family and friends and sometimes of alternative medical practitioners to meet their health-care needs.

INTERVENTIONS

Up to this point, we have examined the interwoven cultural and structural factors that complicate immigrants' use of medical services. Many anthropologists working with immigrants also attempt to "do something" with their research, to apply what they have learned to policy issues or toward improving conditions for the people with whom they have conducted research (Farmer 1999). There are many ways to accomplish this task. One is to work toward changing public policies and laws that restrict immigrants' use of medical services. Anthropological findings can inform legislation and be brought to bear in lawsuits. Anthropologists sometimes work directly with immigrants in non-governmental agencies, providing services and knowledge to assist individuals in the acquisition of care. Another approach is through the development of intervention programs that test a theory of how best to introduce changes.

Medical interventions often seek to change existing beliefs and behaviors, typically focusing on the patient. I have helped develop and implement an intervention with the goal of introducing biomedical beliefs about breast-cancer risks in a culturally appropriate and sensitive manner. Although I believe that we were successful, my experiences also made clear to me both the strengths and weaknesses of such interventions, particularly the focus on individuals instead of the broader, societal factors influencing immigrants' use of medical services. After a brief overview of the intervention, I will discuss critical problems with this approach.

Using the knowledge we gained from ethnographic interviews with Mexican and Salvadoran immigrant women, we developed an intervention aimed at introducing biomedical ideas about risk factors for breast cancer and increasing their practice of breast self-examination and routine mammography (Chavez, Hubbell, and Mishra 1999; Mishra et al. 1998). The intervention took into account the population's relatively low levels of formal education, low income, and preference for the Spanish language. Moreover, we felt that it was imperative to incorporate the Latinas' beliefs into the intervention rather than dismiss them as silly or folkloric. In addition, we were sensitive to the concept that the separation of health problems from a target population's belief systems and daily routines may diminish the effectiveness of health education efforts (Bandura 1982). Finally, we wanted to design an intervention that would have the best chance to change not only knowledge and attitudes but also behavior.

With these considerations in mind, we modeled the intervention on Bandura's theory of behavioral change (Bandura 1977, 1982) and on Freire's empowerment pedagogy (Freire 1970, 1971). In brief, Bandura's theory predicts that individuals will change their self-efficacy (beliefs about their own power, their own abilities) after they have mastered a task and experienced its effectiveness. An increased sense of self-efficacy leads to changes in behavior that may produce improved outcomes. For example, a woman is more likely to perform breast self-examination if she feels competent to do it. If a clinician validates a woman's findings, she will feel more competent in routine self-examination. The intervention also employs lessons learned by Paulo Freire during his literacy campaigns in developing countries, based on Bandura's theoretical perspective. Latinas in our study share many cultural and socio-economic attributes, such as low levels of formal education, with groups that have already been helped by his empowering pedagogy. Freire found that individuals with low educational attainment absorb new information best when it is presented in a way that relates to their current environment and life circumstances. Therefore, the educational process should allow students to introduce into the educational setting any issues that relate to their broader social context and affect their beliefs about the health problem (in this case, breast cancer). The educator then empowers the students to make breast cancer control their own problem instead of the educator's. Through this strategy, the educator and the participants become involved in an interactive process that leads to more information sharing about breast cancer–related beliefs and enables the women to become actively involved in a problem-solving process that may result in their improved health.

The theoretical model for the intervention stressed the need for the learner to "own the problem." Freire developed what he termed a "problem-posing" educational method. He contrasted the problem-posing method with the banking concept of education, wherein "knowledge is a gift bestowed by those who consider themselves knowledgeable upon those whom they consider to know nothing" (Freire 1970). He explains that the banking concept reinforces the individuals' fatalistic perception of their situation and, consequently, does not allow students to shape their own actions to achieve needed change. By contrast, the problem-posing method presents a particular situation to students as a problem to be solved by the group. This model of learning encourages the individual to analyze the way she perceives reality. Within this framework, the educational process involves "give and take" communication. In an open dialog with the educator, students can internalize and evaluate critically the information they receive. Given such an educational environment, students become intimately involved in the subject, and the solutions that are developed will likely be applicable to their own lives.

We pilot-tested an empowerment-model intervention in a university-affiliated community clinic in Orange County. During each session, a health educator posed questions designed to encourage thought and discussion about the potential impact of breast cancer on the lives of the participants, about risk factors and symptoms of breast cancer, and about prevention and treatment of the disease. The educator then guided the group to come up with solutions to the problem of breast-cancer control. We obtained measures of breast cancer–related knowledge, attitudes, and practices before, immediately following, and six weeks after the intervention in the experimental group and in a con-

224

trol group that did not receive the intervention. Results of this pilot test enabled us to determine the effectiveness of the empowerment methodology in improving breast-cancer control among Latinas.

The results of our pilot test have been published elsewhere (Chavez, Hubbell, and Mishra 1999; Mishra et al. 1998). Suffice it to say that we were successful in our efforts to introduce new ideas and methods to detect breast lumps without denigrating pre-existing beliefs. However, a major strength of our approach was also a major limitation. The intervention we developed works well with small groups. It relies on individuals to transmit their new understandings to relatives and friends in a snowball effect. This is a very time-consuming method. Although it may have effectively changed beliefs and behaviors of individuals, it did nothing to alter the structural obstacles encountered by Mexican immigrant women, and other low-income people, when seeking medical services. We were faced with a very real dilemma. We could increase awareness of the positive value of preventive care and use of cancer-screening exams and, thus, the desire to obtain such care. However, we could do nothing about the cost of medical care, financial screening, lack of medical insurance, English language skills, and immigration status, to name a few of the structural barriers for Mexican immigrant women.

We did "a little good" but realized, with frustration, that only fundamental changes in embedded societal inequalities would have a real and lasting impact on immigrants' lives and well-being (Farmer 1999). Ultimately, many of the greatest threats to immigrant health and their use of medical services lie outside their own beliefs and behaviors. These are related to the growing gulf between the haves and have-nots in American society. Stephen Bezruchka (2001), an M.D. who teaches at the University of Washington's School of Public Health, summed up the problem well: "Research during the last decade has shown that the health of a group of people is not affected substantially by individual behaviors such as smoking, diet and exercise, by genetics or by the use of health care. In countries where basic goods are readily available, people's life span depends on the hierarchical structure of their society, that is, the size of the gap between rich and poor."

Medical interventions focusing on the individual may make positive, important incremental changes in individual lives. However, immigrants (and many poor citizens) would benefit hugely from higher wages, mandatory medical insurance provided by employers, a national health-care system, increased funding of ESL (English as a Second Language) classes, more enforcement of fair labor standards and practices, and even a greater public recognition that immigrants are not a drain on social services but are contributing members of society.

MEDICAL ANTHROPOLOGY AND IMMIGRATION— A MUTUAL BENEFIT

Finally, medical anthropology and immigration research are not mutually exclusive interests. They are mutually beneficial. My own research has been an example of this point. An attention to medically related issues and problems has helped me better understand the immigrant experience. The first study I conducted on immigration had, as a special component, the use of medical services (Chavez 1984; Chavez, Cornelius, and Jones 1985). At the time, public discourse characterized immigrants, especially Mexicans, as over-utilizing medical resources and becoming a burden on society. Our study sought to introduce empirical research into the debate. Even though the impetus for our research was to fill what we perceived was a gap in knowledge, it quickly became clear that health beliefs and health care were important in the lives of the people we interviewed. Their experiences, fears, and frustrations applied to them not just as immigrants but also as human beings suffering illness, injuries, and stresses in their lives. The formidable obstacles they faced in trying to alleviate these problems were not theirs alone but were extreme examples of obstacles also encountered by low-income and marginalized citizens.

It is here that immigration studies and medical anthropology are so mutually beneficial; ultimately, both are about understanding the human experience. Because our research seeks to be holistic in its approach and perspective, it is wise to remember that health and use of medical services are not separate from working conditions, living conditions, the politics of belonging to society, and the allocation of resources and benefits. We cannot fully understand the range of meanings and limitations of concepts such as citizenship, community, and social integration without attending to the health and well-being of immigrants.

Notes

Acknowledgments: An earlier version of this chapter was prepared for the seminar "Anthropology and Contemporary Immigration," organized by Nancy Foner and held at the School of American Research, in Santa Fe, New Mexico, from October 7 to 11, 2001. I am indebted to all the participants and the anonymous reviewers for their generous suggestions and comments, and especially to Nancy Foner. I am also grateful for Cathy Ota's thoughtful comments. Any limitations in this chapter are mine alone.

1. Kleinman suggests eight questions: What do you call the problem? What do you think has caused the problem? Why do you think it started when it did? What do you think the sickness does? How severe is the sickness? What kind of treatment do you think the patient should receive? What are the chief problems the sickness caused? What do you fear most about the sickness?

2. See Dressler (1996, 1999) and Janes (1990) for a discussion on the impact of stress on migrants' well-being. See also Cervantes, Salgado de Snyder, and Padilla (1989) for the incidence of post–traumatic stress disorder among refugees and labor migrants from Mexico and Central America.

3. Trained bilingual women interviewers from the Field Research Corporation in San Francisco conducted the telephone survey from September 1992 to March 1993.

8

Anthropologists, Migrants, and Health Research
Confronting Cultural Appropriateness

Jennifer S. Hirsch

And if a stranger sojourns with thee in thy land, thou shalt not wrong
him....The stranger that dwell with you shall be to you as one born
among you, and thou shalt love him as thyself, for you were strangers
in the land of Egypt.

—*Leviticus, 19:33–34*

In the autumn of 2000, I received a frantic phone call from an epidemiologist at the Centers for Disease Control and Prevention (CDC).
She was investigating a syphilis outbreak among Mexican migrants in
rural Alabama and told me that the CDC team was having trouble getting the infected men to speak with them. She wondered whether I, as
an anthropologist, could suggest the best way to approach these men. It
seemed that she wanted me to let her in on the secret handshake. As a
putative expert not just on Mexican migrants in general but also—even
better—on Mexican migrants and infectious diseases, what could I tell
her that would make them trust her enough to talk?

Anthropologists who conduct research with migrant groups sometimes find themselves called on to explain the behavior or experiences
of the people with whom they work, either in the court of public opinion or in official discussions about policy formation. This is true in not
only the area of health and medical services research but also any area
in which public policy might conceivably draw on academic research

(for example, see *Boston Globe,* June 29, 2001; *Newsday,* September 15, 1999 and March 20, 2001; *New York Times,* May 31, 1998; *Columbus Dispatch,* March 25, 1998; *Washington Post,* March 22, 1998).

This chapter attempts to sort through several issues involved in deciding how to respond when called on. To a non-anthropologist, it might seem obvious that an anthropologist, when asked about migrant health, would talk about culture. However, within the discipline, we have moved far from the idea that the proper domain of a cultural anthropologist is exclusively culture. Medical anthropologists Nancy Scheper-Hughes (1992), Paul Farmer (1999), and Richard Parker (2001) have argued recently that the reach of both our theoretical and our applied work has been hobbled by an over-investment in the importance of cultural difference. Critical medical anthropologists, however, have largely failed to explore the way in which the knowledge we produce is shaped not only by our own theoretical frameworks but also by the desires of the audiences to whom we are, or might be, speaking. Regardless of theoretical advances in the discipline, anthropologists in public health continue to face the fact that people call in an anthropologist when they want to hear about culture—and in particular, about culture as a barrier to complying with certain desirable behavior (as in the opening anecdote). The demand for "culturological" explanations exists independently of our willingness to produce them.

As we develop a research agenda for anthropology and migration, it is urgent to draw on recent developments in anthropological theory and practice, but it is equally urgent to consider how the knowledge we produce fits into broader political economies of knowledge, serving certain political agendas and silencing others. In this chapter, I make this point primarily through an exploration of different ways in which public health research on migrants has incorporated the concept of culture. As I discuss in the conclusion, though, this point applies more broadly to other substantive areas of the ethnography of immigration. Shweder (see Chapter 9) argues that anthropologists might "rise to the moral challenges posed by cultural migration" by using our position as experts on cultural diversity to help our evermore multicultural society "distinguish between a defensible pluralism and the indefensible position of radical relativism." Here, I make a different point about culture and the moral challenges of migration. Without denying the critical role we can play in fighting ethnocentrism, I caution that exaggerating the importance of culture as a determinant of health outcomes can do a real disservice to those for whom we presume to speak.

In this chapter, I propose that we conduct research on migrant health within a framework of "liberation anthropology" as a way of resisting the demand for the very sort of anthropological work on culture and health that the CDC epidemiologist asked me to provide. (As I will explain, the pat answer she seemed to be seeking promotes a limited understanding of the determinants of ill health.) In *Death without Weeping*, Nancy Scheper-Hughes (1992) writes about how a variety of factors—social inequality, political oppression, the social myopia of physicians, and the poor's own variously constituted reasons for avoiding acknowledging that they are on the brink of starvation—have created an epidemic of *nervos* in rural northeastern Brazil, in which people perceive their illness to be primarily characterized by emotional fragility, treatable by pills rather than by food. As part of an attempt to develop a "liberation medicine" that parallels Latin American experiments in liberation theology, she suggests that another option exists and that medicine can be a "critical practice of freedom" (1992:215). Doctors can work to alleviate both physical suffering and the social inequalities that produce it. As she writes, "We might have the basis for a liberation medicine, a new medicine, like a new theology, fashioned out of hope" (1992:215).

Scheper-Hughes' work also suggests the possibility of an anthropology of liberation; a key role for the ethnographer-writer is to give "voice, as best she can, to those who have been silenced" (1992:28). Liberation anthropology, however, would involve not just a sensitive form of ethnographic storytelling and a keener ear for community members' pain. It would also involve, like liberation theology, a commitment to social analysis that reveals the underlying causes of suffering and ill health, including the pathogenic role of social inequality (Farmer 1999:5). To contribute to the broader project of liberation anthropology, medical anthropologists must explore cultural influences on health and healing, but they must also go far beyond this.

In the first part of this chapter, I argue that the nature of ethnography in immigrant communities obliges us to embrace the role of spokesperson and advocate. Unless we agree that we should answer when asked, there is little point in discussing the political implications of whatever response we might craft. Next, I discuss how public health has integrated the concept of culture and examine the political implications of these cultural explanations of health. I argue that when anthropologists who work on migrant health are asked to provide explanations about culture and health, we should push to reframe the question so that it explores more broadly the determinants of migrant health. In the third section, I use examples from my own research with Mexican migrants in Atlanta to demonstrate how we might do this and thus produce theoretically sophisticated research that articulates clearly with critical policy questions—in other words, how we can not only provide grist for the culture mill but also raise questions about the prevailing models of determinants of immigrant health, about the interests served by an oversimplified model of culture, and, ultimately, about the politics of knowledge about immigrant health.

ETHICS, ETHNOGRAPHY, AND RESEARCH WITH MIGRANTS

Our ethical obligations to the migrants who are the subjects of our research stem from three sources: (1) our general ethical responsibility as social science researchers to avoid harm to our subjects, (2) the ways in which the particular vulnerabilities of our immigrant subjects may facilitate entrée into their communities, and (3) the dependence of Americans on the exploitation of immigrant labor for our very high material standard of living.

In a sense, my invocation of the idea of liberation anthropology is merely a translation of anthropologists' primary ethical responsibility, as stated in the ethics statement of the American Anthropological Association (AAA): "To avoid harm or wrong, understanding that the development of knowledge can lead to change which may be positive or negative for the people or animals worked with or studied" (AAA 1998:section IIIA1, paragraph 2). The liberation anthropology framework adds a level of critical reflection, however, to the principle that we should first do no harm. It suggests that the onus is on us not merely to avoid exploiting migrants as individuals but also to reflect on how our work can be used to the detriment of their communities.[1] Our representations of immigrant communities can shape what the American public thinks about these communities and thus cause material damage or produce real benefits for those same communities. Our history as a discipline in the area of research on race and ethnicity should remind us of the importance of thinking critically about the political implications of the knowledge we generate.

The political and economic vulnerability of many immigrant communities adds another level of obligation to our generic responsibility to consider the implications of how we represent the communities with which we work. The Code of Federal Regulations for the Protection of Human Subjects (1991) specifies that research with vulnerable populations, such as children, prisoners, and pregnant women, be subject to a higher level of review. The reasoning is that where the risk is greater, the benefit to be gained from such research must also be greater in order to justify the research. To some extent, this may be true of all immigrants who, as individuals and communities, feel apprehension related to how the stories we tell about them to the broader American public might affect their ability to find work and housing and coexist peacefully with other groups.

Some may feel more vulnerable, however, to the winds of public opinion than others. Indian software engineers in southern California have less reason to care about how their non-immigrant neighbors perceive them than do Mexican migrants in Cobb County, Georgia, where an English-only law has been debated, off and on, since the late 1990s. However, given that many of those software engineers may be in the United States on temporary visas and that the number of these visas is set every year by Congress, they also have reason to worry about making a good impression on their local and national neighbors.

The disparity in language skills and access to resources between researchers and our immigrant subjects may also make immigrants feel less able to reject our advances than they would in their sending communities. During seven months in rural Mexico conducting research on gender, sexuality, and reproductive health in a migrant-exporting community, I usually felt that those I visited welcomed me as a pleasant distraction but that all I had to offer them was the marginal prestige conferred by a visit from *la gringa* (which I inferred from the hurt looks of those who asked why I never visited them) and my willingness to serve as a courier, taking letters, cards, and small gifts between

Degollado and El Fuerte and Atlanta. As with any anthropologist from a rich country working among the poor, there was always the possibility that people spoke with me because they wanted to extract gifts or even money from a well-funded anthropologist trying to develop rapport. Occasionally, I did bring gifts to the women I interviewed, and I was usually happy to buy ice cream, some tacos, or an *agua fresca* for their children. In general, though, I needed them more than they needed me: They spoke the language perfectly and were the insiders.

Furthermore, when far from home, we are subject to constraints of politeness imposed upon guests. If we speak out too often, too vociferously, or against the wrong people, we may face problems with visa renewal, research permits, and access to the very people with whom we have invested so much time in developing rapport. Even in Mexico, which, although far from being a perfect democracy, is hardly a totalitarian society, one acquaintance constantly threatened to invoke Article 33 of the constitution and have me thrown out of the country.[2] Although he was joking (and Article 33 is seldom invoked), he made it clear to me that he resented my presence, that he thought I was a bad influence on his wife, and that I was a guest in his community.

The limited usefulness of anthropologists on foreign soil stands in sharp contrast to their influence on native turf. Although I repeatedly explained to my informants in Atlanta that I was conducting research in order to complete a doctorate in public health and anthropology, several referred to my studies as *trabajo social* (social work). Given the tasks I performed for them, it is not surprising that they thought of me as a free, full-time social worker who had adopted several families in their immediate community. To gain entrée into the community and establish a framework for regular participant observation, I made doctor's appointments, drove women on errands, and translated in a variety of settings.[3] My help, in and of itself, was not exploitative, but this method of establishing relationships with an immigrant community suggests a very different interpersonal power dynamic than one in which the anthropologist arrives at a field site knowing nobody, barely speaking the language, and having little sense of local norms and customs. Favors provided in the normal course of ethnographic fieldwork—even when offered with the best intentions—may influence migrants to consent to the interview process or to answer specific questions out of fear that if they do not cooperate the anthropologist would cease to offer these favors. These small gestures to ease the pain of settlement may make entry into communities in the United States easier than in places where we are visitors.[4] Therefore, a potential for exploitation is inherent in a fieldwork relationship with immigrants such as the ones I shared with my informants—but the opportunity to do good is greater because our voices count for so much more than they might elsewhere.[5]

A final layer of obligation is created by the ways in which all Americans, anthropologists included, enjoy the fruits of immigrant labor —every $1.99 head of romaine lettuce, $3.99 basket of out-of-season strawberries, or boneless chicken breast we buy was likely touched by the hand of an immigrant. The 4,000-square-feet mini-mansions that sprouted up across the Atlanta metropolitan area in the 1990s would have been unaffordable to the middle class were they not built largely by immigrant hands. The immigrant labor that makes goods, services, and real estate so affordable contains an infrequently acknowledged cost. In 1999, more than half of the fifty construction fatalities in Atlanta occurred among Latinos (*Mundo Hispanico,* June 7, 2000; *Atlanta Journal Constitution,* September 4, 2000b). Nationally, Latinos (many of whom are immigrants) are over-represented in our nation's most hazardous industries (*New York Times,* July 16, 2001). In Atlanta, a Mexican immigrant recently fell to his death during the construction of Emory's Whitehead research building, which I pass daily on the way to my office. Of course, in this age of global capitalism we can trace the relationship between the American standard of living and worldwide exploitation, and the same has been true at least since the age of Mercantilism (see Mintz 1985). Still, it is harder to look away from the damage this does to real bodies when these bodies live right next door. Anthropologists conducting research with migrants will likely disagree on the best way to discharge these ethical obligations. However, because of the political and individual vulnerability of many immigrants, together with the ways in which we benefit from the fruits of their labor, anthropologists who work with immigrants cannot easily ignore the imperative to see themselves as advocates, not just researchers.

CULTURE AND PUBLIC HEALTH

My suggestion that engaging in ethnographic work with migrants inherently commits us to advocacy does not mean that all anthropologists must engage with the legislative process or become community organizers. In keeping with my proposal for an anthropology of liberation, even those anthropologists who see their work as purely academic should consider the political implications of the knowledge they generate. In this section of the chapter, I turn a critical eye on the way the concept of culture has been applied in public health, exploring the concept of cultural appropriateness and discussing some possible reasons for the current enthusiasm for cultural explanations of health behavior. In doing so, I argue that although a real demand exists for immigration research that looks at cultural influences on health, medical anthropologists should be wary of thinking that our most valuable contribution to the anthropology of migration is to produce research on the health beliefs of various migrant communities. True, this may be the product in greatest demand from public health agencies, thus translating most easily into fundable research projects, but it seems worthwhile to distinguish between work that is valued in the marketplace and work that expresses our own most dearly held values.

Over the past four decades, international public health research and programs have increasingly acknowledged how culture shapes the success of public health programs. Often they have looked to anthropologists as experts in community structure and local beliefs (see Coreil and Mull 1990). More recently, minority and migrant health advocates and those charged with serving America's increasingly diverse population have embraced the idea of making health services culturally appropriate and health providers culturally competent. However, the simplistic models of culture employed with increasing frequency in public health research and interventions are leagues from the theoretical state of the art in medical anthropology, which emphasizes the interweaving of culturally constructed beliefs and structurally influenced access to services and living conditions (for example, see Chapter 7; Chavez et al. 2001). I argue here that to conduct unreflexively research that will be used in the pursuit of cultural appropriateness runs the risk of doing a real disservice to those whom we claim to want to help.

The intense focus on culturally appropriate health services and prevention programs cries out for critical analysis because it represents the premier policy discourse through which much of the public sector recognizes and ascribes meaning to differences in immigrant groups.[6] An analysis of government publications promoting cultural appropriateness reveals a simplistic concept of culture, but the problem with cultural appropriateness is not only what it shows but also what it fails to highlight.[7] It suggests that the critical problems with immigrant health relate to health services that are not offered according to the various tastes and preferences of immigrant groups, instead of acknowledging that, in all too many cases, immigrants live in unhealthy conditions, work at dangerous jobs, and have very limited access to health services.

The National Center for Cultural Competence, a federally funded center at Georgetown University, defines *cultural competence* as the capacity to "(1) value diversity, (2) conduct self-assessment, (3) manage the dynamics of difference, (4) acquire and institutionalize cultural knowledge, and (5) adapt to diversity and the cultural contexts of the communities they serve" (from Cross et al. 1989, cited in Goode 2001). Training providers in cultural competence is one step towards providing services that are culturally appropriate—that is, appealing and intelligible to the target population. Inevitably, advocates for cultural competence and cultural appropriateness (for example, Bureau of Primary Health Care n.d.; Cohen and Goode 1999; Goode 2001; Office of Minority Health October 1998, January 2000, February/March 2001) provide statistical and anecdotal evidence of the increasing ethnic diversity of the United States due to immigration and frame cultural competence as a necessary response. For example, the cover article in an OMH (January 2000:1–2) newsletter describes the problems faced by an elderly Bosnian woman with terminal cancer admitted to a health facility: "'She doesn't read, speak or understand English, her Muslim faith requires modesty during physical exams, and cultural beliefs make her family members shy away from discussing end-of-life matters. Many providers are looking for guidance on how to respond to these situations appropriately,' said Julia Puebla Fortier, principal investigator with Resources for Cross Cultural Health Care."

Cultural competence, then, is intended to solve the problem of cultural difference. That this draws on, at least implicitly, decades of research on culture, health, and illness produced by medical anthropologists becomes explicit from even a cursory look at a list of reasons for the necessity of cultural competence provided by one policy brief (Cohen and Goode 1999). These include variation in ethnomedical models and patterns of resort (that is, the patterns in which people self-treat and use health-care services), the diversity of preferences regarding traditional and allopathic medicine, the effect of bias and discrimination within the health-care system, and the under-representation of culturally and linguistically diverse groups in the service delivery system. Although the last two issues have not been major topics of concern to medical anthropologists (for an exception, see Maternowska 2000), the first two have been among the field's most prominent research topics for the past several decades (see Brown 1998; Johnson and Sargent 1990).

The problem with cultural competence is not just the historically static, oversimplified concept of culture deployed in these programs. Cultural appropriateness may make services more attractive to those who are eligible, promoting a consumer-choice approach to improving the public's health, but it does nothing for those who are left out in the cold by the free market. Furthermore, it implies that cultural beliefs are the cause of ill health and, therefore, that programs catering to those beliefs or communicating in a way that acknowledges them can improve people's health. The focus on their beliefs fails to acknowledge that these groups frequently lack the power to transform the conditions in which they live, labor, and reproduce and that it is these conditions, instead of exotic cultural forms, that are the underlying causes of poor health.

Two examples of successful, culturally competent programs give a fuller idea of what cultural competence entails. Sonrisitas (Little Smiles) is an oral-health promotion program sponsored by Colectivo Saber, a school and a community-based organization in San Diego, California. As described in the OMH newsletter (February/March 2001:12), "*Sonrisitas* is a culturally appropriate program that relies on the traditional Latino *promotoras* model to change behavior and educate the community about dental health. The model uses the natural support system that exists within the Latino community. It is an informal system that helps people and families, utilizes existing resources as well as alternative sources of support, and is based on *confianza* (confidence) and *respecto* [sic] (respect). Latinos value interpersonal relationships and turn to individuals to confide in. To assure the success of our *promotoras* model, the community we serve has to respect and have confidence in our promotoras and our message."

It is certainly true that the Latino community may have a "natural support system," but the discussion of the program does not acknowledge the other demands that living in a low-resource community can place on this support system. It also does not acknowledge that the reason a community-based oral-health promotion program is so important for Latinos is that so few have access to dental insurance or, for that matter, to any health insurance. The article further notes that *promotoras* and parents worked together to design the program and that "working together in a collaborative effort is one attribute of the Latino culture. *Colectivismo* (working together) is associated with high levels of personal interdependence and facilitates working in unison to problem solve issues that affect the community.... *Familismo*, seeing the family as the primary social unit and support system, is an important Latino characteristic. The value works to keep parents open to education and information programs that will assist them in keeping the family healthy and well" (OMH February/March 2001:12).

The program review concludes by noting that "in true Latino fashion, the classes conclude with a graduation *fiesta* where the whole family is invited and the participants receive a diploma!" Throughout, the references to Latino values suggest a vision of culture as timeless, unchanging, and internally homogeneous. That sort of approach to culture raises a red flag for most anthropologists, but the larger problems are the lack of contextualization and the idea that fiestas and family values—instead of, say, community mobilization about lack of access to care—are the most productive approaches to improving migrant health.

Cultural Competence: A Journey, a glossy publication produced by the Bureau of Primary Health Care (1999), explains and promotes the concept of culturally appropriate services through examples of how health programs have made themselves more attractive to their target populations. The Park Ridge Family Health Center, in Sunset Park, Brooklyn, is highlighted in a passage titled "Celebrating Competence: Gold Fish

Are Lucky." The population in the late 1980s was primarily Spanish-speaking, but Sunset Park is now home to many Chinese, as well as increasing numbers of Russians, Poles, and Arabic-speaking Muslims. The report notes that most Sunset Park residents avoided the local community health center in spite of its multilingual signs. Executive Director Jim Stiles described how he reacted by doing "a myriad of things that show that we want to be a provider for our neighborhood." These included putting Chinese lettering on the signs outside the clinic and redecorating the interior: "In the center of the waiting room at the Park Ridge Family Health Center, for example, is a fish tank. It improved the atmosphere, officials thought, helped patients to relax, and provided a Feng Shui element of water and sound. But when Chinese patients came to the center, which serves a wide-ranging mix of ethnicities, they were uncomfortable with the tank. It held the wrong kind of fish—gold and yellow fish are needed for luck. So out went the tropicals and in went the gold fish. But there was something else wrong. The tank was sitting under a skylight, and the sun streaming in removed the color and the fortuity from the fish. A shade was installed to cover the skylight." The remaining pages of *Cultural Competence* provide examples of culturally competent service provision elsewhere. The Minnesota Indian Board of Health was open to "healing ceremonies, vision quests, herbal remedies, and visits to a sweat lodge." A community health center in Seattle provided Chinese patients with acupuncture and Southeast Asian refugees with culturally appropriate treatment for post–traumatic stress disorder. The local radio station broadcast a series of dramatic novellas for the Spanish-speaking community in South Dade County, Florida. Latina women suffering from hypertension could take a dance class with salsa music in Oakland, California.

The underlying logic is that cultural competence is necessary because of increased immigration, that targeted efforts towards individual migrant groups will improve the health of the nation as a whole. On one level, of course, cultural competence is hardly a bad thing. Indeed, it is an improvement over its implied alternative, cultural incompetence. Under the rubric of improving cultural competence, Latino community advocates in Atlanta have made real gains, including effective resistance to (and the eventual repeal of) an English-only

ordinance for signs in Cobb County, increased access to higher education for non-citizen children who graduate from Georgia high schools,
shelters for day laborers, attention by the Federal Occupational Safety
and Health Administration to the high proportion of construction
fatalities among Latino workers, and, most recently, a collaborative
effort to increase compliance with Title VI of the 1964 Civil Rights Act
by ensuring that clinics receiving federal funding provide adequate
access to medical interpretation.

The emphasis on cultural competence, however, can lead to problematic assumptions about how best to improve immigrant health. For
one, to suggest that people who "have culture" need special programs
to entice them to use health services seems mildly patronizing.
Presumably, "culture free," white, native-born Americans do not.
Improving health services for those who qualify for government-
funded care is praiseworthy but does little to help the millions of immigrants who are not provided with health insurance by either the
individuals and companies for whom they work or the government to
which they pay taxes. In Georgia alone, the thousands of Mexican
women who give birth every year have not been eligible for prenatal
care from Medicaid since the 1996 federal welfare reform. Another
reason to be wary of overemphasizing the health beliefs of migrant
groups is that popular representations of these groups can use their
sexual, nutritional, or healing practices as a way of exoticizing them.
For example, a recent article in the *Atlanta Journal Constitution* (April
17, 2002) opens by describing "horror stories" that have followed the
Hmong in America: "There was the Hmong Shaman in Fresno, Calif.,
who chanted incantations while a German shepherd puppy was publicly bludgeoned. And the Hmong mother in St. Paul, Minn., who
strangled her six children to death. And there have been many other
incidents—of Hmong exorcisms and opium use, polygamy and kidnap
marriages...." Of course, not all writing about migrants' health in the
popular press sensationalizes their supposed beliefs and behaviors.
However, articles such as this one remind us that ethnographic descriptions of cultural variability in health and healing can be used to emphasize our newest neighbors' most exotic aspects, instead of what we all
have in common.

Even beyond debates about the role of culture in shaping access to health care, focusing on health care as a determinant of overall health overlooks the role of underlying structural factors. Immigrants are typically (but, of course, not always) poor. They are also over-represented among the uninsured and in the nation's most hazardous occupations, such as construction, farming, meat processing, and garment work (see Frumkin, Walker, and Friedman-Jimenez 1999; *New York Times* July 16, 2001). Many live in substandard housing in neighborhoods with the heaviest burden of environmental contamination. Poorer health outcomes are more common among people marked by ethnic or racial difference, but acknowledging this cultural difference will not make these immigrants healthier.

The most problematic aspect of the cultural competence paradigm is that it reifies racial and ethnic differences as the key explanatory variables to which we must attend and reduces the salience of social class factors. Research that explores ethnomedical models of health so that program directors can construct a separate, appropriately decorated clinic for each new ethnic interest group does not do nearly as much to improve the health of our nation's immigrants as would some exploration of what these immigrants have in common with poor, working and non-working blacks and whites, for whom "health disparities" are the inevitable outcome of income disparities. The focus on ethnic and cultural differences makes health services an area in which ethnic groups inevitably compete for resources. The interweaving of health services and identity politics works against the recognition of the shared inequalities faced by all the poor, native and immigrant alike. This obscuring of the pathogenic role of social inequality is not just a theoretical point. Health services, along with schools and the marketplace, are critical institutional contexts in which newcomers learn about life in America. One of the key take-home lessons of culturally appropriate services is that developing an ethnic identity in America means learning to vie with other minority groups for a piece of the federally funded pie.

Those committed to an anthropology of liberation, therefore, should be wary of conducting research on the exotic health beliefs of immigrants that will be used for the development of culturally appropriate health services. Rather, the liberation anthropology response is to analyze the public health epistemologies that, for various political, historical, methodological, and theoretical reasons, have come to privilege individual behavior and individual-level risk factors over structural ones (see Krieger 2000; Watney 1999). Cultural competence is the product of well-meaning advocates for minority and immigrant health whose vision of the reach of public health is limited by the current state of the field. They attribute problems to the system's inability to serve certain groups and conceive of solutions that only change the behavior of individuals instead of the system as a whole. The cultural appropriateness framework represents an enormous amount of hard work motivated by genuine concern for and commitment to improving the health of immigrants and the under-served. My goal here is not to be superciliously critical of these dedicated public servants but to show how the current individualist bias in public health limits their efforts. Our job as critical ethnographers should be to point out the political implications of the cultural appropriateness worldview in a way that is intelligible to non-anthropologists.

A second task for the liberation-minded anthropologist is to set his or her sights on the institutions with which migrants come in contact—in this case, to produce an anthropology of public health and health care in the United States. An anthropology of public health might usefully explore why culture has gained such a prominent place of late in the explanatory models of researchers and practitioners. Others have noted how the current appetite for work on cultural factors shaping health draws on material factors such as the changing demographics of the American population (OMH 1998) and on the fact that early HIV prevention efforts are widely understood to have failed because of a lack of sensitivity to cross-cultural variation in sexuality (Parker 2001; Parker and Aggleton 1999; Vance 1991). Widespread popular embrace of the idea that culture matters deserves further reflection. Anthropologists can contribute to the move towards cultural appropriateness in health services in a variety of ways. Rather than merely answer the questions people are most likely to ask us (reporting the necessary information about cultural values and beliefs so that practitioners can shape their programs accordingly), we should pose two questions of our own: Why are people so interested in culture? What else, other than culture, shapes immigrant health? Both of these questions are fundamental for a liberation anthropology approach to migrant health. Answering the first enables us to explore critically the way in which both theoreticians and practitioners have confused cultural difference with structural violence (Farmer 1999:85). Answering the second helps us move beyond this limited vision of culture to describe more accurately the interrelationships of culture, social inequality, and ill health.

REPRESENTING IMMIGRANT CULTURES

That the concept of culture is misused is hardly reason to turn our back on it altogether. In the following section, I draw some lessons from my own research on US-Mexico migration, migrant health, and cultural creativity, focusing particularly on the special contributions careful ethnography can make to our understanding of the interrelationships of culture, political economy, migration, and health. In addition to generating health research that reframes questions about cultural influences, medical anthropologists can push our dialog with the public in the direction of liberation anthropology by presenting ourselves not only as experts on cultural influences on health but also as experts in community-based health research. In describing anthropological research on migrant health in this way, I suggest that we answer people's questions about health in migrant communities by asking the following four questions: (1) What do you mean by "community," and how is that community internally stratified? (2) What institutional or structural factors shape health in this community? (3) Given these external constraints, what health-seeking strategies do people craft? (4) How are things different for the people of this "community" who live elsewhere? By addressing these four questions, we can produce research that better represents the full range of anthropological contributions to health research. What follows explores these questions for one group and draws on my dissertation research, conducted in Atlanta and Mexico in 1995 to 1997, as well as on several other projects with Atlanta's Mexican migrant community.

In response to the first question, ethnography can make a critical contribution by describing the internal diversity of migrant communities and demonstrating the relevance of this diversity for health behaviors and beliefs. My dissertation was designed as a study to compare the dynamics of gender, sexuality, and reproductive health among Mexican migrants in Atlanta and their sisters or sisters-in-law in the rural Mexican-sending community. The project grew out of my long-term interest in how the social constructions of gender and sexuality shape reproductive health practices. It also aimed to contribute to the developing transnational perspective on cross-border communities and migrants' shifting and strategic constructions of identity by showing the influence of specific places and the constraints of social context, which have been often lost from view. As the data collection proceeded, I came to see that although differences in social context contributed to behavioral and cultural variation between women in the two places, a here-versus-there comparison was limited by an unexamined assumption that Mexico-US migration involved moving from a traditional setting to a more modern one.[8] Social science research on migration has been so absorbed in the question of how things change when people move across space that we have sometimes forgotten that the places from which they come are not frozen in a distant, traditional time. Along these lines, I found that migration-related changes in gender and sexuality needed to be placed in the context of a broader, historical transformation in marriage and gender in Mexico. As I discuss in *A Courtship after Marriage: Sexuality and Love in Mexican Transnational Families,* these dual trajectories of change can be summed up by two phrases I heard repeatedly throughout the course of my fieldwork: *"Ya no somos tan dejadas como las de antes"*—"We are no longer as easily pushed around as women of the past"—and *"En el norte, la mujer manda"*—"In the United States, women give the orders" (Hirsch 2003).

This Mexican transformation in the social construction of gender was reflected in generational differences in marital ideals. Women born in the 1920s, 1930s, and 1940s in rural western Mexico described marital relationships there as based on respect, obligation, clear hierarchies of age and sex, and the fulfillment of a strictly gendered division of labor. Their daughters, born in the 1960s and 1970s, described unions organized around ideals of cooperation and shared decision-making, sexual and emotional intimacy, and a less rigid (although hardly egalitarian) distribution of authority. (Even though at a disadvantage in terms of socially structured access to resources, the older women were certainly not submissive, exerting influence in subtle, and sometimes not so subtle, ways, and their daughters were not quite as powerful as they made themselves out to be [Hirsch 2003].) The younger couples I knew, in both Mexico and Atlanta, described how sexual intimacy created and strengthened marital bonds. Differences between the younger and older women's stories show that mutually pleasurable sex has come to be understood as a source of marital harmony, not just a way of producing children and keeping a man's attention from straying. Recalling question one, above, the internal diversity in this community's notions of sexuality, then, were not only due to the rural communities' increasing integration into migrant circuits but also to the changes in rural Mexico itself—and the family lives and relationships there. The profound social and economic changes in this region of Mexico are intimately linked to migration, but to credit migration alone for these changes would be a mistake.

The vast social changes that produced this shift to a more companionate model of marriage have also (not surprisingly) produced diversity in health beliefs, such as women's understanding of their reproductive physiology. For example, Magdalena, a forty-eight-year-old woman of great wisdom but little formal education, explained that infertility is caused by a woman's remaining open *(abierta)* after childbirth, so a baby cannot stick to the inside of her womb. Isabel, twenty years Magdalena's junior and educated at a private Catholic high school in a nearby provincial city, had markedly different views. When I asked her about women who are stuck "open" and need traditional massage to become pregnant again, she looked at me as though I were an idiot and said that women who don't get pregnant must not be ovulating regularly and should have their hormone levels checked by a doctor. Isabel lives in Mexico, but her sisters Blanca and Patricia live in Atlanta, as does Magdalena. Blanca and Patricia's ideas about fertility and reproduction, however, resemble Isabel's much more than they do their neighbor Magdalena's. A well-meaning clinician in Georgia who studies traditional Mexican ethnomedical models, such as those to which Magdalena ascribes, in order to communicate better with his or her patients would hardly find cultural competence useful if the patient in question happened to be Blanca or Patricia. Social class and generational differences create internal diversity in a cultural group, so it is misleading to speak of a culture as a unified whole, as the cultural appropriateness approach often does.

Gender, another critical line of fragmentation in these communities, provides further reason to ask people what they mean by "community." Gender differences in interpretation of culturally constructed beliefs about marital sexuality highlight the importance of exploring socially constructed disparities in power within cultural groups. In rural Mexico and in Atlanta, younger Mexican women have come to see infidelity not just as evidence of a lack of respect (as their mothers did) but also as a profound breach of the intimacy on which marriage is based (Hirsch, et al. 2002). Younger women call on the cultural framework of companionate marriage to question men's right to extramarital sex and men's supposed inability to domesticate their desire. Although many of the younger women's husbands shared some of their ideas about marital companionship and sexual intimacy, most did not embrace the idea that men's infidelity had become unacceptable. Indeed, many men felt that the savvy modern husband should exercise extra caution to keep his misbehavior from his wife. In a social context in which men frequently spend nine or ten months a year apart from their wives while they work as migrant laborers in the United States, gender differences in attitudes towards infidelity have critical implications for the prevention of sexually transmitted diseases, including HIV. The differences in how men and women interpret the meaning of infidelity within companionate marriage remind us that intracultural differences in beliefs are a product of both individual choice and socially structured access to power. Medical anthropologists should insist that portraits of migrant cultures seek out the tensions and disagreements within cultural groups and explore how social stratification shapes these tensions, rather than accept a socially flat portrayal of cultural influences on health. These examples about infidelity and infertility suggest that anthropological research on migrant health can make a valuable contribution by adding complexity to pat statements about what Mexicans—and other migrant groups—believe.

Looking beyond Cultural Factors

In addition to producing more nuanced portrayals of the diversity of health beliefs within migrant communities, medical anthropologists should explore the importance of beliefs relative to other factors in shaping actual behavior, thereby answering the second question about how structural factors influence health. In my dissertation research, for example, although I found Mexican women's fertility goals to be similar in Mexico and the United States, striking differences emerged in preferred ways to achieve those goals. Of the thirteen women I interviewed in Atlanta, seven relied on a modern method such as the pill or IUD. Among their sisters or sisters-in-law in Degollado and El Fuerte, only one had tried such a method, and she discontinued it quickly after being invited to be godmother to a friend's daughter at her first communion. (To be a godparent, you must take communion, and you cannot take communion unless you have confessed. No priest in this region of Mexico would allow a woman with only three children to use an IUD unless a pregnancy would mean her certain death.) The difference in contraceptive preferences is largely the product of differences in the organization of certain key social institutions (the Catholic church, the family, the labor market, the health sector) in rural Mexico and the United States (see Hirsch and Nathanson 2001). Also, a different value is attached to fertility in the two locations. In Mexico, fertility is a precious resource that women fear will be impaired by the side effects of the pill or the IUD. In Atlanta, women weigh the risk of an unplanned child more heavily, wary about the effects on their ability to work outside the home. They also feel greater freedom to choose a method to which their partner objects.[9]

Inevitably, an ethnography of immigrant experience is an ethnography of America. To draw a more rounded picture, we must not only work with immigrants but also include ethnographic (and demographic) studies of the institutions that shape their lives, in order to understand the context within which they make specific choices. The example above highlights the importance of institutions. To attribute the difference in contraceptive practices solely to migration-related cultural changes, such as a change in the value of fertility, would be a mistake. In terms of health institutions, this would mean an anthropology of public health, rather than merely *in* public health. Studying the structure, organization, and constraints imposed by the institutions with which migrants negotiate is the only way to understand their options—and we cannot reasonably interpret studies of individual choices and preferences without information about the (perhaps limited) options available.

Another example that highlights the role of structural factors comes from my research on social ties and HIV risk among Mexican migrant men in Atlanta, which explored how cultural factors (such as men's ideas about masculinity, sexuality, and marriage) and social factors (migrant experience, social networks, and loneliness) shaped men's likelihood of engaging in sexual relationships while they were in Atlanta as temporary labor migrants.[10] The ethnographic and survey data from this pilot study suggest that both social and cultural factors shape men's HIV behaviors (Hirsch and Yount 2001), but in the end what put these men at risk for HIV infection was that they were in the United States (the risk of HIV infection is much lower in rural Mexico). They were forced to migrate and take low-status jobs here on account of dire economic conditions in their home communities and long-standing economic and political inequalities between the United States and Mexico. I make this point not to deprive these men of any agency (after all, some men engaged in extramarital sex and others did not) but to argue that we should attend to not only the choices individuals make but also the broad social and economic forces that limit their options.

Following Paul Farmer's (1999) lead, I have come to be more concerned with the institutional determinants of health than with cultural factors. To explore these institutional determinants of health, I am developing a project, in collaboration with the Hispanic Health Coalition (an Atlanta grassroots Latino health advocacy group) and Atlanta's Mexican consulate, that aims to improve occupational safety and health among day laborers in the construction industry. Nationally, Latinos are over-represented among worksite fatalities (*New York Times,* July 16, 2001). Locally, more than 50 percent of deaths in the construction industry occur among Hispanics (*Atlanta Journal Constitution,* September 4, 2000).[11] When I discussed plans for the project with my colleagues at the Hispanic Health Coalition, their first response was to focus on the cultural barriers to improving occupational safety and health. "You know," some members of the coalition told me, "back home we never worry about things like that. People ride around in the back of trucks in Mexico, even little children. We are not used to taking precautions, wearing masks and things."

Of course, using infant car seats, wearing seat belts, taking cholesterol-lowering drugs, and exercising daily reflect a different worldview and ability to control one's fate than piling into the back of a pickup for an impromptu trip to town and eating tacos in the plaza. Such differences in behavior are not just a product of culture, however. Latino immigrants readily learn to use car seats and buy car insurance when clear institutional supports are in place to encourage their doing so. Most day laborers have little control over the conditions in which they work and even less opportunity to develop task-specific skills that would make it easier for them to carry out their work safely. While the research project is still under development, we hope to educate *contratistas* (contractors) and *subcontratistas* (subcontractors) about workplace safety and their legal obligations to provide a safe working environment.

Negotiating Modernity through Medicine

The third question we might ask as we map out a liberatory approach to medical anthropology research with migrants is how individual strategies are formed at the crucible of culturally constructed beliefs and structural or institutional constraints. For health research, this means looking at how people negotiate strategically through the various systems of service provision. It also implies an open-ended exploration of the goals shaping these strategies. Of course, one goal of seeking health services is to achieve or maintain physical health, but we risk missing a rich symbolic dimension of health behaviors if we assume that this is the only (or even the primary) determinant of health-seeking behavior.

The sight of her growing fetus, for example, fascinated Mercedes, a young Mexican woman in Atlanta. She cajoled me into calling her obstetrician's office and reporting that she was having symptoms of premature labor, solely so that she could have an emergency ultrasound at twenty weeks to learn the baby's sex. She then had me accompany her to the office as a translator. Her evident delight afterwards was not just because she could begin knitting in the appropriate color. She loved the technology, savoring her peek into the future at her baby-to-be and her ability to manipulate the medical system (and me) to give her this opportunity. Other Mexican women I met in Atlanta found it laughable that some women in Georgia broke the law in order to have babies at home (home birth is illegal in Georgia). They did not understand why anyone would choose to have a baby as their mothers did, at home with the *partera*. For them, a physician-assisted, medicated delivery marks middle-class status. The women who come to Atlanta want to deliver in a hospital because they believe that it is safest and because it is the only way to get a birth certificate. Also, they see access to technology as a measure of their successful adaptation to American society. They are making health-care choices that indicate their desire to be modern women.

Learning what people are trying to achieve through their use of specific services helps us see health-seeking behavior as an act of consumption, a way of constructing and performing modern or traditional identity. Even among the poor and uninsured, issues of identity and belonging may be played out through the use of health services. For example, when immigrants prefer traditional healers to allopathic practitioners, how is this related to a preference for services that are familiar and affordable? To what extent are these healing rituals also rituals of identity? Conversely, what are the cultural and social factors that lead to the sort of ethnomedical syncretism we see across the spectrum of American society? In exploring the weaving together of traditional and allopathic approaches, we should push for a theoretical framework that embraces both Mercedes' intense desire for an extra ultrasound and many Americans' fascination with massage, acupuncture, and herbal remedies. Although structural factors (such as employment that provides health insurance) are one explanatory factor, people's desire to position themselves in relation to modernity (expressed through medical technology) also seems important.

Discussions of culture's influence on immigrant health-seeking behavior often assume a fixed set of cultural beliefs that correlate directly with a certain set of behaviors. In contrast, an agency-oriented approach to immigrants' use of the American health-care system suggests that a preference for traditional medicine, for clinics with good *feng shui*, is not inevitable. It is better to start out by investigating immigrants' strategies—including the way they make health-care choices as a way to express who they are, or who they are becoming—as they navigate through the health-care system's many barriers. Questions about how migrants' health-care choices express identity are closely linked, of course, to questions about citizenship, eligibility for Medicaid, and the broader economic structure of the health-care sector. To the extent that culture and identity shape the decisions migrants make about how to heal themselves, however, we should also attend to the possible linkages among modernity, medical technology, and immigrant identity.

Calling for Comparative Research on Migrant Health

Finally, after we describe and explain how the combination of external constraints, shared beliefs, and individual goals shapes health-seeking behaviors in a specific migrant community, the fourth question I suggest would push us toward comparative research, which can highlight the influence of social context in numerous ways. In spite of the recent flourishing of multi-sited ethnographic fieldwork in migrant communities, we still do not know much about how people's lives change as a result of short-term, long-term, and permanent moves between one country and another. Also, there are real challenges to doing even this multi-sited work well. I would argue, however, that it is also crucial to "nest" these multi-sited studies of migration and social and cultural change within studies of cultural and social transformation in the places from which migrants come. My own research on the interweaving of generational and migration-related changes in marriage, sexuality, and reproduction suggests that gaining a clear purchase on how people's lives change with migration is impossible without having some idea of the cultural and social transformations underway in their home country. Given the logistical challenges of finding enough time to do extended fieldwork in one location, much less multiple sites, one solution might be to promote more cross-fertilization and collaboration between migration researchers and anthropologists (or other social scientists) who have conducted—and can conduct in the future—long-term fieldwork in the societies from which large numbers of migrants come.

Comparative studies are vital to unpack and problematize the dominance outside anthropology of purely cultural explanations of migrant health and to help us think more clearly about, and make more useful policy contributions to, the role of culture in migrant settlement. A second kind of comparative work—cross-national comparisons of immigrants, for example, in Canada and the United States (countries with

related streams of immigrants but very different health-care systems)—
would help evaluate the role of culture and the importance of cultural
appropriateness, relative to other determinants of migrant health.
Third, within the United States, comparisons of the experiences of
migrant groups and non-immigrants can also shed light on the relative
roles of various explanatory factors in shaping immigrant health. The
studies should also be designed to bring out the role of social class
among immigrants and non-immigrants alike. To do this well, of
course, it is necessary to foster collaboration among anthropologists
who specialize in different ethnic groups.

Fourth, we need comparisons across locations within the United
States. Much of what we know about migrants is based on research in
Miami, Los Angeles, and New York. Newer migrant-receiving locations
provide markedly different contexts (see Brettell, Chapter 6); migrants
arrive at a particular historical, political, and economic moment in
time. The high rates of construction fatalities among Latinos in
Atlanta, for example, may be related to the low rates of unionization in
the construction trades. In areas where construction work is more heavily unionized (and therefore harder for newcomers to penetrate),
there may be less reliance on day laborers who do not have the chance
to develop task-specific skills. Atlanta ranks high nationally in pedestrian fatalities, and pedestrian fatalities have been a particular problem
among Mexican immigrants (CDC 1999; *Atlanta Journal Constitution*,
September 4, 2000a). This may be less of a problem in cities that have
invested more heavily than Atlanta in sidewalks and public transportation. Furthermore, the physical geography of Atlanta, with its limited
opportunities for safe walking, has important implications for obesity, a
critical area of Latino health. It may not be possible to disentangle all
the complex differences between being the millionth Mexican man to
arrive in pre–Immigration Reform and Control Act, post-recession
California in 1984 and being the 150,000th to arrive in post-Olympic,
pre-recession Atlanta fifteen years later.[12] However, generalizing from
one situation to the next is ill-advised without taking into account the
many contextual factors shaping migrants' experiences and health outcomes.

Jennifer S. Hirsch

CONCLUSION

In this chapter I have argued that the ethical obligations we incur by working with migrants in our own country require us to reflect on the political implications of the knowledge we produce. I applied this critical perspective to anthropological research on migrant health, suggesting that cultural appropriateness—and, more broadly, any research that focuses exclusively on how culture shapes migrant health—is unlikely to contribute to the broader project of liberation anthropology. To push for research on migrant health that advances the broader goals of liberation anthropology, I make two broad recommendations: first, that we turn our critical faculties toward an analysis of the questions we are asked, exploring why culture has come to hold such a prominent place in the explanatory frameworks of health professionals, and second, that we insist on portraying culture in a more nuanced fashion and view it as only one of many factors influencing migrant health. Drawing on examples from my fieldwork in Atlanta and rural western Mexico, I have illustrated how attention to internal social stratification in migrant communities, the social institutions within which migrants navigate, the ways that people use the health arena in making claims about traditional or modern identities, and comparative research design can lead to ethnographic research characterized by a more theoretically sophisticated understanding of the relationship between culture and health. Attending to these factors will also, I have suggested, guide us to produce research that contributes to a liberation anthropology agenda by highlighting, rather than obscuring, how structures of power shape migrant experience.

A conclusion that applies more generally to the anthropology of migration is that all research with migrants is political—political because the questions people ask us derive from a desire to see how migrants will fit into American society, political because the answers we give can be used to argue for or against specific programs or services that will shape the trajectories of migrant settlement. Whether we conduct research on schools (see Stepick and Stepick, Chapter 5), health services (see Chavez, Chapter 7), labor markets, or transnational social institutions or write about the theories scholars use to frame this research (see Glick Schiller, Chapter 4), we ought to frame our research explicitly as part of a larger project of liberation anthropology rather than hide behind the mantle of science to avoid acknowledging the political aspects of our work. Some might argue that, by admitting we are driven by a specific politics, we will delegitimize our findings in the policy arena. Theoretical developments in our field, such as the push for situated knowledge, make clear that conducting research free from bias is impossible. Just as importantly, critical theories provide the tools to expose the costs of research that explores, for example, cultural influences on health without looking more broadly at the pathogenic role of social inequality (Farmer 1999:5). By deliberately considering the agendas served by the knowledge we generate, we can place our research in the service of a vision of America in which we welcome not just the hands that labor for us but also the bodies for which we must care, the minds we must educate, and the hearts whose dreams may not be that different from our own.

Notes

Acknowledgments: The fieldwork on which this chapter draws was generously supported by the Andrew Mellon Foundation through a grant to the Department of Population Dynamics at Johns Hopkins University, the National Science Foundation Program in Cultural Anthropology (SBR-9510069) and the International Migration Program at the Social Science Research Council, and the Emory Center for AIDS Research. I also gratefully acknowledge support from the Fogarty International Center at the National Institutes of Health via its ongoing support for the Emory AIDS International Training and Research Program (NIH#1 D43 TW01042-02). I also acknowledge, in writing this chapter, my very great debt to my dear friend and mentor, Michael Francis Jiménez (August 14, 1948, to September 1, 1991), who on a chilly fall day in 1986 brought an auditorium full of naive, ambitious, self-involved Princeton undergraduates to tears as he lectured about the fall of the Allende regime. Throughout his too brief career, he taught many of us a first, unforgettable lesson about the histories of power, the power of history, and the possibility of doing academic work that matters.

1. The administrative and legal apparatus that has evolved in recent years to ensure that research is consistent with federal guidelines for the protection of human subjects is primarily concerned with the protection of individual rights, whereas here I am pointing to our responsibility to the community. On the issue of community-oriented research ethics, see King, Henderson, and Stein 1999;

National Bioethics Advisory Commission (NBAC) 2001.

2. Article 33 is a provision in the Mexican constitution under which foreigners who are a threat to national security can be deported.

3. The need for interpreters (and drivers) is particularly acute in Atlanta because of the very weak public transportation system and the relative recency of the large Spanish-speaking community. There is a real paucity of second-generation bilingual professionals who can be hired by the health system *(Atlanta Journal Constitution,* July 2, 2001; Sebert 2000; Georgia Department of Human Resources 1994).

4. This balance of power may be particularly skewed in newer migrant-receiving locations, such as Atlanta, where few non-Latinos speak Spanish. In communities with a longer history of migration, more US-born people (as well as, of course, more second-generation immigrants) may speak the native language of these new groups and be able to provide these small favors. For many Mexicans in Atlanta, though, I am the first *gringo* they have met who speaks Spanish.

5. A standard clause in the consent forms used to ensure human subjects' protection in clinical and public health research informs the potential participant that access to services or programs will not depend on willingness to participate in research. To some extent, it might be possible to create an ethnographic parallel to this by offering translation and advocacy to those we interview formally and those we do not. To the extent that we use participant observation as a method of data collection, however, anyone who requests our aid becomes both a potential recipient of favors from us and a potential research subject.

6. Improving the cultural competence of health services is one cornerstone of a recent initiative of the Department of Health and Human Services, "Eliminating Racial and Ethnic Disparities in Health." The initiative, which parallels in focus the current ten-year plan for national health goals *(Healthy People 2010),* concentrates on reducing or eliminating racial or ethnic disparities in health access and outcomes in six areas: infant mortality, cancer screening and management, cardiovascular disease, diabetes, HIV/AIDS, and immunizations (see http://www.omhrc.gov/rah).

7. My data on cultural appropriateness and cultural competence are from *Closing the Gap,* the newsletter of the Federal Office of Minority Health (OMH); the website describing the Department of Health and Human Services' program "Eliminating Racial and Ethnic Disparities in Health"; publications of the National Center for Cultural Competence at Georgetown University; and a publication from the Bureau of Primary Health Care, *Cultural Competence: A Journey.*

8. As I discuss elsewhere, my initial impulse to look at migration and cultural change (in this specific case, migration and gender) was typical of a genre of migration research that looks at the changes associated with migration without inquiring adequately into how the places from which people come might be subject to historical transformation (Hirsch 2003). Linda Anne Rebhun, in her research on love and cultural transformation in rural northeastern Brazil (1999:2), talks about how her informants perceived modernity and geography as interwoven according to a spatial wheel of time in which more urban, centrally located places, in and of themselves, were perceived to be more modern, generating more modern modes of action, thought, and relationships. More rural locations were perceived to be more resistant to change, more remote not just in space but also in time. If we are interested in working with people as they move across space, we need to be alert to our own tendencies to subscribe to these folk ideas about space and time. We must look as hard for rural modernities in sending communities as for urban ones in the United States.

9. Women in rural Mexico have better access to family planning than do their peers in urban Atlanta. They do not face the barriers of language and transportation that immigrants encounter, and several methods (Depo and oral contraceptive pills) are even available over the counter, without the additional barrier (albeit an important one from a preventive-health point of view) of the pap smear.

10. The study "Mexican Men in the Urban South: Social Ties and HIV Risk" was supported through a pilot grant from the Emory Center for AIDS Research.

11. Without knowing what percentage of construction workers in Georgia are Hispanic, we cannot know for sure whether they are under- or over-represented among fatalities. Given that Hispanics represent only about 5 percent of the state's overall population, it seems a good guess that this statistic is cause for alarm.

12. The Immigration Reform and Control Act, which became US federal law in 1986, was intended to limit immigration from Mexico to the United States by imposing strict penalties on those who employed immigrants lacking legal permission to work.

9

The Moral Challenge in Cultural Migration

Richard A. Shweder

Coming to terms with diversity in an increasingly multicultural world has become one of the most pressing public policy projects for liberal democracies in the early twenty-first century. One way to come to terms with diversity is to try to understand the scope and limits of toleration for variety at different national sites where immigration from foreign lands has complicated the cultural landscape. This chapter examines a series of legal and moral questions about the proper response to norm conflict between mainstream populations and cultural minority groups (including old and new immigrants), with special reference to disputed cases that have arisen in the recent history of the United States.

A SPLINTERED WORLD?

Clifford Geertz (2000) has remarked that "positioning Muslims in France, Whites in South Africa, Arabs in Israel, or Koreans in Japan are not altogether the same sort of thing. But if political theory is going to be of any relevance at all in the splintered world, it will have to have something cogent to say about how, in the face of a drive towards a destructive integrity, such structures can be brought into being, how they can be sustained, and how they can be made to work."

By the phrase "the splintered world," Clifford Geertz means our contemporary world of borderless capitalism, in which globalization has become a motivating (albeit controversial) ideal. In that world, not only are goods (including cultural goods and symbols) and financial capital encouraged to travel more freely across national frontiers but labor also moves internationally (although with highly variable and fewer degrees of freedom).

Of course, we are not talking here just of Muslims in France or Koreans in Japan, but also of Thais in Israel, Bangladeshis in Saudi Arabia, Angolans in South Africa, Nicaraguans in Costa Rica, Guatemalans in Mexico, Mexicans in the United States, Gambians in Norway, and so forth. In our splintered world at the end of the twentieth century, more than 125 million people (including at least 27 million political refugees) lived outside their country of birth or citizenship—an all-time high. About one-third of that international migration moved in the direction of the seven wealthiest countries in the world, including the United States and Canada. About 50 percent moved across national borders within the third world (Martin 1996).

As a footnote, I should mention that although 125 million (or so) may be an all-time high in numbers of people living abroad, the deep or long-term significance of that number is not entirely transparent. To remember that internationalism is neither a new thing nor an irreversible process may even be a useful corrective to some of the grandiosity, utopianism, and presentism of the current discourse about globalization, cosmopolitanism, and the free flow of everything. The last great push to globalize the world and promote free trade and labor migration in the late nineteenth century came to a halt with World War I. This was followed by protectionism, isolationism, and nationalist fervor. It remains to be seen whether we are witnessing something new in the organization of a world system or are compulsively repeating a deep historical cycle, another swing of the internationalism/nationalism, free trade/restrictive tariff, open borders/closed borders pendulum—déjà vu, all over again. (Concerning similarities and differences in immigration waves across two centuries; see Foner [2000] and Suárez-Orozco [2000].)

Even now, in these heady, high-tech, on-line days of so-called borderless capitalism and expanding global markets, a little caution in the face of visionary claims about a new transnational, neo-liberal world order might be wise. There is, of course, much talk about the dissolution of national boundaries. For the moment, there is a clear pulse in the direction of increasing international labor flows (foreign workers make up one-seventh of the labor force of South Africa and a majority of the labor force in some West Asian nations). To splinter things further, political refugees displaced by civil wars and local conflicts are living all over the place.

Nevertheless, it remains a fact that approximately 98 percent of the people on the planet Earth have stayed put, in the sense that they live in the country where they were born or where they are citizens (Martin 1996). Many of them believe that there are too many splinters (that is, foreigners) around, therefore Clifford Geertz's mention of "a drive towards a destructive integrity." At least some of the 2 percent on the move are making some of the settled 98 percent, who want to feel at home in their culture, nervous about the future of their way of life, and vice versa. Vice versa because when some of those 2 percent arrive in a foreign land, they may well be told either to conform to local cultural norms or go away.

THE DRIVE TOWARDS A DESTRUCTIVE INTEGRITY

"A drive towards a destructive integrity" is an arresting (even if tendentious) expression. By this, I take it that Clifford Geertz means the inclination of dominant cultural groups to demand and/or require culturally different immigrant minority groups to alter their way of life and assimilate their tastes, values, and practices to mainstream cultural norms. This drive includes the use of the state's coercive power to "cleanse" the local national scene of genuine cultural diversity.

For example, in the predominately Christian regions of Northern Europe, Islam is perceived as a real or potential danger. In those countries, even center-left political leaders may voice attitudes evoking images of strident "cultural nationalism." The *New York Times* journalist Roger Cohen has described the plight of Turks in Denmark (Cohen 2000; also see Ewing 2000 and Wikan 2000 on Islam in other parts of Europe). Cohen notes that even the then–prime minister of Denmark, a social democrat, has asserted "that he could not accept certain 'aspects of the Islamic religion' like interrupting work with prayer." "It must be clear," the prime minister announced, "that in Denmark we work in the workplace." Roger Cohen goes on to remark that "European governments, uneasy about an influx of foreigners [from Muslim countries], now say these immigrants must resolve the contradictions [between cultures] by embracing the culture of their adoptive lands. The bureaucrats have focused on arranged marriages as disastrous; they hinder integration, offend Western values and encourage immigrant ghettos, or so officials say. They also bring more immigrants because 'family unification' is one of the few legal ways left to get into Europe." "The message is clear," writes Cohen, "Conform at work and at marriage." The journalist goes on to report that because the Danish government estimated that 90 percent of Danish Turks found wedding partners in Turkey, it "passed legislation this year to deter any immigrant younger than twenty-five from bringing a foreign spouse to Denmark."

That idea—conform to mainstream cultural beliefs and practices about work and family, or stay away—is not just a European attitude. "Cultural differences are beautiful," comments Marceline Walter, who directs community education in the New York State Administration for Children's Services, "but they have nothing to do with the law. We can't possibly have a set of laws for Americans, a set of laws for immigrants, and a set of laws for tourists" (quoted in Ojito 1997).

The strong assimilationist stance (a drive towards a destructive integrity?) of the sort expressed in those comments is not the only possible response to immigrants who bring with them unfamiliar or even alien beliefs and practices. National attitudes towards cultural differences tend to be contingent on current social, economic, and political circumstances, on the history of the nation's engagement with minority groups, and on the legal and ethical normative regime in place. Nevertheless, a more facilitative, "live and let live," pluralistic or accommodative impulse of the sort expressed, for example, by Supreme Court Justice William Brennan has also been voiced in some liberal democracies. Justice Brennan (in *Michael H.* v. *Gerald D.*, 491 US 110, 141 [1989], dissenting) remarks: "We are not an assimilative, homogeneous society, but a facilitative, pluralistic one, in which we must be willing to abide someone else's unfamiliar or even repellent practice because the same tolerant impulse protects our own idiosyncrasies." I am reminded here of a remarkable public service advertisement in the early days of television in the 1950s. During my childhood in the New York metropolitan area, a jingle that was played on the air linked patriotism to tolerance: "George Washington loved good roast beef. Chaim Solomon loved fish. When Uncle Sam served liberty, they both enjoyed the dish." It also seems noteworthy that as we entered the twenty-first century, the Immigration and Naturalization Service (INS) of the United States published a document titled "What Are the Benefits and Responsibilities of Citizenship?" This states that "America becomes stronger when all its citizens respect the different opinions, cultures, ethnic groups, and religions found in this country. Tolerance for differences is also a responsibility of citizenship."

In this chapter I try to address, in part, the pluralist challenge of Clifford Geertz and Mr. Justice William Brennan. I was greatly assisted in this task by my participation in recent years in a Social Science Research Council Working Group, "Ethnic Customs, Assimilation and American Law" (recently renamed "Law and Culture") (www.ssrc.org). The Working Group has brought legal scholars, normative theorists, and empirical social scientists (mostly anthropologists and social psychologists) in contact with one another's way of thinking and talking about diversity. In the context of Working Group meetings, legal scholarship and social science research are brought to bear on the practical question of what shape multiculturalism can, and should, take in liberal democratic societies in the contemporary world. Variations are examined in the legal resources and ethical traditions of different liberal democracies with regard to the question of how much cultural diversity will be possible, given the history of this or that particular normative (legal/ethical) regime in this or that particular land (see Shweder, Minow, and Markus 2002).

We have taken a look at how liberal democracies handle key issues such as church and state, parental rights and children's rights, and individual rights and group rights. How do countries distinguish between matters that should be kept private (and, therefore, away from the gaze of the state) and matters that should be public (therefore becoming candidates for government surveillance, scrutiny, regulation, or intervention)? Are the techniques used by parents to socialize, discipline, and develop moral character in their children (for example, spankings or tests of courage involving ordeals) a private family affair, or should these be monitored and subject to regulation by the state? Any physical punishment of children by their parents is a crime in Norway, but not so in India or the United States. How do the legal and ethical resources and traditions of different nation-states with regard to those issues (church/state, individual rights/group rights, parental rights/children's rights, private matters/public matters) have a bearing on the social and political management of diversity when dominant cultures and minority cultures collide?

As Geertz implies (more or less as an aside), it is "not altogether the same sort of thing" as one migrates away from the normative regime of one liberal democracy (for example, Norway or Germany) and becomes a subject of the normative regime of another (for example, India or the United States). In this instance, at least, in cases involving the management and treatment of cultural differences, national borders do matter and no global normative regime exists.

Just ask the Turks living in Berlin. Many will tell you that they are freer to practice and promote Islam in public spaces in Germany than in Turkey. In Turkey, religion is officially considered a totally private matter that should be kept at home and out of all public domains. In Germany, Christianity (and perhaps some day soon, Islam) is legitimately (that is, legally) promoted in the public schools (Ewing 2000). In other words, different normative regimes are associated with the relationship of the mosque/church/temple and the state in Turkey and Germany. Looking at church/state norms in the United States, one finds that they differ in various ways from the normative regimes defining and constraining the debates about the issue in both Germany and Turkey. The normative/legal/moral regimes regulating and managing "difference" are not the same, even across liberal democracies.

THE SCOPE AND LIMITS OF TOLERANCE—
A NORMATIVE AGENDA FOR ANTHROPOLOGY

My main aim in this chapter is to raise a normative question: How much cultural diversity ought to be possible within the confines of a liberal democracy such as the United States of America? Also, I want to point to instances where cultures have collided, resulting in deep reflection on what one might mean by *pluralism* or *tolerance* in a liberal democracy such as the United States.

Let me start by acknowledging that the type of normative question I am raising is not the type that anthropologists are accustomed to analyzing systematically. Of course, many anthropologists hold strong personal views on the topic. Most non-anthropologists probably assume that most anthropologists have high regard for cultures other than their own and are prepared to offer a defense of other ways of life against any "drive towards a destructive integrity."

This assumption, however, is not necessarily correct. Within the discipline of American anthropology are activists involved in the international human rights movement. The use of a discourse of human rights within anthropology is complex, and that discourse is by no means consistent, rigorous, or intellectually coherent (for a discussion of the muddles in the past and present official stances of the American Anthropological Association (AAA) towards a human rights perspective, see Engle 2002). Nevertheless, among contemporary American anthropologists are human rights activists who reject the notions of group rights, or parental rights, or rights to local self-determination and are suspicious of the idea of a basic "right to culture" (see Cohen and Bledsoe 2002; Wikan 2000). They are far more interested in the application of some notion of universal individual rights to "save the children" of other cultures from their own parents and to legitimize "humanitarian interventions" by international organizations. They want to use the idea of universal human rights to protect individuals, especially women and children, from cultural practices that are thought to be patriarchal, oppressive, or inequitable in some regard. These cultural practices include polygamy, bride price, arranged marriage, veiling, the sequestering or seclusion of females, and the cosmetic genital surgeries associated with gender identity ceremonies or adult initiation in parts of East and West Africa. (For an overview of the human rights–versus–culture debates, see Minow 2000; Okin 1999; for a critique of the supposed opposition between rights and culture, see Volpp 2001). Such human rights activists can be quite scornful of other cultures and may even be interested in sanctioning or criminalizing those who engage in what they take to be "barbaric practices." These days, at least some anthropologists embrace one form or other of what was once called "the civilizing project."

Moreover, within American anthropology are significant theoretical currents and principled positions running against the professional posing of questions about the legitimate scope for cultural tolerance. One such current, the neo-positivists in anthropology, might well reject the question precisely because it is normative instead of empirical. Stay away from moral or normative questions about what ought to be, the principled positivist might declare, for such questions are outside the realm of any anthropologist's scientific competence.

Another current—the postculturalists, anti-culturalists, and skeptical postmodernists in anthropology—has, in so many ways (and by now, for so many years), been calling for a deeply corrosive reading of all representations of "others." These anthropologists have raised doubts about the reality and existence of bounded groups. Under the banner of a critique of "essentialism," "monumentalism," or "Orientalism," or of just plain stereotyping, they have become critical of all attempts to portray members of other cultures with any characteristic face. The postculturalists have been working very hard to subjectivize or dissolve the very ideas of ethnic group "identity" and of objective ethical "truth." At this point, one can hardly expect them to see the point of trying to give an answer to moral questions about how much cultural diversity ought to be allowed within the confines of a liberal democratic nation state. Nevertheless, in our current splintered world, this is the kind of question that anthropologists—at least those who continue to be pro-cultural—are going to have to address more and more, if for no other reason than that in a splintered world, cultures sometimes collide, often to the detriment of immigrant minority groups.

A LIBERAL DEMOCRACY SUCH AS THE UNITED STATES OF AMERICA

At the moment, legal scholars in the United States are far ahead of anthropologists in constructing a normative language or justificatory discourse for addressing issues of cultural accommodation and the limits of tolerance (for example, see Stolzenberg 1993). This is not surprising. A liberal democracy such as the United States imagines itself to be a haven for religious and cultural diversity. It imagines itself to be a land where the state does not take collective, official, or public positions (and is therefore "neutral") concerning the religious beliefs and related practices and cultural traditions of those entitled to citizenship and political participation. It imagines itself to be a place where citizenship as an American has only weak or minimal implications for the way you lead your private life, for the type of associations you form, for the way you raise your children. It imagines itself to be a "law and order" society, in which, at the end of the day, the interpretation, refinement, and redefinition of the limits of liberty and pluralism within the liberal democratic framework of the United States are left to the courts and legal scholars.

For the sake of argument, let me say more about what I mean by "the framework" of liberal democracy in the United States. In Michael McConnell's monumental essay on the origins of the Exercise of Religion clauses of the First Amendment of the Constitution of the United States ("Congress shall make no law respecting an establishment of religion, or prohibiting the free exercise thereof"), he writes the following: "The central conception of liberalism, as summarized in the Declaration of Independence, is that government is instituted by the people in order to secure their rights to life, liberty and the pursuit of happiness. Governmental powers are limited to those needed to secure these legitimate ends. In contrast to both ancient and modern non-liberal regimes, government is not charged with the promotion of the good life for its citizens. Except as needed for mutual protection and a limited class of common interests, government must leave the definition of the good life to private institutions, of which family and church are the most conspicuous. Even in the absence of a free exercise clause, liberal theory would find the assertion of government power over religion illegitimate, except to the extent necessary for the protection of others" (McConnell 1990:1465).

McConnell's condensed description of the character of liberal democracy in the United States is useful for several reasons. First, it reminds us that not every democratic society is liberal. Democratic societies are those in which the reigning norms, laws, rules, and regulations express the will of the people (typically, but not always, as determined by a majority vote), but there is no guarantee that the will of the people will be liberal in character. Democracies, that is, polities, whose norms express the will of the people become liberal democracies precisely to the extent that people will their society to be organized in a particular way, namely, in a way that guarantees certain basic liberties (freedom of association, freedom of expression, freedom of religious practice, freedom to have and raise a family) and various protections (against harm, discrimination, coercion, abuse) to all members of the society in their pursuit of a good life.

Second, the statement reminds us that in any liberal democracy a balance must be struck between two, often contradictory, liberal impulses. On the one hand is the impulse to leave individuals free to live their lives by their own personal, cultural, or religious lights. On the other hand is the equally liberal impulse to protect those who are vulnerable from harm, exploitation, and abuse and to make use of the coercive power of the state in the furtherance of certain "common interests."

Third, McConnell's formulation leaves unspecified the exact content and limits of that "limited class of common interests" that are the legitimate objects of government power. Even given McConnell's conception of the importance of limiting government power in a liberal democratic society, at least some aspects of life that might be thought to be part of a definition of the good life are ceded by him to the public realm. In other words, there are exceptions to the principle that "government is not charged with the promotion of the good life for its citizens"; the discovery, definition, and defense of goodness is not entirely a private affair.

By McConnell's own account, aspects of the good life that are in the public realm include a common interest in safety, life, and liberty and in maintaining the conditions (nondiscrimination, protection from abuse or exploitation) that make the pursuit of happiness possible for individuals. Other aspects (McConnell, writing as a neo-conservative, implies *most* aspects) of the good life are left to private institutions—individuals, families, and religious organizations—to define and promote by and for themselves.

Yet, quite notably, little is said about how to determine the scope and limits of those common interests that legitimate the state's involvement. Is one's personal health a private matter? Is it a common interest justifying government surveillance and regulation in the name of public health? How about the religious training or moral education of one's children? How much, and which part, of a child's general education is part of the common interest? How much, and which parts, should be shielded and protected from state intervention? Should the definition and promotion of virtue be handed over to the public realm in the name of justice and the defense of common interests, or should character development and value training be left in the control of families and parents?

McConnell's description of the nature of liberal democracy in the United States is useful precisely because a crucial and difficult question appears to be left wide open: What are the rightful limits on the power of those who govern to define and promote the good life? This is the philosophical territory where much of the ideological action and political dispute within liberal democracies take place, over questions about whether to extend or restrict the use of the state's coercive power to define the obligations and duties of its citizens in various aspects of their lives (sexuality, dress, discipline, health, work, family, education, religion, values, and so forth).

For a variety of reasons, I believe that no transcendental, purely objective, or universal answer exists to the question regarding which parts of the definition of the good life should be privately defined and which publicly defined. If an answer exists, it is not an answer that can be known with certainty, at least not by mere mortals. In this area of political and social theorizing, there is much room for disagreement. The boundary between what ought to be private and what ought to be public is fuzzy. It is drawn at different points in different legal and moral traditions, which is one reason that liberal democratic societies are not identical in the extent to which the role of those who govern is kept limited. If nothing else, liberal democratic nations are likely to differ in the extent to which the meaning of a good life is left up to individuals, families, and religious organizations to define privately. Such differences among liberal democracies produce different experiences for immigrant minority groups when public conflicts arise over cultural practices that offend the sensibilities of mainstream or dominant groups. The focus in this chapter, however, is on the normative scope of multiculturalism within one particular liberal democracy, the United States. How should that liberal democracy, given its legal and ethical traditions and unique history of encounters with "others," react to recently arrived minority groups whose cultural beliefs (ideas about what is good, true, beautiful, and efficient) and related practices collide with the cultural beliefs and practices of dominant or mainstream cultural groups? I engage that question by interrogating four cases from the recent history of the United States.

THE AMISH IN WISCONSIN

I am going to start with the famous and relatively recent prosecution of a cultural minority group that migrated to the United States more than two hundred years ago and whose members fundamentally reject the beliefs, values, and way of life of most contemporary Americans. In 1972, the US Supreme Court reviewed a legal case (*Wisconsin* v. *Yoder et al.*, 406 US 205; all relevant quotations here are from that Court decision) in which Amish parents who were members of the Old Order Amish religion and the Conservative Amish Mennonite Church were indicted for violating the state of Wisconsin's compulsory school attendance law. The law required that all children in Wisconsin go to school until age sixteen. Three Amish parents were prosecuted for failing to send their sons and daughters to school beyond the eighth grade and for keeping them on the farm. By staying on the farm, the boys learned the skills associated with occupational life in a rural Amish community, and, crucially, they learned to value manual work and physical labor (and perhaps bible reading) over other types of human pursuits. The girls learned the skills associated with domesticity and the responsibilities of motherhood and family life. Both the boys and the girls were prepared for a voluntary, late-adolescent baptism (a kind of religious and cultural commitment ceremony) and were more fully initiated into the beliefs, virtues, and values of the Amish way of life.

The Amish, as you probably know, are Mennonites and trace their spiritual lineage back to the Swiss, German, and Dutch Anabaptists of the sixteenth century, a heterodox Christian sect. As described by the US Supreme Court, the Anabaptists "rejected institutionalized churches and sought to return to the early simple, Christian life, de-emphasizing material success, rejecting the competitive spirit, and seeking [even back then] to insulate themselves from the modern world." An essential feature of the Amish defense was their dedication to a long-standing tradition or way of life that, in itself, was a way of making manifest and expressing certain sincerely held religious beliefs that had remained more or less constant for centuries. They claimed that exposing their kids to the values, practices, social environment, and curriculum of a modern Wisconsin high school would threaten their way of life.

The First Amendment to our Constitution bars the government from either establishing religion (for example, favoring one religion over another, creating a state religion, providing sponsorship or financial support to religion) or interfering with the free exercise of religion. At this moment in the evolution of our legal tradition, two interpretations of the true meaning of the free-exercise clause are hotly contested (Eisenberg 2002; Eisgruber and Sager 1994a and b, 1996; McConnell 1990; Souter 1993).

According to one interpretation (which I shall dub *the authority of religious conscience* interpretation), the injunction that Congress shall make no law prohibiting the free exercise of religion has the following meaning: In the absence of a sufficiently compelling, secular public need (for example, public safety), the government should grant exemptions (for example, to the Amish) from general legal obligations that conflict with religious duties, assuming that those religious duties are matters of conscience that can be traced to sincerely held religious beliefs.

According to the second interpretation (which I shall dub *the nondiscrimination* interpretation), the injunction has the following meaning: All citizens are entitled to equal liberty such that no law shall be written that deliberately discriminates against them or displays hostility towards them because of their sincerely held religious beliefs (and related practices).

According to the second view, the free-exercise clause expresses a principle of nondiscrimination, and little more. It should not be interpreted as a statement of privilege (a claim for exemption from general legal obligations) for practices related to sincerely held religious beliefs or perceived obligations to God. According to that (nondiscrimination) interpretation, a law that happens to have a negative effect on the practices of a particular religious group does not necessarily violate constitutional guarantees of religious freedom. By that reading of the free-exercise clause, a law—for example, one prohibiting all forms of animal slaughter (perhaps on grounds of cruelty to animals)—would not necessarily be a violation of religious liberty, even if, in effect, it criminalized the ritual sacrifice of animals in religious ceremonies. It would not run afoul of the free-exercise clause as long as the law was formally neutral (displayed in its wording, or on its face, no particular hostility to religion or to particular religious groups) and was generally applied to all citizens (hunters, pest-control experts, slaughter houses, members of religious groups, and so on).

Whatever one's interpretation of the true meaning of the free-exercise clause, any challenge to the constitutionality of a law or statute in the name of free exercise of religion must begin with the identification of the sincerely held religious beliefs associated with a group, community, or "church." In relationship to those sincerely held religious beliefs, conscientious assertions of religious duties of various sorts (obligations to God in contrast to obligations to the state) can then be derived and assessed, and questions concerning the interests of the state, the degree of facial neutrality of the law, and so forth, can be evaluated.

In the case of the Amish, the relevant sincerely held religious belief was their literal interpretation of a particular biblical injunction from the Epistle of Paul to the Romans, which, in the context of studies of immigration, reads like a fundamental anti-assimilation principle. That injunction, "be not conformed to this world," was held by the Amish parents, by expert witnesses, and ultimately by the Court to be central to the Amish faith and was identified as a pervasive religious principle regulating the entire Amish way of life.

Any anthropological or historical summary of the Amish is likely to make note of certain distinctive features of their cultural community, including a religiously motivated pacifism, a rejection of the idea of oaths, and the conduct of religious services (often in the German language) at home rather than in churches. One central aim of the Amish cultural community (its core rationale) is to restore a way of life that members of the Amish community associate with the Christianity of apostolic times. Therefore, they reject many beliefs, values, virtues, and material objects (telephones, radios, cars, televisions) we associate with life in the modern world, and they strictly limit their contacts with the non-Amish world. Parents want to perpetuate their way of life by passing on their own way of seeing and being in the world to their children. In that regard, they strongly discourage certain kinds of exposure to the outside world and disapprove of marriage outside the faith. They have an interest in preserving their religious and cultural tradition, which depends, in large part, on their ability to recruit adherents from the next generation.

The state of Wisconsin thought that the Amish, like everyone else, should send their kids to school beyond the eighth grade. Also, the state thought that Amish parents, like everyone else, should not be permitted to shield their children from useful knowledge and keep them "ignorant." The state argued that its system of compulsory education was uniformly and generally applied to all families in Wisconsin. They argued that the system was not created with any animus towards the Amish and (it was argued) that the educational system served important public needs, providing not only preparation for intelligent citizenship and a productive life in society but also the opportunity to benefit from a modern secondary school education, regardless of the wishes of one's parents.

Justice White put it this way: "In the present case the State is not concerned with the maintenance of an educational system as an end in itself, it is rather attempting to nurture and develop the human potential of its children, whether Amish or non-Amish: to expand their knowledge, broaden their sensibilities, kindle their imagination, foster a spirit of free inquiry, and increase their human understanding and tolerance. It is possible that most Amish children will wish to continue living the rural life of their parents.... Others, however, may wish to become nuclear physicists, ballet dancers, computer programmers, or historians, and for these occupations formal training will be necessary."

Justice William O. Douglas, in his famous partial dissent from the opinion of the Court, wondered whether there really is or should be an identity of interest between parents and their children. The required high school education would make transcending one's family and social background easier. He wanted to hear more from the kids, only one of whom, Frieda Yoder, had testified about her own degree of commitment to the Amish way of life. "The parents are seeking to vindicate not only their own free exercise claims, but also those of their high-school-age children," Justice Douglas wrote in his dissent. "If the parents in this case are allowed a religious exemption, the inevitable effect is to impose the parents' notion of religious duty upon their children.... I think the children should be entitled to be heard. While the parents, absent dissent, normally speak for the entire family, the education of the child is a matter on which the child will often have decided views. He may want to be pianist or an astronaut or an oceanographer. To do so he will have to break from the Amish tradition. It is the future of the student, not the future of the parents that is imperiled by today's decision. If a parent keeps his child out of school beyond the grade school, then the child will be forever barred from entry into the new and amazing world of diversity that we have today."

It is not very difficult to imagine contemporary human rights activists extending Justices White and Douglas's "there but for fortune goes you or goes I" line of argument and expressing a related sense of regret about Frieda Yoder's loss of certain options. Frieda Yoder might well have become a feminist activist, scornful of the sex-role differentiation within the Amish community, if only the state had been able to compel her parents to enroll her in a Wisconsin secondary school in the late 1960s and early 1970s.

As you have undoubtedly inferred, the US Supreme Court granted the Amish an exemption from the compulsory education laws of Wisconsin. In an opinion written by Justice Burger (but supported by most of the liberal judges on the Court), the Court balanced the interests of the state in universal education against the rights of American citizens to religious liberty and to follow the dictates of a religious conscience. The state's interest in education was fully acknowledged by the Court. Nevertheless, the required extra years of schooling beyond eighth grade did not seem essential because the Amish learned useful skills at home and were self-sufficient and potentially employable (as carpenters or farmers, for example) had they chosen to venture out into the modern world. By eighth grade, they knew how to read, write, and count, and there was no evidence that they could not discharge the responsibilities of citizenship.

Moreover, their religious beliefs were sincere. Their way of life, which gave substance to their beliefs and made manifestly obvious their sincerity, was a recognizable, long-standing, and, the Court seemed to suggest, even an admirable tradition, which was truly threatened by the compulsory education law of Wisconsin. If Amish children are forced to go to school until age sixteen, the Court concluded, "they must either abandon belief and be assimilated into society at large or be forced to migrate to some other, more tolerant region." Therefore, in 1972 the scale tilted heavily on the side of the Amish, although that Court decision remains controversial to this day.

Notably, the decision granting an exemption to the Amish relied on an authority of religious conscience interpretation of the free exercise of religion clause of the Bill of Rights and expressed some skepticism about the nondiscrimination point of view. In the opinion of the Court, the Wisconsin school-attendance requirement did apply uniformly and generally to all citizens of the state. It did not, on its face, discriminate against religions or against the Amish (it made no mention of the Amish and was not written with the Amish in mind). Also, it was motivated by a perfectly legitimate secular concern.

However, those conditions of generality and formal neutrality—and, therefore, apparent nondiscrimination—were judged to be insufficient for disposing of the case. According to the Court, "a regulation neutral on its face may, in its application, nonetheless offend the constitutional requirement for government neutrality, if it unduly burdens the free exercise of religion." (See Markus, Steele, and Steele 2000 on problems with formal neutrality, or "colorblindness," in the treatment of racial minorities.) The Court called for doctrinal flexibility and a realistic, case by case–based application of the First Amendment's religion clauses. The opinion went on to say that "the Court must not ignore the danger that an exception from a general obligation of citizenship on religious ground may run afoul of the Establishment Clause [favoring Amish Mennonites over other religions, who have not been exempted from the law, for example], but that danger cannot be allowed to prevent any exception no matter how vital it may be to the protection of values promoted by the right of free exercise."

Anthropology has much to learn from the careful study of cases such as *Wisconsin* v. *Yoder et al.* (1972) and, also, much to contribute to the development of the normative discourse about "difference" that emerges out of cases of this type.

For example, the Court was impressed that the Amish had remained committed to religious beliefs to which their forebears had adhered for 300 years and to a way of life that had remained constant ("perhaps some would say static," the Court wrote) for a long time. In several ways, a conception of culture (as a shared and relatively stable conception of the sacred made manifest in everyday practice) not unlike that developed by Emile Durkheim in *The Elementary Forms of the Religious Life* (and also not unlike the conception of culture disparaged by skeptical postmodernists and anti-culturalists in contemporary anthropology) carried the day for the Amish in their fight against the state. Had a skeptical postmodern anthropologist or human rights activist been called as an "expert witness," what would he or she have said? That Yoder is merely an individual who has multiple selves and has manufactured or socially constructed a fictive communal past? That Amish practices are in constant flux and don't deserve deference or protection? That the less control any parent has over a child's socialization the better, especially for those antiquated Amish patriarchs?

The Court reasoned as follows:

> In evaluating those claims [the alleged violation of their religious freedom by the compulsory education law] we must be careful to determine whether the Amish religious faith and their mode of life are, as they claim, inseparable and interdependent. A way of life, however virtuous and admirable, may not be interposed as a barrier to reasonable state regulation of education if it is based on purely secular considerations; to have the protection of the Religion Clauses, the claims must be rooted in religious belief. Although a determination of what is a "religious" belief or practice entitled to constitutional protection may present a most delicate question, the very concept of ordered liberty precludes allowing every person to make his own standards on matters of conduct in which society as a whole has important interests. Thus, if the Amish asserted their claims because of their subjective evaluation and rejection of the contemporary secular values accepted by the majority, much as Thoreau rejected the social values of his time and isolated himself at Walden Pond, their claims would not rest on a religious basis. Thoreau's choice was philosophical and personal rather than religious, and such belief does not rise to the demands of the Religion Clauses.

That comment, distinguishing between religious versus non-religious sincerely held beliefs, bothered Justice Douglas. In his partial dissent, he reminded the Court that in other decisions the Court had already expanded the concept of religious belief to include any sincere and meaningful belief that occupied a parallel place in the conscience of its possessor to that filled by the idea of "God." Justice Douglas had in mind a Supreme Court decision concerning conscientious objection to military service (see Eisenberg 2002 for an argument about the expansion of the free-exercise clause to include all conscientious beliefs, whether or not theologically based). Emile Durkheim's anthropological approach to the analysis of cultural communities as "churches" based on a core set of shared ideas held to be "sacred" and set apart from the profane aspects of life would seem to provide a firm anthropological basis for this type of judicial reasoning.

An instructive feature of the opinion of the Court, at least for minority groups seeking to position themselves within American society, is that the Court seemed to be impressed with the Amish way of life, perhaps even to the point of romanticizing Amish culture. This was not a court that was in the mood to take a decision that might bring an end to the Amish way of life. Not only were the judges impressed that the Amish had been around a long time or that their religious beliefs were sincere, but the Court also noted that "the Amish qualities of reliability, self-reliance and dedication to work" would be readily marketable in today's society. The Court remarked that the Green County Amish (of Wisconsin) had never been known to commit crimes or receive public assistance, and none were unemployed. In fact, the Court commended Amish communities and asserted that they are "singularly parallel and reflect many of the virtues of Jefferson's idea of the 'sturdy yeoman' who would form the basis of what he [Thomas Jefferson] considered as the ideal of a democratic society. Even their idiosyncratic separateness exemplifies the diversity we profess to admire and encourage." One is tempted by the following speculation: The Amish might have been assisted in their case by the Court's perception that they were a small, industrious, non-threatening, and virtue-minded minority group. The Court seemed to value having Amish in our midst, nostalgically reminding us of an imagined time when the world was less competitive, less hectic, and less modern.

Stating its judicial opinion in a way that warms the heart of at least this anthropological pluralist, the Court wrote as follows: "We must not forget that in the Middle Ages important values of the civilization of the Western World were preserved by members of religious orders who isolated themselves from all worldly influences against great obstacles. There can be no assumption that today's majority is 'right' and the Amish and others like them 'wrong.' A way of life that is odd or even erratic but interferes with no rights or interests of others is not to be condemned because it is different."

Finally, the Court rededicated itself to what it saw as an enduring principle of the constitutional tradition of the United States: The government's role is not to save children from either their parents or themselves (by requiring Amish children to be educated in Wisconsin high schools or increasing the odds that Frieda Yoder will grow up to become a cosmopolitan feminist). It is up to parents, not the state, the Court argued, to raise children and guide their religious education, and we should not leave it up to the government to determine the religious future of a child. In the United States, it is presumed that children belong to their parents and not to the state.

A SANTERIA CHURCH IN FLORIDA

I have discussed the Amish schooling case at some length because it represents a moment in legal history when the authority of religious conscience interpretation of the free exercise of religion clause was put to work in defense of a minority cultural tradition. Also, it is a model case for a pluralistic anthropology of cultural migration. The 1972 case of *Wisconsin* v. *Yoder et al.* concerned a long-residing, unorthodox, white Christian minority group of Northern European origin whose members were "different" because they refused to be up-to-date in the modern world. The next case (Church of the Lukumi Babalu Aye and Ernesto Pichardo, *Petitioners* v. *City of Hialeah;* 508 US 520 [1993]), which I shall merely sketch, is even more recent. (All relevant quotations here are from that court decision.) It concerns new immigrants from Cuba (and Haiti) who moved into the city of Hialeah, Florida, and proposed to start a Santeria church (the Church of the Lukumi Babalu Aye, Inc.), in which their worship and devotion would include the ritual sacrifice of animals. In particular, within the confines of their religious establishment, they planned to feed their hungry gods (or *Orishas*) by means of the sacrifice of goats, sheep, chickens, pigeons, doves, ducks, guinea pigs, and turtles.

Santeria ("the way of the Saints") is a syncretic religion combining aspects of West African Yoruba spiritualism with a Catholic iconography of saints. A devout member of a Santeria church believes that he or she has a personal relationship to the *Orishas*—who are powerful, but not immortal, spirits represented through the figures of Catholic saints—and that the *Orishas* depend for their survival on animal sacrifice. It is a religious duty of believers in the Santeria religion to nurture the *Orishas,* to feed them and keep them alive. The Santeria religion originally developed in Cuba among former slave populations and has spread to Haiti, Brazil, and more recently to the United States, especially New York and Florida.

When the newly arrived *Orisha* worshippers of Florida proposed to open a church, they quickly discovered some hazards of living in a local democracy that is not liberal. The city council of Hialeah held an emergency public meeting at which, in a democratic atmosphere conducive to expressions of religious intolerance, the chaplain of the local police department declared that Santeria was a sin, "foolishness," "an abomination to the Lord," and the worship of "demons." He told the city council, "We need to be helping people and sharing with them the truth that is found in Jesus Christ." He exhorted the city council "not to permit this church to exist."

Shortly after the emergency public meeting, the city council zoned out the Santeria church by means of an ordinance prohibiting animal slaughter outside areas designated for slaughterhouses, although an exception was made for the practice of Jewish Kosher slaughter in the City of Hialeah. Additionally, the city council criminalized the Santeria religious rituals by means of ordinances making it illegal to kill animals for reasons other than food consumption. The newly enacted laws were written in such a way as to protect the practices of various interested parties. Exemptions were granted to local hunters, those who construct buildings in which they slaughter animals for human consumption, pest-control specialists who kill mice, skunks, squirrels, and other animals, and local farmers who kill small numbers of hogs and cattle for purposes other than food consumption.

The Santeria church challenged the ordinance in court. A number of animal rights organizations sided with the city and opposed the Santeria immigrants. The Supreme Court of the United States ultimately ruled unanimously in favor of the church, after six years of litigation. Although the decision of the Supreme Court was unanimous, it is noteworthy that they had to reverse earlier decisions of the US District Court and the US Court of Appeals. Both lower courts had ruled in favor of the city and against the church.

This decision has several other noteworthy features. The Court made note of the role of animal sacrifice in the history of religions. It pointed out, reiterating a core principle of "free exercise" legal doctrine, that "although the practice of animal sacrifice may seem abhorrent to some, religious beliefs need not be acceptable, logical, consistent, or comprehensible to others in order to merit First Amendment protection."

Despite the fact that both lower courts had supported the city ordinances, the Supreme Court justices thought that the case was easy, precisely because the ordinances were neither neutral nor general in their application and seemed to have as their object "the suppression of Santeria's central element, animal sacrifice." The Court opinion states, "the latter ordinances' various prohibitions, definitions and exemptions demonstrate that they were 'gerrymandered' with care to proscribe religious killings of animals by Santeria church members but to exclude almost all other animal killings." The Court also judged that various legitimate government interests, such as public health issues with respect to the disposal of organic garbage, could be served without a prohibition on all Santeria sacrificial practice. If the free exercise clause of the First Amendment was intended to do anything, the Court asserted, it was to protect religious minorities from precisely this type of persecution by the state. Why that was not obvious to the lower courts is not explained.

A less obvious although crucial feature of the Santeria decision is the historical shift in the normative status of the nondiscrimination interpretation of the free-exercise clause that had taken place since 1972. The *Wisconsin* v. *Yoder Court of 1972* leaned heavily on the authority of religious conscience interpretation and was prepared to weigh and balance the claims of religious obligation related to sincerely held religious beliefs against the legitimate claims and important interests of the secular state. By 1993, however, much had changed.

In a watershed case in 1990 (*Employment Division* v. *Smith;* 494 US 892 [1990]), in a plurality decision written by Justice Antonio Scalia, the multiply divided Court adopted the nondiscrimination approach to religious liberty jurisprudence. It announced that under the free-exercise clause, a law that burdens religious practice need not be justi-fied by a compelling government interest if it is formally neutral and of general applicability. In the case of Smith, members of the Native American Church in the state of Oregon were denied government employment benefits because they had engaged in work-related mis-conduct; namely, they had violated an Oregon law prohibiting the use of illegal drugs (in this case, peyote). The Court supported that denial of benefits. It argued that the law making peyote use (and other drugs) illegal was not a violation of the free-exercise rights of members of the Native American Church because the point of the free-exercise clause is to prohibit discrimination or persecution on religious grounds. Because the law was formally neutral (no animus to Native Americans was apparent in its wording) and was generally applied to all citizens of the state, it did not run afoul of the First Amendment.

The Smith ruling produced a storm of protest from Congress and from religious organizations around the country. The Court's nondis-crimination approach to religious liberty resulted in the following nor-mative rule: A formally neutral, generally applicable law does not violate the free-exercise clause even when no compelling government interest is at stake and even when the law has the (unintended) effect of treating a religious practice, such as Native American peyote use, as against the law. Under that interpretation, as Justice David Souter has suggested, even Catholic communion might be vulnerable to legal penalties, should the age of Prohibition return and a law be written that neutrally and generally prohibits all consumption of alcohol. By the way, during the last age of Prohibition in the United States, the law forbidding the consumption of alcohol was written with an explicit exemption for "wine for sacramental purposes." Dominant, powerful, or well-connected groups (for example, the Catholic Church during the age of Prohibition) have a way of getting their interests represented to lawmakers, who either do not pass the law, out of fear that it might be universally applied, or pass the law with explicit exceptions and exemptions. This is one of the ways that small immigrant minority groups, whose interests may be poorly represented in the halls of government, are at a disadvantage in a law-and-order society.

In outraged response to the 1990 Smith Peyote case decision, Congress passed the Religious Freedom Restoration Act (RFRA), which President Clinton signed into law. The act mandated for the courts something very much like the authority of religious conscience reading of the free-exercise clause, in which the clause (as Justice Souter has put it) "safeguards a right to engage in religious activity free of unnecessary governmental interference." The US Supreme Court subsequently declared RFRA unconstitutional, a violation of the separation of congressional powers from judicial powers. (For a variety of views on Smith, RFRA, and the meaning of the religion clauses, see Eisenberg 2002; Eisgruber and Sager 1994a and b, 1996; McConnell 1990; Sager 2000.)

In any case, the Smith ruling and its nondiscrimination interpretation of religious liberty was the law of the land when the City of Hialeah tried to prohibit Santeria animal sacrifice within its territory. In that case, the nondiscrimination interpretation of religious freedom worked well to protect the Santeria church, precisely because the city ordinances were neither neutral (hostility towards a religion was facially apparent) nor generally applied. The case seemed easy. Nevertheless, the minority on the Smith Court, of whom Justice Souter is perhaps the most outspoken and eloquent, is clearly waiting for an opportunity to revisit the Smith decision. This is apparent from Justice Souter's concurring opinion in the Santeria animal sacrifice case, in which he outlines a line of attack on the nondiscrimination interpretation of religious freedom in the United States. He leaves us wondering what the Smith plurality on the Court would have said about ritual sacrifice in a Santeria church if the City of Halileah had passed a formally neutral law prohibiting all animal slaughter for any purpose and applied it generally and across the board, with no exemptions for anyone, including the Santerias.

The normative regime that is going to emerge out of current conflicts over the interpretation of that single important clause in the First Amendment to the Constitution is going to be consequential. It is going to make a difference in the scope permitted to unfamiliar or alien cultural practices related to sincerely held and self-defining sacred/religious-cultural beliefs. It is going to make a difference in the construction, management, and handling of "differences" in an increasingly multicultural national scene.

AFGHANS IN MAINE

My next example comes from a legal case in the state of Maine (*State of Maine* v. *Mohammed Kargar*, 679 A.2d 81). In a multicultural, law-and-order society such as the United States, the law of the land often presupposes and codifies the substantive beliefs, values, emotional reactions, aesthetic standards, and pictures of the world peculiar to those cultural groups who are mainstream and have the most power. This can be hazardous for members of immigrant minority groups, as was the case in 1985, when the state legislature of Maine wrote a law making criminal any sexual act with a minor (non-spouse) under the age of fourteen. Those who wrote the law went on, in their wisdom, to define a sexual act as, among other things, "direct physical contact between the genitals of one and the mouth...of another."

Hence, in 1993, when Mr. Mohammad Kargar, an Afghani refugee who had been residing in the United States for three years, was seen kissing the genitals of his eighteen-month-old son, he found the police descending on his home. He was arrested, convicted of gross sexual assault in Superior Court, and prohibited from seeing his family while the case was appealed. Three years later, his conviction was overturned by the State Supreme Court, which relied heavily on cultural analysis. In this case, fidelity in ethnographic representation made a difference in the outcome of the case.

As it turns out, kissing the genitals of a young child is common-place in Mr. Kargar's cultural community and is viewed there as a sign of love and affection. It is precisely the father's willingness to kiss what is viewed as an unclean or unholy part of the body (a place where uri-nation takes place) that makes the act such a powerful display of love. The gesture is so socially endorsed and "normal" in Mr. Kargar's local Afghan community that pictures representing that type of show of affection are proudly displayed in family photo albums. After taking testimonies from members of the relevant local cultural network and expert witnesses, it was possible for the Supreme Court of Maine to construct an alternative understanding of Mr. Kargar's act. With insights into local meanings and the "native point of view," they were able to view it as a symbolic action with positive connotations rather than as an act of physical abuse.

Although the Supreme Court of Maine ultimately vindicated Mohammad Kargar, the whole process and legal ruling were at great cost to the defendant. The court made no suggestion that the law be amended to make room for alternative cultural understandings of sexuality and touching and gave no assurance that other Afghani residents of Maine will not have the police knocking on their doors.

Perhaps this case seems exotic to you. Perhaps it makes you nervous, given your own local cultural sensibilities. Given that many of you are anthropologists or social scientists, perhaps you are especially alert to the hazards of ethnocentrism and are able, or at least willing, to try to bracket your own socialized moral and emotional reactions and see things from an alternative point of view. Unfortunately for immigrant minority groups, feeling-laden and morally outraged ethnocentric misreadings of their customary or habitual actions and underlying intentions by members of dominant majority groups are more common than one supposes. The consequences can be devastating, especially for members of minority groups. That alone ought to be reason enough for cultural anthropologists (at least those who are still pro-cultural) to share what we know about other cultures with the public and play a part in normative public policy debates. Being slow to judge others and getting one's ethnographic facts straight can be virtues, as will become even more apparent in a moment.

SOMALIS IN SEATTLE

My fourth and final example is not yet a legal case in the United States, but now on the books is a federal law criminalizing a particular cultural practice that is commonplace among immigrants from certain parts of Africa. Sooner or later some African parent is going to be prosecuted, and at that time the constitutionality of the law may well be tested.

Unless you are an anthropologist who knows a good deal about East and West African gender identity and coming-of-age ceremonies, you may find this final example very difficult to think about in an open-minded way. I believe that this is largely because of the way the practice has been represented in a global discourse that bears little relationship to informed anthropological accounts. Many Americans who cherish their liberal democracy like to think of themselves as pluralists who value diversity and believe that tolerance of cultural differences is good. Nevertheless, when families arrive in their midst from Somalia, Egypt, the Sudan, Sierra Leone, Mali, the Gambia, or Ethiopia, these same liberal Americans begin to sound like that police chaplain from the City of Hialeah—the one who called Santeria animal sacrifice a sin, an abomination, who said not to let it happen here. I have in mind the reaction of dominant groups in the United States to families such as the Somali refugees who arrived in Seattle in the early 1990s. These families wanted to continue doing what is done in Somalia. They wanted (by their own lights) to improve the bodies and further the normal social development of both their sons and daughters by means of a cosmetic genital surgery.

When a doctor at the Harbor View Medical Center in Seattle asked a pregnant Somali women whether she would like to have her child circumcised if is it a boy, the woman replied, "Yes, and if it is a girl, too" (Coleman 1998). The hospital happened to be one that is sensitive to cultural issues and has a significant inner-city minority group clientele. A committee was formed to look into the possibility of a minor, medically safe female circumcision procedure that might be made available to immigrants from cultures in which circumcision for both males and females is the cultural ideal and is viewed as an essential ingredient of normal growth and gender development. The Harbor View committee proposed to do the procedure, with the informed consent of both the parents and the child, when the child became approximately twelve years old, under hygienic conditions and with a local anesthesia. From a medical point of view, the proposed procedure was less intrusive than a typical male circumcision performed in the United States. Nevertheless, when news was leaked that Harbor View, a respected medical institution affiliated with the University of Washington, was contemplating this step, the local mainstream non-immigrant community went ballistic. Congresswoman Patricia Schroeder warned the medical center that it might be prosecuted under a federal law that she herself had sponsored.

The relevant law was passed by Congress in September 1996 and went into effect in March 1997. The law criminalizes "female genital mutilation" and penalizes with fines and/or prison sentence (up to five years) anyone who knowingly engages in surgery on any parts of the genitals of a female who is under eighteen years of age. The law explicitly states that in punishing offenders, no account shall be taken of their belief that the surgery is required as a matter of custom or ritual. Such wording suggests a law written with the explicit aim of suppressing a cultural practice associated with immigrants from Africa. It is noteworthy that the law was passed without any public hearings. It was passed without seeking expert testimony from any anthropologist who had studied female initiation or gender identity issues in East and West Africa, or from anyone else. Absolutely no attempt was made to represent or understand the point of view of the many African peoples for whom cosmetic genital surgery (for males and females) is as central to their cultural identities and sense of well-being as (male) circumcision is for Jews and for Muslims.

Faced with a potential lawsuit, negative publicity on the local news channels nightly, and many expressions of intolerance toward African peoples who "mutilate" their own children, the Harbor View Medical Center withdrew its tentative proposal for a genital surgery option for the female children of African immigrants.

The reasons for the intolerance are obvious and can be directly related to the representations of the practice of female genital surgeries that have dominated the press in the First World and have been widely disseminated by anti-FGM (female genital mutilation) activist organizations and lobbying groups. If you read and believe the literature put out by anti-FGM activists, what African peoples are said to do is, indeed, horrifying. If you read and believe that literature, you must think that Africa is a "dark continent" where for hundreds, if not thousands, of years African parents have been murdering and maiming their daughters and depriving them of the capacity for a sexual response. You must believe that African parents (mothers and fathers) are either monsters ("mutilators" of their children) or fools (incredibly ignorant of the health consequences of their own child-rearing practices and the best interests of their children) or that African women are weak and passive and live under the thumb of cruel, loathsome, or barbaric African men.

There is a powerful impulse within a liberal democracy such as the United States to leave people free to live their lives according to their own views of what is good, true, beautiful, or effective—but not if what they choose to do does great harm to those who are innocent, vulnerable, and not in a position to make choices for themselves. If such representations were accurate, who would not want to "save the children" and bring the practice of cosmetic genital surgeries to an end. But are they accurate? Compare such horrifying representations of the African "other" in our midst with the accounts of four anthropologists who know something about Africa, the practice of female circumcision, or both. (For a more detailed and thorough examination of this topic, see Shweder 2002.)

This is what Robert Edgerton (1989:40), an expert on East African history and contemporary society, says about the practice of female circumcision in Kenya in the 1920s and 1930s, at a time under British colonial rule when Christian missionaries and colonial administrators tried unsuccessfully to wipe it out. Then, nearly half of all Kenyan ethnic groups circumcised both girls and boys. In Kenya in the 1920s and 1930s, the surgery typically occurred around adolescence. It should be noted that across and within African ethnic groups, the age at which cosmetic genital surgeries for boys and girls are performed varies (any time from birth to the late teenage years) and the style and degree of surgery vary, too (in the case of girls, from a cut in the prepuce covering the clitoris to the complete "smoothing out" of the genital area by removing all visible parts of the clitoris and all external labia). In a few ethnic groups (especially in the Sudan and Somalia), the smoothing out operation is sometimes concluded by stitching closed the vaginal opening with the aim of enhancing fertility, protecting the womb, and tightening the vagina (so as to increase the capacity to give and experience sexual pleasure during intercourse in high-fertility populations of women whose vaginal canal has been widened or loosened by multiple births) (see Boddy 1982, 1989, 1996; Gruenbaum 2001). The stitching (aimed at creating something like a truss), referred to as "infibulation" or "Pharaonic circumcision," has received enormous attention (much of it lurid and sensational) in the global anti-FGM literature. In reality, this procedure is rare or non-existent in most parts of Africa and is the exception, not the rule, across the continent. In Kenya and most parts of East and West Africa, a more typical cosmetic genital surgery might involve the removal of some or all of the visible parts of the clitoris and either partial or complete removal of the labia minora. In general, and at a minimum, any form of African genital surgery leaves in tact at least 50 percent of the total tissue structure of the clitoris. This is because much of the tissue structure of the clitoris (at least 50 percent) is internal, below the surface, and not readily visible and is therefore not removed during the surgery, which may help to explain why circumcised women can experience sexual pleasure and have orgasms.

Assessing the consequences of female genital surgeries in Kenya during the 1920s and 1930s, Edgerton remarks that the operation was performed without anesthesia and was very painful, "yet most girls bore it bravely and few suffered serious infection or injury as a result. Circumcised women did not lose their ability to enjoy sexual relations, nor was their child-bearing capacity diminished. Nevertheless the practice offended Christian sensibilities." Edgerton's is but one of several anthropological statements that call into question the accuracy of the nightmarish discourse of the current global anti-FGM campaigns.

This is what Sandra Lane and Robert Rubinstein (1996:35) say about the practice today in Egypt, where approximately 85–90 percent of females and males are circumcised:

> An important caveat, however, is that many members of societies that practice traditional female genital surgeries do not view the result as mutilation. Among these groups, in fact, the resulting appearance is considered an improvement over female genitalia in their natural state. Indeed, to call a woman uncircumcised, or to call a man the son of an uncircumcised mother, is a terrible insult and noncircumcised adult female genitalia are often considered disgusting. In interviews we conducted in rural and urban Egypt and in studies conducted by faculty of the High Institute of Nursing, Zagazig University, Egypt, the overwhelming majority of circumcised women planned to have the procedure performed on their daughters. In discussions with some fifty women we found only two who resent and are angry at having been circumcised. Even these women do not think that female circumcision is one of the most critical problems facing Egyptian women and girls.

> In the rural Egyptian hamlet where we have conducted field-
> work some women were not familiar with groups that did not
> circumcise their girls. When they learned that the female
> researcher was not circumcised their response was disgust
> mixed with joking laughter. They wondered how she could
> have thus gotten married and questioned how her mother
> could have neglected such an important part of her prepara-
> tion for womanhood.

This is what Carla Obermeyer (1999:92, 95), an epidemiologist and medical anthropologist at Harvard University, says after a recent massive review of the medical and demographic literature on the health consequences of the cultural practice: "On the basis of the vast literature on the harmful effects of genital surgeries, one might have anticipated finding a wealth of studies that document considerable increases in mortality and morbidity. This review could find no incontrovertible evidence on mortality, and the rate of medical complications suggest that they are the exception rather than the rule.... In fact, studies that systematically investigate the sexual feelings of women and men in societies where genital surgeries are found are rare, and the scant information that is available calls into question the assertion that female genital surgeries are fundamentally antithetical to women's sexuality and incompatible with sexual enjoyment."

Arguably the most systematic, large-scale, and scientifically rigorous study of the medical consequences of female genital surgeries in Africa is the Medical Research Council investigation of the reproductive health consequences of the practice (Morison et al. 2001). The study was published after Obermeyer's literature review, although its findings are consistent with her conclusions. The study was conducted in the Gambia, where the surgery most typically involves an excision of the visible part of the clitoris and either a partial or complete excision of the labia minora. The study systematically compared circumcised with uncircumcised women. More than 1,100 women (ages fifteen to fifty-four) from three ethnic groups (Mandinka, Wolof, and Fula) were interviewed and given gynecological examinations and laboratory tests. In the annals of the literature, this is rare data on the consequences of female genital operations.

Overall, very few differences were discovered in the reproductive health status of circumcised women versus uncircumcised women. Of the women who were uncircumcised, 43 percent reported menstrual problems, compared with 33 percent for circumcised women. The difference was not statistically significant. Of the women who were uncircumcised, 56 percent had a damaged perineum, compared with 62 percent for circumcised women. Again, the difference was not statistically significant. There were a small number of statistically significant differences, for example, more syphilis (although not a lot of syphilis) among uncircumcised women and a higher level of one particular kind of bacterial infection among circumcised women. In general, from the point of view of reproductive health consequences, there was not much to write home about. As noted in the research report, the supposed morbidities (such as infertility, painful sex, vulval tumors, menstrual problems, incontinence, and most endogenous infections) often cited by anti-FGM advocacy groups as common long-term problems of female circumcision did not distinguish women who had the surgery from those who did not. Yes, 10 percent of circumcised Gambian women in the study were infertile, but the level of infertility was exactly the same for the uncircumcised Gambian women in the study. The authors (Morison et al. 2001:651) caution anti-FGM activists against exaggerating the morbidity and mortality risks of the practice. In addition, circumcised Gambian women expressed high levels of support for the practice. The authors of the study write, "When women in our study were asked about the most recent circumcision operation undergone by a daughter, none reported any problems" (2001:651).

Finally, this is what Fuambai Ahmadu (2000), an anthropologist at the London School of Economics and Political Science, says about her own ritual initiation in Sierra Leone: "It is difficult for me—considering the number of ceremonies I have observed, including my own—to accept that what appear to be expressions of joy and ecstatic celebrations of womanhood in actuality disguise hidden experiences of coercion and subjugation. Indeed, I offer that the bulk of Kono women who uphold these rituals do so because they want to—they relish in the supernatural powers of their ritual leaders over against men in society, and they embrace the legitimacy of female authority and particularly, the authority of their mothers and grandmothers."

Ms. Ahmadu grew up in the United States after her parents migrated here when she was five years old. As a young adult, at age twenty-two, she returned to Sierra Leone to be initiated like all other Kono women. Speaking at the AAA meetings in Chicago four years ago, she remarked, "I also share with feminist scholars and activists campaigning against the practice a concern for women's physical, psychological and sexual well-being, as well as with the implications of these traditional rituals for women's status and power in society. Coming from an ethnic group [the Kono of Eastern Sierra Leone] in which female (and male) initiation and circumcision are institutionalized and a central feature of culture and society and having myself undergone this traditional process of becoming a 'woman,' I find it increasingly challenging to reconcile my own experiences with prevailing global discourses on female circumcision."

None of this type of testimony was sought or heard before Patricia Schroeder and the Congress wrote a law designed to make this type of initiation illegal. For the most part, anthropologists who are most knowledgeable about African circumcision practices have been hesitant to step forward, speak out, and educate the public about this cultural practice, although this may be changing (for example, see Obermeyer 1999; Shell-Duncan and Hernlund 2000).

Consider two types of hypothetical cases (also described in Shweder 2002), a real instance of which may one day come forward in our courts.

Imagine an African mother who lives in the United States and holds the following convictions: She believes that her daughters, as well as her sons, should be able to improve their looks and their marriage prospects, enter into a covenant with God, and be honored as adult members of the community, via circumcision. Imagine that her proposed surgical procedure (for example, a cut in the prepuce that covers the clitoris) is no more substantial from a medical point of view than the customary American male-circumcision operation. Why should we not extend that option to the Kono parents of girls, as well as to the Jewish parents of boys. Principles of gender equity, due process before the law, religious and cultural freedom, and family privacy would seem to support the option. Or is one going to argue that gender equity requires that male circumcision be criminalized as well, thereby attempting (as anti–male circumcision activists in Canada and the

United States are promoting) to eradicate a practice that has been central to Judaism and Islam for thousands of years?

Imagine a sixteen-year-old female Somali teenager living in Seattle who believes that a genital alteration would be "something very great." She likes the look of her mother's body and her recently circumcised cousin's body far better than she likes the look of her own. She wants to be a mature and beautiful woman, Somali-style. She wants to marry a Somali man or, at least, a man who appreciates the intimate appearances of an initiated woman's body. She wants to show solidarity with other African women who express their sense of beauty, civility, and feminine dignity in this way, and she shares their sense of aesthetics and seemliness. She reviews the medical literature and discovers that the surgery can be done safely, hygienically, and with no great effect on her sexual capacities. After consultation with her parents and the full support of other members of her community, she elects to carry on the tradition. In a society that endorses sex-change operations, breast enhancements, nose jobs, and a vast array of cosmetic surgeries, what principle of justice demands that her cultural heritage and ideals for the human body be criminalized and brought to an end?

CONCLUSION

In this chapter on the moral challenge of cultural migration for liberal democracies, I have discussed four types of controversial cases: school refusal among the Amish of Wisconsin, animal sacrifice in a Santeria church in Florida, touching and physical contact among Afghans in Maine, and female genital surgeries for Somalis in Seattle. I have focused on these four cases with a very special purpose in mind: to draw attention to aspects of the ethical and moral national regime that delimits the space within which tolerance of cultural difference is possible in the United States. In examining these cases, I do not mean to suggest that immigrant minority groups have had an unusually hard time maintaining their cultural practices in the United States. Indeed, some have argued that the United States has been far more accommodating of difference than have other societies in the world and has absorbed large numbers of immigrants without great difficulty (Cohen and Bledsoe 2002). To the extent that this is true, it may have something to do, in part, with the way US legal and ethical traditions treat issues such as the free exercise of religion, family privacy, parental rights, and so forth. It may have something to do with the relatively decentralized nature of normative regimes in the United States, where it is sometimes possible to change location and migrate to "a more tolerant region." Nearly half the states in the United States, although not Oregon, have made legal exceptions for the sacramental use of peyote by members of the Native American Church.

My main aim, however, has been merely to raise questions about the scope of cultural tolerance in a liberal democracy such as the United States. Whether anthropology as a discipline will rise to the moral challenges posed by cultural migration remains to be seen. Inevitably and increasingly, public policy debates will address difficult issues about the shape multiculturalism ought to take. Will anthropology discipline itself to be a scholarly discipline that faithfully represents the native point of view? Will it work to combat ethnocentrism in the law by educating the general public about the moral decency and rationality of "others"? Will anthropology engage a normative agenda for a multicultural society in an informed and rigorous way, trying to distinguish between a defensible pluralism and the indefensible position of radical relativism that says whatever is, is okay? Or will the main message of contemporary anthropology be that we should live in a world of individuals without groups? That everything is in flux and unbounded? That Frederick Nietzsche was right about custom being false consciousness and tradition bad faith? That not only is the idea of God dead but also the idea of culture? Will the message of cultural anthropology be that attachment to the heritage of one's ancestors does not and should not matter any more? I hope not. This is a good time for anthropology to reclaim and defend its interest in the value of cultural differences, which is one way American cultural anthropology can begin to rediscover its soul.

Acknowledgments

I wish to express my gratitude to the members of the Social Science Research Council Working Group on Ethnic Customs, Assimilation, and American Law [recently renamed "Law and Culture"] for educating me about the issues discussed in this chapter. I believe that because I have been inspired over the years by conversations with colleagues such as David Chambers, Jane Cohen, Arthur Eisenberg, Martha Minow, Alison Renteln, and Larry Sager, I was able to work up the courage to engage in this type of analysis of legal cases.

References

Abelmann, N., and J. Lie
1995   *Blue Dreams: Korean Americans and the Los Angeles Riots.* Cambridge, Mass.:
        Harvard University Press.

Abusharaf, R. M.
2002   *Wanderings: Sudanese Migrants and Exiles in North America.* Ithaca, N.Y.:
        Cornell University Press.

Acherman-Chor, D.
2001   Becoming Comprehensive: Organizational Cultures, Tracking Practices and
        Equality of Opportunity. Ph.D. diss., Florida International University,
        Miami.

Adler, R.
n.d.   *Yucatecans in Dallas, Texas: Breaching the Border, Bridging the Distance.* Boston:
        Allyn and Bacon, in press.

Ahmadu, F.
2000   Rites and Wrongs: Excision and Power among Kono Women of Sierra
        Leone. In *Female "Circumcision" in Africa: Culture, Change and Controversy,*
        edited by B. Shell-Duncan and Y. Hernlund, Boulder, Col.: Lynne Rienner.
        (Also presented in the panel "Female Genital Cutting: Local Dynamics of a
        Global Debate," November 18, 1999, 98th Annual Meeting of the American
        Anthropological Association, Chicago.)

Ainslie, R.
1998   Cultural Mourning, Immigration, and Engagement: Vignettes from the
        Mexican Experience. In *Crossings: Mexican Immigration in Interdisciplinary
        Perspectives,* edited by M. Suárez-Orozco, Cambridge, Mass.: David
        Rockefeller Center for Latin American Studies, Harvard University Press.

Alba, R., and N. Denton
2002   The Old and New Landscapes of Diversity: Residential Patterns of
        Immigrant Minorities. Paper presented at the Social Science Research
        Council workshop "Immigration, Race and Ethnicity: Then to Now,"
        San Jose, Cal.

References

Alba, R., and V. Nee

1999   Rethinking Assimilation Theory for a New Era of Immigration. In *The Handbook of International Migration: The American Experience,* edited by C. Hirschman, P. Kasinitz, and J. DeWind, New York: Russell Sage Foundation.

2003   *Remaking the American Mainstream.* Cambridge, Mass.: Harvard University Press.

Alba, R. D., J. R. Logan, B. J. Stults, G. Marzan, and W. Zhang

1999   Immigrant Groups in the Suburbs: A Reexamination of Suburbanization and Spatial Assimilation. *American Sociological Review* 64:446–460.

Ali-Ali, N., R. Black, and K. Koser

2001   The Limits to "Transnationalism": Bosnian and Eritrean Refugees in Europe as Emerging Transnational Communities. *Ethnic and Racial Studies* 24 (4):601–618.

American Anthropological Association (AAA)

1998   *Code of Ethics.* Arlington, Va.: American Anthropological Association.

Anctil, P.

1984   Double Majorité et Multiplicité Ethnoculturelle à Montréal. *Recherches Sociographiques* 25:441–450.

Anderson, B.

1993   The New World Disorder. *New Left Review* 193 (May/June):2–13.

1994   Exodus. *Critical Inquiry* 20 (winter):314–327.

Andreas, P.

2000   *Border Games: Policing the U.S.-Mexico Divide.* Ithaca, N.Y.: Cornell University Press.

Andreas, P., and T. Snyder, eds.

2000   *The Wall around the West: States Borders and Immigration Controls in North America and Europe.* Lanham, Md.: Rowman & Littlefield.

Anzaldúa, G.

1990   *Making Face, Making Soul/Haciendo Caras: Creative and Critical Perspectives by Women of Color.* San Francisco: Aunt Lute.

Appadurai, A.

1996   *Modernity at Large: Cultural Dimensions of Globalization.* Minneapolis: University of Minnesota Press.

1988   Introduction: Place and Voice in Anthropological Theory. *Cultural Anthropology* 3:16–20.

1990   Disjuncture and Difference in the Global Economy. *Public Culture* 2 (2):1–24.

Apter, D.

1965   *The Politics of Modernization.* Chicago: University of Chicago Press.

Arensberg, C.

1965   *Culture and Community.* New York: Harcourt, Brace & World.

Arvizu, S.

2001   Building Bridges and Empowerment: Anthropological Contributions to Diversity and Educational Practices. In *Cultural Diversity in the United States,* edited by I. Susser and T. Patterson, pp. 391–404. Malden, Mass.: Blackwell Publishers.

Asad, T.

1973   Introduction. In *Anthropology and the Colonial Encounter,* edited by T. Asad. London: Ithaca Press.

Atlanta Journal and Constitution

2000a   Fixes Afoot to Make Buford Highway Safer for Pedestrians. September 4.

2000b   OSHA Targets Alarming Rise in On-the-Job Fatalities. September 4.

2001   Clinics Scrambling for Interpreters. July 2.

2002   Rural Roots Bring Hmong to Georgia, Atlanta and the World. April 17.

Bach, R., and L. Schraml

1982   Migration, Crisis and Theoretical Conflict. *International Migration Review* 16 (2):320–41.

Bacon, J.

1996   *Life Lines: Community, Family and Assimilation among Asian Indian Immigrants.* New York: Oxford University Press.

Baer, H. A.

2001   *Biomedicine and Alternative Healing Systems in America: Issues of Class, Race, Ethnicity and Gender.* Madison: The University of Wisconsin Press.

Bailey, B.

2001   *Language, Race and Negotiation of Identity: A Study of Dominican Americans.* New York: LFB Scholarly Publishing.

Bandura, A.

1977   Self-Efficacy: Toward a Unifying Theory of Behavioral Change. *Psychological Review* 84:191–215.

1982   Self-Efficacy Mechanism in Human Agency. *American Psychologist* 37:122–147.

Barnes, J. A.

1954   Class and Committees in a Norwegian Island Parish. *Human Relations* 7:39–58.

1969   Networks and Political Processes. In *Social Networks in Urban Situations,* edited by J. C. Mitchell, pp. 51–76. Manchester: Manchester University Press.

Basch, L.

1987   The Vincentians and Grenadians: The Role of Voluntary Associations in Immigrant Adaptation to New York City. In *New Immigrants in New York,* edited by N. Foner, pp. 159–194. New York: Columbia University Press.

2001   Transnational Relations and the Politics of National Identity: An Eastern Caribbean Case Study. In *Islands in the City: West Indian Migration to New York,* edited by N. Foner, pp. 117–141. Berkeley: University of California Press.

Basch, L., N. Glick Schiller, and C. Szanton Blanc
1994   *Nations Unbound: Transnational Projects, Postcolonial Predicaments, and Deterritorialized Nation States.* Langhorne, Pa.: Gordon and Breach.

Basch, L., R. Wiltshire, W. Wiltshire, and J. Toney
1990   *Caribbean Regional and International Migration: Transnational Dimensions.* Ottawa, Canada: International Development Research Centre.

Bauman, Z.
1998   *Globalization: The Human Consequences.* New York: Columbia University Press.

Baylis, J., and S. Smith
1997   *The Globalization of World Politics.* New York: Oxford University Press.

Benmayor, R., R. M. Torruellas, and A. L. Juarbe
1997   Claiming Cultural Citizenship in East Harlem: "Si Esto Puedo Ayudar a la Comunidad Mía...." In *Latino Cultural Citizenship,* edited by W. W. Flores and R. Benmayor, pp. 154–209. Boston: Beacon Press.

Berger, J., and J. Mohr
1975   *A Seventh Man: The Story of a Migrant Worker in Europe.* Harmondsworth, UK: Penguin Books.

Berk, M. L., C. L. Schur, L. R. Chavez, and M. Frankel
2000   Health Care Use among Undocumented Latino Immigrants: Is Free Health Care the Main Reason Why Latinos Come to the United States? A Unique Look at the Facts. *Health Affairs* 19:51–64.

Bezruchka, S.
2001   Is Our Society Making You Sick? *Newsweek,* February 26.

Bhabha, H.
1996   Embodied Rights: Gender Persecution, State Sovereignty, and Refugees. *Public Culture* 9:3–32.

Boas, F.
1911a   *Changes in Bodily Form of Descendants of Immigrants.* Reports of the Immigration Commission, 61st Congress, 2nd Session, Senate Document No. 208. Vol. 38. Washington, D.C.: Government Printing Office.

1911b   *The Mind of Primitive Man.* New York: Macmillan.

1940   *Race, Language and Culture.* New York: Free Press.

Boddy, J.
1982   Womb as Oasis: The Symbolic Context of Pharaonic Circumcision in Rural Northern Sudan. *American Ethnologist* 9:682–698.

1989   *Wombs and Alien Spirits: Women, Men and the Zar Cult in Northern Sudan.* Madison: University of Wisconsin Press.

1996   Violence Embodied? Circumcision, Gender Politics, and Cultural
        Aesthetics. In *Rethinking Violence against Women,* edited by R. E. Dobash and
        R. P. Dobash, Thousand Oaks, Cal.: Sage Publications.

Bodnar, J.
1985   *The Transplanted: A History of Immigrants in Urban America.* Bloomington:
        Indiana University Press.

Bodnar, J., M. Weber, and R. Simon
1982   *Lives of Their Own: Blacks, Italians, and Poles in Pittsburgh, 1900–1960.*
        Urbana: University of Illinois Press.

Body-Gendrot, S., and M. Martiniello
2000   *Minorities in European Cities: The Dynamics of Social Integration and Social
        Exclusion at the Neighbourhood Level.* New York: St. Martins Press.

Boissevain, J., and H. Grotenberg
1986   Culture, Structure and Ethnic Enterprise: The Surinamese of Amsterdam.
        Ethnic and Racial Studies 9:1–22.

Borjas, G.
1999   *Heaven's Door: Immigration Policy and the American Economy.* Princeton, N.J.:
        Princeton University Press.

Borneman, J.
1986   Emigres as Bullets/Immigration as Penetration: Perceptions of the
        Marielitos. *Journal of Popular Culture* 20:73–92.

Borofsky, R., F. Barth, R. Shweder, L. Rodseth, N. Stolzenberg
2001   WHEN: A Conversation about Culture. *American Anthropologist* 103:432–446.

Boston Globe
2001   Migration's Disruption of Children Weighed Most Youngsters Apart from
        At Least One Parent. June 29, third edition, National/Foreign section.

Boswell, T. D.
1994   *The Cubanization and Hispanicization of Metropolitan Miami.* Miami: The
        Cuban American Policy Center.

Bourne, R.
1916   Trans-national America. *Atlantic Monthly* 118:86–97.

Bower, B.
1993   Mind-Survival Link Emerges from Death Data. *Science News* 144:293.

Bozzoli, B.
1983   Marxism, Feminism, and South African Studies. *Journal of South African
        Studies* 9 (2):139–171.

Brandes, S.
1975   *Migration, Kinship, and Community: Tradition and Transition in a Spanish
        Village.* New York: Academic Press.

REFERENCES

Brennan, D.
2001   Tourism in Transnational Places: Dominican Sex Workers and German
        Sex Tourists Imagine One Another. *Identities: Global Studies in Culture and
        Power* 7 (4):621–663.

Brettell, C. B.
1981   Is the Ethnic Community Inevitable? A Comparison of the Settlement
        Patterns of Portuguese Immigrants in Toronto and Paris. *Journal of Ethnic
        Studies* 9:1–17.

1999   *The City as Context: Approaches to Immigrants and Cities.* Proceedings of
        Metropolis International Workshop, September 28–29, Luso-American
        Development Foundation, Lisbon.

2000a   Theorizing Migration in Anthropology: The Social Construction of
        Networks, Identities, Communities, and Globalscapes. In *Migration Theory:
        Talking across Disciplines,* edited by C. Brettell and J. Hollifield, pp. 97–136.
        New York: Routledge.

2000b   Urban History, Urban Anthropology, and the Study of Migration in Cities.
        City and Society 12:129–138.

Brettell, C. B., and P. de Berjeois
1992   Anthropology and the Study of Immigrant Women. In *Seeking Common
        Ground: Multidisciplinary Studies of Immigrant Women in the United States,*
        edited by D. Gabaccia, pp. 41–63. Westport, Conn.: Greenwood Press.

Brettell, C. B., and J. Hollifield, eds.
2000   *Migration Theory: Talking across Disciplines.* New York: Routledge.

Brown, K. M.
1999   Staying Grounded in a High-Rise Building: Ecological Dissonance and
        Ritual Accommodation in Haitian Vodou. In *Gods of the City,* edited by
        R. Orsi, pp.79–102. Bloomington: Indiana University Press.

Brown, P. J., ed.
1998   *Understanding and Applying Medical Anthropology.* Mountain View, Cal.:
        Mayfield Publishing Co.

Bruner, E.
1970   Medan: The Role of Kinship in an Indonesian City. In *Peasants in Cities,*
        edited by W. Mangin, pp. 122–134. Boston: Houghton Mifflin.

Bryce-LaPorte, R. S.
1993   Voluntary Immigration and Continuing Encounters between Blacks: The
        Post-Quincentenary Challenge. *Annals, AAPSS* 530 (November):28–41.

Bryceson, D., and U. Vuorela, eds.
2002   *The Transnational Family: New European Frontiers and Global Networks.*
        Oxford: Berg Publishers Limited.

Buechler, J. M., ed.
1976   Women and Migration. *Anthropological Quarterly* 49 (special issue).

Buijs, G.

1993   *Migrant Women.* Oxford: Berg Publishers Limited.

Burawoy, M.

1991a   Reconstructing Social Theory. In *Ethnography Unbound,* edited by
M. Burawoy et al., Berkeley: University of California Press.

1991b   The Extended Case Method. In *Ethnography Unbound,* edited by
M. Burawoy et al., Berkeley: University of California Press.

1998   The Extended Case Method. *Sociological Theory* 16 (1):4–33.

Bureau of Primary Health Care

1999   *Cultural Competence: A Journey.* New Orleans: Health Resources and Services
Administration, Department of Health and Human Services, and
Spectrum Unlimited.

Calavita, K.

1992   *Inside the State: The Bracero Program, Immigration and the INS.* New York:
Routledge.

1996   The New Politics of Immigration: "Balanced-Budget Conservatism" and
the Symbolism of Proposition 187. *Social Problems* 43:284–305.

Camarillo, A.

2002   Black and Brown in Compton: Demographic Change, Suburban Decline,
and Intergroup Relations in a South Central Los Angeles Community,
1950–2000. Paper presented at the Social Science Research Council workshop "Immigration, Race and Ethnicity: Then to Now," San Jose, Cal.

Canclini, N.

1995   *Hybrid Cultures: Strategies for Entering and Leaving Modernity,* translated by
C. Chippari and S. López. 1989. Reprint, Minneapolis: University of
Minnesota Press.

Caplan, N., M. H. Choy, and J. K. Whitmore

1989   *The Boat People and Achievement in America: A Study of Family Life, Hard Work,
and Cultural Values.* Ann Arbor: The University of Michigan Press.

1991   *Children of the Boat People: A Study of Educational Success.* Ann Arbor: The
University of Michigan Press.

1992   Indochinese Refugee Families and Academic Achievement. *Scientific
American* (February):36–42.

Carter, D.

1997   *States of Grace: Senegalese in Italy and the New European Immigration.*
Minneapolis: University of Minnesota Press.

Cary, F. C., ed.

1996   *Urban Odyssey: A Multicultural History of Washington, D.C.* Washington:
Smithsonian Institution Press.

Castles, S.

1984   *Here for Good.* London: Pluto Press.

Castles, S., and A. Davidson

2000   *Citizenship and Migration: Globalization and the Politics of Belonging.* New York: Routledge.

Castles, S., and M. J. Miller

1998   *The Age of Migration: International Population Movements in the Modern World,* 2d ed. New York and London: The Guilford Press.

Centers for Disease Control (CDC)

1999   Pedestrian Fatalities—Cobb, Dekalb, Fulton, and Gwinett Counties, Georgia, 1994–1998. *Morbidity and Mortality Weekly Report* 48:601–605.

Cervantes, R. C., V. N. Salgado de Snyder, and A. M. Padilla

1989   Posttraumatic Stress in Immigrants from Central America and Mexico. *Hospital and Community Psychiatry* 40:615–619.

Chagnon, N. A.

1997   *Yanomamo,* 5th ed. Fort Worth, Tex.: Harcourt Brace College Publishers.

Chamberlain, M.

2002   Language, Identity and Caribbean Families: Transnational Perspectives. Paper presented at the conference "Caribbean Migration in Metropolitan Countries: Identity, Citizenship and Models of Integration," Maison de Sciences de l'Homme, Paris.

Chan, S.

1990   European and Asian Immigration into the United States in Comparative Perspective: 1820s to 1920s. In *Immigration Reconsidered: History, Sociology, and Politics,* edited by V. Yans-McLaughlin, New York: Oxford University Press.

Chavez, L. R.

1984   Doctors, Curanderos, and Brujas: Health Care Delivery and Mexican Immigration in San Diego. *Medical Anthropology Quarterly* 15:31–37.

1992   *Shadowed Lives: Undocumented Immigrants in American Society.* (2d ed. 1998) Fort Worth, Tex.: Harcourt Brace and Jovanovich College Publishers.

1997   Immigration Reform and Nativism: The Nationalist Response to the Transnationalist Challenge. In *Immigrants Out! The New Nativism and the Anti-Immigrant Impulse in the United States,* edited by J. F. Perea, pp. 61–77. New York: New York University Press.

1998   *Shadowed Lives.* New York: Harcourt Brace.

2001   *Covering Immigration: Popular Images and the Politics of the Nation.* Berkeley: University of California Press.

Chavez, L. R., W. A. Cornelius, and O. W. Jones

1985   Mexican Immigrants and the Utilization of Health Services. *Social Science and Medicine* 21:93–102.

Chavez, L. R., E. T. Flores, and M. Lopez-Garza

1992   Undocumented Latin American Immigrants and U.S. Health Services: An

Approach to a Political Economy of Utilization. *Medical Anthropology Quarterly* 6: 6–26.

Chavez, L. R., F. A. Hubbell, J. M. McMullin, R. G. Martinez, and S. I. Mishra
1995   Structure and Meaning in Models of Breast and Cervical Cancer Risk Factors: A Comparison of Perceptions among Latinas, Anglo Women and Physicians. *Medical Anthropology Quarterly* 9:40–74.

Chavez, L. R., F. A. Hubbell, and S. I. Mishra
1999   Ethnography and Breast Cancer Control. In *Anthropology in Public Health: Bridging Differences in Culture and Society,* edited by R. A. Hahn, pp. 117–141. New York and Oxford: Oxford University Press.

Chavez, L. R., F. A. Hubbell, S. I. Mishra, and R. B. Valdez
1997   Undocumented Immigrants in Orange County, California: A Comparative Analysis. *International Migration Review* 31:88–107.

Chavez, L. R., J. M. McMullin, S. I. Mishra, and F. A. Hubbell
2001   Beliefs Matter: Cultural Beliefs and the Use of Cervical Cancer Screening Tests. *American Anthropologist* 103:1114–1129.

Chavez, L. R., and V. M. Torres
1994   The Political Economy of Latino Health. In *The Anthropology of Hispanic Groups in the United States.* Houston, Tex.: Arte Publico Press.

Chaze, W., G. Black, S. Peterson, G. White, and J. Hogue
1983   Our Big Cities Go Ethnic. *US News & World Report* 94 (11):49–53.

Chen, H.
1992   *Chinatown No More: Taiwan Immigrants in Contemporary New York.* Ithaca, N.Y.: Cornell University Press.

Chock, P. P.
1996   No New Women: Gender, "Alien," and "Citizen" in the Congressional Debate on Immigration. *PoLar* 19 (1):1–9.

Cinel, D.
1982   *From Italy to San Francisco: The Immigrant Experience.* Stanford, Cal.: Stanford University Press.

Clark, R. L., J. Passel, W. N. Zimmerman, and M. E. Fix
1994   *Fiscal Impact of Undocumented Aliens: Selected Estimates for Seven States.* Washington, D.C.: The Urban Institute.

Cleeland, N., and L. Romney
1999   Latinos Find Luck in Vegas. *Los Angeles Times,* November 30.

Clifford, J.
1994   Diasporas. *Cultural Anthropology* 9 (3):302–337.

Coatsworth, J.
2002   Globalization, Growth and Equality since Columbus. Lecture delivered to the Harvard-Ross Seminar "Globalization and Education," Harvard University, Cambridge, Mass., October.

REFERENCES

Code of Federal Regulations
1991   Title 45, Part 46, Protection of Human Subjects (45 CFR 46), revised June 18 (effective August 19).

Cohen, A.
1969   *Custom and Politics in Urban Africa: A Study of Hausa Migrants in Yoruba Towns.* Berkeley: University of California Press.
1993   *Masquerade Politics: Explorations in the Structure of Urban Cultural Movements.* Berkeley: University of California Press.

Cohen, E., and T. D. Goode
1999   *Rationale for Cultural Competence in Primary Health Care.* Policy Brief 1. Washington, D.C.: National Center for Cultural Competence.

Cohen, J. M., and C. Bledsoe
2002   Immigrants, Agency and Allegiance: Notes from Anthropology and from the Law. In *Engaging Cultural Differences: The Multicultural Challenge in Liberal Democracies,* edited by R. A. Shweder, M. Minow, and H. R. Markus, New York: Russell Sage Foundation.

Cohen, Robin
1997   *Global Diasporas: An Introduction.* Seattle: University of Washington Press.

Cohen, Roger
2000   For "New Danes," Differences Create a Divide. *New York Times,* December 18.

Cole, J.
1997   *The New Racism in Europe: A Sicilian Ethnography.* Cambridge: Cambridge University Press.

Coleman, D. L.
1998   The Seattle Compromise: Multicultural Sensitivity and Americanization. *Duke Law Review* 47:717–783.

Collins, P.
1990   *Black Feminist Thought.* Boston: Hyman.

Colson, E.
1971   *The Social Consequences of Resettlement.* Manchester: Manchester University Press.

Columbus Dispatch
1998   Immigrant Success: Why Sanjay Can Read Better Than Johnny. March 25.

Conway, D., A. Bailey, and M. Ellis
2001   Gendered and Racialized Circulation–Migration: Implications for Poverty and Work Experience of New York's Puerto Rican Women. In *Migration, Transnationalization, and Race in a Changing New York,* edited by H. Cordero-Guzman, R. Smith, and R. Grosfoguel, Philadelphia: Temple University Press.

Coreil, J., and J. D. Mull, eds.
1990   *Anthropology and Primary Health Care.* Boulder, Col.: Westview Press.

Cornelius, W.

1992   From Sojourners to Settlers: The Changing Profile of Mexican Immigration in the United States. In *U.S.-Mexico Relations: Labor Market Interdependence,* edited by J. Bustamante, C. Reynolds, and R. Hinojosa Ojeda, Stanford, Cal.: Stanford University Press.

1998   The Structural Embeddedness of Demand for Mexican Immigrant Labor: New Evidence from California. In *Crossings: Mexican Immigration in Interdisciplinary Perspectives,* edited by M. Suárez-Orozco, Cambridge, Mass.: David Rockefeller Center for Latin American Studies, Harvard University Press.

Cornelius, W., P. Martin, and J. Hollifield

1994   *Controlling Immigration: A Global Perspective.* Stanford, Cal.: Stanford University Press.

Cross, T., B. Bazron, R. Dennis, and M. Isaacs

1989   Towards a Culturally Competent System of Care, Vol. I. Washington, D.C.: Georgetown University Center for Child and Human Development (also known as Georgetown University Child Development Center), CASSP Technical Assistance Center.

Dandler, J., and C. Medeiros

1988   Temporary Migration from Cochabamba, Bolivia to Argentina: Patterns and Impact in Sending Areas. In *When Borders Don't Divide: Labor Migration and Refugee Movements in the Americas,* edited by P. Pessar, pp. 8–41. New York: Center for Migration Studies.

D'Andrade, R.

1984   Cultural Meaning Systems. In *Culture Theory,* edited by R. A. Schweder and R. A. Levine, pp. 88–119. Cambridge: Cambridge University Press.

Davis, M.

1992   *City of Quartz: Excavating the Future of Los Angeles.* New York: Vintage Books.

Dehyle, D.

1987   Learning Failure: Tests as Gatekeepers and the Culturally Different Child. In *Success or Failure?: Learning and the Language Minority Student,* edited by H. T. Trueba, pp. 85–108. New York: Newbury House Publishers, Harper and Row.

Delgado-Gaitan, C.

1987   Parent Perceptions of School: Supportive Environments for Children. In *Success or Failure?: Learning and the Language Minority Student,* edited by H. T. Trueba, pp. 131–155. Cambridge, Mass.: Newbury House Publishers.

Delgado-Gaitan, C., and H. Trueba, eds.

1991   *Crossing Cultural Borders: Education for Immigrant Families in America.* New York: The Falmer Press.

De Vos, G.

1992   *Social Cohesion and Alienation: Minorities in the United States and Japan.* Boulder, Col.: Westview Press.

REFERENCES

DeWind, J.

2000 Immigration Studies and the Social Science Research Council. In *Immigration Research for a New Century: Multidisciplinary Perspectives,* edited by N. Foner, R. Rumbaut, and S. Gold, pp. 69–75. New York: Russell Sage Foundation.

di Leonardo, M.

1984 *The Varieties of Ethnic Experience: Kinship, Class, and Gender among California Italian-Americans.* Ithaca, N.Y.: Cornell University Press.

1998 *Exotics at Home.* Chicago: University of Chicago Press.

Diminescu, D.

2002 "La Marginalité Bon Marché": Le Cas Des Mobilités Roumaines en Europe. Paper presented at the Colloquim Economie de bazaar les métropoles euroméditerraneennes, Aix-en-Provence.

Donato, K.

1992 Understanding U.S. Immigration: Why Some Countries Send Women and Others Send Men. In *Seeking Common Ground: Multidisciplinary Studies of Immigrant Women in the United States,* edited by D. Gabaccia, pp. 159–184. Westport, Conn.: Praeger.

Donnelly, N. D.

1994 *Changing Lives of Refugee Hmong Women.* Seattle: University of Washington Press.

Dressler, W. W.

1996 Culture, Stress, and Disease. In *Medical Anthropology: Contemporary Theory and Method,* edited by C. F. Sargent and T. M. Johnson, pp. 252–271. Westport, Conn.: Praeger.

1999 Modernization, Stress, and Blood Pressure: New Directions in Research. *Human Biology* 71:583–605.

Durand, J.

1998 Migration and Integration. In *Crossings: Mexican Immigration in Interdisciplinary Perspectives,* edited by M. Suárez-Orozco, Cambridge, Mass.: David Rockefeller Center for Latin American Studies, Harvard University Press.

Dussel, E. P.

2000 *Polarizing Mexico: The Impact of Liberalization.* New York: Lynne Rienner.

Dwyer, D.

1983 *Women and Income in the Third World: Implications for Policy.* International Programs Working Paper 18. New York: The Population Council.

Eades, J.

1987 Anthropologists and Migrants: Changing Models and Realities. In *Migrants, Workers, and the Social Order,* edited by J. Eades, pp.1–16. London: Tavistock.

Eames, E., and J. Goode

1977   *Anthropology of the City.* Englewood Cliffs, N.J.: Prentice-Hall.

Ebaugh, H., and J. S. Chafetz

2000   *Religion and the New Immigrants: Continuities and Adaptations in Immigrant Congregations.* Walnut Creek, Cal.: AltaMira Press.

Eckert, P.

1989   *Jocks and Burnouts: Social Categories and Identity in the High School.* New York: Teachers College Press.

Eckholm, E.

2001   District in Beijing to Shut Schools for Migrants. *New York Times,* October 31.

Edgerton, R. B.

1989   *Mau Mau: An African Crucible.* New York: The Free Press.

Eisenberg, A. N.

2002   Accommodation and Coherence: In Search of a Unified Theory for Adjudicating Claims of Faith, Conscience and Culture. In *Engaging Cultural Differences: The Multicultural Challenge in Liberal Democracies,* edited by R. A. Shweder, M. Minow, and H. R. Markus, New York: Russell Sage Foundation.

Eisenhart, M., and M. E. Graue

1993   Constructing Cultural Differences and Educational Achievement in Schools. In *Minority Education: Anthropological Perspectives,* edited by E. Jacob and C. Jordan, pp. 165–179. Norwood, N.J.: Ablex.

Eisgruber, C., and L. Sager

1994a   The Vulnerability of Conscience: The Constitutional Basis for Protecting Religious Conduct. *University of Chicago Law Review* 61.

1994b   Why the Religious Freedom Restoration Act Is Unconstitutional. *New York University Law Review* 69.

1996   Unthinking Religious Freedom. *Texas Law Review* 74.

Ellis, M.

2001   A Tale of Five Cities? Trends in Immigrant and Native-Born Wages. In *Strangers at the Gates: New Immigrants in Urban America,* edited by R. Waldinger, pp. 117–158. Berkeley: University of California Press.

England, S.

1999   Negotiating Race and Place in the Garifuna Diaspora: Identity Formation and Transnational Grassroots Politics in New York City and Honduras. *Identities: Global Studies in Culture and Power* 6 (1):38–46.

Engle, K.

2002   From Skepticism to Embrace: Human Rights and the American Anthropological Association, 1947–1999. In *Engaging Cultural Differences: The Multicultural Challenge in Liberal Democracies,* edited by R. A. Shweder, M. Minow, and H. R. Markus, New York: Russell Sage Foundation.

REFERENCES

Epstein, A. L.

1958   *Politics in an African Urban Community.* Manchester: Manchester University
        Press.

1969   The Network and Urban Social Organization. In *Social Networks in Urban
        Situations: Analyses of Personal Relationships in Central African Towns,* edited
        by J. C. Mitchell, pp. 77–116. Manchester: Manchester University Press.

Epstein, A. L., ed.

1967   *The Craft of Social Anthropology.* London: Tavistock.

Espenshade, T., ed.

1997   *Keys to Successful Immigration: Implications of the New Jersey Experience.*
        Washington, D.C.: The Urban Institute Press.

Espiritu, Y. L.

1997   *Asian-American Women and Men: Labor, Laws and Love.* Thousand Oaks, Cal.:
        Sage Publications.

2001   We Don't Sleep Around like White Girls Do: Family, Culture, and Gender
        in Filipina American Lives. *Signs* 26 (2):415-440.

Evans-Pritchard, E. E.

1962   *Social Anthropology and Other Essays.* New York: Free Press of Glencoe.

Ewing, K. P.

2000   Legislating Religious Freedom: Muslim Challenges to the Relationship
        between "Church" and "State" in Germany and France. *Daedalus: Journal of
        the American Academy of Arts and Sciences* ("The End of Tolerance: Engaging
        Cultural Differences" issue) 129:31–54.

Fadiman, A.

1997   *The Spirit Catches and You Fall Down.* New York: Farrar Straus and Giroux.

Faist, T.

2000a   *The Volume and Dynamics of International Migration and Transnational Spaces.*
        Oxford: Oxford University Press.

2000b   Transnationalization in International Migration: Implications for the Study
        of Citizenship and Culture. *Ethnic and Racial Studies* 23 (2):189–222.

Falicov, C.

1998   *Latino Families in Therapy: A Guide to Multicultural Practice.* New York: Guilford.

Farmer, P.

1992   *AIDS and Accusation: Haiti and the Geography of Blame.* Berkeley: University
        of California Press.

1999   *Infections and Inequalities: The Modern Plagues.* Berkeley: University of
        California Press.

Feldman-Bianco, B.

1992   Multiple Layers of Time and Space: The Construction of Class, Race,
        Ethnicity, and Nationalism among Portuguese Immigrants. In *Towards a
        Transnational Perspective on Migration: Race, Class, Ethnicity and Nationalism*

Reconsidered, edited by N. Glick Schiller, L. Basch, and C. Blanc-Szanton, pp. 145–174. New York: New York Academy of Sciences.

Fernández-Kelly, M. P., and A. García

1990   Power Surrendered, Power Restored: The Politics of Home and Work among Hispanic Women in Southern California and Southern Florida. In *Women, Politics and Change,* edited by L. A. Tilly and P. Gurin, pp. 130–149. New York: Russell Sage Foundation.

Fernández-Kelly, M. P., and R. Schauffler

1994   Divided Fates: Immigrant Children in a Restructured U.S. Economy. *International Migration Review* 28:662–689.

Ferree, M. M.

1990   Between Two Worlds: German Feminist Approaches to Working-Class Women and Work. In *Feminist Research Methods: Exemplary Readings in the Social Sciences,* edited by J. McCarl Nielsen, pp. 174–192. Boulder, Col.: Westview Press.

Fix, M. E., and J. S. Passel

1999   *Trends in Noncitizens' and Citizens' Use of Public Benefits Following Welfare Reform: 1994–97.* Washington, D.C.: Urban Institute.

Foner, N.

1973   *Status and Power in Rural Jamaica: A Study of Educational and Political Change.* New York: Teachers College Press.

1978   *Jamaica Farewell: Jamaican Migrants in London.* Berkeley: University of California Press.

1983   *Jamaican Migrants: A Comparative Perspective on the New York and London Experience.* Occasional Paper No. 36. New York: Center for Latin American and Caribbean Studies, New York University.

1985   Race and Color: Jamaican Migrants in London and New York. *International Migration Review* 19:708–727.

1986   Sex Roles and Sensibilities: Jamaican Women in New York and London. In *International Migration: The Female Experience,* edited by R. J. Simon and C. B. Brettell, pp. 133–151. Totowa, N.J.: Rowman and Allanheld.

1987a   The Jamaicans: Race and Ethnicity among Jamaicans in New York City. In *New Immigrants in New York,* edited by N. Foner, pp. 195–218. New York: Columbia University Press.

1987b   Introduction: New Immigrants and Changing Patterns in New York City. In *New Immigrants in New York,* edited by N. Foner, pp. 1–33. New York: Columbia University Press.

1998a   Towards a Comparative Perspective on Caribbean Migration. In *Caribbean Migration: Globalised Identities,* edited by M. Chamberlain, pp. 47–60. London: Routledge.

1998b   West Indian Identity in the Diaspora. *Latin American Perspectives* 25:173–188.

1999   The Immigrant Family: Cultural Legacies and Cultural Changes. In *The Handbook of International Migration*, edited by C. Hirschman, P. Kasinitz, and J. DeWind, pp. 257–264. New York: Russell Sage Foundation.

2000   *From Ellis Island to JFK: New York's Two Great Waves of Immigration.* New Haven, Conn., and New York: Yale University Press and Russell Sage Foundation.

2001a   West Indian Migration to New York: An Overview. In *Islands in the City: West Indian Migration to New York*, edited by N. Foner, pp. 1–22. Berkeley: University of California Press.

2001b   New Immigrants in a New New York. In *New Immigrants in New York*, edited by N. Foner, pp. 1–32. 2d ed. New York: Columbia University Press.

2001c   Immigrant Commitment to America, Then and Now: Myths and Realities. *Citizenship Studies* 5:27–40.

2001d   Transnationalism: Then and Now. In *Migration, Transnationalization, and Race in a Changing New York*, edited by H. Cordero-Guzman, R. Smith, and H. R. Gosfoguel, pp. 35–57. Philadelphia: Temple University Press.

2002   Response. Forum: Old and New Immigrants: On Nancy Foner's From Ellis Island to JFK. *Journal of American Ethnic History* 21:102–119.

Foner, N., ed.

2001e   *New Immigrants in New York.* 2d ed. New York: Columbia University Press.

2001f   *Islands in the City: West Indian Immigration to New York.* Berkeley and Los Angeles: University of California Press.

Foner, N., R. Rumbaut, and S. Gold

2000   Immigration and Immigration Research in the United States. In *Immigration Research for a New Century: Multidisciplinary Perspectives*, edited by N. Foner, R. Rumbaut, and S. Gold, pp. 1–19. New York: Russell Sage Foundation.

Foster, G., and R. V. Kemper

1974   Introduction: A Perspective on Anthropological Fieldwork in Cities. In *Anthropologists in Cities*, edited by G. Foster and R. V. Kemper, pp. 1–17. Boston: Little Brown.

Fournier, M., M. Rosenberg, and D. White

1997   *Quebec Society: Critical Issues.* Scarborough, Ontario: Prentice Hall Canada Inc.

Fouron, G., and N. Glick Schiller

1997   Haitian Identities at the Juncture between Diaspora and Homeland. In *Caribbean Circuits: New Directions in the Study of Caribbean Migration*, edited by P. Pessar, pp. 127–159. New York: Center for Migration Studies.

2001a   The Generation of Identity: Redefining the Second Generation within a Transnational Social Field. In *Migration, Transnationalization, and Race in a Changing New York*, edited by H. Cordero-Guzman, R. Smith, and R. Grosfoguel, pp. 58–86. Philadelphia: Temple University Press.

2001b   All in the Family: Gender, Transnational Migration, and the Nation-State.
          Identities: Global Studies in Culture and Power ("Gendering Transnational
          Spaces" special issue) 7 (4):539–582.

Fox, R. G.
1977   *Urban Anthropology: Cities in Their Cultural Settings.* Englewood Cliffs, N.J.:
          Prentice-Hall.

Fredrickson, G.
1997   *The Comparative Imagination.* Berkeley: University of California Press.

Freeman, J.
1995   *Changing Identities: Vietnamese Americans, 1975–1995.* Boston: Allyn and Bacon.

Freire, P.
1970   Cultural Action and Conscientization. *Harvard Educational Review*
          40:452–477.
1971   Education as Cultural Action: An Introduction. In *Conscientization for
          Liberation,* edited by L. M. Colonnese, pp. 109–122. Washington, D.C.:
          Division for Latin America, United States Catholic Conference.

Frey, W. H.
2001   *Melting Pot Suburbs: A Census 2000 Study of Suburban Diversity.* Center on
          Urban & Metropolitan Policy, the Brookings Institution, Census 2000 Series.

Friedman, T.
2000   *The Lexus and the Olive Tree: Understanding Globalization.* New York: Anchor
          Books.

Frisken, G., L. S. Bourne, G. Gad, and R. A. Murdie
2000   Social Sustainability: The Toronto Experience. In *The Social Sustainability of
          Cities: Diversity and the Management of Change,* edited by M. Polese and
          R. Stren, pp. 68–97. Toronto: University of Toronto Press.

Frumkin, H., E. D. Walker, and G. Friedman-Jimenez
1999   Minority Workers and Communities. *Occupational Medicine: State of the Art
          Reviews* 14 (3):495–517.

Fuglerud, O.
1999   *Life on the Outside: The Tamil Diaspora and Long Distance Nationalism.*
          London: Pluto Press.

Gabaccia, D.
1992   Introduction. In *Seeking Common Ground: Multidisciplinary Studies of
          Immigrant Women in the United States,* edited by D. Gabaccia, pp. xi–xxvi.
          Westport, Conn.: Greenwood Press.
1994   *From the Other Side: Women, Gender, and Immigrant Life in the U.S.,
          1820–1990.* Bloomington: Indiana University Press.

Gamio, M.
1930   *Mexican Immigration to the United States.* Chicago: University of Chicago Press.

1931   *The Mexican Immigrant: His Life Story.* Chicago: University of Chicago Press.

Garcia, C.

1992   *Dreaming in Cuban.* New York: Ballantine.

Gardner, K., and R. Grillo, eds.

2002   Transnational Households and Ritual. *Global Networks* 2 (special issue):179–262.

Garrison, V., and C. I. Weiss

1979   Dominican Family Networks and United States Immigration Policy: A Case Study. *International Migration Review* 12 (2):264–283.

Geertz, C.

1973a   *The Interpretation of Cultures.* New York: Basic Books.

1973b   Religion as a Cultural System. In *The Interpretation of Cultures,* edited by C. Geertz, pp. 87–126. New York: Basic Books.

1983   *Local Knowledge.* New York: Basic Books.

1995   *After the Fact: Two Countries, Four Decades, One Anthropologist.* Cambridge, Mass.: Harvard University Press.

1997   The Next Thirty-Five Years of Anthropology. *The Sciences* 37 (November/December):3.

2000   *Available Light: Anthropological Reflections on Philosophic Topics.* Princeton, N.J.: Princeton University Press.

Georges, E.

1992   Gender, Class, and Migration in the Dominican Republic: Women's Experiences in a Transnational Community. *Towards a Transnational Perspective on Migration: Race, Class, Ethnicity and Nationalism Reconsidered,* edited by N. Glick Schiller, L. Basch, and C. Blanc-Szanton, pp. 81–100. New York: New York Academy of Sciences.

Georgia Department of Human Resources

1994   Access to Health Care by Limited English Proficient Populations in Georgia: A Report of the Bilingual Health Initiative Task Force. Atlanta, Ga.: Division of Public Health.

Germain, A., J. Archambault, B. Blanc, J. Charbonneau, F. Dansereau, and D. Rose

1995   Cohabitation Interethnique et Vie de Quartier. *Études et Recherches,* no. 12. Québec: Ministère des Affaires Internationales, de l'Immigration et des Communautés Culturelles.

Germain, A., and D. Rose

2000   *Montréal: The Quest for a Metropolis.* New York: John Wiley & Sons.

Gerstle, G.

1999   Liberty, Coercion and the Making of Americans. In *The Handbook of International Migration: The American Experience,* edited by C. Hirschman, P. Kasinitz, and J. DeWind, pp. 275–293. New York: Russell Sage Foundation.

Gibson, M.

1987   The School Performance of Immigrant Minorities: A Comparative View.

Anthropology and Education Quarterly 18 (4):262–275.

1988   *Accommodation without Assimilation: Sikh Immigrants in an American High School.* Ithaca, N.Y.: Cornell University Press.

1991   Ethnicity, Gender and Social Class: The School Adaptation Patterns of West Indian Youths. In *Minority Status and Schooling: A Comparative Study of Immigrant and Involuntary Minorities,* edited by M. A. Gibson and J. U. Ogbu, pp. 169–203. New York: Garland Publishing, Inc.

1993   The School Performance of Immigrant Minorities: A Comparative View. In *Minority Education: Anthropological Perspectives,* edited by E. Jacob and C. Jordan, pp. 113–128. Norwood, N.J.: Ablex.

Gibson, M., and J. Ogbu, eds.

1991   *Minority Status and Schooling: A Comparative Study of Immigrant and Involuntary Minorities.* New York: Garland Publishing, Inc.

Giddens, A.

2000   *Runaway World: How Globalization Is Reshaping Our Lives.* New York: Routledge.

Glazer, N., and D. P. Moynahan

1970   *Beyond the Melting Pot.* Cambridge, Mass.: MIT Press.

Glenn, E. N.

1986   *Issei, Nisei, War Bride: Three Generations of Japanese-American Women in Domestic Service.* Philadelphia: Temple University Press.

Glick Schiller, N.

1999a   Transmigrants and Nation-States: Something Old and Something New in the U.S. Immigrant Experience. In *The Handbook of International Migration: The American Experience,* edited by C. Hirschman, P. Kasinitz, and J. DeWind, pp. 94–119. New York: Russell Sage Foundation.

1999b   Who Are These Guys?: A Transnational Perspective on National Identities. In *Identities on the Move: Transnational Processes in North America and the Caribbean Basin,* edited by L. Goldin, pp. 15–43. Houston: University of Texas Press.

1999c   Transnational Nation-States and Their Citizens: The Asian Experience. In *Globalisation and the Asia Pacific: Contested Territories,* edited by P. Dicken, P. Kelley, L. Kong, K. Olds, and H. W. Yeung, pp. 202–218. London: Routledge.

Glick Schiller, N., L. Basch, and C. Blanc-Szanton, eds.

1992a   *Towards a Transnational Perspective on Migration: Race, Class, Ethnicity and Nationalism Reconsidered.* Annals of the New York Academy of Sciences 645. New York: New York Academy of Sciences.

1992b   Towards a Definition of Transnationalism. In *Towards a Transnational Perspective on Migration: Race, Class, Ethnicity and Nationalism Reconsidered,* edited by N. Glick Schiller, L. Basch, and C. Blanc-Szanton, pp. ix–xiv. New York: New York Academy of Sciences.

1992c   Transnationalism: A New Analytic Framework for Understanding Migration. In *Towards a Transnational Perspective on Migration: Race, Class, Ethnicity and Nationalism Reconsidered,* edited by N. Glick Schiller, L. Basch, and C. Blanc-Szanton, pp. 1–24. New York: New York Academy of Sciences.

1995   From Immigrant to Transmigrant: Theorizing Transnational Migration. *Anthropology Quarterly* 68 (1):48–63.

Glick Schiller, N., J. DeWind, M. Brutus, C. Charles, G. Fouron, and A. L. Thomas

1987   All in the Same Boat? Unity and Diversity among Haitian Immigrants. In *Caribbean Life in New York City,* edited by C. Sutton and E. Chaney, pp. 167–184. Staten Island, N.Y.: Center for Migration Studies.

Glick Schiller, N., and G. Fouron

1990   Everywhere We Go We Are in Danger: Ti Manno and the Emergence of a Haitian Transnational Identity. *American Ethnologist* 17 (2):329–347.

1998   Transnational Lives and National Identities: The Identity Politics of Haitian Immigrants. In *Transnationalism from Below,* edited by M. P. Smith and L. Guarnizo, pp. 130–161. New Brunswick, N.J.: Transaction Publishers.

1999   Terrains of Blood and Nation: Haitian Transnational Social Fields. *Ethnic and Racial Studies* 22 (2):340–366.

2001a   *Georges Woke Up Laughing: Long Distance Nationalism and the Search for Home.* Durham, N.C., and London: Duke University Press.

2001b   I Am Not a Problem without a Solution: Poverty, Transnational Migration, and Struggle. In *New Poverty Studies: The Ethnography of Politics, Policy and Impoverished People in the United States,* edited by J. Goode and J. Maskovsky, pp. 321–361. New York: New York University Press.

Gluckman, M.

1958   Analysis of a Social Situation in Modern Zululand. Rhodes-Livingston Papers No. 28. Manchester: Manchester University Press.

1961   Anthropological Problems Arising from the African Industrial Revolution. In *Social Change in Modern Africa,* edited by A. Southall, pp. 67–83. London: Oxford University Press.

1967   Introduction. In *The Craft of Social Anthropology,* edited by A. L. Epstein, pp. xi–xx. London: Tavistock.

Gold, S. J.

1992   *Refugee Communities: A Comparative Field Study.* Newbury Park, Cal.: Sage Publications.

Goldberg, B.

1992   Historical Reflections on Transnationalism, Race, and the American Immigrant Saga. In *Towards a Transnational Perspective on Migration: Race, Class, Ethnicity and Nationalism Reconsidered,* edited by N. Glick Schiller, L. Basch, and C. Blanc-Szanton, pp. 201–216. New York: New York Academy of Sciences.

Goldring, L.

1998   The Power of Status in Transnational Social Fields. In *Transnationalism from Below,* edited by M. P. Smith and L. Guarnizo, pp. 165–195. New Brunswick, N.J.: Transaction Publishers.

2001   The Gender and Geography of Citizenship in Mexico-U.S.: Transnational Spaces. *Identities: Global Studies in Culture and Power* 7 (4):501–537.

Goldsmith, M. F.

1989   As Farmworkers Help Keep America Healthy, Illness May Be Their Harvest. *Journal of the American Medical Association* 261:3207–3213.

Gonzalez, N.

1986   Giving Birth in America: The Immigrant's Dilemma. In *International Migration: The Female Experience,* edited by R. Simon and C. Brettell, pp. 241–253. Totowa, N.J.: Rowman and Allanheld.

1988   *Sojourners of the Caribbean: Ethnogenesis and Ethnohistory of the Garifuna.* Urbana: University of Illinois Press.

1992   *Dollar, Dove, and Eagle: One Hundred Years of Palestinian Migration in Honduras.* Ann Arbor: University of Michigan Press.

Goode, J.

1990   A Warm Welcome to the Neighborhood: Community Responses to Immigrants. *Urban Anthropology* 19:125–153.

Goode, J., and J. A. Schneider

1994   *Reshaping Ethnic and Racial Relations in Philadelphia: Immigrants in a Divided City.* Philadelphia: Temple University Press.

Goode, T. D.

2001   *Engaging Communities to Realize the Vision of One Hundred Percent Access and Zero Health Disparities: A Culturally Competent Approach.* Policy Brief 4. Washington, D.C.: National Center for Cultural Competence.

Gottdiener, M., C. C. Collins, and D. R. Dickens

1999   *Las Vegas: The Social Production of an All-American City.* Malden, Mass.: Blackwell Publishers.

Graham, P.

2001   Political Incorporation and Re-Incorporation: Simultaneity in the Dominican Migrant Experience. In *Migration, Transnationalization, and Race in a Changing New York,* edited by H. Cordero-Guzman, R. Grosfoguel, and R. Smith, pp. 87–108. Philadelphia: Temple University Press.

Grasmuck, S., and P. Pessar

1991   *Between Two Islands: Dominican International Migration.* Berkeley: University of California Press.

Grenier, G., and A. Stepick

1992   *Miami Now! Immigration, Ethnicity, and Social Change.* Gainesville: University Presses of Florida.

Griffith, D.
1985   Women, Remittances and Reproduction. *American Ethnologist* 12 (4):676–690.

Grillo, R., B. Riccio, and R. Salih
2000   *Here or There? Contrasting Experiences of Transnationalism: Moroccans and Senegalese in Italy.* Sussex: Centre for the Comparative Study of Culture, Development, and the Environment.

Gross, J., D. McMurray, and T. Swedenburg
1996   Arab Noise and Ramadan Nights: Rai, Rap, and Franco-Magrebi Identities. In *Displacement, Diaspora, and Geographies of Identity,* edited by S. Lavie and T. Swedenburg, pp. 119–155. Durham, N.C.: Duke University Press.

Gruenbaum, E.
2001   *The Female Circumcision Controversy: An Anthropological Perspective.* Philadelphia: University of Pennsylvania Press.

Guarnizo, L.
1997a   "Going Home": Class, Gender, and Household Transformation among Dominican Return Migrants. In *Caribbean Circuits: New Directions in the Study of Caribbean Migration,* edited by P. Pessar, pp. 13–60. New York: Center for Migration Studies.
1997b   The Emergence of a Transnational Social Formation and the Mirage of Return Migration among Dominican Transmigrants. *Identities: Global Studies in Culture and Power* 4 (2):281–322.

Guarnizo, L., A. Portes, and W. Haller
2002   From Assimilation to Transnationalism: Determinants of Transnational Political Action among Contemporary Migrants. Working Paper Series. Center for Migration and Development, Princeton University, Princeton, N.J.

Guarnizo, L., A. I. Sanchez, and E. Roach
1999   Mistrust, Fragmented Solidarity and Transnational Migration: Colombians in New York City and Los Angeles. *Ethnic and Racial Studies* 22:367–396.

Guarnizo, L., and M. P. Smith
1998   The Locations of Transnationalism. In *Transnationalism from Below,* edited by M. P. Smith and L. Guarnizo, pp. 3–34. New Brunswick, N.J.: Transaction Publishers.

Guccone, J., and A. Blankstein
2002   Faith Healer Charged in O.C. Man's Death. *Los Angeles Times,* October 31.

Guest, K.
2003   *God in Chinatown: Religion and Survival in New York's Evolving Immigrant Community.* New York: New York University Press.

Gulick, J.
1967   *Tripoli: A Modern Arab City.* Cambridge, Mass.: Harvard University Press.

1975   The City as Microcosm of Society. *Urban Anthropology* 4:5–15.

1984   The Essence of Urban Anthropology: Integration of Micro and Macro Perspectives. *Urban Anthropology* 13:295–306.

Guo, Z.

2000   *Ginseng and Aspirin: Health Care Alternatives for Aging Chinese in New York.* Ithaca, N.Y.: Cornell University Press.

Gupta, A., and J. Ferguson

1992   Beyond "Culture": Space, Identity, and the Politics of Difference. *Cultural Anthropology* 7:6–23.

1997a   Discipline and Practice: The "Field" as Site, Method, and Location in Anthropology. In *Anthropological Locations: Boundaries and Grounds of a Field Science*, edited by A. Gupta and J. Ferguson, pp. 1–46. Berkeley: University of California Press.

Gupta, A., and J. Ferguson, eds.

1997b   *Culture, Power, Place: Explorations in Critical Anthropology.* Durham, N.C.: Duke University Press.

Gutierrez, D.

1998   Ethnic Mexicans and the Transformation of "American" Social Space: Reflections on Recent History. In *Crossings: Mexican Immigration in Interdisciplinary Perspectives*, edited by M. Suárez-Orozco, Cambridge, Mass.: David Rockefeller Center for Latin American Studies, Harvard University Press.

Hackett, B. N.

1996   We Must Become Part of the Larger American Family: Washington's Vietnamese, Cambodians, and Laotians. In *Urban Odyssey: A Multicultural History of Washington, DC*, edited by F. C. Cary, pp. 276–291. Washington: Smithsonian Institution Press.

Haines, D. W., ed.

1989   *Refugees as Immigrants: Cambodians, Laotians and Vietnamese in America.* Totowa, N.J.: Rowman and Littlefield.

1996   *Refugees in America in the 1990s.* Westport, Conn.: Greenwood Press.

Haines, D. W., and C. Mortland, eds.

2001   *Manifest Destinies: Americanizing Immigrants and Internationalizing Americans.* Westport, Conn.: Praeger.

Handlin, O.

1951   *The Uprooted.* Boston: Little, Brown.

Hannerz, U.

1980   *Exploring the City.* New York: Columbia University Press.

Hardt, M., and A. Negri

2000   *Empire.* Cambridge, Mass.: Harvard University Press.

Harris, M.

1979   *Cultural Materialism: The Struggle for a Science of Culture.* New York: Vintage Books.

Harrison, F.

1997   The Gendered Politics and Violence of Structural Adjustment: A View from Jamaica. In *Situated Lives: Gender and Culture in Everyday Life,* edited by L. Lamphere, H. Ragoné, and P. Zavella, pp. 451–468. New York: Routledge.

Hartsock, N.

1987   The Feminist Standpoint: Developing the Ground for a Specifically Feminist Historical Materialism. In *Feminism and Methodology,* edited by S. Harding, pp. 157–180. Bloomington: University of Indiana Press.

Harvey, D.

1989   *The Condition of Postmodernity: An Enquiry into the Conditions of Cultural Change.* New York: Blackwell Publishers.

Haynes, D. V.

1997   Illegal Pharmacies Thrive in Some Immigrant Areas. *Chicago Tribune,* March 14.

Heckman, F.

2001   *Effectiveness of National Integration Strategies toward Second-Generation Migrant Youth in a Comparative European Perspective.* Final Report, Targeted Socio-Economic Research Programme, ERB-SOE2-CT97-3055, Directorate General Science, Research, and Development, European Commission, Brussels.

Hendricks, G.

1974   *The Dominican Diaspora: From the Dominican Republic to New York City— Villagers in Transition.* New York: Teachers College Press.

Hepner, R.

1998   The House That Rasta Built: Church-Building and Fundamentalism among New York Rastafarians. In *Gatherings in Diaspora: Religious Communities and the New Immigration,* edited by R. S. Warner and J. G. Wittner, pp. 197–234. Philadelphia: Temple University Press.

Hernandez, D. J., and E. Charney, eds.

1998   *From Generation to Generation: The Health and Well-Being of Children in Immigrant Families.* Washington, D.C.: National Academy Press.

Hirsch, J. S.

2000   In El Norte La Mujer Manda: Gender, Generation, and Geography in a Mexican Transnational Community. In *Immigration Research for a New Century,* edited by N. Foner, R. Rumbaut, and S. Gold, pp. 369–389. New York: Russell Sage Foundation.

2003   *A Courtship after Marriage: Gender, Sexuality and Love in a Mexican Migrant Community.* Berkeley: University of California Press.

Hirsch, J. S., J. Higgins, M. Bentley, and C. Nathanson.
2002   The Cultural Constructions of Sexuality: Marital Infidelity and STD/HIV Risk in a Mexican Migrant Community. *American Journal of Public Health* 92 (8):1227–1237.

Hirsch, J. S., and C. A. Nathanson
2001   Some Traditional Methods Are More Modern Than Others: Rhythm, Withdrawal and the Changing Meanings of Sexual Intimacy in Mexican Companionate Marriage. *Culture, Health and Sexuality* 3 (4):413–428.

Hirsch, J. S., and K. M. Yount
2001   "Because He Misses His Normal Life Back Home": Social and Cultural Influences on Mexican Migrant's HIV Risk Behavior. Paper presented at the Annual Meeting of the American Anthropological Association, Washington, D.C.

Hirschman, C., P. Kasinitz, and J. DeWind, eds.
1999   *The Handbook of International Migration.* New York: Russell Sage Foundation.

Holliday, K. V.
2001   Botanicas in Orange County: Alternative Spaces of Healing. Paper presented on the panel "The Phenomenology of Religious Experience" at the Annual Meeting of the American Anthropological Association, Washington, D.C.

Hollifield, J. F.
2000   The Politics of International Migration: "How Can We Bring the State Back In?" In *Migration Theory: Talking across Disciplines,* edited by C. B. Brettell and J. F. Hollifield, pp. 137–186. New York: Routledge.

Holmes, S. A.
1998   Immigration Fuels Strong Growth in Many U.S. Metropolitan Areas. *New York Times,* 1 January.

Holtzman, J.
2000   *Nuer Journeys, Nuer Lives: Sudanese Refugees in Minnesota.* Boston: Allyn and Bacon.

Hondagneu-Sotelo, P.
1994   *Gendered Transitions: Mexican Experiences of Immigration.* Berkeley: University of California Press.

1995   Women and Children First. *Socialist Review* 25 (1):169–190.

1999   Introduction: Gender and Contemporary U.S. Immigration. *American Behavioral Scientist* 42 (4):565–576.

2001   *Domestica: Immigrant Workers Cleaning and Caring in the Shadows of Affluence.* Berkeley: University of California Press.

Hondagneu-Sotelo, P., and E. Avila
1997   "I'm Here, but I'm There": The Meanings of Latina Transnational Motherhood. *Gender and Society* 11 (5):548–569.

Hopkins, M., and N. Donnelly, ed.

1993   *Selected Papers on Refugee Issues—II.* Arlington, Va.: American Anthropological Association.

Houston, M., R. Kramer, and J. M. Barrett

1984   Female Predominance of Immigration to the United States since 1930: A First Look. *International Migration Review* 18 (4):908–963.

Howe, I.

1976   *World of Our Fathers.* New York: Simon and Schuster.

Howe, L.

1990   Urban Anthropology: Trends in Its Development since 1920. *Cambridge Anthropology* 14:37–66.

Huddle, D.

1993   The Costs of Immigration. Press release by Carrying Capacity Network, July.

Hurh, W. M., and K. C. Kim

1984   *Korean Immigrants in America: A Structural Analysis of Ethnic Confinement and Adhesive Adaptation.* Rutherford, N.J.: Farleigh Dickinson University.

Inda, J. X., and R. Rosaldo

2002a   Introduction: A World in Motion. In *The Anthropology of Globalization: A Reader,* edited by J. X. Inda and R. Rosaldo, pp. 1–34. Malden, Mass.: Blackwell Publishers.

Inda, J. X., and R. Rosaldo, eds.

2002b   *The Anthropology of Globalization: A Reader.* Oxford: Blackwell Publishers.

Inglis, C., and L. Manderson

1991   Turkish Immigrants in Australia. In *Minority Status and Schooling: A Comparative Study of Immigrant and Involuntary Minorities,* edited by M. A. Gibson and J. U. Ogbu, pp. 97–130. New York: Garland Publishing.

Itzigsohn, J.

2000   Immigration and the Boundaries of Citizenship: The Institutions of Immigrants' Political Transnationalism. *International Migration Review* 34:1126–1154.

2002   The Formation of Latino/a Panethnic Identities. Paper presented at the Social Science Research Council workshop "Immigration, Race, and Ethnicity: Then to Now," San Jose, Cal.

Itzigsohn, J., C. Fore, E. Hernandez, and O. Vasquez

1999   Mapping Dominican Transnationalism. *Ethnic and Racial Studies* 22:316–319.

2002   Incorporation and Transnationalism among Dominican Immigrants. Paper presented at the conference "Caribbean Migrations toward Metropolitan Countries: Identity, Citizenship, Models of Integration," Maison des Sciences de l'Homme, Paris, June 20–22.

Jameson, F., and M. Miyoshi, eds.

1998   *The Cultures of Globalization.* Durham, N.C.: Duke University Press.

Janes, C. R.
1990   *Migration, Social Change, and Health: A Samoan Community in Urban California.* Stanford, Cal.: Stanford University Press.

Jen, G.
1991   *Typical American.* Boston: Houghton Mifflin.

Johnson, H.
1996   *Undocumented Immigration to California: Year 1980–1993.* San Francisco: Public Policy Institute of California.

Johnson, K. R.
1995   Public Benefits and Immigration: The Intersection of Immigration Status, Ethnicity, Gender, and Class. *UCLA Law Review* 42:1509–1575.

Johnson, T. M., and C. F. Sargent
1990   *Medical Anthropology: Contemporary Theory and Method.* New York: Praeger.

Jones-Correa, M.
1998   Different Paths: Gender, Immigration, and Political Participation. *International Migration Review* 32 (2):357–388.

Kao, G., and M. Tienda
1995   Optimism and Achievement: The Educational Performance of Immigrant Youth. *Social Science Quarterly* 96:1–19.

Kasinitz, P.
1992   *Caribbean New York: Black Immigrants and the Politics of Race.* Ithaca, N.Y.: Cornell University Press.

Kasinitz, P., J. Battle, and I. Miyares
2001   Fade to Black? The Children of West Indian Immigrants in Southern Florida. In *Ethnicities: Children of Immigrants in America,* edited by R. Rumbaut and A. Portes, pp. 267–300. Berkeley: University of California Press.

Kasinitz, P., and J. Freidenberg-Herbstein
1987   The Puerto Rican Parade and West Indian Carnival: Public Celebrations in New York City. In *Caribbean Life in New York City: Sociocultural Dimensions,* edited by C. Sutton and E. Chaney, pp. 327–349. New York: Center for Migration Studies.

Kasinitz, P., J. Mollenkopf, and M. C. Waters
2002   Becoming American/Becoming New Yorkers: The Experience of Assimilation in a Majority Minority City. *International Migration Review* 36:1020–1036.

Kearney, M.
1986   From the Invisible Hand to Visible Feet: Anthropological Studies of Migration and Development. *Annual Review of Anthropology* 15:331–361.

1991   Borders and Boundaries of the State and Self at the End of Empire. *Journal of Historical Sociology* 4 (1):52–74.

1995   The Local and the Global: The Anthropology of Globalization and Transnationalism. *Annual Review of Anthropology* 24:547–565.

REFERENCES

2000   Transnational Oaxacan Indigenous Identity: The Case of Mixtecs and
            Zapotecs. *Identities: Global Studies in Culture and Power* 7 (2):173–195.

Kelherer, W.

2000   Making Home in the Irish/British Borderlands: The Global and the Local
            in a Conflicted Social Space. *Identities: Global Studies in Culture and Power* 7
            (2):139–172.

Kemper, R.

1977   *Migration and Adaptation: Tzintzuntzan Peasants in Mexico City.* Beverly Hills,
            Cal.: Sage Publications.

Kemper, R. V., and J. R. Rollwagen

1996   Urban Anthropology. Vol. 4 of *Encyclopedia of Cultural Anthropology.*
            pp. 1337–1344. New York: Henry Holt and Company.

Kibria, N.

1993   *Family Tightrope: The Changing Lives of Vietnamese Americans.* Princeton, N.J.:
            Princeton University Press.

2002   *Becoming Asian American: Second-Generation Chinese and Korean American
            Identities.* Baltimore, Md.: Johns Hopkins University Press.

Kim, S.

1984   Seeking a Dialogue by Koreans, Blacks. *Los Angeles Times,* June 8.

King, A., ed.

1997   *Culture, Globalization, the World System: Contemporary Conditions for the
            Representation of Identity.* New York: Cambridge University Press.

King, N., G. Henderson, and J. Stein

1999   *Beyond Regulations: Ethics in Human Subjects Research.* Chapel Hill: University
            of North Carolina Press.

Kivisto, P.

2001   Theorizing Transnational Immigration. *Ethnic and Racial Studies* 24
            (4):549–577.

Kleinberg, O., and G. De Vos

1973   *Migration: Report of the Research Conference on Migration, Ethnic Minority
            Status, and Social Adaptation.* Rome: United Nations Social Research
            Institute.

Kleinman, A.

1980   *Patients and Healers in the Context of Culture.* Berkeley: University of
            California Press.

1988   *The Illness Narratives: Suffering, Healing, and the Human Condition.* New York:
            Basic Books.

Klimt, A.

2000   Enacting National Selves: Authenticity, Adventure, and Disaffection in the
            Portuguese Diaspora. *Identities: Global Studies in Culture and Power* 6
            (4):513–550.

Kloosterman, R. C.

1998   Migration in the Netherlands and the Emerging Post Industrial Social
        Divide in Urban Areas. In *Immigration, Integration and Cities: Exploring the
        Links.* pp. 73–89. Paris: OECD Proceedings.

Kloosterman, R., J. Van der Leun, and J. Rath

1999   Mixed Embeddedness: (In)formal Economic Activities and Immigrant
        Businesses in the Netherlands. *International Journal of Urban and Regional
        Research* 23 (2):252–266.

Koltyk, J.

1998   *New Pioneers in the Heartland: Hmong Life in Wisconsin.* Boston: Allyn and
        Bacon.

Konczal, L.

1999   *Assimilating into Hispanic America: The Case of Nicaraguan Immigrant
        Adolescents.* Working Paper 4. Miami: Immigration and Ethnicity Institute,
        Florida International University.

2001   The Academic Orientation of First and Second Generation Nicaraguan
        Immigrant Adolescents. Ph.D. diss., Florida International University, Miami.

Kottak, C.

1999   *Mirror for Humanity: A Concise Introduction to Cultural Anthropology.* 2d ed.
        New York: McGraw Hill.

Kraly, E. P., and I. Miyares

2001   Immigration to New York: Policies, Population, and Patterns. In *New
        Immigrants in New York,* edited by N. Foner, pp. 33–79. 2d ed. New York:
        Columbia University Press.

Kramer, B. J.

1991   Education and American Indians: The Experience of the Ute Indian
        Tribe. In *Minority Status and Schooling: A Comparative Study of Immigrant and
        Involuntary Minorities,* edited by M. A. Gibson and J. U. Ogbu, pp. 287–307.
        New York: Garland Publishing.

Kraut, A. M.

1994   *Silent Travelers: Germs, Genes, and the "Immigrant Menace."* Baltimore, Md.:
        Johns Hopkins University Press.

Krieger, N.

2000   Epidemiology and Social Sciences: Towards a Critical Reengagement in
        the 21st Century. *Epidemiologic Reviews* 22 (1):155–163.

Kroeber, A.

1944   *Configurations of Culture Growth.* Berkeley and Los Angeles: University of
        California Press.

Kuper, A.

1999   *Culture: The Anthropologist's Account.* Cambridge, Mass.: Harvard University
        Press.

Kwong, P.

1987   *The New Chinatown.* New York: Hill and Wang.

1996   *The New Chinatown.* Revised ed. New York: Hill and Wang.

1998   *Forbidden Workers: Illegal Chinese Immigrants and American Labor.* New York: New Press.

LaFromboise, F., H. Coleman, and J. Gerton

1998   Psychological Impact of Biculturalism: Evidence and Theory. In *Readings in Ethnic Psychology,* edited by P. Organista, K. Chun, and G. Martin, New York: Routledge.

Laguerre, M.

1984   *American Odyssey: Haitians in New York City.* Ithaca, N.Y.: Cornell University Press.

Lamphere, L.

1987   *From Working Daughters to Working Mothers: Immigrant Women in a New England Industrial Community.* Ithaca, N.Y.: Cornell University Press.

Lamphere, L., ed.

1992   *Structuring Diversity: Ethnographic Perspectives on the New Immigrants.* Chicago: University of Chicago Press.

Lamphere, L., and A. Stepick, eds.

1994   *Newcomers in the Workplace.* Philadelphia: Temple University Press.

Landale, N. S., and R. S. Oropesa

1995   *Immigrant Children and the Children of Immigrants: Inter- and Intra-Group Differences in the United States.* Research Paper 95-02. East Lansing: Population Research Group, Michigan State University.

Landale, N. S., R. S. Oropesa, and B. K. Gorman

1997   *Immigration and Infant Health: Birth Outcomes of Immigrant and Native Women.* University Park, Pa.: Population Research Institute and Department of Sociology, Pennsylvania State University, and National Research Council Board on Children, Youth, and Families.

Landolt, P.

2001   Salvadoran Economic Transnationalism: Embedded Strategies for Household Maintenance, Immigrant Incorporation, and Entrepreneurial Expansion. *Global Networks* 1 (3):217–241.

Lane, S. D., and R. A. Rubinstein

1996   Judging the Other: Responding to Traditional Female Genital Surgeries. *Hastings Center Report* 26:31–40.

Lechner, F., and J. Boli, eds.

1999   *The Globalization Reader.* New York: Bladwell.

Lee, C.

1995   *Native Speaker.* New York: Riverhead.

Lee, C., and G. DeVos

1981   *Koreans in Japan: Cultural Continuities and Minority Status.* Berkeley and Los
        Angeles: University of California Press.

Lee, E.

1966   A Theory of Migration. *Demography* 3:47–57.

Lee, Y.

1991   Koreans in Japan and the United States. In *Minority Status and Schooling:
        A Comparative Study of Immigrant and Involuntary Minorities,* edited by
        M. A. Gibson and J. U. Ogbu, pp. 131–167. New York: Garland Publishing.

Leeds, A.

1973   Locality Power in Relation to Supralocal Power Institutions. In *Urban
        Anthropology,* edited by A. Southall, pp. 15–41. New York: Oxford University
        Press.

Lesher, D., and P. McDonnell

1996   Wilson Calls Halt to Much Aid for Illegal Immigrants. *Los Angeles Times,*
        August 28.

Lesser, J.

1999   *Negotiating National Identity: Immigrants, Minorities, and the Struggle for
        Ethnicity in Brazil.* Durham, N.C.: Duke University Press.

Lessinger, J.

1992   Investing or Going Home: A Transnational Strategy among Indian
        Immigrants in the United States. In *Towards a Transnational Perspective on
        Migration,* edited by N. Glick Schiller, L. Basch, and C. Blanc-Szanton,
        pp. 54–80. New York: The New York Academy of Sciences.

1995   *From the Ganges to the Hudson: Indian Immigrants in New York City.* Boston:
        Allyn and Bacon.

2003   "Religious" Violence in India: Ayodhya and the Hindu Right. In *The State,
        Identity, and Violence: Political Disintegration in the Post-Cold War World,*
        edited by R. B. Ferguson, London: Routledge.

Levitt, P.

2000   Migrants Participate across Borders: Toward an Understanding of Forms
        and Consequences. In *Immigration Research for a New Century,* edited by
        N. Foner, R. Rumbaut, and S. Gold, pp. 459–479. New York: Russell Sage
        Foundation.

2001a   *The Transnational Villagers.* Berkeley and Los Angeles: University of
        California Press.

2001b   Between God, Ethnicity, and Country: An Approach to the Study of
        Transnational Religion. Paper presented at Social Science Research
        Council workshop "Transnational Migration: Comparative Perspectives,"
        Princeton University, Princeton, N.J.

REFERENCES

Levitt, P., and M. C. Waters, eds.

2002   *The Changing Face of Home: The Transnational Lives of the Second Generation.*
        New York: Russell Sage Foundation.

Lewis, O.

1959   *Five Families: Mexican Case Studies in the Culture of Poverty.* New York: Basic Books.

1966   *La Vida: A Puerto Rican Family in the Culture of Poverty—San Juan and New
        York.* New York: Random House.

Li, W.

1998   Anatomy of a New Ethnic Settlement: The Chinese Ethnoburb in Los
        Angeles. *Urban Studies* 35:479–501.

Light, I.

1972   *Ethnic Enterprise in America: Business Welfare among Chinese, Japanese and
        Blacks.* Berkeley: University of California Press.

Lindstrom, D.

1991   The Differential Role of Family Networks in Individual Migration
        Decisions. Paper presented at the Annual Meeting of the Population
        Association of America, Washington, D.C.

Little, K.

1965   *West African Urbanization: A Study of Voluntary Associations.* Cambridge:
        Cambridge University Press.

1973   *African Women in Towns: An Aspect of Africa's Social Revolution.* Cambridge:
        Cambridge University Press.

Lock, M., and N. Scheper-Hughes

1996   A Critical-Interpretive Approach in Medical Anthropology: Rituals and
        Routines of Discipline and Dissent. In *Medical Anthropology: Contemporary
        Theory and Method,* edited by C. F. Sargent and T. M. Johnson, pp. 41–70.
        Westport, Conn.: Praeger

Low, S.

1996   The Anthropology of Cities: Imagining and Theorizing the City. *Annual
        Review of Anthropology* 25:383–409.

1997   Theorizing the City. *Critique of Anthropology* 17:403–409.

1999   *Theorizing the City: The New Urban Anthropology Reader.* New Brunswick, N.J.:
        Rutgers University Press.

Lowe, L.

1996   *Immigrant Acts: On Asian-American Cultural Politics.* Durham, N.C.: Duke
        University Press.

Lowie, R. H.

1937   *The History of Ethnological Theory.* New York: Farrar & Rinehart.

Mahler, S. J.

1995a   *American Dreaming: Immigrant Life on the Margins.* Princeton, N.J.: Princeton
        University Press.

1995b   *Salvadorans in Suburbia: Symbiosis and Conflict.* Boston: Allyn and Bacon.

1998   Theoretical and Empirical Contributions toward a Research Agenda for Transnationalism. In *Transnationalism from Below,* edited by M. P. Smith and L. Guarnizo, pp. 64–100. New Brunswick, N.J.: Transaction Publishers.

2001   Transnational Relationships: The Struggle to Communicate across Borders. *Identities: Global Studies in Culture and Power* ("Gendering Transnational Spaces" special issue) 7 (4):583–620.

Mahler, S., and P. Pessar

2001   Gendered Geographies of Power: Analyzing Gender across Transnational Spaces. *Identities: Global Studies in Culture and Power* 7 (4):441–459.

Mahler, S., and P. Pessar, eds.

2001   *Identities: Global Studies in Culture and Power* ("Gendering Transnational Spaces" special issue) 7 (4).

Maira, S. M.

2002   *Desis in the House: Indian American Youth Culture in New York City.* Philadelphia: Temple University Press.

Malkki, L.

1992   National Geographic: The Rooting of Peoples and the Territorialization of National Identity among Scholars and Refugees. *Cultural Anthropology* 7:24–44.

Manning, R. D.

1998   Multicultural Washington D.C.: The Changing Social and Economic Landscape of a Post Industrial Metropolis. *Ethnic and Racial Studies* 21:328–354.

Marcus, G.

1986   Contemporary Problems of Ethnography in the Modern World System. In *Writing Culture,* edited by J. Clifford and G. Marcus, Berkeley: University of California Press.

Margolis, M.

1994   *Little Brazil: An Ethnography of Brazilian Immigrants in New York.* Princeton, N.J.: Princeton University Press.

1998   *An Invisible Minority: Brazilians in New York City.* Boston: Allyn and Bacon.

Markides, K. S., and J. Coreil

1986   The Health of Hispanics in the Southwestern United States: An Epidemiological Paradox. *Public Health Reports* 101:253–265.

Markowitz, F.

1993   *A Community in Spite of Itself: Soviet Jewish Emigrés in New York.* Washington, D.C.: Smithsonian Institution Press.

Markus, H. R., C. Steele, and D. Steele

2000   Colorblindness as a Barrier to Inclusion: Assimilation and Nonimmigrant Minorities. *Daedalus: Journal of the American Academy of Arts and Sciences* ("The End of Tolerance: Engaging Cultural Differences" issue) 129:233–259.

Martin, M. K., and B. Voorheis

1975   *Female of the Species.* New York: Columbia University Press.

Martin, P.

1995   Proposition 187 in California. *International Migration Review* 24:255–263.

1996   Increasing Numbers of Migrants Challenge Policymakers Worldwide.
        Population Today 2 (5).

Martinez, R. G., L. R. Chavez, and F. A. Hubbell

1997   Purity and Passion: Risk and Morality in Latina Immigrants' and
        Physicians' Beliefs about Cervical Cancer. *Medical Anthropology* 17:337–362.

Massey, D.

1994   *Space, Place and Gender.* Minneapolis: University of Minnesota Press.

Massey, D. S.

1987   The Ethnosurvey in Theory and Practice. *International Migration Review* 21
        (4):1498–1522.

1999   Why Does Immigration Occur? A Theoretical Synthesis. In *The Handbook
        of International Migration: The American Experience,* edited by C. Hirschman,
        P. Kasinitz, and J. DeWind, pp. 34–52. New York: Russell Sage Foundation.

Massey, D. S., R. Alacón, J. Durand, and H. González

1987   *Return to Atzlan: The Social Process of International Migration from Western
        Mexico.* Berkeley: University of California Press.

Massey, D. S., and N. Denton

1993   *American Apartheid.* Cambridge, Mass.: Harvard University Press.

Massey, D. S., J. Durand, and N. Malone

2002   *Beyond Smoke and Mirrors: Mexican Immigration in an Era of Economic
        Integration.* New York: Russell Sage Foundation.

Maternowska, C.

2000   A Clinic in Conflict: A Political Economy Case Study of Family Planning
        in Haiti. In *Contraception across Cultures: Technologies, Choices, Constraints,*
        edited by A. Russell, E. Sobo, and M. Thompson, pp. 103–128. Oxford:
        Berg Publishers.

Mato, D.

1997   On Global and Local Agents and the Making of Transnational Identities
        and Related Agendas in "Latin" America. *Identities: Global Studies in Culture
        and Power* (Transnational Processes: Situated Identities" special issue) 4
        (2):167–212.

Matsuoka, A., and J. Sorenson

2000   *Ghosts and Shadows: Construction of Identity and Community in an African
        Diaspora.* Toronto: University of Toronto Press.

Matthei, L. M., and D. A. Smith

1998   Belizean "Boys 'n the Hood"? Garifuna Labor Migration and Transnational

Identity. In *Transnationalism from Below*, edited by M. P. Smith and L. E. Guarnizo, pp. 270–290. New Brunswick, N.J.: Transaction Publishers.

Matute-Bianchi, M. E.

1986   Ethnic Identities and Patterns of School Success and Failure among Mexican-Descent and Japanese-American Students in a California High School: An Ethnographic Analysis. *American Journal of Education* 95 (1):233–255.

Maurer, B.

1995   Orderly Families for the New Economic Order: Belonging and Citizenship in the British Virgin Islands. *Identities: Global Studies in Culture and Power* ("Sanctioned Identities" special issue, edited by J. Collier and B. Maurer) 2 (1–2):149–171.

Mayer, P.

1961   *Townsmen or Tribesmen: Conservation and the Process of Urbanization in a South African City*. London: Oxford University Press.

McAlister, E.

1998   The Madonna of 115th Street Revisited: Vodou and Haitian Catholicism in the Age of Transnationalism. In *Gatherings in Diaspora: Religious Communities and the New Immigration*, edited by R. S. Warner and J. G. Wittner, pp. 123–160. Philadelphia: Temple University Press.

McConnell, M. W.

1990   *The Origins and Historical Understanding of Free Exercise of Religion*. Harvard Law Review 103:1410–1517.

McDonnell, P. J.

1997   Prop. 187 Found Unconstitutional by Federal Judge. *Los Angeles Times*, November 15.

McGuire, M. B.

1988   *Ritual Healing in Suburban America*. New Brunswick, N.J.: Rutgers University Press.

McMullin, J. M., L. R. Chavez, and F. A. Hubbell

1996   Knowledge, Power and Experience: Variation in Physicians' Perceptions of Breast Cancer Risk Factors. *Medical Anthropology* 16:295–317.

Meillassoux, C.

1981   *Maidens, Meal, and Money: Capitalism and the Domestic Community*. Cambridge: Cambridge University Press.

Meintel, D.

1997   Les Comportements Linguistiques et la Nouvelle Pluriethnicité Montréalaise. *Etudes Canadiennes/Canadian Studies* 45:83–93.

2000   Identity Issues among Young Adults of Immigrant Background in Montreal. *Horizontes* (Brésil) 14:13–38.

Meintel, D., V. Piché, D. Juteau, and S. Fortin

1997   *Le Quartier Côte-des-Neiges à Montréal.* Montréal: L'Harmattan.

Menjívar, C.

1999   The Intersection of Work and Gender: Central American Immigrant
        Women and Employment in California. *American Behavioral Scientist* 42
        (4):601–627.

2000   *Fragmented Ties: Salvadoran Immigrant Networks in America.* Berkeley:
        University of California Press.

2002   The Ties That Heal: Guatemalan Immigrant Women's Networks and
        Medical Treatment. *International Migration Review* 36:437–466.

Merton, R.

1968   *Social Theory and Social Structure.* 1957. Reprint, New York: Free Press.

Micklethwait, J., and A. Wooldridge

2000   *A Future Perfect: The Challenge and Hidden Promise of Globalization.* New York:
        Times Books.

Mignolo, W.

1998   Globalization, Civilization Processes, and the Relocation of Languages and
        Cultures. In *The Cultures of Globalization,* edited by F. Jameson and
        M. Miyoshi, pp. 32–53. Durham, N.C.: Duke University Press.

Mills, M. B.

1997   Contesting the Margins of Modernity: Women, Migration, and
        Consumption in Thailand. *American Ethnologist* 24 (1):37–61.

Mills, N., ed.

1994   *Arguing Immigration: Are New Immigrants a Wealth of Diversity...or a Crushing
        Burden?* New York: Touchstone.

Min, P. G.

1996   *Caught in the Middle: Korean Communities in New York and Los Angeles.*
        Berkeley: University of California Press.

1998   *Changes and Conflicts: Korean Immigrant Families in New York.* Boston: Allyn
        and Bacon.

Minow, M.

2000   About Women, About Culture: About Them, About Us. *Daedalus: Journal
        of the American Academy of Arts and Sciences* ("The End of Tolerance:
        Engaging Cultural Differences" issue) 129:125–146.

Mintz, S.

1985   *Sweetness and Power: The Place of Sugar in Modern History.* New York: Penguin
        Books.

Miranda, M. L.

1997   *A History of Hispanics in Southern Nevada.* Reno and Las Vegas: University of
        Nevada Press.

Mishra, S. I., F. A. Hubbell, L. R. Chavez, R. J. Magana, P. Nava, and R. B. Valdez

1998 Breast Cancer Control among Latinas: Evaluation of a Theory-Based Educational Program. *Health Education and Behavior* 5:653–670.

Mitchell, J. C.

1956 *The Kalela Dance: Aspects of Social Relationships among Urban Africans in Northern Rhodesia.* Rhodes-Livingston Paper No. 27. Manchester: Manchester University Press.

1966 Theoretical Orientations in Urban African Studies. In *The Social Anthropology of Complex Societies,* edited by M. Banton, pp. 37–68. London: Tavistock.

1969 *Social Networks in Urban Situations: Analyses of Personal Relationships in Central African Towns.* Manchester: Manchester University Press.

1973 Distance, Transportation, and Urban Involvement in Zambia. In *Urban Anthropology: Cross-Cultural Studies of Urbanization,* edited by A. Southall, pp. 287–314. New York: Oxford University Press.

Mittleman, J., ed.

1996 *Globalization: Critical Reflections.* Boulder, Col.: Lynne Reinner.

2000 *The Globalization Syndrome.* Princeton, N.J.: Princeton University Press.

Moch, L. P.

1992 *Moving Europeans: Migration in Western Europe since 1650.* Bloomington: Indiana University Press.

Mohanty, C.

1991 Cartographies of Struggle: Third World Women and the Politics of Struggle. In *Third World Women and the Politics of Feminism,* edited by C. Mohanty, A. Russo, and L. Torres, pp. 1–47. Bloomington: University of Indiana Press.

Mollenkopf, J. H.

1999 Urban Political Conflicts and Alliances: New York and Los Angeles Compared. In *The Handbook of International Migration: The American Experience,* edited by C. Hirschman, P. Kasinitz, and J. DeWind, pp. 412–422. New York: Russell Sage Foundation.

Molotch, H., W. Freudenberg, and K. Paulsen

2000 History Repeats Itself, but How? City Character, Urban Tradition, and the Accomplishment of Place. *American Sociological Review* 65:791–822.

Molyneux, M.

1999 The Politics of the Cuban Diaspora in the United States. In *The United States and Latin America: The New Agenda,* edited by J. Bulmer-Thomas and J. Dunkerley, Cambridge, Mass: DRCLAS and Harvard University Press.

Moore, K.

1975 The City as Context: Context as Process. *Urban Anthropology* 4:17–25.

REFERENCES

Morawska, E.

1987   Sociological Ambivalence: The Case of Eastern European Peasant-Immigrant Workers in America, 1980s–1930s. *Qualitative Sociology* 10 (3):225–250.

1989   Labor Migrations of Poles in the Atlantic World Economy, 1880–1914. *Comparative Studies in Society and History* 31 (2):237–270.

2001a   Structuring Migration: The Case of Polish Income-Seeking Travelers to the West. *Theory and Society* 3:47–80.

2001b   Disciplinary Agendas, Analytic Strategies, and Objectivity of (Im)Migration Research: Advantages of Interdisciplinary Knowledge. Paper presented at Social Science Research Council workshop "Transnational Migration: Comparative Perspectives," Princeton University, Princeton, N.J.

Morgan, J.

2001   Un-Equal Opportunity: Sex and School among First and Second Generation Mexican Immigrant Adolescent Girls. Ph.D. diss., Florida International University, Miami.

Morgan, S., and E. Colson, eds.

1987   *People in Upheaval.* New York: Center for Migration Studies.

Morison, L., C. Scherf, G. Ekpo, K. Pain, B. West, R. Coleman, and G. Walraven

2001   The Long-Term Reproductive Health Consequences of Female Genital Cutting in Rural Gambia: A Community-Based Survey. *Tropical Medicine and International Health* 6:643–653.

Morokvasic, M.

1984   Birds of Passage Are Also Women. *International Migration Review* 18 (4):886–907.

1993   "In and Out" of the Labor Market: Immigrant and Minority Women in Europe. *New Community* 19 (3):459–483.

1996   Entre L'Est et L'Ouest, Des Migrations Pendulaires. In *Migrants: Les Nouvelle Mobilit,* edited by M. Morokvasic and H. Rudolph, pp. 119–157. Paris: L'Harmattan.

Morsey, S. A.

1996   Political Economy in Medical Anthropology. In *Medical Anthropology: Contemporary Theory and Method,* edited by C. F. Sargent and T. M. Johnson, pp. 21–40. Westport, Conn.: Praeger.

Moya, J.

1998   *Cousins and Strangers: Spanish Immigrants in Buenos Aires, 1850–1930.* Berkeley: University of California Press.

Muller, T.

1998   Immigration and Urban Areas: The United States Experience. In *Immigration, Integration and Cities: Exploring the Links.* pp. 33–47. Paris: OECD Proceedings.

Mundo Hispanico

2000   Casi La Mitad de Los Obreros Muertos Son Hispanos. 7 June.

Murnane, R., and F. Levy

1996   *Teaching the New Basic Skills.* New York: Free Press.

Myers, D.

1998   Dimensions of Economic Adaptation by Mexican-Origin Men. In
Crossings: Mexican Immigration in Interdisciplinary Perspectives, edited by
M. Suárez-Orozco, Cambridge, Mass.: David Rockefeller Center for Latin
American Studies, Harvard University Press.

Nader, R., ed.

1993   *The Case against Free Trade: GATT, NAFTA, and the Globalization of Corporate
Power.* New York: North Atlantic Books.

Naples, N.

1997   The "New Consensus" on the Gendered "Social Contract." The 1987–1988
US Congressional Hearings on Welfare Reform. *Signs* 22 (4):907–945.

Nash, J.

1986   A Decade of Research on Women in Latin America. In *Women and Change
in Latin America,* edited by J. Nash and H. Safa, pp. 3–21. South Hadley,
Mass.: Bergin and Garvey Publishers.

Nash, J., and M. P. Fernández Kelly, eds.

1983   *Women, Men, and the International Division of Labor.* Albany: State University
of New York Press.

National Bioethics Advisory Commission (NBAC)

2001   *Ethical and Policy Issues in Research Involving Human Participants.* August,
Bethesda, Md.

National Health Foundation (NHF)

1995   *Barriers to Health Care for U.S. Citizen Children of Undocumented Parents.* Los
Angeles.

National Research Council (NRC)

1997   *The New Americans: Economic, Demographic and Fiscal Effects of Immigration.*
Washington, D.C.: National Academy Press.

1998   *From Generation to Generation: The Health and Well-Being of Children in
Immigrant Families.* Washington, D.C.: National Academy Press.

National Science Foundation (NSF)

1995   Cultural Anthropology and Human Capital: Anthropology's Role in the
NSF Initiative on Human Capital, June 27–28, Arlington, Va.

Nelson, N.

1978   Female-Centered Families: Changing Patterns of Marriage and Family
among Buzaa Brewers of Mathare Valley. *African Urban Studies* 3:85–104.

1992   The Women Who Have Left and Those Who Stay Behind. In *Gender and Migration in Developing Countries,* edited by Sylvia Chant, pp. 109–138. London: Bayhaven Press.

New York Newsday

1999   Asian Population Spikes in Queens: Census Shows Big Boost in Diversity in '90s. September 15, Queens edition.

2001   In Queens, "Microcosm of the World," Areas among Most Diverse in the City. March 20, Queens edition.

New York Times

1998   What Shall We Ask Of Immigrants? May 31, section 4.

1999   Wanted: American Physicists, July 23, A27.

2001   Hispanic Workers Die at Higher Rate. July 16.

Ng, F.

1993   *Bone.* New York: Harper Collins.

Ng, M.

1998   *Eating Chinese Food Naked.* New York: Scribner.

Nyiri, P.

1999   *New Chinese Migrants in Europe: The Case of the Chinese Community in Europe.* Aldershot, UK: Ashgate.

Obermeyer, C. M.

1999   Female Genital Surgeries: The Known, the Unknown, and the Unknowable. *Medical Anthropology Quarterly* 13:79–106.

Office of Minority Health (OMH), US Dept. of Health and Human Services

1998   *Closing the Gap* (October).

2000   Moving toward Consensus on Cultural Competency in Health Care. *Closing the Gap* (January):1–2.

2001   Dental Program Brings Latino Values to California Community. *Closing the Gap* (February/March):12.

Ogbu, J.

1974   *The Next Generation: An Ethnography of Education in an Urban Neighborhood.* New York: Academic Press.

1978   *Minority Education and Caste: The American System in Cross-Cultural Perspective.* New York: Academic Press.

1982   Cultural Discontinuities and Schooling. *Anthropology and Education Quarterly* 13 (4):290–307.

1983   Minority Status and Schooling in Plural Societies. *Comparative Education Review* 27 (2):168–190.

1987a   Variability in Minority Responses to Schooling: Nonimmigrants vs. Immigrants. In *Interpretive Ethnography of Education: At Home and Abroad,* edited by G. Spindler and L. Spindler, pp. 255–278. Hillsdale, N.J.: Lawrence Erlbaum.

1987b   Variability in Minority School Performance: A Problem in Search of an
Explanation. *Anthropology and Education Quarterly* 19:312–334.

1991   Immigrant and Involuntary Minorities in Comparative Perspective. In
*Minority Status and Schooling: A Comparative Study of Immigrant and
Involuntary Minorities,* edited by M. A. Gibson and J. U. Ogbu, pp. 3–33.
New York: Garland Publishing.

1993   Variability in Minority School Performance: A Problem in Search of an
Explanation. In *Minority Education: Anthropological Perspectives,* edited by
E. Jacob and C. Jordan, pp. 83–111. Norwood, N.J.: Ablex.

Ogbu, J., and M. Matute-Bianchi
1986   Understanding Socio-Cultural Factors: Knowledge, Identity, and School
Adjustment. In *Beyond Language: Social and Cultural Factors in Schooling
Language Minority Students.* Sacramento, Cal.: Department of Education.

Ojito, M.
1997   Culture Clash: Foreign Parents, American Child Rearing. *New York Times,*
June 29.

Okin, S. M.
1999   *Is Multiculturalism Bad for Women?* Princeton, N.J.: Princeton University
Press.

Olsen, L.
1997   *Made in America: Immigrant Students in Our Public Schools.* New York: New Press.

Olwig, K. F.
1997   Cultural Sites: Sustaining a Home in a Deterritorialized World. In *Siting
Culture: The Shifting Anthropological Object,* edited by K. F. Olwig, and
K. Hastrup, pp. 17–38. London: Routledge.

2001   New York as a Locality in a Global Family Network. In *Islands in the City:
West Indian Migration to New York,* edited by N. Foner, pp. 142–160.
Berkeley: University of California Press.

O'Meara, P., H. Mehlinger, and M. Krain, eds.
2000   *Globalization and the Challenges of the New Century: A Reader.* Bloomington:
Indiana University Press.

Ong, A.
1987   *Spirits of Resistance and Capitalist Discipline: Factory Women in Malaysia.*
Albany: State University of New York Press.

1992   Limits to Cultural Accumulation: Chinese Capitalists on the American
Pacific Rim. In *Towards a Transnational Perspective on Migration,* edited by
N. Glick Schiller, L. Basch, and C. Blanc-Szanton, pp. 125–143. New York:
The New York Academy of Sciences.

1999   *Flexible Citizenship: The Cultural Logics of Transnationality.* Durham, N.C.:
Duke University Press.

REFERENCES

Orfield, G.

1998   Commentary. In *Crossings: Mexican Immigration in Interdisciplinary Perspectives*, edited by M. Suárez-Orozco, Cambridge, Mass.: David Rockefeller Center for Latin American Studies, Harvard University Press.

2002   Commentary. In *Latinos: Remaking America*, edited by M. Suárez-Orozco and M. Páez, Berkeley and London: University of California Press.

Organization for Economic Cooperation and Development (OECD)

1998   *Immigrants, Integration and Cities: Exploring the Links.* Paris: OECD Proceedings.

Ortner, S. B.

1991   Reading America: Preliminary Notes on Class and Culture. In *Recapturing Anthropology*, edited by R. G. Fox, pp. 163–190. Santa Fe, N.Mex.: School of American Research Press.

1996   *Making Gender: The Politics and Erotics of Culture.* Boston: Beacon Press.

Padilla, E.

1958   *Up from Puerto Rico.* New York: Columbia University Press.

Pan, P. P.

1999   At Home in Chirilagua, VA: Salvadoran Leaves Old Village, Finds New One in US. *The Washington Post,* December 6.

Park, K.

1996   Use and Abuse of Race and Culture: Black-Korean Tension in America. *American Anthropologist* 98 (3):492–498.

1997   *The Korean American Dream: Immigrants and Small Business in New York City.* Ithaca, N.Y.: Cornell University Press.

Parker, R.

2001   Sexuality, Culture and Power in HIV/AIDS Research. *Annual Reviews in Anthropology* 30:163–179.

Parker, R., and P. Aggleton

1999   *Culture, Society and Sexuality: A Reader.* London: UCL Press.

Parkin, D.

1974   Congregational and Interpersonal Ideologies in Political Ethnicity. In *Urban Ethnicity*, edited by A. Cohen, pp. 119–158. London: Tavistock.

Paulston, R. G.

1977   Separate Education as an Ethnic Survival Strategy: The Finlandssvenska Case. *Anthropology and Education Quarterly* 8 (3):181–188.

Peacock, J.

1986   *The Anthropological Lens.* Cambridge: Cambridge University Press.

Pedraza, S.

1996   Origins and Destinies: Immigration, Race, and Ethnicity in American History. In *Origins and Destinies: Immigration, Race, and Ethnicity in America*, edited by S. Pedraza and R. Rumbaut, pp. 1–20. Belmont, Cal.: Wadsworth.

Pérez, L.

1986   Immigrant Economic Adjustment and Family Organization: The Cuban Success Story Reexamined. *International Migration Review* 20:4–20.

Perry, W. J.

1923   *The Children of the Sun.* London: Methuen.

Pessar, P. R.

1984   The Linkage between the Household and the Workplace in the Experience of Immigrant Women in the United States. *International Migration Review* 18:1188–1211.

1986   The Role of Gender in Dominican Settlement in the United States. In *Women and Change in Latin America*, edited by J. Nash and H. Safa, pp. 273–294. South Hadley, Mass.: Bergin and Garvey Publishers.

1995a   On the Homefront and in the Workplace: Integrating Immigrant Women into Feminist Discourse. *Anthropological Quarterly* 68 (1):37–47.

1995b   *A Visa for a Dream: Dominicans in the United States.* Boston: Allyn and Bacon.

1995c   The Elusive Enclave: Ethnicity, Class, and Nationality among Latino Entrepreneurs in Greater Washington, DC. *Human Organization* 54:383–392.

1999a   Engendering Migration Studies: The Case of New Immigrants in the United States. *American Behavioral Scientist* 42 (4):577–600.

1999b   The Role of Gender, Households, and Social Networks in the Migration Process: A Review and Reappraisal. In *The Handbook of Migration Studies,* edited by C. Hirschman, P. Kasinitz, and J. DeWind, pp. 53–70. New York: Russsell Sage Foundation.

2001   Women's Political Consciousness and Empowerment in Local, National, and Transnational Contexts: Guatemalan Refugees and Returnees. *Identities: Global Studies in Culture and Power* 7:461–500.

Pessar, P. R., and P. M. Graham

2001   The Dominicans: Transnational Identities and Local Politics. In *New Immigrants in New York*, edited by N. Foner, pp. 251–273. 2d ed. New York: Columbia University Press.

Petersen, W.

1968   Migration. In *International Encyclopedia of the Social Sciences.* New York: Macmillan.

Phinney, J.

1998   Ethnic Identity in Adolescents and Adults: Review of Research. In *Readings in Ethnic Psychology,* edited by P. B. Organista, K. Chun, and G. Martin, New York: Routledge.

Phizacklea, A., ed.

1983   *One-Way Ticket: Migration and Female Labour.* Boston: Routledge and Kegan Paul.

REFERENCES

Plotnicov, L.

1967   *Strangers to the City: Urban Man in Jos, Nigeria.* Pittsburgh: University of Pittsburgh Press.

Portes, A.

1997   Immigration Theory for a New Century: Some Problems and Opportunities. *International Migration Review* 31:799–825.

2001   Introduction: The Debates and Significance of Immigrant Transnationalism. *Global Networks* 1 (3):181–194.

Portes, A., ed.

1996   *The New Second Generation.* New York: Russell Sage Foundation.

Portes, A., and R. Bach

1985   *Latin Journey: Cuban and Mexican Immigrants in the United States.* Berkeley: University of California Press.

Portes, A., L. Guarnizo, and P. Landolt

1999   Introduction: Pitfalls and Promises of an Emergent Field. *Ethnic and Racial Studies* 22 (2):217–237.

Portes, A., W. Haller, and L. E. Guarnizo

2002   Transnational Entrepreneurs: An Alternative Form of Immigrant Economic Adaptation. *American Sociological Review* 67:278–298.

Portes, A., and D. MacLeod

1996a   Educational Progress of Children of Immigrants: The Roles of Class, Ethnicity, and School Context. *Sociology of Education* 69:255–275.

1996b   What Shall I Call Myself? Hispanic Identity Formation in the Second Generation. *Ethnic and Racial Studies* 19 (3):373–396.

Portes, A., and R. G. Rumbaut

1993   The Educational Progress of Children of Immigrants. Release No. 2 of the project "Children of Immigrants, the Adaptation Process of the Second Generation." Unpublished paper. Department of Sociology, Johns Hopkins University, Baltimore, Md.

1996   *Immigrant America.* 2d ed. Berkeley: University of California Press.

2001   *Legacies: The Story of the Immigrant Second Generation.* Berkeley and London: University of California Press; New York: Russell Sage Foundation.

Portes, A., and R. Schauffler

1996   Language and the Second Generation: Bilingualism Yesterday and Today. In *The New Second Generation*, edited by A. Portes.New York: Russell Sage Foundation.

Portes, A., and A. Stepick

1993   *City on the Edge: The Transformation of Miami.* Berkeley: University of California Press.

Portes, A., and C. Truelove

1987   Making Sense of Diversity: Recent Research on Hispanic Minorities in the United States. *American Review of Sociology* 13:359–385.

Portes, A., and M. Zhou

1992   Gaining the Upper Hand: Economic Mobility among Immigrant and Domestic Minorities. *Ethnic and Racial Studies* 15 (4):491–522.

1993   The New Second Generation: Segmented Assimilation and Its Variants. *Annals of the American Academy of Political and Social Sciences* 530:74–95.

Prashad, V.

2000   *The Karma of Brown Folk.* Minneapolis: University of Minnesota Press.

Press, I.

1979   *The City as Context: Urbanism and Behavioral Constraints in Seville.* Urbana: University of Illinois Press.

Ramirez, B.

1997   Histoire et Histoires dans la Métropole Québécoise: Le Quartier Côte-des-Neiges. In *Le Quartier Côte-des-Neiges à Montréal,* edited by D. Meintel, V. Piché, D. Juteau, and S. Fortin, pp. 53–76. Montréal: L'Harmattan Inc.

Rapport, N., and J. Overing

2000   *Social and Cultural Anthropology: The Key Concepts.* New York: Routledge.

Rath, J., and R. Kloosterman

2000   Outsiders' Business: A Critical Review of Research on Immigrant Entrepreneurship. *International Migration Review* 34:657–681.

Ravenstein, E. G.

1885   The Laws of Migration. *Journal of the Statistical Society* 48:167–235.

1889   The Laws of Migration. *Journal of the Statistical Society* 82:214–301.

Rebhun, L. A.

1999   *The Heart Is Unknown Country: Love in the Changing Economy of Northeast Brazil.* Stanford, Cal.: Stanford University Press.

Redfield, R.

1955   *The Little Community: Viewpoints for the Study of a Human Whole.* Chicago: University of Chicago Press.

1967   *The Primitive World and Its Transformations.* 1953. Reprint, Ithaca, N.Y.: Cornell University Press.

Reiter, R., ed.

1975   *Towards an Anthropology of Women.* New York: Monthly Review Press.

Reitz, J. G.

1998   *Warmth of the Welcome: The Social Causes of Economic Success for Immigrants in Different Nations and Cities.* Boulder, Col.: Westview Press.

Repak, T.

1995   *Waiting on Washington: Central American Workers in the Nation's Capital.* Philadelphia: Temple University Press.

Reyna, S.

1994   Literary Anthropology and the Case against Science. *Man* 29:555–581.

2002   *Connections: Brain, Mind, and Culture in a Social Anthropology.* London: Routledge.

Reza, H. G.

1999   Prescription Drugs Flow in Illegal Tide. *Los Angeles Times,* February 27.

Rhodes, L. A.

1996   Studying Biomedicine as a Cultural System. In *Medical Anthropology: Contemporary Theory and Method,* edited by C. F. Sargent and T. M. Johnson, pp. 165–180. Westport, Conn.: Praeger.

Rhor, M.

2001   Philadelphia Plan Seeks "Replacement People," Immigrants the Answer, Council Told. *Philadelphia Inquirer,* May 17.

Richman, K.

1992   "Lavalas at Home/Lavalas for Home": Inflections of Transnationalism in the Discourse of Haitian President Aristide. In *Towards a Transnational Perspective on Migration,* edited by N. Glick Schiller, L. Basch, and C. Blanc-Szanton, pp. 189–200. New York: The New York Academy of Sciences.

Robben, A.

n.d.   *Hitting Where It Hurts Most: The Traumatization of Argentine Society.* Berkeley: University of California Press.

Roberts, B.

1978   *Cities of Peasants: The Political Economy of Urbanization in the Third World.* London: E. Arnold.

Roberts, K.

1985   Household Labour Mobility in a Modern Agrarian Economy: Mexico. In *Labour Circulation and the Labour Process,* edited by G. Standing, pp. 358–381. London: Croom Helm.

Rollwagen, J.

1975   Introduction: The City as Context, A Symposium. *Urban Anthropology* 4:1–4.

Rollwagen, J., ed.

1990   Southeast Asian Refugees in the United States. *Urban Anthropology* 16 (special issue):273–304.

Roosens, E.

1989   *Creating Ethnicity: The Process of Ethnogenesis.* Newbury Park, Cal.: Sage Publications.

Rosaldo, M.

1980   The Use and Abuse of Anthropology: Reflections on Feminism and Cross-Cultural Understanding. *Signs* 5 (3):389–417.

Rosaldo, M., and L. Lamphere, eds.

1974   *Women, Culture, and Society.* Stanford, Cal.: Stanford University Press.

Rosaldo, R.

1989   *Culture and Truth: The Remaking of Social Analysis.* Boston: Beacon Press.

Rostow, W. W.

1960   *The Stages of Economic Growth, A Non-Communist Manifesto.* Cambridge: Cambridge University Press.

Rothman, H.

1998   *Devil's Bargains: Tourism in the Twentieth-Century American West.* Lawrence: University of Kansas Press.

2002   *Neon Metropolis: How Las Vegas Started the Twenty-First Century.* New York: Routledge.

Rothstein, F., and M. Blim, eds.

1992   *Anthropology and the Global Factory: Studies of the New Industrialization in the Late Twentieth Century.* New York: Bergin and Garvey.

Rouse, R.

1986   Migration and Family Politics in Family Life: Divergent Projects and Rhetorical Strategies in a Mexican Migrant Community. Paper presented at the Annual Meeting of the American Anthropological Association, Philadelphia.

1991   Mexican Migration and the Social Space of Postmodernism. *Diaspora* 1 (spring):8–23.

1992   Making Sense of Settlement: Class Transformation, Cultural Struggle, and Transnationalism among Mexican Migrants in the United States. In *Towards a Transnational Perspective on Migration: Race, Class, Ethnicity and Nationalism Reconsidered,* edited by N. Glick Schiller, L. Basch, and C. Blanc-Szanton, pp. 25–52. New York: New York Academy of Sciences.

1995   Thinking through Transnationalism: Notes on the Cultural Politics of Class Relations in the Contemporary United States. *Public Culture* 7:353–402.

Rubel, A. J., and M. R. Hass

1996   Ethnomedicine. In *Medical Anthropology: Contemporary Theory and Method,* edited by C. F. Sargent and T. M. Johnson, pp. 113–130. Westport, Conn.: Praeger.

Rubel, A. J., C. W. O'Nell, and R. Collado Ardon

1984   *Susto: A Folk Illness.* Berkeley: University of California Press.

REFERENCES

Rumbaut, R. G.

1995   The New Californians: Comparative Research Findings on the Educational Progress of Immigrant Children. In *California's Immigrant Children*, edited by R. Rumbaut and W. Cornelius, La Jolla, Cal.: Center for US-Mexican Studies.

1996   Ties That Bind: Immigration and Immigrant Families in the United States. In *Immigration and the Family: Research and Policy on U.S. Immigrants,* edited by A. Booth, A. Crouter, and N. Landale, Mahwah, N. J.: Lawrence Erlbaum.

1997a   Assimilation and Its Discontents: Between Rhetoric and Reality. *International Migration Review* 31:923–960.

1997b   Parodoxes (and Orthodoxies) of Assimilation. *Sociological Perspectives* 40:481–511.

Rumbaut, R. G., L. R. Chavez, R. Moser, S. Pickwell, and S. Wishik

1988   The Politics of Migrant Health Care: A Comparative Study of Mexican Immigrants and Indochinese Refugees in San Diego. *Research in the Sociology of Medicine* 7:143–202.

Rumbaut, R., and A. Portes, eds.

2001   *Ethnicities: Children of Immigrants in America.* Berkeley: University of California Press.

Rumbaut, R. G., and J. R. Weeks

1989   Children of Immigrants: Is "Americanization" Hazardous to Infant Health? In *Children of Color: Research, Health, and Public Policy Issues,* edited by B. M. Lester, H. E. Fitzgerald, and B. Zuckerman, New York: Garland.

Rutheiser, C.

1996   *Imagineering Atlanta: The Politics of Place in the City of Dreams.* London and New York: Verso.

1999   Making Place in the Nonplace Urban Realm: Notes on the Revitalizaiton of Downtown Atlanta. In *Theorizing the City: The New Urban Anthropology Reader,* edited by S. Low, pp. 317–341. New Brunswick, N.J.: Rutgers University Press.

Sager, L.

2000   The Free Exercise of Culture: Some Doubts and Distinctions. *Daedalus: Journal of the American Academy of Arts and Sciences* ("The End of Tolerance: Engaging Cultural Differences" issue) 129:193–208.

Salazar-Parreñas, R.

2001   *Servants of Globalization: Women, Migration and Domestic Work.* Stanford, Cal.: Stanford University Press.

Salzman, P.

1999   *The Anthropology of Real Life: Events in Human Experience.* Prospect Heights, Ill.: Waveland Press.

Sanjek, R.

1998   *The Future of Us All: Race and Neighborhood Politics in New York City.* Ithaca, N.Y.: Cornell University Press.

2000   Color-Full before Color Blind: The Emergence of Multiracial Neighborhood Politics in Queens, New York City. *American Anthropologist* 102:762–772.

Sanjek, R., and S. Gregory, eds.

1994   *Race.* New Brunswick, N.J.: Rutgers University Press.

Sassen, S.

1988   *The Mobility of Labor and Capital: A Study in International Investment and Labor Flow.* New York: Cambridge University Press.

1991   *The Global City: New York, London, Tokyo.* Princeton, N.J.: Princeton University Press.

1996   Toward a Feminist Analytics of the Global Economy. *Indiana Journal of Global Legal Studies* 4 (1):7–41.

1998   *Globalization and Its Discontents: Essays on the Mobility of People and Money.* New York: The New Press.

Saxenian, A.

1999   *Silicon Valley's New Immigrant Entrepreneurs.* San Francisco: Public Policy Institute of California.

Schapera, I.

1947   *Migrant Labour and Tribal Life: A Study of Conditions in the Bechuana Protectorate.* Oxford: Oxford University Press.

Schensul, S., J. Schensul, and M. LeCompte

1999   *Essential Ethnographic Methods: Observations, Interviews, and Questionnaires.* Walnut Creek, Cal.: Altamira.

Scheper-Hughes, N.

1992   *Death without Weeping: The Violence of Everyday Life in Brazil.* Berkeley: University of California Press.

Schildkrout, E.

1974   Ethnicity and Generational Differences among Urban Immigrants in Ghana. In *Urban Ethnicity,* edited by A. Cohen, pp. 187–222. London: Tavistock.

Schissel, B., R. Wannter, and J. S. Frideres

1989   Social and Economic Context and Attitudes toward Immigrants in Canadian Cities. *International Migration Review* 23:289–308.

Schlosser, E.

2001   *Fast Food Nation.* Boston: Houghton Mifflin.

Schmink, M.

1984   Household Economic Strategies: Review and Research Agenda. *Latin American Research Review* 19 (3):87–101.

REFERENCES

Schmitt, E.
2001   To Fill In Gaps, Shrinking Cities Seek a New Wave of Foreigners. *New York Times,* May 30.

Schneider, J.
1990   Defining Boundaries, Creating Contacts: Puerto Rican and Polish Presentation of Group Identity through Ethnic Parades. *Journal of Ethnic Studies* 18:33–57.

Schwartz, B., ed.
1967   *Caste in Overseas Indian Communities.* San Francisco: Chandler.

Scollon, R., and S. Scollon
1981   *Narrative, Literacy, and Face in Interethnic Communication.* Norwood, N.J.: Ablex.

Scudder, T., and E. Colson
1982   From Welfare to Development. In *Involuntary Migration and Resettlement: Problems and Responses of Dislocated People,* edited by A. Hansen and A. Oliver-Smith, pp. 267–287. Boulder, Col.: Westview.

Sebert, A.
2000   Needs Assessment for Reproductive Health among Latinas: Cobb, DeKalb, Fulton, and Gwinnett Counties, Georgia. Master's thesis, University of Michigan, Ann Arbor.

Seguin, A., and A. Germain
2000   The Social Sustainability of Montreal: A Local or a State Matter. In *The Social Sustainability of Cities: Diversity and the Management of Change,* edited by M. Polese and R. Stren, pp. 39–67. Toronto: University of Toronto Press.

Sen, A.
2000   Global Doubts. Commencement address presented at Harvard University, Cambridge, Mass., June 8.

Shack, W. A.
1973   Urban Ethnicity and the Cultural Process of Urbanization in Ethiopia. In *Urban Anthropology: Cross-Cultural Studies of Urbanization,* edited by A. Southall, pp. 251–286. New York: Oxford University Press.

Shah, N.
2001   *Contagious Divides: Epidemics and Race in San Francisco's Chinatown.* Berkeley: University of California Press.

Shell-Duncan, B., and Y. Hernlund, eds.
2000   *Female "Circumcision" in Africa: Culture, Change and Controversy.* Boulder, Col.: Lynne Rienner.

Shimahara, N. K.
1991   Social Mobility and Education: Burakumin in Japan. In *Minority Status and Schooling: A Comparative Study of Immigrant and Involuntary Minorities,* edited by M. A. Gibson and J. U. Ogbu, pp. 327–353. New York: Garland Publishing.

Shogren, E.

1996   Clinton's Signature Launches Historical Overhaul of Welfare. *Los Angeles Times,* August 23.

Shokeid, M.

1988   *Children of Circumstances: Israeli Emigrants in New York.* Ithaca, N.Y.: Cornell University Press.

Shukla, S.

1997   Feminisms of the Diaspora Both Local and Global: The Politics of South Asian Women against Domestic Violence. In *Women Question Politics,* edited by C. Cohen, K. Jones, and J. Tronto, pp. 269–283. New York: New York University Press.

Shweder, R.

2000   What about "Female Genital Mutilation"? and Why Understanding Culture Matters in the First Place. *Daedalus* 129:209–232.

2001   Rethinking the Object of Anthropology and Ending Up Where Kroeber and Kluckhohn Began. *American Anthropologist* 103:437–440.

2002   What about "Female Genital Mutilation"? and Why Understanding Culture Matters in the First Place. In *Engaging Cultural Differences: The Multicultural Challenge in Liberal Democracies,* edited by R. A. Shweder, M. Minow, and H. R. Markus, New York: Russell Sage Foundation.

Shweder, R., M. Minow, and H. Markus, eds.

2000   Introduction to *Daedalus* 129 ("The End of Intolerance: Engaging Cultural Differences" special issue):v–ix.

2002   *Engaging Cultural Differences: The Multicultural Challenge in Liberal Democracies.* New York: Russell Sage Foundation.

Sider, G.

1992   The Contradictions of Transnational Migration: A Discussion. In *Towards a Transnational Perspective on Migration: Race, Class, Ethnicity and Nationalism Reconsidered,* edited by N. Glick Schiller, L. Basch, and C. Blanc-Szanton, pp. 231–240. New York: New York Academy of Sciences.

Silverman, S.

2002   The American Tradition: Bringing Anthropology into the Modern World (1925–1975). Paper presented at the conference "Four Traditions in Anthropology," Max Planck Institute for Social Anthropology, Halle/Saale, Germany.

Simon, J.

1989   *The Economic Consequences of Immigration.* Oxford: Basil Blackwell.

Simon, R., and C. Brettell, eds.

1986   *International Migration: The Female Experience.* Totowa, N.J.: Rowman and Allanheld.

Simons, R. C., and C. C. Hughes, eds.

1985   *The Culture-Bound Syndromes: Folk Illnesses of Psychiatric and Anthropological Interest.* Boston: D. Reidel.

Singer, A., and A. Brown

2001   Washington, D.C. In *Encyclopedia of American Immigration,* edited by J. Ciment, pp. 974–982. Armonk, N.Y.: M. E. Sharpe.

Singer, A., S. Friedman, I. Cheung, and M. Price

2001   *The World in a Zip Code: Great Washington, D.C. as a New Region of Immigration.* Survey series, April. Washington: The Brookings Institution.

Skrbis, Z.

1999   *Long Distance Nationalism: Diasporas, Homelands and Identities.* Aldershot, UK: Ashgate.

Skutnabb-Kangas, T.

1981   Guest Worker or Immigrant—Different Ways of Reproducing an Underclass. *Journal of Multilingual and Multicultural Development* 2:89–115.

Small, C.

1997   *Voyages: From Tongan Villages to American Suburbs.* Ithaca, N.Y.: Cornell University Press.

Smart, A., and J. Smart

1998   Transnational Social Networks and Negotiated Identities in Interactions between Hong Kong and China. In *Transnationalism from Below,* edited by M. P. Smith and L. Guarnizo, pp. 103–128. New Brunswick, N.J.: Transaction Publishers.

Smith, G. E.

1933   *The Diffusion of Culture.* London: Watts.

Smith, M. P., and L. Guarnizo

1998   *Transnationalism from Below.* New Brunswick, N.J.: Transaction Publishers.

Smith, R. C.

1998   Transnational Localities: Community, Technology, and the Politics of Membership within the Context of Mexico-U.S. Migration. In *Transnationalism from Below,* edited by M. P. Smith and L. Guarnizo, pp. 196–240. New Brunswick, N.J.: Transaction Publishers.

Smith, R. T.

2001   Caribbean Families: Questions for Research and Implications for Policy. In *Caribbean Families in Britain and the Trans-Atlantic World,* edited by H. Goulbourne and M. Chamberlain, pp. 48–62. London: Macmillan Education.

Smith-Hefner, N.

1999   *Khmer American.* Berkeley: University of California Press.

Soja, E. W.

1992   The Stimulus of a Little Confusion: A Contemporary Comparison of
        Amsterdam and Los Angeles. In *After Modernism: Global Restructuring and
        the Changing Boundaries of City Life,* edited by M. P. Smith, pp. 17–38. New
        Brunswick, N.J.: Transaction Publishers.

1996   Los Angeles, 1965–1992: From Crisis-Generated Restructuring to
        Restructuring-Generated Crisis. In *The City: Los Angeles and Urban Theory
        at the End of the Twentieth Century,* edited by A. J. Scott and E. W. Soja,
        pp. 426–464. Berkeley: University of California Press.

Soros, G.

2002   *On Globalization.* New York: Public Affairs.

Soto, I. M.

1987   West Indian Child Fostering: Its Role in Migrant Exchanges. In *Caribbean
        Life in New York City: Sociocultural Dimensions,* edited by C. R. Sutton and
        E. M. Chaney, pp. 131–149. Staten Island, N.Y.: Center for Migration
        Studies.

Souter, D.

1993   Concurring Opinion in Church of the Lukumi Babalu Aye, Inc. and
        Ernesto Pichardo, *Petitioners* v. *City of Hialeah,* No. 91-948, Supreme Court
        of the United States, 508 US 520.

Soysal, Y.

1994   *Limits to Citizenship: Migrants and Postnational Membership in Europe.*
        Chicago: University of Chicago Press.

Stafford, S. B.

1987   The Haitians: The Cultural Meaning of Race and Ethnicity. In *New
        Immigrants in New York,* edited by N. Foner, pp. 131–158. New York:
        Columbia University Press.

Stasiulis, D.

1999   Relational Positionality of Nationalisms, Racisms and Feminisms. In
        Between Women and Nation, edited by N. Alarcon, C. Kaplan, and
        M. Moallem, pp. 182–218. Durham, N.C.: Duke University Press.

Steinberg, L., B. Bradford Brown, and S. Dornbusch

1996   *Beyond the Classroom: Why School Reform Has Failed and What Parents Need to
        Do.* New York: Simon and Schuster.

Stepick, A.

1998   *Pride against Prejudice: Haitians in the United States.* Boston: Allyn and Bacon.

Stepick, A., G. Grenier, M. Castro, and M. Dunn

2003   *This Land Is Our Land: Immigrants and Power in Miami.* Berkeley: University
        of California Press.

Stepick, A., and C. D. Stepick

1994   *Preliminary Haitian Needs' Assessment: Report to the City of Miami.* Miami: Immigration and Ethnicity Institute, Florida International University.

1999   *The Academic Orientations of Native-Born and Immigrant Minority Adolescents: Research Proposal.* Working Paper Number 1. Miami: Immigration and Ethnicity Institute, Florida International University.

Stepick, A., C. D. Stepick, E. Eugene, D. Teed, and Y. Labisserie

2001   Shifting Identities and Inter-Generational Conflict: Growing Up Haitian in Miami. In *Ethnicities: Children of Immigrants in America,* edited by R. Rumbaut and A. Portes, pp. 229–266. Berkeley: University of California Press.

Stiglitz, J.

2002   A Fair Deal for the World. *New York Review of Books,* May 23.

Stoller, P.

1999   *Jaguar.* Chicago: University of Chicago Press.

2001   West Africans: Trading Places in New York. In *New Immigrants in New York,* edited by N. Foner, pp. 229–250. 2d ed. New York: Columbia University Press.

2002   *Money Has No Smell: The Africanization of New York City.* Chicago: University of Chicago Press.

Stolzenberg, N. M.

1993   "He Drew a Circle That Shut Me Out": Assimilation, Indoctrination and the Paradox of a Liberal Education. *Harvard Law Review* 106:581–667.

Suárez-Orozco, C.

2000   Identities under Siege. In *Cultures under Siege: Collective Violence and Trauma,* edited by A. Robben and M. Suárez-Orozco, New York: Cambridge University Press.

Suárez-Orozco, C., and M. M. Suárez-Orozco

1994   The Cultural Psychology of Hispanic Immigrants. In *Handbook of Hispanic Cultures in the United States: Anthropology,* edited by T. Weaver, pp. 129–146. Houston: Arte Publico Press.

1995   *Transformations: Migration, Family Life, and Achievement Motivation among Latino Adolescents.* Stanford, Cal.: Stanford University Press

Suárez-Orozco, C., and M. M. Suárez-Orozco, eds.

2001   *Children of Immigration.* Cambridge, Mass.: Harvard University Press.

Suárez-Orozco, M.

1987a   Towards a Psychosocial Understanding of Hispanic Adaptation to American Schooling. In *Success or Failure?: Learning and the Language Minority Student,* edited by H. T. Trueba, pp. 156–168. Cambridge, Mass.: Newbury House Publishers.

1987b   Becoming Somebody: Central American Immigrants in U.S. Inner-City

Schools. *Anthropology and Education Quarterly* 18 (4):287–299.

1987c   Hispanic Americans: Comparative Considerations and the Educational Problems of Children. *International Migration* 25 (2):141–164.

1987d   Transformations in Perception of Self and Social Environment in Mexican Immigrants. In *People in Upheaval*, edited by S. Morgan and E. F. Colson, pp. 129–143. New York: Center for Migration Studies.

1989a   Psychosocial Aspects of Achievement Motivation among Recent Hispanic Immigrants. In *What Do Anthropologists Have to Say about Dropouts?* edited by H. T. Trueba, G. Spindler, and L. Spindler, pp. 99–116. New York: The Falmer Press.

1989b   *Central American Refugees and U.S. High Schools: A Psychosocial Study of Motivation and Achievement.* Stanford, Cal.: Stanford University Press.

1990   Migration and Education: United States—Europe Comparisons. In *Status Inequality: The Self in Culture*, edited by G. A. De Vos and M. Suárez-Orozco, Newbury: Sage Publications.

1991a   Immigrant Adaptation to Schooling: A Hispanic Case. In *Minority Status and Schooling: A Comparative Study of Immigrant and Involuntary Minorities*, edited by M. A. Gibson and J. U. Ogbu, pp. 37–61. New York: Garland Publishing.

1994   Anxious Neighbors: Belgium and Its Immigrant Minorities. In *Controlling Immigration: A Global Perspective*, edited by W. Cornelius, P. Martin, and J. Hollifield, Stanford, Cal.: Stanford University Press.

1996   Unwelcome Mats. *Harvard Magazine*, July/August.

1999   Latin American Immigration to the United States. In *The United States and Latin America: The New Agenda*, edited by V. Bulmer-Thomas and J. Dunkerley, Cambridge, Mass.: David Rockefeller Center for Latin American Studies, Harvard University Press.

2000   Everything You Ever Wanted to Know about Assimilation but Were Afraid to Ask. *Daedalus: Journal of the American Academy of Arts and Sciences* 129:1–31 ("The End of Tolerance: Engaging Cultural Differences" issue).

Suárez-Orozco, M., ed.

1991b   Migration, Minority Status, and Education: European Dilemmas and Responses in the 1990s. Theme issue of the *Anthropology and Education Quarterly*, 22 (2):1–32.

1998   *Crossings: Mexican Immigration in Interdisciplinary Perspectives.* Cambridge, Mass.: David Rockefeller Center for Latin American Studies, Harvard University Press.

Suárez-Orozco, M., and M. Páez. eds.

2002   *Latinos: Remaking America.* Berkeley, Cal., and Cambridge, Mass: The University of California Press and the David Rockefeller Center for Latin American Studies, Harvard University.

REFERENCES

Suárez-Orozco, M., C. Suárez-Orozco, and D. Qin-Hilliard, eds.

2001a   *The New Immigration: Interdisciplinary Perspectives Vol. 1.* New York:
Routledge.

2001b   *The New Immigration: Interdisciplinary Perspectives Vol. 2.* New York:
Routledge.

2001c   *The New Immigration: Interdisciplinary Perspectives Vol. 4.* New York:
Routledge.

2003   *The New Immigration Millennium Reader.* New York: Routledge.

Sutton, C.

1987   The Caribbeanization of New York City and the Emergence of a
Transnational Sociocultural System. In *Caribbean Life in New York:
Sociocultural Dimensions,* edited by C. Sutton and E. Chaney, pp. 15–30.
New York: Center for Migration Studies.

1992   Some Thoughts on Gendering and Internationalizing Our Thinking about
Transnational Migrations. In *Towards a Transnational Perspective on
Migration: Race, Class, Ethnicity and Nationalism Reconsidered,* edited by
N. Glick Schiller, L. Basch, and C. Blanc-Szanton, pp. 241–249. New York:
New York Academy of Sciences.

Sutton, C., and E. Chaney, eds.

1987   *Caribbean Life in New York City: Sociocultural Dimensions.* New York: Center
for Migration Studies.

Sutton, C., and S. Makiesky

1987   Migration and West Indian Racial and Ethnic Consciousness. In *Caribbean
Life in New York City: Sociocultural Dimensions,* edited by C. Sutton and
E. Chaney, pp. 92–116. New York: Center for Migration Studies.

Taylor, A.

2002   Globalization, Trade and Development: Some Lessons from History.
Working Paper 9326. National Bureau of Economic Research.

Taylor, J. E.

1986   Differential Migration, Networks, Information, and Risk. In *Research in
Human Capital and Development,* edited by O. Stark, pp. 147–171.
Greenwich, Conn.: JAI Press.

Terry, D.

1997   Makeshift Pharmacies Are Dispensing Death. *Los Angeles Times,* March 29.

Thistlewaite, F.

1964   Migration from Europe Overseas in the Nineteenth and Twentieth
Centuries. In *Population Movements in Modern European History,* edited by
H. Moeller, pp. 73–92. New York: Macmillan.

Tienda, M., S. A. Smith, and V. Ortiz

1987   Industrial Restructuring, Gender Segregation, and Sex Differences in
Earnings. *American Sociological Review* 52 (April):195–210.

Titus, D.

2001   High Stakes Down Under for Indigenous Peoples: Learning from Maori Education in New Zealand: An Outsiders Perspective. Presented at the Annual Meeting of the National Association for Multicultural Education, Las Vegas, Nev.

Tölölyan, K.

1991   The Nation State and Its Others: In Lieu of a Preference. *Diaspora* 1 (1):3–7.

2001   Elites and Institutions in the Armenian Transnation. Paper presented at Social Science Research Council workshop "Transnational Migration: Comparative Perspectives," Princeton University, Princeton, N.J.

Tomlinson, S.

1983   *Ethnic Minorities in British Schools: A Review of the Literature, 1960–82.* London: Heinemann.

1989   Ethnicity and Educational Achievement in Britain. In *Different Cultures, Same School: Ethnic Minority Children in Europe,* edited by L. Eldering and J. Kloprogge, pp. 15–37. Amsterdam: Swets and Zeitlinger.

Trueba, H. T.

1987a   Culturally Based Explanations of Minority Students' Academic Achievement. *Anthropology and Education Quarterly* 19:270–287.

1987b   *Success or Failure?: Learning and the Language Minority Student.* Cambridge, Mass.: Newbury House Publishers.

1989   Rethinking Dropouts: Culture and Literacy for Minority Student Empowerment. In *What Do Anthropologists Have to Say about Dropouts?* edited by H. T. Trueba, G. Spindler, and L. Spindler, pp. 27–42. New York: The Falmer Press.

Trueba, H. T., L. Jacobs, and E. Kirton

1990   *Cultural Conflict and Adaptation: The Case of Hmong Children in American Society.* New York: The Falmer Press.

Trueba, H. T., G. Spindler, and L. Spindler, eds.

1989   *What Do Anthropologists Have to Say about Dropouts?* New York: The Falmer Press.

Tsuda, T.

1996   Strangers in the Ethnic Homeland. Ph.D. diss., University of California at Berkeley.

2003   *Strangers in the Ethnic Homeland: Japanese Brazilian Return Migration in Transnational Perspective.* New York: Columbia University Press.

Turkle, S.

1997   *Life on Line: Identity in the Age of the Internet.* New York: Touchstone.

Turner, B. S.

1987   *Medical Power and Social Knowledge.* Beverly Hills, Cal.: Sage Publications.

REFERENCES

Turner, V.

1957   *Schism and Continuity in an African Society.* Manchester: Manchester
University Press for Rhodes-Livingstone Institute.

United Nations High Commissioner for Refugees (UNHCR)

2003   Basic Facts. http://www.unhcr.ch/cgi-bin/texis/vtx/basics.

United States Bureau of the Census

1999   *Profile of the Foreign-Born Population in the United States: 1997.* Washington,
D.C.: Current Population Reports.

van Dijk, R.

2002   Religion, Reciprocity, and Restructuring Family Responsibility in the
Ghanaian Pentecostal Diaspora. In *The Transnational Family: New European
Frontiers and Global Networks,* edited by D. Bryceson and U. Vuorela,
pp. 173–196. Oxford: Berg Publishers Limited.

Van Velsen, J.

1967   The Extended Case Method and Situational Analysis. In *The Craft of Social
Anthropology,* edited by A. L. Epstein, pp. 129–149. London: Tavistock.

Vance, C.

1991   Anthropology Rediscovers Sexuality: A Theoretical Comment. *Social Science
and Medicine* 33 (8):875–884.

Vernon, S. W., B. C. Tilley, A. V. Neale, and L. Steinfeldt

1985   Ethnicity, Survival, and Delay in Seeking Treatment for Symptoms of
Breast Cancer. *Cancer* 55:1563–1571.

**Vernon, S. W., V. G. Vogel, S. Halabi, G. L. Jackson, R. O. Lundy, and
G. N. Peters**

1992   Breast Cancer Screening Behaviors and Attitudes in Three Racial/Ethnic
Groups. *Cancer* 69:165–174.

Vertovec, S.

n.d.   Transnational Communities Programme. http://www.transcomm.ox.ac.uk/
introduc.htm.

Vickerman, M.

1999   *Crosscurrents: West Indian Immigrants and Race.* New York: Oxford University
Press.

Visweswaran, K.

1997   Histories of Feminist Ethnography. *Annual Review of Anthropology*
26:591–621.

Volpp, L.

2001   Feminism versus Multiculturalism. *Columbia Law Review* 101
(5):1181–1218.

Waitzkin, H.

1983   *The Second Sickness: Contradictions of Capitalist Health Care.* New York: Free
Press.

Walbridge, L.

1996   *Without Forgetting the Imam: Lebanese Shi'Ism in an American Community.*
        Detroit: Wayne State University Press.

Waldinger, R.

1989a   Immigration and Urban Change. *Annual Review of Sociology* 15:211–232.

1989b   Structural Opportunity or Ethnic Advantage: Immigrant Business
        Development in New York. *International Migration Review* 23:48–72.

1996   From Ellis Island to LAX: Immigrant Prospects in the American City.
        International Migration Review 30 (4):1078–1085.

1997   Social Capital or Social Closures? Immigrant Networks in the Labor
        Market. Working Paper Series 26. Lewis Center for Regional Policy
        Studies, University of California, Los Angeles.

2001   Strangers at the Gates. In *Strangers at the Gates: New Immigrants in Urban
        America,* edited by R. Waldinger, pp. 1–29. Berkeley: University of
        California Press.

Waldinger, R., H. Aldrich, and R. Ward, eds.

1990   *Ethnic Entrepreneurs: Immigrant and Ethnic Business in Western Industrial
        Societies.* Newbury Park, Cal.: Sage Publications.

Waldinger, R., and M. Bozorgmehr, eds.

1996   *Ethnic Los Angeles.* New York: Russell Sage Foundation.

Waldinger, R., and C. Der-Martirosian

2001   The Immigrant Niche: Pervasive, Persistent, Diverse. In *Strangers at the
        Gates: New Immigrants in Urban America,* edited by R. Waldinger,
        pp. 228–271. Berkeley: University of California Press.

Wallace, W.

1971   *Logic of Science in Sociology.* New York: Aldine de Gruyter.

Warner, R. S., and J. G. Wittner, eds.

1998   *Gatherings in Diaspora: Religious Communities and the New Immigration.*
        Philadelphia: Temple University Press.

Warren, P. M.

1999   O.C. Is Rated near Top in Health Study: Officials Credit Affluence,
        Demographics for Good News. *Los Angeles Times,* January 12.

Washington Post

1998   Success Predicted for Immigrants' Children. March 22, final edition, section A.

Waters, M. C.

1999   *Black Identities: West Indian Immigrant Dreams and American Realities.*
        Cambridge, Mass.: Harvard University Press.

2000   The Sociological Roots and Multidisciplinary Future of Immigration
        Research. In *Immigration Research for a New Century: Multidisciplinary
        Perspectives,* edited by N. Foner, R. Rumbaut, and S. Gold, pp. 44–48. New
        York: Russell Sage Foundation.

2001   Growing Up West Indian and African American: Gender and Class
Differences in the Second Generation. In *Islands in the City: West Indian
Migration to New York,* edited by N. Foner, pp. 193–215. Berkeley: University
of California Press.

Watney, S.

1999   Safer Sex as Community Practice. In *Culture, Society and Sexuality: A
Practical Beginning,* edited by R. Parker and P. Aggleton, London:
University College of London Press.

Watson, J. L., ed.

1977   *Between Two Cultures.* Oxford: Basil Blackwell.

Weber, T.

1999   Lethal Drug Trade: Unsafe Medicines from Mexico; Back-Room Shops Sell
Latino Immigrants Dangerous Remedies without Warnings of Sometimes-
Fatal Side Effects. *Los Angeles Times,* May 23.

Wellmeier, L.

1998   Saint Eulalia's People in Exile: Maya Religion, Culture, and Identity in Los
Angeles. In *Gatherings in Diaspora,* edited by R. S. Warner and J. G. Wittner,
pp. 97–122. Philadelphia: Temple University Press.

Werbner, P.

1996   Stamping the Earth with the Name of Allah: Zikr and the Sacralizing of
Space among British Muslims. In *Making Muslim Space in North America and
Europe,* edited by B. Metcalf, pp. 167–185. Berkeley: University of
California Press.

Westwood, S., and P. Bhachu, eds.

1988   *Enterprising Women: Ethnicity, Economy, and Gender Relations.* London:
Routledge.

Whiteford, L. M.

1996   Political Economy, Gender, and the Social Production of Health and
Illness. In *Gender and Health: An International Perspective,* edited by
C. F. Sargent and C. B. Brettell, pp. 242–259. Upper Saddle River, N.J.:
Prentice Hall.

Wikan, U.

2000   Citizenship on Trial: Nadia's Case. *Daedalus: Journal of the American Academy
of Arts and Sciences* ("The End of Tolerance: Engaging Cultural
Differences" issue) 129:55–76.

2002   *Generous Betrayal: Politics of Culture in the New Europe.* Chicago: University of
Chicago Press.

Williams, R. I., N. J. Binkin, and E. J. Clingman

1986   Pregnancy Outcomes among Spanish-Surname Women in California.
American Journal of Public Health 76:387–391.

Williamson, J.

2002   Winners and Losers over Two Centuries of Globalization. Working Paper 9161. National Bureau of Economic Research.

Wilson, W.

1997   *When Work Disappears: The World of the New Urban Poor.* New York: Vintage Books.

Wiltshire, R.

1992   Implications of Transnational Migration for Nationalism: The Caribbean Example. In *Towards a Transnational Perspective on Migration: Race, Class, Ethnicity and Nationalism Reconsidered,* edited by N. Glick Schiller, L. Basch, and C. Blanc-Szanton, pp. 175–188. New York: New York Academy of Sciences.

Wimmer, A., and N. Glick Schiller

2002a   Methodological Nationalism and Beyond: Nation-State Building, Migration and the Social Sciences. *Global Networks* 2 (4):301–334.

2002b   Methodological Nationalism and the Study of Migration. *Archives of European Sociology* XLIII (2):217–240.

Woldemikael, T.

1985   Opportunity versus Constraint: Haitian Immigrants and Racial Ascription. *Migration Today* 13 (4):7–12.

1989   *Becoming Black American: Haitians and American Institutions in Evanston, Illinois.* New York: AMS Press.

Wolf, E.

1982   *Europe and the People without History.* Berkeley: University of California Press.

Wolpe, H.

1975   The Theory of Internal Colonialism: The South African Case. In *Beyond the Sociology of Development,* edited by I. Oxaal, T. Barnett, and D. Booth, pp. 229–252. London: Routledge and Kegan Paul.

Wong, B.

1982   *Chinatown: Economic Adaptation and Ethnic Identity of the Chinese.* New York: Holt, Rinehart and Winston.

1998   *Ethnicity and Entrepreneurship: The New Chinese Immigrants in the San Francisco Bay Area.* Boston: Allyn and Bacon.

Wood, C.

1981   Structural Change and Household Strategies: A Conceptual Framework for the Study of Rural Migration. *Human Organization* 40 (4):338–343.

1982   Equilibrium and Historical-Structural Perspectives on Migration: A Comparative Critique with Implications for Future Research. *International Migration Review* 16 (2):298–319.

REFERENCES

World Bank

2001   Assessing Globalization. http://www.worldbank.org/html/extdr/pb/
globalization/paper1.htm.

Wright, C.

1995   Gender Awareness in Migration Theory: Synthesizing Actor and Structure
in Southern Africa. *Development and Change* 26:771–791.

Wyman, M.

1993   *Round-Trip to America: The Immigrants Return to Europe, 1880–1930.* Ithaca,
N.Y.: Cornell University Press.

Yalçin-Heckman, L.

1997   The Perils of Ethnic Associational Life in Europe: Turkish Migrants in
Germany and France. In *The Politics of Multiculturalism in the New Europe:
Racism, Identity and Community,* edited by T. Modood and P. Werbner,
pp. 95–110. London: Zed.

Yanigisako, S.

1985   *Transforming the Past: Tradition and Kinship among Japanese-Americans.*
Stanford, Cal.: Stanford University Press.

Yi, D., and L. Jack

1999   Manslaughter Charge Filed in Probe of Illegal Clinic. *Los Angeles Times,*
July 21.

Yu, E.

1982   The Low Mortality Rates of Chinese Infants: Some Plausible Explanations.
Social Science and Medicine 16:253–265.

Yuan, D. Y.

1966   Chinatown and Beyond: The Chinese Population in Metropolitan New
York. *Phylon* 23:321–332.

Zain, A.

2002   Negotiated Muslim Space: The Incorporation of West African Muslims in
New York City. Paper presented at the conference "Religion and
Immigrant Incorporation in New York," New School University, New York.

Zane, W.

1999   Spiritual Baptists in New York City: A View from the Vincentian
Converted. In *Religion, Diaspora, and Cultural Identity: A Reader in the
Anglophone Caribbean,* edited by J. W. Pulis, pp. 125–151. Amsterdam:
Gordon and Breach.

Zavella, P.

1987   *Women's Work and Chicano Families.* Ithaca, N.Y.: Cornell University Press.

1997   The Tables Are Turned: Immigration, Poverty, and Social Conflict in
California Communities. In *Immigrants Out! The New Nativism and the Anti-
Immigrant Impulse in the United States,* edited by J. F. Perea, pp. 136–161.
New York: New York University Press.

Zentella, A.

2002   Latin@Languages and Identities. In *Latinos: Remaking America,* edited by
        M. Suárez-Orozco and M. Páez, Berkeley: University of California Press.

Zhan, M.

2001   Does It Take a Miracle? Negotiating Knowledge, Identities, and
        Communities of Traditional Chinese Medicine. *Cultural Anthropology*
        16:453–480.

Zhou, M.

1992   *Chinatown: The Socioeconomic Potential of an Urban Enclave.* Philadelphia:
        Temple University Press.

1994   Chinatown Revisited: Community-Based Organizations, Immigrant
        Families, and the Younger Generation. Working Paper no. 67. New York:
        Russell Sage Foundation.

Zhou, M., and C. Bankston

1994   Social Capital and the Adaptation of the Second Generation: The Case of
        Vietnamese Youth in New Orleans. *International Migration Review* 28
        (winter):821–845.

1998   *Growing Up American: How Vietnamese Children Adapt to Life in the United
        States.* New York: Russell Sage Foundation.

Zhou, M., and J. Gatewood

2000   Introduction. In *Contemporary Asian America: A Multidisciplinary Reader,*
        edited by M. Zhou and J. Gatewood, pp. 1–46. New York: New York
        University Press.

Zinn, M. B., M. Baca, L. Weber Cannon, E. Higginbotham, and B. Thornton Dill

1986   The Exclusionary Practices in Women's Studies. *Signs* 11:290–303.

Index

and, 62; obligation created by public benefits of, 235; service economy and, 182–83, 188; stigmatization of, 57; studies of urban labor market and, 179–84. *See also* economy
immigrant medical beliefs: brought from parent culture, 200; of Chinese on birth years/diseases link, 204–5; conflict between US and Hmong, 201, 203–4; of Mexican immigrants on breast cancer risk factors, 209–11, 210*t*; of Mexicans suffering from *susto* (soul loss), 204; more compassionate model of Mexican marriage and, 246; popular representations of Hmong, 241; relative to other factors in shaping behavior, 247–50; selected folk illnesses included in, 202*t*; studies on cultural models/disease and, 208–11; unregulated health care providers (folk healers) and, 218–19, 220–22. *See also* medicinal knowledge
immigrant minorities: autonomous, 133, 160n.5; caste-like, 133–34; three types of, 133
immigrants: cultural beliefs/medicinal knowledge brought by, 200; defining terminology of, 16, 159n.1; heterogeneous population of US, 63–65; medical screening of, 207; new transnational pattern of, 56; percent with bachelor's degree or higher (2000) of US, 64*fig*; percent with less than ninth grade completed (2002) of US, 65*fig*; preference for "migrant" or "transmigrant" terminology, 16; relationships between African Americans and, 194nn.10, 12; selected folk

illnesses found among US, 202*t*; social stigma of diseases associated with, 207–8; sojourner pattern of, 55–56; US debate over providing medical services to, 197–99. *See also* first-generation; migrants; second-generation
immigrant women: accounts of gains after migration, 38–39; emancipation and, 85–93; as largely absent from immigration studies, 77–78; responsibilities to transmit/maintain ethnic traditions, 91–93; scholarship on, 78–79. *See also* gender; Mexican immigrant women
immigration: causes/consequences of large-scale, 57–60; examining role of religion in, 33–34; family reunification factor in, 58, 59; globalization as triggering, 46–47, 52–54; high proportion of people returning home (1890s–1910s) from US, 55; history of anthropological studies of US, 14–22; impact on American culture by, 43n.13; as movement across space, 56; popular destinations for recent US, 43n.14–44n.14; as pressing contemporary social issue, 3–4; study of changing social/cultural patterns due to US, 17–18. *See also* population movements
immigration studies: anthropology and early post-war years of, 9–14; calling for comparative research in, 252–53; contributions of anthropologists to, 54–55; evolving division of labor in interdisciplinary, 75–76; interdisciplinary exchanges in, 5–9; migrant research, 229–44; mix of methods used in, 158–59;

mutual benefits of medical anthropology studies and, 226; women as largely absent from, 77–78. *See also* anthropological studies; medical anthropology studies; transnational migration studies
instrumental culture, 66
INS (US Immigration and Naturalization Service), 263
interdisciplinary exchanges: development of new conceptual frameworks using, 75; evolving division of labor in, 75–76; immigration studies and contributions of, 5–9; mixed methods of immigration research and, 158–59; pull of discipline and push toward, 23–25; studies of immigration using, 5–9; transnational migration studies using, 6, 99, 103–4
internal migration, 56–57
international migration, 56
International Migration Review (Sutton and Chaney), 14
interview research technique, 23, 26
"Is the Ethnic Community Inevitable?" (Brettell), 163
Italian immigrants (late nineteenth century), 168
Itzigsohn, J., 118

Jaguar (Stoller), 21
Jamaican female immigrants, 88
Jewish identity, 107
Jewish immigrants (late nineteenth century), 168

Kikuyu women, 81–82
kinship patterns: among first-generation vs. second-generation, 12; gendered approach to, 82; in urban context, 12. *See also* immigrant families/households; marriage; social networks
Kleinman, A., 203

School of American Research
Advanced Seminar Series

PUBLISHED BY SAR PRESS

PUBLISHED BY SAR PRESS

URUK MESOPOTAMIA & ITS NEIGHBORS:
CROSS-CULTURAL INTERACTIONS IN THE
ERA OF STATE FORMATION
  Mitchell S. Rothman, ed.

CATASTROPHE & CULTURE: THE
ANTHROPOLOGY OF DISASTER
  Susanna M. Hoffman &
  Anthony Oliver-Smith, eds.

TIKAL: DYNASTIES, FOREIGNERS,
& AFFAIRS OF STATE: ADVANCING
MAYA ARCHAEOLOGY
  Jeremy A. Sabloff, ed.

REMAKING LIFE & DEATH: TOWARD AN
ANTHROPOLOGY OF THE BIOSCIENCES
  Sarah Franklin & Margaret Lock, eds.

GRAY AREAS: ETHNOGRAPHIC
ENCOUNTERS WITH NURSING HOME
CULTURE
  Philip B. Stafford, ed.

PUBLISHED BY CAMBRIDGE UNIVERSITY PRESS

DREAMING: ANTHROPOLOGICAL AND
PSYCHOLOGICAL INTERPRETATIONS
  Barbara Tedlock, ed.

THE ANASAZI IN A CHANGING
ENVIRONMENT
  George J. Gumerman, ed.

REGIONAL PERSPECTIVES ON THE OLMEC
  Robert J. Sharer & David C. Grove, eds.

THE CHEMISTRY OF PREHISTORIC
HUMAN BONE
  T. Douglas Price, ed.

THE EMERGENCE OF MODERN HUMANS:
BIOCULTURAL ADAPTATIONS IN THE
LATER PLEISTOCENE
  Erik Trinkaus, ed.

THE ANTHROPOLOGY OF WAR
  Jonathan Haas, ed.

THE EVOLUTION OF POLITICAL SYSTEMS
  Steadman Upham, ed.

CLASSIC MAYA POLITICAL HISTORY:
HIEROGLYPHIC AND ARCHAEOLOGICAL
EVIDENCE
  T. Patrick Culbert, ed.

TURKO-PERSIA IN HISTORICAL
PERSPECTIVE
  Robert L. Canfield, ed.

CHIEFDOMS: POWER, ECONOMY, AND
IDEOLOGY
  Timothy Earle, ed.

PUBLISHED BY UNIVERSITY OF CALIFORNIA PRESS

WRITING CULTURE: THE POETICS
AND POLITICS OF ETHNOGRAPHY
  James Clifford &
  George E. Marcus, eds.

PUBLISHED BY UNIVERSITY OF ARIZONA PRESS

THE COLLAPSE OF ANCIENT STATES AND
CIVILIZATIONS
Norman Yoffee &
George L. Cowgill, eds.

PUBLISHED BY UNIVERSITY OF NEW MEXICO PRESS

RECONSTRUCTING PREHISTORIC PUEBLO
SOCIETIES
William A. Longacre, ed.

NEW PERSPECTIVES ON THE PUEBLOS
Alfonso Ortiz, ed.

STRUCTURE AND PROCESS IN LATIN
AMERICA
Arnold Strickon &
Sidney M. Greenfield, eds.

THE CLASSIC MAYA COLLAPSE
T. Patrick Culbert, ed.

METHODS AND THEORIES OF
ANTHROPOLOGICAL GENETICS
M. H. Crawford & P. L. Workman, eds.

SIXTEENTH-CENTURY MEXICO:
THE WORK OF SAHAGUN
Munro S. Edmonson, ed.

ANCIENT CIVILIZATION AND TRADE
Jeremy A. Sabloff &
C. C. Lamberg-Karlovsky, eds.

PHOTOGRAPHY IN ARCHAEOLOGICAL
RESEARCH
Elmer Harp, Jr., ed.

MEANING IN ANTHROPOLOGY
Keith H. Basso & Henry A. Selby, eds.

THE VALLEY OF MEXICO: STUDIES IN
PRE-HISPANIC ECOLOGY AND SOCIETY
Eric R. Wolf, ed.

DEMOGRAPHIC ANTHROPOLOGY:
QUANTITATIVE APPROACHES
Ezra B. W. Zubrow, ed.

THE ORIGINS OF MAYA CIVILIZATION
Richard E. W. Adams, ed.

EXPLANATION OF PREHISTORIC CHANGE
James N. Hill, ed.

EXPLORATIONS IN ETHNOARCHAEOLOGY
Richard A. Gould, ed.

ENTREPRENEURS IN CULTURAL CONTEXT
Sidney M. Greenfield, Arnold Strickon,
& Robert T. Aubey, eds.

THE DYING COMMUNITY
Art Gallaher, Jr. &
Harlan Padfield, eds.

SOUTHWESTERN INDIAN RITUAL DRAMA
Charlotte J. Frisbie, ed.

LOWLAND MAYA SETTLEMENT PATTERNS
Wendy Ashmore, ed.

SIMULATIONS IN ARCHAEOLOGY
Jeremy A. Sabloff, ed.

CHAN CHAN: ANDEAN DESERT CITY
Michael E. Moseley & Kent C. Day, eds.

SHIPWRECK ANTHROPOLOGY
Richard A. Gould, ed.

ELITES: ETHNOGRAPHIC ISSUES
George E. Marcus, ed.

THE ARCHAEOLOGY OF LOWER CENTRAL
AMERICA
Frederick W. Lange &
Doris Z. Stone, eds.

LATE LOWLAND MAYA CIVILIZATION:
CLASSIC TO POSTCLASSIC
Jeremy A. Sabloff &
E. Wyllys Andrews V, eds.

Photo by Katrina Lasko

Participants in the School of American Research advanced
seminar "Anthropology and Contemporary Immigration,"
Santa Fe, New Mexico, October 7–11, 2001.
From left: Richard Shweder, Patricia Pessar, Josh DeWind,
Jennifer Hirsch, Nina Glick Schiller, Leo Chavez,
Caroline Brettell, Alex Stepick, and Nancy Foner.
Not Pictured: Marcelo Suárez-Orozco